G.A. HENTY
December 8, 1832 — November 16, 1902

THE DASH FOR KHARTOUM

A

TALE OF THE NILE EXPEDITION

by

G. A. Henty

ILLUSTRATED BY JOSEPH NASH, R.I.
AND JOHN SCHÖNBERG

ALSO INCLUDED IN THIS EDITION,
CAMP LIFE IN ABYSSINIA
BY G. A. HENTY

PRESTONSPEED PUBLICATIONS

Historiac Dona Repertum

Pennsylvania

A note about our name: Preston/Speed Publications
In an age where it has become fashionable to denigrate fathers,
we have decided to honor ours. Our name is in loving memory
of Preston Louis Schmitt and Speed - Lester Herbert Maynard
("Speed" is a nickname that was earned for prowess in baseball).

Published July 14, 1892 by
BLACKIE & SON, LONDON

Blackie & Son Title Page Date: 1891

Heirloom Hardcover Edition ISBN 1-887159-41-X
Popular Softcover Edition ISBN 1-887159-40-1
Printed in the U.S.A.

PRESTON/SPEED PUBLICATIONS
51 Ridge Road
MILL HALL, PENNSYLVANIA   17751
(570) 726-7844
www.prestonspeed.com
2000

INTRODUCTION:

G. A. Henty's life was filled with exciting adventure. Completing Westminster School, he attended Cambridge University. Along with a rigorous course of study, Henty participated in boxing, wrestling and rowing. The strenuous study and healthy, competitive participation in sports prepared Henty to be with the British army in Crimea, as a war correspondent witnessing Garibaldi fight in Italy, visiting Abyssinia, being present in Paris during the Franco-Prussian war, in Spain with the Carlists, at the opening of the Suez Canal, touring India with the Prince of Wales (later Edward VII) and a trip to the California gold fields. These are only a few of his exciting adventures.

G. A. Henty lived during the reign of Queen Victoria (1837-1901) and began his story telling career with his own children. After dinner, he would spend an hour or two in telling them a story that would continue the next day. Some stories took weeks! A friend was present one day and watched the spell-bound reaction of his children suggesting that he write down his stories so others could enjoy them. He did. Henty wrote numerous books plus stories for magazines and was dubbed as "The Prince of Story-Tellers" and "The Boy's Own Historian." One of Mr. Henty's secretaries reported that he would quickly pace back and forth in his study dictating stories as fast as the secretary could record them.

Henty's stories revolve around a fictional boy hero during fascinating periods of history. His heroes are diligent, courageous, intelligent and dedicated to their country and cause in the face, at times, of great peril. His histories, particularly battle accounts, have been recognized by historian scholars for their accuracy. There is nothing dry in Mr. Henty's stories and thus he removes the drudgery and laborious task often associated with the study of history.

Henty's heroes fight wars, sail the seas, discover land, conquer evil empires, prospect for gold, and a host of other exciting adventures. They meet famous personages like Josephus, Titus, Hannibal, Robert the Bruce, Sir William Wallace, General Marlborough, General Gordon, General Kitchner, Robert E. Lee, Frederick the Great, the Duke of Wellington, Huguenot leader Coligny, Cortez, King Alfred, Napoleon, and Sir Francis Drake just to mention a *few*. The heroes go through the fall of Jerusalem, the Roman invasion of Britain, the Crusades, the Viking invasion of Europe, the Reformation in various countries, the Reign of Terror, etc. In short, Henty's heroes live through tumultuous historic eras meeting the leaders of that time. Understanding the culture of the time period becomes second nature.

Preston/Speed Publications is delighted to offer again the works of G. A. Henty. Action-packed exciting adventure awaits adults and a whole new generation. The books have been reproduced with modern type-setting. However, the original grammar, spellings and punctuation remains the same as the original versions.

FOREWORD

George Alfred Henty and Charles George Gordon were contemporaries, indeed less than eight weeks separate their birth dates. Both served their country with the British army in the Crimea; Henty in the Hospital Commissariat and Gordon with the Royal Engineers. Henty went on into journalism but Gordon remained in the army rising to the rank of General. He gained an early reputation as an able map maker and surveyor and this talent he put to good use wherever he was posted. His last years were spent attempting to secure a lasting peace in Sudan and then in supervising the withdrawal of the British. Using a blend of mercy and justice he had suppressed the slave trade and attempted to bring native tribes together in opposition to the Mahdi. As an Englishman serving his Queen in a distant land, he was doing his duty, but when Khartoum was beseiged he desperately needed reinforcements. He appealed to the British government; 200 men would have been enough to assist him at that early state of the siege. William Ewart Gladstone, Prime Minister in 1884, was slow to initiate a British Expedition to assist Gordon. He felt Gordon had gone beyond his service to his country in taking up the cause of another nation and that he was really in no great danger. As news of the approaching Mahdi's hostile force filtered back to England H.M. Queen Victoria telegraphed Lord Hartington, at the War Office 'Gordon is in danger. You are bound to save him.' She then told Gladstone 'if not for humanity's sake, for the honour of the Government and nation, Gordon must not be abandoned.'

Khartoum was under siege for almost a year. Lord

Wolseley, a personal friend of both G. A. Henty and General Gordon, assembled an expeditionary force and set out from Wadi Halfa in November. He felt deeply that Charlie Gordon should be rescued, but on 26 January the Mahdi's forces over-ran Khartoum, butchering to death everyone. Wolseley arrived two days later and was shattered to learn of Gordon's horrible death. On his return to England, Wolseley corresponded earnestly with Henty on a number of military matters.

Gordon had been a sincere God-fearing man whose strong belief in Christianity and its principles was to sustain him throughout his military career. For reading matter outside his office he always turned to his Bible for in its pages he firmly believed was truth. Gordon never embraced any Christian sect and this was borne out in Khartoum fourteen years after his death when four service chaplains stood at his grave-side. An Anglican, a Roman Catholic, a Presbyterian and a Methodist shared the solemnities which were concluded with the Sudanese playing 'Abide with me', Gordon's favourite hymn.

————————————

The English Public School reached its zenith in mid Victorian times. Growing out of a network of old endowed schools which had provided a good all-around Christian-based education, public schools developed into large expensive boarding establishments whose pupils came from the well-to-do classes of all parts of the country and the empire. Pupils were prepared for entry to the ancient universities or for public service, military or civil. These schools were characterised by the high standards of order and discipline administered, to the great extent by the elder pupils themselves. Some boys, appointed as monitors, were put in responsible peer-management positions. The term Public School was first used in 1860 when the seven senior ones were given as Eton, Winchester, Westminster, Harrow,

Rugby, Charterhouse and Shrewsbury; but the name has also been applied to more than 20 others including Cheltenham College and to some girls' schools which were run on similar lines.

Boarding accomodation was provided in 'houses' at every public school. Boys arriving to start school age 13, were put into houses run by a master and his wife. The boys stayed there for the duration of their education, leaving at the age of eighteen. Inter house rivalry was encouraged with competitions not only in academic subjects but also in all sports. Sport was considered to be character-building. Attainment of the honour was all-important and would set in good stead the young man as he went on into adult life.

In the second chapter of *The Dash for Khartoum* Henty dispatches Rupert and Edgar to Cheltenham College, a minor English Public School where they experience a rigorous regime of education and sport. Henty's elder son Charles Gerald had studied at Cheltenham College only a few years prior to these two fictional lads. An inside knowledge was undoubtedly useful in setting the school scene but Henty, the great oarsman and boxer, seems less able in his writing to cast the magical spell of cricket, that peculiarly English summer pastime. Cricket is more than just a game, it is a way of life. Playing the game requires greater disciplined skill from its participants than just a match between two teams of eleven men fielding, batting and bowling. It is about absorbing etiquette, learning rules, being part of teamwork strategies; in fact, cricket embraces the whole code of conduct of the true Englishman.

Another sport with which Henty seemed less familiar was rugby football. He was aware of terminology and rules but the way Henty regarded both cricket and rugby football was as a bystander and not as an enthusiastic player or supporter. Had he been either of these he would not have compromised this part of the story with erroneous comment which may have led to misunderstandings by later generations of readers. It should also be remembered that since this book was published rules for both sports have been changed, and terminology is different. On most continents nowadays rugby is called rugby football. The British alone call the game soccer — football. This causes confusion in countries where football is now a game more closely allied to that of rugby football.

––––––––––––––––––

The *Dash for Khartoum* was published on 14 July 1891 and within six months had sold 6465 copies, a record number for any Henty novel up to that date. Indeed its popularity continued for many years and it was not re-issued by Blackie in their cheaper edition until the 1920s.

Henty saw no need to explain background history to this story as it had only happened in the previous decade, but he chose to start at the very beginning of the lives of his two young heroes. The book opens with confusion as to the identity of two babies, an oft-used scene-setting introduction which bears a striking resemblance to the opening of *The Gondoliers*, an operetta by Gilbert and Sullivan, first performed at the Savoy Theatre, London on 7 December 1889. It worked for them and it works for Henty, but the story he tells this time is too modern in date to be brought to a traditional Henty conclusion. He cannot relate how these lads move ever onward into successful middle age. He cannot even marry them to daughters of the regiment because by the end of the story, they have still not attained the age of 25 which was considered to be the earliest respectable age for marriage and inheritance!

––––––––––––––––––

As a special correspondent with the *Standard*, a London newspaper, Henty had been in Abyssinia in 1868. His reports later formed the basis for *The March to Magdala*, a detailed war history, one of two he wrote. He also submitted for publication a short account of life at camp which first appeared in *The Cornhill Magazine* and was later rewritten for Volume II of *Union Jack*. Henty was second to none as a storyteller, particularly when using his local knowledge and personal experience to establish authenticity.

In the preface letter to his 'dear lads', G. A. Henty seized this opportunity to offer guidance on the pitfalls of hasty decision making. He strongly recommends one's father as the best friend in whom to confide whenever the going is tough or the way uncertain. A century on, Henty's young heroes are still our role models.

Ann J. King
Fox Hall, Kelshall. Herts. England
   historian and life-long collector of the works of
   G. A. Henty, who is searching for a new biographical
   study of Henty

The women placed herself in his way.

PREFACE.

MY DEAR LADS,

The story of the Nile Expedition is so recent that no word of introduction is necessary to the historical portion of the tale. The moral, such as it is, of the story of the two lads brought up as brothers is — Never act in haste, for repentance is sure to follow. In this case great anxiety and unhappiness were caused through a lad acting as he believed for the best, but without consulting those who had every right to a voice in the matter. That all came right in the end in no way affects this excellent rule, for all might have gone wrong. We are often misled by a generous impulse, more often perhaps than by an evil one, but the consequences may be just as serious in the one case as the other. When in trouble you should always go freely to your best friends and natural advisers, and lay the case fully before them. It may be that, if the trouble has arisen from your own fault, you will have to bear their temporary displeasure, but this is a small thing in comparison with the permanent injury that may arise from acting on your own impulse. In most cases, cowardice lies at the bottom of concealment, and cowardice is of all vices the most contemptible; while the fear of the displeasure of a parent has ruined many a boy's life.

Therefore, when you are in serious trouble always go to your best friend, your father, and lay the case frankly and honestly before him; for you may be sure that present displeasure and even punishment are but small things in comparison with the trouble that may arise from trying to get out of the difficulty in other ways.

Yours sincerely,

G. A. HENTY

CONTENTS

ILLUSTRATIONS

THE DASH FOR KHARTOUM:
A TALE OF THE NILE EXPEDITION

CHAPTER I
MIXED!

In a room in the married non-commissioned officers' quarters in the cantonments at Agra, a young woman was sitting looking thoughtfully at two infants who lay sleeping together on the outside of a bed with a shawl thrown lightly over them. Jane Humphreys had been married about a year. She was the daughter of the regimental sergeant-major, and had been a spoilt child. She was good looking, and had, so the wives and daughters of the other non-commissioned officers said, laid herself out to catch one of the young officers of the regiment, and was bitterly disappointed at the failure of her efforts.

The report may have been untrue, for Jane Farran was by no means popular with the other women, taking far too much upon herself, as they considered, upon the strength of her father's rank, and giving herself airs as if she were better than those around her. There were girls in the regiment just as good looking as she was without any of her airs and tempers. Why should she set herself up above the rest?

THE DASH FOR KHARTOUM

When, however, Sergeant-major Farran died suddenly
of sunstroke after a heavy field-day, whatever plans and hopes
his daughter may have entertained came to an end. Her
name and that of her mother were put down among the
women to be sent, with the next batch of invalids, home to
England, and she suddenly accepted the offer of marriage
of young Sergeant Humphreys, whose advances she had
previously treated with scorn. They were married six weeks
later, on the day before her mother was to go down by train
with a party of invalids to Calcutta. The universal opinion
of the women in the regiment was that the sergeant had got
a bad bargain.

"No man of spirit," one of them said, "would have taken
up with a girl who only accepted him because she could not
do any better. She has got her temper written in her face,
and a nice time of it he is likely to have."

It may have been true that Jane Humphreys had during
her father's lifetime had her ambitions, but she was a clever
woman and adapted herself to her circumstances. If, as the
sergeant-major's daughter, she had given herself airs, and
had thrown herself in the way of the young officers, and had
been light and flighty in her manner, all this was changed as
soon as she was married, and even the most censorious were
obliged to admit that she made Sergeant Humphreys a better
wife than they had expected. His home was admirably kept,
the gay dresses that had been somewhat beyond her station
were cut up and altered, and she dressed neatly and quietly.

She was handy with her fingers, her things always fitted
her well, and she gained the approbation of the officers'
wives, who had previously looked upon her with some
disfavour as a forward young person. She made every effort
to get on good terms with the wives of the other non-
commissioned officers, and succeeded at last in overcoming
the prejudice which, as Jane Farran, she had excited. There
was no doubt that she was a clever woman, and it was equally
beyond doubt that she completely managed her husband.
She was much his superior in education, and possessing far

greater abilities could twist him round her little finger, although she did it so cleverly that he never suspected that he was the victim of such an operation.

A month previous to the opening of the story she had been confined of a boy, and two days later Mrs. Clinton, the wife of the captain of her husband's company, also became a mother. Before the week was over Mrs. Clinton was taken dangerously ill, and as it was impossible for her to nurse her child, the surgeon of the regiment recommended that it should be given into the charge of the sergeant's wife, as she, being a strong and healthy young woman, could very well nurse it as well as her own. It was a month after this that Sergeant Humphreys, returning to his quarters, found his wife sitting by the side of the bed on which the two infants were asleep. "They are as alike as two peas," he said as he looked at them.

"I am sure I wonder, Jane, that you know which is which!"

Mrs. Humphreys' answer did not seem to the point. "Captain Clinton is a rich man, is he not, John?"

"Yes; they say he came into a grand estate two years ago when his father died, and that like enough he will leave the regiment when it goes home next year."

"Then one of those babies will be a rich man, and the other –" and she stopped.

"The other will, I hope, be a non-commissioned officer in the 30th Foot one of these days," the sergeant said. Jane looked up at her husband. There was no touch of envy or discontent in his voice. She was about to speak but checked herself.

"Which is yours, John?" she asked a moment later, returning to his first remark.

"I am sure I could not tell," he said with a laugh. "Babies are mostly pretty much alike, and as these two are just the same age, and just the same size, and have both got gray eyes and light coloured hair – if you can call it hair, – and no noses to speak of, I don't see a pin's point of difference."

THE DASH FOR KHARTOUM

A month later a small party were assembled in Captain Clinton's bungalow. Mrs. Humphreys was standing with a baby in each arm. Mrs. Clinton was lying upon a sofa crying bitterly. Captain Clinton was walking up and down the room, hot and angry. The surgeon of the regiment was standing grave and sympathetic by Mrs. Clinton.

Sergeant Humphreys was in the attitude of attention by the door, with an anxious troubled expression on his face.

"What in the world is to be done, doctor?" Captain Clinton asked. "I never heard of such a thing, it is a most serious business."

"I can quite see that," the doctor replied. "When Mrs. Humphreys came to me and asked me to break the news to you, I told her at once that it was a terrible business. I own that I do not see that she is altogether to blame, but it is a most unfortunate occurrence. As I have just told you, she had, when she put the children to bed, put your child in one of her baby's night-gowns, as it happened there were none of your child's clean. In the morning she took them out and laid them on a rug on the ground before beginning to wash and dress them. She went out to the canteen to get something for her husband's breakfast, and when she returned she could not remember the order in which she had taken them out of bed and laid them down, and could not distinguish her own child from yours."

"You must remember, Mrs. Humphreys," Captain Clinton broke in; "think it over, woman. You must remember how you laid them down."

"Indeed, I do not, sir; I have been thinking all the morning. I had nursed them two or three times during the night, and of course had changed their position then. I never thought about their having the same night-gowns on. If I had, of course I should have been more careful, for I have said to my husband over and over again that it was only by their clothes that I should know them apart, for if they had been twins they could not be more alike."

MIXED!

"This is downright maddening!" Captain Clinton exclaimed, pacing up and down the room. "And is there no mark nor anything by which they can be recognized? Why, bless me, woman, surely you as a mother ought to know your own child!"

Mrs. Humphreys shook her head. "I have nursed them both, sir, and which is mine and which is yours I could not say to save my life."

"Well, put the children down on that sofa," Captain Clinton said, "and take yourself off for the present; you have done mischief enough for a lifetime. I will let you know what we decide upon later on."

"Well, doctor, what on earth is to be done?" he asked after the door had closed upon the sergeant and his wife. "What do you think had best be done, Lucy?"

But Mrs. Clinton, who was but just recovering from her illness, was too prostrated by this terrible blow to be able to offer any suggestion.

"It is a terrible business indeed, Clinton," the doctor said, "and I feel for you most deeply. Of course the possibility of such a thing never entered my mind when I recommended you to let Mrs. Humphreys act as its foster-mother. It seemed at the time quite a providential circumstance that she too should be just confined, and in a position to take to your baby. The only possible suggestion I can offer is that you should for a time bring up both boys as your own. At present they are certainly wonderfully alike, but it is probable that as they grow up you will see in one or other of them a likeness to yourself or your wife, and that the other will take after its own parents. Of course these likenesses do not always exist, but in nine cases out of ten some resemblance can be traced between a boy and one or other of his parents."

"That certainly seems feasible," Captain Clinton said in a tone of relief. "What do you say, dear? It is only bringing up the two children for a time till we are able to be certain which is our own. The other will have had the advantage of a good education and so on, and of course it will be our business to give him a good start in life."

5

"It will be awful having the two children, and not knowing which is our own."

"It will be very unpleasant," Captain Clinton said soothingly; "but, you see, in time you will come to care for them both just as if they had been twins."

"That will be almost as bad," Mrs. Clinton cried feebly. "And suppose one gets to love the wrong one best?"

"We won't suppose that, dear; but if we love them both equally, we will, when we find out which is ours, treat the other as an adopted child and complete his education, and start him in life as if he were so. Fortunately the expense will be nothing to us."

"But this woman has a right to one of them."

"She does not deserve to have one," Captain Clinton said angrily; "but of course we must make some arrangement with her. She is bound to do her best to repair the terrible mischief her carelessness has caused. Well, doctor, we will think it over for an hour or two, but certainly your suggestion seems by far the best for us to adopt."

"The hussy!" the doctor said as he walked away to his quarters. "I am more than half inclined to believe that she has done it on purpose. I never liked the jade before she married, though I own that she has turned out better than I expected. But I always thought her a designing and artful young woman, and gave her credit for plenty of brains, and what could suit her purpose better than this change of children? She would see that in the first place she would get her own boy well brought up, and perhaps provided for, with all sorts of chances of making money out of the affair. It may have been an accident, of course, but if so, it was a wonderfully fortunate one for her."

Such was the opinion among the women of the regiment when the news became known, and Jane Humphreys was speedily made aware of the fact by the change in their manner towards her. They had, however, but small opportunity for demonstrating their opinion, for Mrs. Humphreys remained shut up as much as possible in her room, and the one or two women who were inclined to take a favourable view of the matter and so called upon her, reported that she was completely prostrated by the occurrence. Among the officers and their families the greatest commiseration was felt for Captain Clinton and his wife, and the matter was discussed at tiffin that day with great animation.

"Don't you think, doctor, that a woman must know her own child?" a young ensign asked.

"Not at all, Arbuthnot; that is to say, not if you mean that she would know it by any sort of maternal instinct. There is no such thing. She has no more means of telling her own infant out of a dozen others of similar complexion, age, and appearance, than she would have of picking out her own pocket-handkerchief out of a dozen others of similar pattern if they were all unmarked."

"But a sheep can pick out his own lamb among a hundred, doctor, and I am sure they are alike as so many peas. Surely that must be maternal instinct?"

"Not in the smallest degree, Arbuthnot. The sheep and other animals possess in a very high degree a sense which is comparatively rudimentary in human beings. I mean, of course, the sense of smell. A sheep knows her lamb, and a cow knows her calf, neither by the sense of hearing or by that of sight. She recognizes it solely and wholly by her sense of smell, just as a dog can track its master's footsteps out of a thousand by the same sense. The two babies are as alike as twins; and I am not surprised that, if they really got mixed, this woman should not be able to detect one from the other."

"It is an awful thing for Clinton," the major said. "Here he has got a splendid estate, and he will never be certain whether his own son or a stranger is going to inherit it after him. It is enough to make a man go out of his mind."

"I don't see that that would be likely to mend matters," the doctor said dryly; "in fact it would lessen the one chance that exists of ever setting the matter straight. As I have told him, though these children are very much alike at present – and indeed most babies are – it is probable that as they grow up there will no longer be any resemblance whatever, and

7

that his own child will develop a likeness either to him or Mrs. Clinton, while the other child will resemble the sergeant or his wife."

"We must hope it will be so," the major said, "though there are lots of fellows who don't resemble in the least either of their parents. But what is Clinton going to do about it?"

"He has not settled yet. His wife was in no condition to discuss the matter, poor lady! My suggestion was that he should bring up both the children as if they were his own, until one or other of them develops this likeness that I was speaking of."

"I suppose that is the best thing they can do, doctor; but it will be an awful business if, as they grow up, no likeness to anybody can be detected in either of them."

"Well, major, although at present it does seem an awful thing, it won't seem so bad at the end, say, of twenty years. They will naturally by that time be as fond of one as the other. The boys, in fact, will be like twins; and I suppose the property can be divided in some such way as it would be were they really in that relation to each other."

"But, you see, doctor," one of the captains said, "Mrs. Humphreys has to be considered to a certain extent too. It is hard on Mrs. Clinton; but if she gets both boys she is certain at any rate that one of them is her son, and Mrs. Humphreys will, by that arrangement, have to lose her child altogether. That seems to me pretty rough on her."

"Well, she brought it on herself," the doctor replied. "The whole thing has arisen from her carelessness."

"Do you think it was carelessness, doctor?" the major asked.

"That is a matter on which I will give no opinion, major. It is one upon which one man can form a judgment as well as another. The thing may very well have happened in the way she describes; and again it may be a very cunningly devised plot on her part. It is evident she had everything to gain by such an accident. She would get her child taken off her hands, educated, and provided for. She would calculate no doubt that she would be their nurse, and would expect, in return for giving up her claim to one or other of them, some very distinct monetary advantages. I do not at all say that the affair was not an accident. Upon the contrary, I admit that it was an accident which might very well happen under the circumstances. What I do say is, nothing could have turned out better for her."

Just as tiffin was finished, Captain Clinton's soldier-servant came into the mess-room with the request that Dr. Parker should go across to his master's bungalow. "Well, doctor," Captain Clinton said as he entered, "in the first place I want you to go up and see my wife, and give her a sedative or something, for she is terribly upset over this affair; and in the next place I want to tell you that we have agreed to take your advice in the matter, and to bring up the two children as our own until we can make out which of the two is our child; then I want your advice as to whether they can be weaned without any damage to their health. My wife is determined upon that point. They shall not be brought up by Mrs. Humphreys. There is no other woman, is there, in the regiment with a young baby?"

The doctor shook his head. "There are one or two with babies, but not with babies young enough for her to take to these. It would certainly be far better that they should have the natural nourishment, but I do not say that they would necessarily suffer from being weaned. Still, you see, Clinton, there is a question whether this woman will consent to part with both the children."

"I quite see that, doctor, and of course I shall be ready to make any money arrangements that will content her."

"I would see the husband, if I were you," the doctor said. "He is a steady, well-conducted young fellow, and however this matter has come about, I quite acquit him of having any share in it. I think you will find it more easy to deal with him than his wife. Unfortunately, you see, there is always a difficulty with adopted children. A father cannot sell away his rights; he may agree to do so, but if he changes his mind afterwards he can back out of his agreement. However he may bind himself never to interfere with it, the fact remains that he has a legal right to the custody of his child. And though Sergeant Humphreys might keep any agreement he might make, the mother might give you no end of trouble afterwards."

"I see all that, doctor, but of the two evils I think the one we propose is the least. My wife says she could not bear to see this woman about the children, and I have a good deal of the same feeling myself. At any rate in her present state of health I wish to spare her all trouble and anxiety as much as I can, and therefore it is better to buy this woman off for the present, even though we may have to run the risk of trouble with her afterwards. Anyhow, something must be done at once. The children have both been squalling for the last hour, though I believe that they have had some milk or something given to them. So I had better send across for Humphreys, the sooner the matter is got over the better."

The young sergeant presently appeared.

"Sit down, sergeant. I want to have a talk with you over this terribly painful business. In one respect I quite understand that it is as painful for you and Mrs. Humphreys as it is for us, but in other respects you are much better off than I am. Not only do I not know which is my child, but I do not know which is heir to my estate; which is, as you will understand, a most serious matter."

"I can quite understand that, sir," the sergeant said quietly.

"The only plan that I can see," Captain Clinton went on, "is that for the present I shall adopt both children, and shall bring them up as my own. Probably in time one of them will grow up with some resemblance to myself or Mrs. Clinton, and the other will show a likeness to you or your wife. In that case I should propose to finish the education of your boy, and then to provide for him by putting him into the army, or such other profession as he may choose; for it would be very unfair after bringing him up and educating him as my own to turn him adrift. Thus, you see, in any case my adoption of him would be greatly to his benefit. I can, of course, thoroughly understand that it will be very hard for you and Mrs. Humphreys to give up your child. Very hard. And I am quite ready to make any pecuniary arrangement with you and her that you may think right. I may say that I do not think that it would be desirable that Mrs. Humphreys should continue as their nurse. I want to consider the boys as my own, and her presence would be constantly bringing up unpleasant remembrances. In the second place I think that it would be better for her that she should not act as their nurse. She would know that one of them is her own, and the separation when it came would be very much more painful than it would be at present. Of course I do not expect an answer from you just at this moment. You will naturally wish to talk it over with her, but I shall be glad if you will let us have an answer as soon as you can, as it is necessary that we should obtain another nurse without loss of time."

"What you say seems to me very fair, Captain Clinton," the sergeant said. "I would give anything, sir, that this shouldn't have happened. I would rather have shot myself first. I can answer for myself, sir, that I accept your offer. Of course, I am sorry to lose the child; but a baby is not much to a man till it gets to know him and begins to talk, and it will be a satisfaction to know that he is in good hands, with a far better look-out than I could have given him. I will see my wife, sir, and let you know in half an hour."

"Do you think that she will consent, Humphreys?"

"I am sure she will," the sergeant said briefly, and then added, "There is nothing else she could do," and saluting he went out of the room.

"He suspects his wife of having done it on purpose," Dr. Parker said, speaking for the first time since the sergeant had entered the room. "I don't say he knows it, but he suspects it. Did you notice how decidedly he said that she would consent? And I fancy up to now she has had her own way in everything."

"Well, what do they say?" Mrs. Humphreys asked as her husband entered the door. He told her shortly the offer that had been made. She laughed scornfully. "A likely thing that! So they are to have both children, and I am not to be

11

allowed even to see them; and they are to pick and choose as to which they like to say is theirs, and we are to be shouldered out of it altogether! It is just as bad for me not to know which is my boy as it is for that woman; but they are to take the whole settlement of things in their hands, my feelings to go for nothing. Of course you told them that you would not let them do such a thing?"

"I did not tell them anything of the sort. I told them that I accepted their proposal, and that I could answer for your accepting it too."

"Then you were never more wrong in your life, John Humphreys!" she said angrily; "I won't consent to anything of the sort. Luck has thrown a good thing in our hands, and I mean to make the most of it. We ought to get enough out of this to make us comfortable for life if we work it well. I did not think that you were such a soft!"

"Soft or not soft, it is going to be done as they propose," her husband said doggedly. "It is burden enough as it is – we have lost our child. Not that I care so very much about that; there will be time enough for more, and children do not add to the comfort of close little quarters like these. But whether we like it or not, we have lost the child. In the next place we shall never hear the end of it in the regiment, and I shall see if I cannot manage to get transferred to another. There will be no standing the talk there will be."

"Let them talk!" his wife said scornfully. "What do we care about their talk!"

"I care a great deal," he said. "And I tell you why, because I know what they will say is true."

"What do you mean?" she asked quickly.

"I mean, Jane, that I know you mixed up those children on purpose."

"How dare you say so!" she exclaimed making a step forward as if she would strike him.

"I will tell you why I say so. Because I went to the drawer this morning before going to parade, and I saw some of Mrs. Clinton's baby's night-gowns in it. Yes, I see they are all in the wash-tub now; but they were there this morning, and when I heard you say you had put the child into one of our baby's night-gowns because it had no clean ones of its own, I knew that you were lying, and that you had done this on purpose."

The woman was silent a moment and then burst out, "You are a greater fool than ever I thought you! I did tell a lie when I gave that reason for putting the child into our baby's gown. When I took the two clean ones out of the drawer I did not notice until I put them on that they were both ours, and then I thought it was not worth while changing again just as the child had got quiet and comfortable. Then when I found what had happened in the morning, I had to make some excuse or other, and that occurred to me as the best. When I came back I did put them all into the wash-tub, clean and dirty, in case any one should come here to see about them. What harm was there in that, I should like to know?"

"You have acknowledged you have told one lie over it; after that you may say what you like, but you need not expect me to believe you."

"Well, why don't you go at once and tell them that you believe that I changed the children on purpose?"

"Because in the first place I cannot prove it, and because in the second case you are my wife, Jane. I took you for better or worse, and whatever you have done it is not for me to round on you. Anyhow, I will do all I can to set this matter straight, and the only way that I see it can be set straight is by doing as Captain Clinton says – by letting him have the two children until they grow up, and then see which of the two is like them and which is like us. What do you want done? I suppose you don't want to have the care of them both. I suppose you don't want to get paid for letting them keep them both, and to have every man and woman in the regiment asking the question, Who sold their child? What is it you do want?"

"I want to go as their nurse."

"Well, then, you cannot do it. It is evident that Mrs. Clinton hates the sight of you, and no wonder; and she won't have you at any price. You had best be contented with what you have got."

"What have I got?" she asked sullenly.

"Well, you have got the trouble of the child off your hands, you have got the knowledge that it will be well taken care of and provided for and made a gentleman of. That ought to be a satisfaction to you anyhow."

"What is that when we might make a nice little fortune out of it?"

"I can see no way of making a fortune," he said, "unless you do know which is which, and offer to tell them if they will pay you for it. In which case, instead of making a fortune you would be likely to find yourself inside a prison for years – and serve you right."

The woman was silent for some time, then she said, "Very well, then, I will agree to their terms; but mind you, I will make money out of it yet." And so Sergeant Humphreys went across to Captain Clinton's bungalow and told him that his wife agreed to give up both children.

"It is by far the best thing for the little chap whichever he may be, and you will be able to do a deal more for him than I ever could. My wife did not quite see the matter at first, but she has come round to my way of thinking. No, sir, we do not want to be paid," as Captain Clinton was about to speak; "as long as I am fit for service we want nothing. Some day, perhaps, when I get past service I may ask you to give me a job as a lodge-keeper or some such post, where I can earn my living."

And so the matter was settled. One of the other officers' wives had already lent her ayah to take care of the children until one could be found for them.

The ready manner in which Sergeant Humphreys had done the only thing in his power to obviate the effects of his wife's carelessness restored him at once to the good opinion of his fellow sergeants and the men, as it was generally allowed that he had done the right thing, and that no one could do more. Opinion, however, was less favourable as to his wife. It was soon evident to all who lived in the non-commissioned officers' quarters that things were not going on well between Sergeant Humphreys and his wife. There were frequent and violent quarrels. The sergeant was often down at the canteen drinking more than was good for him. One day Captain Clinton sent for him. "Sergeant, I am sorry to say that I hear from the sergeant-major that you were drunk last night, and that you have several times been the worse for liquor. It is not a formal complaint, but I thought it better to talk to you. You have always been a very steady man, and I should be sorry in the extreme if anything should happen which would cause you to be brought before the colonel. I have no doubt this affair has troubled you greatly, and that it is entirely owing to that that you have become unsettled. Try to pull yourself round, man. You know that nobody attributes the slightest shadow of blame to you in the matter."

"Thank you, sir. I was coming to see you if you hadn't sent for me, to say that I wished to give up my stripes and return to the ranks. I know I shall be degraded if I don't do it of my own free-will, and I would rather go down than be sent down."

"But what will your wife do? It would be a great change to her, Humphreys."

"My wife has made up her mind to go home, sir, and I think it is the best thing she can do. She will never be comfortable in the regiment, and to say the truth we are not comfortable together. She says that she has friends in England she will go and stay with, and I think it is best to let her go. I would rather cut my hand off than ask for anything for myself, but as I am sure that it is for the best that she should go, and as I don't hear of any invalids or women going home at present, I should be very much obliged if you would lend me twenty pounds. I have got thirty laid by, and fifty will be enough to send her across by rail to Bombay, pay her passage home, and leave her twenty pounds in hand when she gets there. I will pay it off so much a month."

"You are welcome to twenty pounds without any talk of repayment, Humphreys. But I wouldn't take any hasty step if I were you. If your wife and you have had a quarrel she may change her mind in a day or two, and think better of it."

"No, sir; I think we are pretty well agreed on the point that she had best go home. People make mistakes sometimes, and I think we both made a mistake when we got married. Anyhow, we have both agreed that it is best to part for a time."

Accordingly three or four days later Mrs. Humphreys left Agra for Bombay, and was seen no more in the regiment. Sergeant Humphreys gave up his stripes and returned to the ranks, and for two years remained there. After his wife had left him he gradually gave up the habit into which he had fallen, and at the end of the two years again became a non-commissioned officer.

He was never heard to speak of his wife after she left him, nor so far as his comrades knew did he ever receive a letter from her. Soon after he had again got his stripes the regiment returned to England, and a month later Captain Clinton sent in his papers and retired from the service.

CHAPTER II
AT CHELTENHAM

EVERYTHING packed and ready, boys?"

"Yes, father, I think so."

"The dog-cart will be at the door at eleven. Be sure and be ready in time. It won't do to miss your train, you know. Well, you have had a pleasant holiday this time, haven't you?"

"Very," both boys replied together. "It has been awfully jolly," one went on, "and that trip in Brittany was certainly the best thing we have done, though we have always enjoyed our holidays. It is ever so much nicer going to out-of-the-way sort of places, and stopping at jolly little inns without any crowd and fuss, than being in those great Swiss hotels as we were last year, where every one was English, and one had to be in at regular times and almost fight to get something to eat. I hope next year you will be able to take us to Norway, as you were saying yesterday. I should think it would be just the same sort of thing as Brittany, only, of course, different sort of scenery, and different language and different people. Madge, you will have to set to and get up Norse to act as our interpreter."

"You are very lazy boys. I had to do all the talking in Brittany. You are supposed to have learnt French longer than I have."

"Oh, yes; supposed. Nobody cares about their French lessons. They make no difference in your place in the school, and so no one takes the trouble to grind at them. Well, come along, let us take a turn round the place for an hour before we start." And the two boys and Madge, who was a year their junior, went out through the French window into the garden.

Captain Clinton walked to the window and looked after them. They were lads any father might be proud of, straight, well-built, handsome English lads of about sixteen. Rupert was somewhat taller than Edgar, while the latter had slightly the advantage in breadth of shoulders. Beyond the fact that both had brown hair and gray eyes there was no marked likeness between them, and their school-fellows often wondered that there should not be more similarity between twins. Both had pleasant open faces, and they were equally popular among their school-fellows. As to which was the cleverest, there were no means of ascertaining; for although both were at Cheltenham together, one was on the modern and the other on the classical side, Captain Clinton having made this arrangement purposely in order that there should be no rivalry between them, and the unpleasantness that sometimes arises when two brothers are at the same school, and one is more clever than the other, was thereby obviated. Rupert was the more lively of the two, and generally did the largest share of talking when they were together; but Edgar, although he talked less, had the more lively sense of humour, and the laughter that broke out in the garden was caused by some quiet remark of his. Captain Clinton turned sharply round upon hearing a sigh from his wife. "Well, Lucy, I know what you are thinking: another holiday over, and we are no nearer to the truth. I own that our plan has failed so far, for I can't see in either of the boys a shadow of resemblance either to you or myself. Some people profess to see likenesses. Mr. Tomline remarked yesterday that he should have known Rupert anywhere as my son, but then Colonel Wilson said the day before that Edgar had got just your expression. I don't see a scrap of likeness either way, and I begin to think, dear, that I don't want to see it."

"No, I don't want to see it either, Percy; I love one as well as the other. Still I should like to know which is our own."

"I used to think so too, Lucy; but I have been doubting for some time about it, and now I am quite sure that I don't want to know. They are both fine lads, and, as you say, we love one just as well as the other. Parental instinct, you see, goes for nothing. I should like to know that one of them was my son, but on the other hand I should be very sorry to know that the other wasn't. I think, dear, that it is much better as it is. We have got two sons instead of one; and after all, the idea that there would be a great satisfaction in the real one inheriting all our landed property has very little in it. There is plenty for them both, and each of them will be just as happy on three thousand a year as he would on six.

"As matters stand now, I have divided the property as nearly as possible equally between them. Madge, of course, will have her share; and I have left it in my will that they shall draw lots which shall have the part with the house and park on it, while the other is to have a sum of money sufficient to build an equally good house on his share of the estate. We can only hope that chance will be wiser than we, and will give the old house to the right boy. However, whether our son or our adopted son, whichever it be which gets it, does not concern me greatly. There is enough for our son to hold a good position and be comfortable and happy. Beyond this I do not trouble. At any rate the grievance, if there is a grievance, is a sentimental one; while it would be a matter of real grief to me should either of them, after having always looked upon us as his parents, come to know that he does not belong to us, and that he has been all along in a false position, and has been in fact but an interloper here. That would be terribly hard for him – so hard that I have ceased to wish that the matter should ever be cleared up, and to dread rather than hope that I should discover an unmistakable likeness to either of us in one or other of them."

"You are right, Percy; and henceforth I will worry no more about it. It would be hard, dreadfully hard, on either of them to know that he was not our son; and henceforth I will, like you, try to give up wishing that I could tell which is which. I hope they will never get to know that there is any doubt about it."

"I am afraid we can hardly hope that," Captain Clinton said. "There are too many people who know the story. Of course it was talked about at every station in India at the time, and I know that even about here it is generally known. No, it will be better some day or other to tell it them ourselves, making, of course, light of the matter, and letting them see that we regard them equally as our sons, and love and care for them alike, and that even if we now knew the truth it could make no difference in our feelings towards them. It is much better they should learn it from us than from anyone else."

At eleven o'clock the dog-cart came to the door. The boys were ready. Captain Clinton drove them to the station four miles away, and in two hours after leaving home they arrived at Cheltenham with a large number of their school-fellows, some of whom had been in the train when they entered it, while others had joined them at Gloucester. At Cheltenham there was a scramble for vehicles, and they were soon at the boarding-house of Mr. River-Smith, which had the reputation of being the most comfortable of the Cheltenham boarding-houses.

There was a din of voices through the house, and in the pleasure of meeting again and of exchanging accounts of how the holidays had been spent, the few lingering regrets that school-time had come round again completely vanished. Then there was a discussion as to the football prospects and who would get their house colours in place of those who had gone, and whether River-Smith's was likely to retain the position it had won by its victories over other houses in the previous season; and the general opinion was that their chances were not good.

"You see," Skinner, the captain of the team, said to a party gathered in the senior boys' study, "Harrison and White will be better than last year, but Wade will of course be a great loss; his weight and strength told tremendously in a scrimmage. Hart was a capital half-back too, and there was no better goal-keeper in the college than Wilson. We have not got any one to take their places, and there are four other vacancies in the team, and in each case those who have left were a lot bigger and stronger than any of the young ones we have got to choose from. I don't know who they will be yet, and must wait for the trial matches before we decide; but I think there is plenty of good material to choose from, and we shall be nearly all up to last year's mark, except in point of weight – there is a terrible falling off there, and we have no one who can fill the place of Wade. He was as strong as a bull; yes, he is an awful loss to us! There was not a fellow in the college who could go through a grease as he could. You remember last year how he rolled those fellows of Bishop's over and carried the ball right through them, and then kicked the deciding goal? That was grand! Why don't some of you fellows grow up like him?" And he looked round reproachfully at his listeners. "Over thirteen stone Wade was, and there is not one of you above eleven and a half – anyhow, not more than a few pounds."

"Why don't you set us an example?" Edgar Clinton asked; and there was a laugh, for the captain of the team was all wire and muscle and could not turn ten stone.

"I am not one of that kind," he said; "but there is Wordsworth, who is pretty near six feet in length, and who, if he gave his mind to it and would but eat his food quietly instead of bolting it, might put some flesh on those spindle-shanks of his and fill himself out till he got pretty near to Wade's weight. A fellow ought to do something for his house, and I call it a mere waste of bone when a fellow doesn't put some flesh on him."

"I can run," Wordsworth said apologetically.

"Yes, you can run when you get the ball," Skinner said in a tone of disgust; "but if a fellow half your height runs up against you, over you go. You must lay yourself out for pudding, Wordsworth. With that, and eating your food more slowly, you really might get to be of some use to the house."

THE DASH FOR KHARTOUM

Wordsworth grumbled something about his having done his share last year.

"It all depends what you think your share is," Skinner said severely. "You did your best, I have no doubt, and you certainly got a good many goals, but that arose largely from the fact that there was nothing tangible in you. You see, you were something like a jointed walking-stick, and, naturally, it puzzled fellows. You have grown wider a bit since then, and must therefore try to make yourself useful in some other line. What we want is weight, and the sooner you put weight on the better. I see Easton has not come yet."

"He never comes until the evening train," another said. "He always declares it has something to do with cross lines not fitting in."

"It takes him so long," Skinner growled, "to fold up his things without a crease, to scent his pocket-handkerchief, and to get his hair to his satisfaction, that you may be quite sure he cannot make an early start. As he is not here, and all the rest that are left out of last year's team are, it is a good opportunity to talk him over. I did not like having him in the team last year, though he certainly did better than some. What do you think? Ought we to have him this year or not? I have been thinking a lot about it."

"I don't care for him," Scudamore said, "but I am bound to say he does put off all that finicking nonsense when he gets his football jersey on, and plays a good, hard game, and does not seem to mind in the least how muddy or dirty he gets. I should certainly put him in again, Skinner, if I were you."

There was a murmur of assent from three of four of the others. "Well, I suppose he ought to play," Skinner said; "but it does rile me to see him come sauntering up as if it was quite an accident that he was there, and talk in that drawling, affected sort of way."

"It is riling," another said; "but besides that I do not think there is much to complain about him, and his making a fool of himself at other times does not affect us so long as he plays well in the team."

"No, I do not know that it does, but all the same it is a nuisance when one fellow keeps himself to himself and never seems to go in for anything. I do not suppose Easton means to give himself airs, but there is nothing sociable about him."

"I think he is a kind-hearted fellow," Edgar Clinton said, speaking, however, with less decision than usual, as became one who was not yet in the first form. "When young Jackson twisted his ankle so badly last term at the junior high jump, I know he used to go up and sit with him, and read with him for an hour at a time pretty near every day. I used often to wish I could manage to get up to him, but somehow I never could spare time; but Easton did, though he was in the college four and was working pretty hard too. I have known two or three other things he has done on the quiet. I don't care for his way of dressing nor for his drawling way of talking, in fact, I don't care for him at all personally; but he is a good-natured fellow in spite of his nonsense."

"Well, then, we must try him again," Skinner said, "and see how he does in the trial matches. There is no certainty about him, that is what I hate; one day he plays up and does uncommonly well, then the next day he does not seem to take a bit of interest in the game."

"I have noticed several times," Scudamore said, "that Easton's play depends very much on the state of the game: if we are getting the best of it he seems to think that there is no occasion to exert himself, but if the game is going against us he pulls himself together and goes into it with all his might."

"He does that," Skinner agreed; "that is what riles me in the fellow. He can play a ripping good game when he likes, but then he does not always like. However, as I said, we will give him another trial."

Half an hour later the subject of the conversation arrived. He was in the first form on the classical side, and was going up at the next examination for Sandhurst. Easton was one of the monitors, but seldom asserted his authority or put himself out in any way to perform the duties of the office. He was dressed with scrupulous care, and no one from his appearance would have said that he had just come off a railway journey. He nodded all round in a careless way as he came in, and there was none of the boisterous friendliness that had marked the meeting of most of the others.

"Affected fool!" Skinner growled to Rupert who was next to him.

"You are a prejudiced beggar, Skinner," Rupert laughed. "You know very well he is not a fool, and I am not at all sure he is affected. I suppose it is the way he has been brought up. There is no saying what you might have been yourself if you had had nurses and people about you who always insisted on your turning out spick-and-span. Well, Easton, what have you been doing with yourself since we saw you last?"

"I have been on the Continent most of the time," Easton said, in the quiet, deliberate tone that was so annoying to Skinner. "Spent most of the time in Germany: had a week at Munich, and the same time in Dresden doing the picture-gallery."

"That must have been a treat," Skinner said sarcastically.

"Yes, it was very pleasant. The worst of it is, standing about so long makes one's feet ache."

"I wonder you did not have a bath-chair, Easton; delicate people go about in them, you know."

"It would be a very pleasant way, Skinner, only I don't think I could bring myself to it."

There was a laugh at his taking Skinner's suggestion seriously.

"What have you been doing, Skinner?"

"I have been up in Scotland climbing hills, and getting myself in good condition for football," Skinner replied shortly.

"Ah, football? Yes, I suppose we shall be playing football this term."

There was another laugh, excited principally by the angry growl with which Skinner greeted this indifference to what was to him the principal feature of the year.

24

AT CHELTENHAM

"I shouldn't mind football," Easton went on, after looking round as if unable to understand what the others were laughing at, "if it wasn't for the dirt. Of course it is annoying to be kicked in the shins and to be squeezed horribly in the greases, but it is the dirt I object to most. If one could but get one's flannels and jerseys properly washed every time it would not matter so much, but it is disgusting to have to put on things that look as if they had been rolled in mud."

"I wonder you play at all, Easton," Skinner said angrily.

"Well, I wonder myself sometimes," Easton said placidly. "I suppose it is a relic of our original savage nature, when men did not mind dirt, and lived by hunting and fighting and that sort of thing."

"And had never learned the nuisance of stiff shirts and collars, and never heard of such a thing as a tailor, and did not part their hair in the middle, Easton, and had never used soap," Skinner broke in.

"No; it must have been beastly," Easton said gravely. "I am very glad that I did not live in those days."

"Ah, you would have suffered horribly if you had, wouldn't you?"

"Well, I don't know, Skinner; I suppose I should have done as other people did. If one does not know the comfort of a wash and a clean shirt, one would not miss it, you see. I have sometimes thought –"

"Oh, never mind what you thought," Skinner broke in out of all patience. "Come, let us go for a walk; it is no use stopping here all this fine afternoon. Let us take a good long spin. I can see half you fellows are out of condition altogether, and the sooner we begin work the better. Will you come, Easton? After lolling about looking at pictures a twelve-mile spin will do you good."

"Thank you, Skinner; I don't know that I want any good done to me. I should not mind a walk, if it is to be a walk; but a walk with you generally means rushing across ploughed fields and jumping into ditches, and getting one's self hot and uncomfortable, and splashing one's self from head to

25

foot. It is bad enough in flannels, but it is downright misery in one's ordinary clothes. But I don't mind a game at rackets, if anyone is disposed for it."

"I will play you," Mossop said. "I want to get my hand in before the racket matches come off."

So they went and put on their flannels and racket shoes, while the rest of the party started for a long walk with Skinner.

"I am glad he has not come," the football captain said as they started; "he drives me out of all patience."

"I don't think you have much to drive out of you, Skinner," Rupert Clinton laughed. "I believe Easton puts about half of it on, on purpose to excite you. I am sure just now I saw a little amusement in his face when he was talking so gravely."

"He will find he has got in the wrong box," Skinner said angrily, "if he tries to chaff me."

A quiet smile was exchanged among the others, for Easton was tall and well built and had the reputation of being the best boxer in the school; and although Skinner was tough and wiry, he would have stood no chance in an encounter with him.

"Well, how did you get on, Mossop?" Scudamore asked as they sat down to tea.

"Easton beat me every game. I had no idea that he was so good. He says he does not intend to play for the racket, but if he did he would have a first-rate chance. I was in the last ties last year and I ought to have a good chance this, but either I am altogether out of practice or he is wonderfully good. I was asking him, and he said in his lazy way that they had got a decent racket-court at his place, and that he had been knocking the balls about a bit since he came home."

"If he is good enough to win," Pinkerton, the captain of the house, said, "he ought to play for the honour of the house. He has never played in any matches here before. I did not know he played at all."

"That is the way with Easton," Edgar Clinton said; "he is good all round, only he never takes trouble to show it. He could have been in the college cricket eleven last year if he liked, only he said he could not spare the time. Though Skinner doesn't think so, I believe he is one of the best in our football team; when he chooses to exert himself he is out and out the best chess player in the house; and I suppose he is safe to pass in high for Sandhurst."

"He is a queer fellow," Pinkerton said, "one never knows what he can do and what he can't. At the last exam Glover said that the papers he sent in were far and away the best, but that he had only done the difficult questions and hadn't sent in any answers at all to the easy ones, so that instead of coming in first he was five or six down the list. I believe myself he did not want to beat me, because if he had he would have been head of the house, and that would have been altogether too much trouble for him. Glover wanted him to go up for the last Indian Civil, and told him he was sure that he could get in if he tried, but Easton said he wasn't fond of heat and had no fancy for India."

"I suppose he was afraid to take the starch out of his collars," Edgar laughed. "Ah! here he is, late as usual."

Easton strolled quietly in and took his place, looking annoyingly fresh and clean by the side of those who had accompanied Skinner on his walk, and who, in spite of vigorous use of clothes brushes, showed signs of cross-country running.

"Have you had a pleasant walk?" he asked calmly.

"Very pleasant," Skinner said, in a tone that defied contradiction. "A delightful walk; just the thing for getting a little into condition."

There was a murmur of assent among the boys who had accompanied him, but there was no great heartiness in the sound; for indeed Skinner had pressed them all to a much higher rate of speed than was pleasant in their ordinary clothes, although they would not have minded it in flannels.

"You all look as if you had enjoyed it," Easton said, regarding them one by one with an air of innocent approval; "warmed yourselves up a bit, I should say. I remark a general disappearance of collars, and Rupert Clinton's face is scratched as if he had been having a contest with some old lady's cat."

"I went head-foremost into a hedge," Rupert laughed. "My foot slipped in the mud just as I was taking off, and I took a regular header into it."

"And what is the matter with your hand, Wordsworth?"

"A beast of a dog bit me. We were going across a field, and the brute came out from a farmhouse. My wind had gone, and I happened to be last and he made at me. Some fool has written in a book that if you keep your eyes fixed upon a dog he will never bite you. I fixed my eye on him like a gimlet but it did not act, and he came right at me and sprang at me and knocked me down and got my hand in his mouth, and I don't know what would have happened if Skinner hadn't pulled a stick out of the hedge, and rushed back and hit him such a lick across the back that he went off yelping. Then the farmer let fly with a double-barrelled gun from his garden; but luckily we were pretty well out of reach, though two or three shots hit Scudamore on the cheek and ear and pretty nearly drew blood. He wanted to go back to fight the farmer, but as the fellow would have reloaded by the time he got there, and there was the dog into the bargain, we lugged him off."

"Quite an adventurous afternoon," Easton said in a tone of cordial admiration, which elicited a growl from Skinner.

"You wish you had been with us, don't you?" he said, with what was meant to be a sneer.

"No, rackets was quite hard work enough for me; and I don't see much fun in either taking a header into a hedge, being bitten by a farmer's dog, or being peppered by the man himself. Still, no doubt these things are pleasant for those who like them. What has become of Templar?"

"He fell into a ditch," Wordsworth said; "and he just was in a state. He had to go up to the matron for a change of clothes. He will be here in a minute, I expect."

"Quite a catalogue of adventures. If I had known beforehand that there was going to be so much excitement I might have been tempted to go with you. I am afraid, Mossop, I have kept you out of quite a good thing."

"There, shut up Easton!" Pinkerton said, for he saw that Skinner was at the point of explosion; "let us have peace and quiet this first night. You have got the best of it, there is no doubt. Skinner would admit that."

"No I wouldn't," Skinner interrupted.

"Never mind whether you would or not, Skinner, it clearly is so. Now, let us change the conversation. For my part I cannot make out why one fellow cannot enjoy football and that sort of thing, and another like to lie on his back in the shade, without squabbling over it. If Skinner had his own way he would never sit quiet a minute, if Easton had his he would never exert himself to walk across the room. It is a matter of taste. I like half and half, but I do not want to interfere with either of your fancies. Now, it is about time to set to work. I expect there are a good many holiday tasks not perfect."

There was a chorus of assent, and the senior boys went off to their private studies, and the juniors to the large study, where they worked under the eye of the house-master.

Skinner's mournful anticipations as to the effect of the want of weight in the football team were speedily verified. The trial matches were almost all lost, the team being fairly borne down by the superior weight of their opponents. There was general exasperation at these disasters, for River-Smith's House had for some years stood high, and to be beaten in match after match was trying indeed. Skinner took the matter terribly to heart, and was in a chronic state of disgust and fury. As Easton observed to Edgar Clinton:

"Skinner is becoming positively dangerous. He is like a Scotch terrier with a sore ear, and snaps at every one who comes near him."

"Still it is annoying," Edgar, who thoroughly sympathized with Skinner, said.

"Well, yes, it is annoying. I am annoyed myself, and it takes a good deal to annoy me. I think we ought to do something."

"Well, it seems to me that we have been doing all we can," Edgar said. "I am sure you have, for it was only yesterday Skinner was holding you up as an example to some of us. He said, 'You ought all to be ashamed of yourselves. Why, look at that lazy beggar Easton, he works as hard as the whole lot of you put together. If it was not for him I should say we had better chuck it altogether.' "

"I observe that Skinner has been a little more civil to me lately," Easton said. "Yes, I do my best. I object to the whole thing, but if one does play one does not like being beaten. I think we had better have a talk over the matter together."

"But we are always talking over the matter," Edgar objected. "All the fellows who had a chance of turning out well have been tried, and I am sure we play up well together. Every one says that we are beaten just because we cannot stand their rushes."

That afternoon the house was badly beaten by the Greenites in the trial match, and as there was a special rivalry between Green's and River-Smith's the disgust not only of the members of the team but of the whole house was very great. Seven of the seniors met after tea in Skinner's study to discuss the situation.

"I don't see anything to be done," Skinner said, after various possible changes in the team had been discussed; "it is not play we want, it is weight. The Greenites must average at least a stone and a half heavier than we do. I have nothing to say against the playing. We simply cannot stand against them; we go down like nine-pins. No, I suppose we shall lose every match this season. But I don't see any use in talking any more about it. I suppose no one has anything further to suggest."

"Well, yes, I have a few words to say," Easton, who had been sitting on the table and had hitherto not opened his lips, remarked in a quiet voice.

"Well, say away."

"It seems to me," Easton went on without paying any regard to the snappishness of Skinner's tone, "that though we cannot make ourselves any heavier, weight is not after all the only thing. I think we might make up for it by last. When fellows are going to row a race they don't content themselves with practice, they set to and train hard. It seems to me that if we were to go into strict training and get ourselves thoroughly fit, it ought to make a lot of difference. We might lose goals in the first half of the play, but if we were in good training we ought to get a pull in the second half. By playing up all we knew at first, and pumping them as much as possible, training ought to tell. I know, Skinner, you always said we ought to keep ourselves in good condition; but I mean more than that, I mean strict training – getting up early and going for a three or four mile run every morning, taking another run in the afternoon, cutting off pudding and all that sort of thing, and going in for it heart and soul. It is no use training unless one does a thing thoroughly."

"Well, one could but try," Skinner said. "There is no reason why one shouldn't train for football just as one does for rowing or running. You are the last fellow I should have expected to hear such a proposal from, Easton, but if you are ready to do it I am sure every one else will be."

There was a cordial exclamation of assent from the others. "Well, of course it will be a horrible nuisance," Easton said regretfully; "but if one does go in for a thing of this sort it seems to me that it must be done thoroughly. And besides, it is very annoying just at the ticklish point of a game, when you would give anything to be able to catch the fellow ahead of you with the ball, to find that your lungs have given out, and that you haven't a cupful of wind left."

"I believe, Easton, that you are a downright humbug," Scudamore said; "and that while you pretend to hate anything like exertion, you are just as fond of it as Skinner is."

"Well, at any rate," Skinner broke in, "we will try Easton's suggestion. From to-night the team shall go into strict training. I will see River-Smith now and get leave for us to go out at six o'clock every morning. We will settle about the afternoon work afterwards. Of course pudding must be given up, and there must be no buying cakes or things of that sort. New bread and potatoes must be given up, and we must all agree never to touch anything to drink between meals. We will try the thing thoroughly. It will be a month before we play our next match with Green's. If we can but beat them I do not care so much about the others. There are two or three houses we should have no chance with if we were to train as fine as a university eight."

The rest of the team were at once informed of the determination that had been arrived at. Had it emanated only from Skinner several of the members might have protested against the hardship of going into training for football, but the fact that Easton had proposed it weighed with them all. If he was ready to take such trouble over the matter no one else could reasonably object, and the consequence was that, although not without a good deal of grumbling at being got up before daylight, the whole team turned out in their flannels and two thick jerseys punctually at six o'clock.

"Here is an egg and half cupful of milk for each of you," Skinner said as they gathered below. "Look sharp and beat up your egg with the milk. Here is a mouthful of biscuit for each. River-Smith said he did not like our going out without taking something before we started, and Cornish, who rowed in the trials at Cambridge, told me that egg and milk was the best thing to take."

Five minutes later, comforted by the egg and milk, the party started.

"We don't want to go at racing speed," Skinner said; "merely a good steady trot to make the lungs play. We don't want to pull ourselves down in weight. I don't think, after the last month's work, we have any fat among us. What we want is wind and last. To-morrow we will turn out with the heaviest boots we have got instead of running shoes. When we can run four miles in them, we ought to be able to keep up pretty fairly through the hardest game of football."

There was a good deal of lagging behind towards the last part of the run, a fact that Skinner pointed out triumphantly as a proof of want of condition, but after a wash and change of clothes all the party agreed that they felt better for the run.

Mr. River-Smith was as much concerned as the boys at the defeats of the house at football, and when they sat down to breakfast the members of the team found that a mutton-chop was provided for each of them. Strict orders had been issued that nothing was to be said outside the house of the football team going into training; and as, for the afternoon's exercise, it was only necessary that every member of the team should take part in football practice, and play up to the utmost, the matter remained a secret. In the first two or three matches played the training made no apparent difference.

"You must not be disheartened at that," Mr. Cornish, who was the "housemaster," told them. "Fellows always get weak when they first begin to train. You will find the benefit presently."

And this was the case. They won the fourth match, which was against a comparatively weak team. This, however, encouraged them, and they were victorious in the next two contests, although in the second their opponents were considered a strong team, and their victory had been regarded as certain.

The improvement in the River-Smithites' team became a topic of conversation in the college, and there were rumours that they had put themselves into regular training, and that some one had seen them come in in a body at seven in the morning after having been for a run. The challenge cup matches were now at hand, and as it happened they were drawn to meet the Greenites, and the match was regarded with special interest throughout the school. The rivalry between the two houses was notorious, and although the

Greenites scoffed at the idea of their being defeated by a team they had before so easily beaten, the great improvement the latter had made gave promise that the struggle would be an exceptionally severe one. Skinner had for some days before looked after the team with extreme vigilance, scarcely letting one of them out of his sight, lest they might eat forbidden things, or in other ways transgress the rules laid down.

"We may not win," he admitted, as they talked over the prospect on the evening before the match, "but at any rate they will have all their work cut out to beat us. I know they are very confident, and of course their weight is tremendously in their favour. Now, mind, we must press them as hard as we can for the first half the game, and never leave them for a single moment. They are sure to get savage when they find they have not got it all their own way, and that will help to pump them. We shall have more left in us the second half than they will, and then will be our chance."

These tactics were followed out, and from the first the game was played with exceptional spirit on both sides; and as the Greenites failed, even by the most determined rushes, to carry the ball into their opponents' goal, the game became, as Skinner had predicted, more and more savage.

The sympathies of the school were for the most part with River-Smith's, and the loud shouts of applause and encouragement with which their gallant defence of their goal was greeted, added to the irritation of the Greenites. When the half-play was called neither party had scored a point, and as they changed sides it was evident that the tremendous pace had told upon both parties.

"Now is our time," Skinner said to his team; "they are more done than we are, and our training will tell more and more every minute. Keep it up hard, and when we see a chance make a big rush and carry it down to their end."

But the Greenites were equally determined, and in spite of the efforts of their opponents, kept the ball at their end of the field.

Then Skinner got it and made a rush. One of the heaviest of the Greenites charged down upon them at full speed, but was encountered by Easton before he reached him, and the two rolled over together. The River-Smithites backed up their leader well, and he was more than half-way down the ground before the Greenites had arrested his progress. Then there was a close scrimmage, and for a time the mass swayed backwards and forwards. But here weight counted for more than wind, and the Greenites were pushing their opponents back when the ball rolled out from the mass.

Edgar Clinton picked it up, and was off with it in a moment, dodging through those who attempted to check his course. He was down near the Greenites' goal before two of them threw themselves upon him together; but his friends were close behind, and after a desperate scrimmage the ball was driven behind the Greenite goal. Some loose play followed, and a Greenite who had the ball threw it forward to one of his own team, who caught it and started running. The River-Smithites shouted "Dead ball!" "Dead ball!" and claimed the point; but the holder of the ball, without heeding the shouts, ran right through followed by the rest of his team, and touched down behind the River-Smith goal. The ball was then brought out and a goal kicked. All this time the River-Smithites had not moved from behind the Greenite goal, but had remained there awaiting the result of their appeal to the umpire, who now at once decided in their favour. Not satisfied with this the Greenites appealed to the referee, who confirmed the decision of the umpire. Too angry to be reasonable, the captain refused to continue the game, and called upon his team to leave the field. They were going, when the derisive shouts of the lookers-on caused them again to alter their intentions, and the game was renewed.

There were ten minutes yet remaining, and for that time the game was played with a fury that caused it to be long memorable in the annals of Cheltenham football. But weight and strength could not prevail over the superior last and coolness of the defenders of the River-Smith goal. Every attempt was beaten off, every rush met, and as no point had been added to the score when time was called, the umpire decided that the game had been won by the River-Smithites by one touchdown to nothing. The captain of the Greenites appealed from the umpire's and referee's decision to the football committee of the college, who gave it against him, and he then appealed to the Rugby Union, who decided that the umpire's decision was perfectly right, and the victory thus remained beyond further contention with the River-Smithites.

CHAPTER III
GONE

B RAVO, Clinton! Well done, indeed!" so shouted one
of the big boys, and a score of others joined in in
chorus.

"Which is Clinton?" a woman who was standing looking
on at the game asked one of the younger boys.

The boy looked up at the questioner. She was a woman
of about forty years old, quietly dressed in black with a gloss
of newness on it.

"I will point him out to you directly. They are all mixed
up again now."

"There are two of them, are there not?" the woman
asked.

"Yes, that's the other; there – that one who has just
picked up the ball and is running with it; there, that's the
other, the one who is just charging the fellow who is trying
to stop his brother."

"Well done!" he shouted, as Edgar's opponent rolled
over.

The woman asked no more questions until the match
was over, but stood looking on intently as the players came
off the ground. Rupert and Edgar were together, laughing
and talking in high spirits; for each had kicked a goal, and
the town boys had been beaten by four goals to one. The
boy to whom she had been speaking had long before strolled
away to another part of the field, but she turned to another
as the Clintons approached.

"Those are the Clintons, are they not?" she asked.

"Yes, and a good sort they are," the boy said heartily.

She stood looking at them intently until they had passed her, then walked away with her eyes bent on the ground, and made her way to a small lodging she had taken in the town. For several days she placed herself so that she could see the boys on their way to and fro between River-Smith's and the college, and watched them at football.

"I wonder who that woman is," Rupert said one day to his brother. "I constantly see her about, and she always seems to be staring at me."

"I thought she stared at me too," Edgar said. "I am sure I do not know her. I don't think I have ever seen her face before."

"She asked me whether you were Clinton the other day when you were playing football. It was just after you had made a run with the ball, and some one shouted, 'Well done, Clinton!' And she asked me which was Clinton, and whether there were not two of them. And of course I pointed you both out," a youngster said who was walking with them.

"That is rum, too," Rupert said. "I wonder who the woman is, Edgar, and what interest she can have in us."

"If she has any interest, Rupert, I suppose she will stop staring some day and speak. Perhaps it is some old servant, though I don't remember her. Well, it is no odds anyway."

Jane Humphreys was much puzzled as to what step she should take first. During all these years she had waited she had always expected that she should have known which was her own child as soon as she set eyes on the boys, and was surprised and disappointed to find that even after a week's stay at Cheltenham, and examining their faces as closely as she could, she had not the slightest idea which was which. She had imagined that she should not only know, but feel an affection for the boy who was her own, and she had fully intended to place him in the position of Captain Clinton's heir, trusting to receive the promise of a large sum from him when he should come into possession.

Now it seemed to her that she cared no more for one than for the other, and that her best plan therefore was to place in the position of heir whichever of them was most likely to suit her purpose. But here, again, she was in a difficulty. If they resembled each other in no other point, they both looked thoroughly manly, straightforward, and honest lads, neither of whom would be likely to entertain any dishonourable proposition. Her intention had been to say to her son, "You are not really the twin brother, as you suppose, of the other. Captain and Mrs. Clinton do not know which of you two is their child." She wondered whether they already knew as much as that. Probably they did. So many people had known of that affair at Agra, that Captain Clinton had probably told them himself. She would tell the boy, "I am the only person in the world who can clear up the mystery. I have the key to it in my hand, and can place either you or the other in the position of sole heir to the estate. I shall expect to be paid a handsome sum from the one I put into possession. Remember, on one hand I can give you a splendid property, on the other I can show you to have been from the first a usurper of things you had no right to – an interloper and a fraud."

It had seemed to her a simple matter before she came down to Cheltenham. Surely no boy in his senses would hesitate a moment in accepting her offer. It had always been a fixed thing in her mind that this would be so, but now she felt that it was not so certain as she before imagined. She hesitated whether she should not defer it, until the boys came of age, and the one she chose could sign a legal document; but she was anxious to leave England, and go right away to America or Australia. Besides, if she had the promise she could enforce its fulfilment. Which boy should she select? She changed her mind several times, and at last determined that she would leave it to chance, and would choose the one whom she next met.

It chanced that Edgar was the first she encountered after having taken this resolution, and it happened that he was walking by himself, having remained in the class-room a few minutes after the rest of the boys had left, to speak to the master respecting a difficult passage in a lesson. The woman placed herself in his way.

"Well, what is it?" he said. "You have been hanging about for the last week. What is it you want?"

"I want to speak to you about something very important."

"Oh, nonsense!" he said. "There is nothing important you can have to tell me."

"Yes, there is; something of the greatest importance. You do not suppose that I should have been here for a week waiting to tell it to you, if it was not."

"Well, I suppose you think it important," he said; "so fire away."

"I cannot tell you now," she said; "it is too long a story. Could you spare me half an hour, young sir? You will not be sorry for it afterwards, I promise you."

Edgar looked impatiently at his watch. He had nothing particular to do at the moment, and his curiosity was excited.

"I can spare it you now," he said.

"I am staying at this address," she said, handing him a piece of paper. "It is not five minutes' walk from here. I will go on, if you will follow me."

"All right," Edgar said, looking at the paper; "though I expect it is some fooling or other." She walked away rapidly, and he sauntered after her. She was standing with the door open when he arrived, and he followed her into a small parlour. He threw himself down into a chair.

"Now, fire away," he said; "and be as quick as you can."

"Before I begin," she said quietly, "will you tell me if you know anything relating to the circumstances of your birth?"

He looked at her in astonishment. "No," he said. "What in the world should I know about the circumstances of my birth?"

"You know that you were born at Agra in India?"

"Of course I know that."

"And your father, Captain Clinton, has never spoken to you about the circumstances?"

Edgar shook his head. "No; I only know that I was born there."

"I should have thought that he would have told you the story," she said; "for there were many knew of it, and you would be sure to hear it sooner or later."

"I do not want to hear of it," he said, leaping to his feet. "If there was anything my father wanted me to know he would tell it to me at once. You do not suppose I want to hear it from anyone else?"

He was making for the door, when she said, "Then you do not know that you are not his son?"

He stopped abruptly. "Don't know I am not his son!" he repeated. "You must be mad."

"I am not mad at all," she said. "You are not his son. Not any relation in the world to him. Sit down again and I will tell you the story."

He mechanically obeyed, feeling overwhelmed with the news he had heard. Then as she told him how the children had become mixed, and how Captain Clinton had decided to bring them up together until he should be able to discover by some likeness to himself or wife which was his son, Edgar listened to the story with a terrible feeling of oppression stealing over him. He could not doubt that she was speaking the truth, for if it were false it could be contradicted at once. There were circumstances too which seemed to confirm it. He recalled now, that often in their younger days his father and mother had asked casual visitors if they saw any likeness between either of the children to them; and he specially remembered how closely Colonel Winterbottom, who had been major in his father's regiment, had scrutinized them both, and how he had said, "No, Clinton, for the life of me I cannot see that one is more like you and your wife than the other." And now this woman had told him that he was not their son; and he understood that she must be this sergeant's wife, and that if he was not Captain Clinton's son she must be his mother.

"You are Mrs. Humphreys, I suppose?" he said in a hard, dry voice when she had ceased speaking.

"I am your mother," she said. He moved as if struck with sudden pain as she spoke, but said nothing.

"I sacrificed myself for your sake," she went on after a pause. "I had them both, and it seemed to me hard that my boy should grow up to be a boy of the regiment, with nothing better to look forward to than to enlist in it some day, while the other, no better in any respect than him, should grow up to be a rich man, with everything the heart could desire, and I determined that he should have an equal chance with the other. I knew that perhaps some day they might find out which was which by a likeness, but that was not certain; and at any rate you would get a good education and be well brought up, and you were sure to be provided for, and when the time should come, if there was still doubt, I could give you the chance of either having the half or all, just as you chose. It was terrible for me to give you up altogether, but I did it for your good. I suffered horribly, and the women of the regiment turned against me. Your father treated me badly, and I had to leave him and come home to England. But my comfort has all along been that I had succeeded; that you were being brought up as a gentleman, and were happy and well cared for."

Edgar sat silent for some time. "How do you know," he asked suddenly, "that it is Rupert and not I who is the real son?"

"One of the infants," she said, "had a tiny mole no bigger than a pin's head on his shoulder, and I was sure that I would always know them apart from that."

"Yes, Rupert has a mark like that," Edgar admitted, for he had noticed it only a short time before.

"Yes," the woman said quietly. "Mrs. Clinton's child had that mark. It was very, very small and scarcely noticeable, but as I washed and dressed them when babies, I noticed it."

"Well, what next?" Edgar asked roughly.

"As I said, my boy," –Edgar winced as she spoke–"it is for you to choose whether you will have half or all the property. If I hold my tongue you will go on as you are now, and they will never know which is their son. If you like to have it all, to be the heir of that grand place and everything else, I have only to go and say that my boy had a mole on his shoulder. There is nothing I would not do to make you happy."

"And I suppose," Edgar said quietly, "you will want some money for yourself?"

"I do not wish to make any bargain, if that is what you mean," she said in an indignant tone. "I know, of course, that you can give me no money now. I suppose that in either case you would wish to help a mother who has done so much for you. I don't expect gratitude at present. Naturally you are upset about what I have told you. Some day when you grow to be a man you will appreciate better than you can now what I have done for you, and what you have gained by it."

Edgar sat silent for a minute or two, and then he rose quietly and said, "I will think it all over. You shall have my answer in a day or two," and without another word left the room and sauntered off.

"What is the matter, Edgar?" Rupert asked two hours later. "I have been looking for you everywhere, and young Johnson has only just said that you told him to tell me you were feeling very seedy, and were going to lie down for a bit."

"I have got a frightful headache, Rupert," Edgar, who was lying with his face to the wall, said. "I am too bad to talk, old fellow; let me alone. I daresay I shall be all right when I have had a night's sleep. Tell River-Smith, will you, that I am seedy, and cannot come down to tea. I do not want the doctor or anything of that sort, but if I am not all right in the morning, I will see him."

Rupert went out quietly. It was something new Edgar's being like this, he never remembered him having a bad headache before. "I expect," he said to himself, "he got hurt in one of those scrimmages yesterday, although he did not say anything about it. I do hope that he is not going to be ill. The examinations are on next week, it will be a frightful

43

nuisance for him to miss them." He went into Edgar's dormitory again the last thing. He opened the door very quietly in case he should be asleep.

"I am not asleep," Edgar said; "I am rather better now. Good-night, Rupert," and he held out his hand. Rupert was surprised at the action, but took his hand and pressed it.

"Good-night, Edgar. I do hope that you will be all right in the morning."

"Good-night, old fellow. God bless you!" and there was almost a sob in the lad's voice.

Rupert went out surprised and uneasy. "Edgar must be worse than he says," he thought to himself. "It is rum of him saying good-night in that way. I have never known him do such a thing before. I wish now that I had asked River-Smith to send round for the doctor. I daresay Edgar would not have liked it, but it would have been best; but he seemed so anxious to be quiet and get off to sleep, that I did not think of it."

The first thing in the morning Rupert went to his brother's dormitory to see how he was. He tapped at the door, but there was no answer. Thinking that his brother was asleep, he turned the handle and went in. An exclamation of surprise broke from him. Edgar was not there and the bed had not been slept in, but was just as he had seen it when Edgar was lying on the outside. On the table was a letter directed to himself. He tore it open.

"My dear Rupert," it began, "a horrible thing has happened, and I shall be off to-night. I have learned that I am not your brother at all, but that I was fraudulently put in that position. I have been writing this afternoon to father and mother. Oh! Rupert, to think that it is the last time I can call them so. They will tell you the whole business. I am writing this by the light of the lamp in the passage, and you will all be up in a few minutes, so I have no time to say more. I shall post the other letter to-night. Good-bye, Rupert! Good-bye, dear old fellow! We have been happy together, haven't we? and I hope you will always be so. Perhaps some day when I have made myself a name – for I have no right to call myself Clinton, and I won't call myself by my real name – I may see you again. I have taken the note, but I know that you won't grudge it me."

Rupert read the letter through two or three times, then ran down as he was, in his night-shirt and trousers, and passed in to the master's part of the private house. "Robert," he said to the man-servant whom he met in the passage, "is Mr. River-Smith dressed yet?"

"He is not finished dressing yet, Master Clinton; at least he has not come out of his room. But I expect he is pretty near dressed."

"Will you ask him to come out to me at once, please?" Rupert said. "It is a most serious business, or you may be sure I should not ask."

The man asked no questions, for he saw by Rupert's face that this must be something quite out of the ordinary way. "Just step into this room and I will fetch him," he said.

In a minute the master came in. "What is it, Clinton,– nothing serious the matter, I hope?"

"Yes, sir, I am afraid it is something very serious. My brother was not well yesterday evening. He said that he had a frightful headache, but he thought it would be all right in the morning, and he went and lay down on his bed. I thought that he was strange in his manner when I went in to say good-night to him; and when I went in this morning, sir, the bed hadn't been slept in and he was gone, and he has left me this note, and it is evident, as you will see, that he is altogether off his head. You see, he fancies that he is not my brother."

The master had listened with the gravest concern, and now glanced hastily through the letter.

" 'Tis strange indeed," he said. "There is no possibility, of course, that there is anything in this idea of his?"

"No, sir, of course not. How could there be?"

"That I cannot say, Clinton. Anyhow the matter is most serious. Of course he could not have taken any clothes with him?"

"No, sir; at least he cannot have got any beyond what he stands in. I should think the matron would not have given him any out, especially as he must have told her that he was ill, or he could not have got into the dormitory."

"I had better see her first, Clinton; it is always well to be quite sure of one's ground. You go up and dress while I make the inquiries."

Rupert returned to the dormitory, finished dressing, and then ran down again. "He has taken no clothes with him, Clinton. The matron says that he went to her in the afternoon and said that he had a splitting headache, and wanted to be quite quiet and undisturbed. She offered to send for the doctor, but he said that he expected that he should be all right in the morning, but that if he wasn't of course the doctor could see him then. So she unlocked the door of the dormitory and let him in. I asked her if he had his boots on. She said no; he was going up in them, contrary to rule, when she reminded him of it, and he took them off and put them in the rack in the wood-closet. I have seen the boot-boy, and he says he noticed when he went there this morning early to clean them, No. 6 rack was empty. So your brother must have come down, after he had gone up to the dormitory, and got his boots.

"Now let us ask a few questions of the servants." He rang the bell, and sent for some of the servants. "Which of you were down first this morning?" he asked.

"I was down first, sir," one of the girls said.

"Did you find anything unusual?"

"Yes, sir. One of the windows downstairs, looking into the yard, was open, though I know I closed it and put up the shutters last night; and John says the door of the yard has been unbolted too, and that the lock had been forced."

The master went out, walked across the yard, and examined the lock.

"There would be no difficulty in opening that on this side," he said to Rupert; "it could be done with a strong pocket-knife easily enough."

"What is to be done, sir?" Rupert asked anxiously. "Shall I telegraph to my father?"

"I think you had better go and see him, Clinton. Your brother probably did not leave the house until twelve o'clock, though he may have gone at eleven. But whether eleven or twelve it makes no difference. No doubt he posted the letter he speaks of the first thing on leaving; but, you see, it is a cross post to your place, and the letter could not anyhow have got there for delivery this morning. You can hardly explain it all by telegram; and I think, as I said, it is better that you should go yourself. I will have breakfast put for you in my study, and I will have a fly at the door. You will be able to catch the eight-o'clock train into Gloucester, and you should be home by eleven."

"You do not think anything could have happened to him?" Rupert asked anxiously.

"No, I do not think that there is any fear of that, Clinton. You see, he has got a fixed idea in his head; he has evidently acted with deliberation. Besides, you see in his letter to you he says he shall not see you until he has made a name for himself. I tell you frankly, Clinton, that my own impression is that your brother is not mad, but that he has – of course I do not know how, or attempt to explain it – but that he has in some way got the idea that he is not your brother. Has he been quite himself lately?"

"Quite, sir; I have seen nothing unusual about him at all."

"Did he seem bright and well yesterday morning?"

"Just the same as usual, sir. I was quite surprised when, just at tea-time, I found that he had gone to lie down with the headache."

"Did he get any letter yesterday?"

"No, sir; we neither of us had any letter, in the morning anyhow. He may have received one in the afternoon, for anything I know."

"I will go and ask Robert," the master said; "he always takes the letters from the letter-bag."

47

"No, Clinton," he went on when he returned; "there were only three letters for the boys in the afternoon mail, and neither of them was for him. He cannot have seen anyone, can he, who could have told him any story that would serve as a foundation for this idea?"

Then an idea flashed across Rupert. "Well, sir, a rather curious thing has happened in the last few days. There has been a woman about here, and it appears she asked one of the boys which were the Clintons; and we have seen her every time we have been out, and we both noticed that she has stared at us in a very strange way. I don't know that that can possibly have anything to do with it. She may have spoken to Edgar yesterday. Of course I cannot say."

"Well, I must be going now. I have told Robert to put your breakfast in my study, and to send the boy for a fly."

"What will you say to the boys, sir?" Rupert asked anxiously.

"There will be no occasion to say anything for a day or two beyond the fact that you are obliged to go home suddenly. I shall only say Clinton, but it will naturally be supposed that I mean both of you. If it gets out that you have gone alone, which it may do, although I shall give strict orders to the contrary, I shall of course mention that we fear that your brother got his head hurt in that football match, and that he has taken up some strange ideas and has gone off. But it is hardly likely that the matter will leak out in any way until you return, or I hear from you. I think you can make yourself quite easy on that score."

It was half-past eleven when Rupert Clinton reached home. On the way he had thought over how he had best break the news quietly to his father, and he got out of the trap that had driven him from the station at the lodge, and made a long circuit so as to reach the stable without being seen from the front windows of the house. He went at once to the old coachman, who was a great ally of the boys. The man uttered an exclamation of astonishment at seeing him.

GONE

"Why, Master Rupert, I thought that you were not coming home for another fortnight. Well, you have given me a start!"

"Look here, Fellows, I have come to see my father about a serious matter, and I want to see him before I see my mother."

"Nothing the matter with Master Edgar, I hope, sir?"

"Yes, it is about him; but I will tell you presently, Fellows, I don't want to lose a minute now. Please go into the house and get my father to come out at once to the stables. Make any excuse you like to bring him out, and as you come along you can tell him I am here."

In five minutes Captain Clinton hurried into the saddle-room, where Rupert was standing. He was pale and agitated.

"What is the matter, Rupert,– has anything happened to Edgar? I know that it must be something very serious or you would never come like this."

"It is serious, father, very serious;" and he told him what had happened, and handed him the letter that Edgar had left.

"You see he has evidently gone out of his mind, father."

Captain Clinton ran his eye over the letter and gave an exclamation of surprise and grief, then he stood for a minute covering his face with his hand. When he removed it Rupert saw that his eyes were filled with tears.

"Poor boy" he murmured. "I see that we have made a terrible mistake, although we did it for the best."

"A mistake, father! Why, is it possible, can it be true that –"

"That Edgar is not your brother, my boy? Yes, it is certain that he is not your brother, though whether he or you is our son we know not."

Rupert stood speechless with astonishment. "One of us not your son!" he said at last in a broken voice. "Oh, father, how can that be?"

"It happened thus, Rupert," Captain Clinton said, and then told him the story of the confusion that had arisen between the children. He then went on: "You see, Rupert,

49

we hoped, your mother and I, at first that we should find out as you grew up, by the likeness one of you might develop to your mother or myself, which was our child; but for some years now, my boy, I have feared rather than hoped to discover a likeness, and have been glad that neither of you took after either of us, as far as we could see. We loved you equally, and could not bear the thought of losing either of you. We had two sons instead of one, that was all; and had one been proved to be ours, we should have lost the other. We intended to tell you in a short time how the matter stood, and that while one was our adopted son and the other our own, we neither knew nor cared which was which, loving you both equally and regarding you both as our own. Indeed we should never have told you about it, had it not been that as the story of the confusion at your birth was known to a great many men who were at that time in India, it was almost sure to come to your ears sooner or later. Had we ever dreamt that it would come like this, of course we should have told you long ago. But how can Edgar have learnt it? Still more, how can anyone have been able to tell him – what even we do not know – that he is not our son?"

"You will know when the letter arrives by the next post, father. But now I have heard the story, I think it must have been told him by a woman;" and he related how they had been watched by a woman who was a stranger to them.

"What was she like, Rupert?"

Rupert described her as well as he was able.

"I have no doubt that it was Mrs. Humphreys, Rupert; she would be about the age you describe, and, allowing for the seventeen years that have passed since I have seen her, like her in appearance. But we had better go in to your mother now, she must be told. I will go in first and break it to her. Of course there is nothing else that can be done until we get Edgar's letter. I will send a man off on horseback to the post-office; we shall get it an hour earlier than if we wait for the postman to bring it."

GONE

It was half an hour before Captain Clinton came out from the drawing-room and called Rupert in. The boy had been telling the news to Madge, having asked his father if he should do so. She had been terribly distressed, and Rupert himself had completely broken down.

"You can come in now, both of you," Captain Clinton said. "Of course, your mother is dreadfully upset, so try and keep up for her sake."

Mrs. Clinton embraced Rupert in silence, she was too affected for speech.

"Do you think," she said after a time in broken tones, "Edgar can have gone with this woman?"

"I don't know, mother; I have not been able to think about it. I should not think he could. I know if it had been me I should have hated her even if she was my mother, for coming after all this time to rob me of your love and father's. I should run away as he has done, I daresay, though I don't know about that; but I would not have gone with her."

"I cannot make out how she could have known which was which," Captain Clinton said, walking up and down the room; "we have never seen any likeness in either of you to ourselves, but it is possible she may have seen a likeness in Edgar to her husband. By the way," he said suddenly, "I must send off a telegram to River-Smith; he, of course, will be most anxious."

He took a telegram form from his desk, and after a minute's hesitation wrote: "No anxiety as to Edgar's mind – can account for his conduct – will write fully to-morrow after I have received his letter – shall keep Rupert here some days." Then putting it in an envelope, he rang the bell and directed the servant to give it to one of the grooms with orders to ride with it at once to the nearest telegraph station.

"Now, Rupert, the best thing you and Madge can do is to go out for a walk. You can know nothing more until the letter arrives, and it will be better for you to be moving about than to be sitting here quietly.

"Your mother had best lie down until the letter comes; it cannot be here until five o'clock."

THE DASH FOR KHARTOUM

Madge and Rupert as they walked talked the matter over in every possible light, the only conclusion at which they arrived being that whoever might be Edgar's father and mother they would always regard him as their brother, and should love him just the same as before.

"I cannot think why he ran away!" Madge exclaimed over and over again. "I am sure I should not run away if I found that I wasn't father and mother's real daughter. They have been everything to me, and I could not love them a bit less if I did know that I was their adopted child instead of being their real one."

"No, certainly not," Rupert agreed; "but then, you see, Madge, Edgar may have thought that he had been adopted, not as childless people sometimes adopt children, but because they could not help adopting him."

"But that wasn't his fault, Rupert."

"No, that wasn't his fault; but I can understand him feeling that it made a great difference. Oh, I wonder what he is doing! I expect he went up to London by the night mail; he would have caught that at Glo'ster. But what could he do when he got there?"

"Oh, I am not thinking about that!" the girl said. "I am thinking what he must feel when he knows father and mother are not his father and mother, and that you and I are not his brother and sister. It must be awful, Rupert."

"It must be awful," Rupert agreed. "I do not know what I should have done had it been me, and you know it might just as well have been me as Edgar. I wish it were five o'clock!"

The afternoon seemed indeed endless to them all. For the last half-hour Rupert and Madge sat at the window gazing across the park for the first sight of the horseman, and at last they exclaimed simultaneously, "There he comes!"

Captain Clinton, who had been sitting by the sofa holding his wife's hand in his, rose. "I will go and meet him," he said.

"Rupert and Madge, you had better go into the library until I call you. I must read it over first to your mother."

GONE

Without a word they went into the other room, and from the window watched Captain Clinton as he walked quickly down the drive to meet the groom. They saw him take the letter, and, as the man rode on towards the stables, open it and stand reading it.

"It is very bad," Madge said almost in a whisper, as she saw her father drop his hand despondently to his side, and then with bent head walk towards the house. Not another word was spoken until Captain Clinton opened the door and called them. Madge had been crying silently, and the tears were running fast down Rupert's cheeks as he sat looking out on to the park.

"You had better read the letter here," Captain Clinton said. "I may tell you what I did not mention before, that there was a strong opinion among many at the time, that the confusion between the children arose, not from accident, as was said, but was deliberate, and this letter confirms that view. This is what has hit Edgar so hard."

The letter was as follows: –

"My dearest father, for I cannot call you anything else, I have just heard about my birth from a woman who calls herself my mother, and who, I suppose, has a right to do so, though certainly I shall never call her or think of her so. She has told me about her child and yours getting mixed, and how you brought both up in hopes of finding out some day which was which.

"Rupert and I had noticed for some days a woman looking at us, and she met me this afternoon and said she had something of extreme importance to tell me. I went with her and she told me the story, and said that I was her son and not yours. I asked her how she knew me from Rupert, and she said that one of us had a small mole on the shoulder. I knew that Rupert had a tiny mole there, and she said that that was the mark by which she knew your son from hers.

"Then, father, she told me that she had done it all on purpose, and had sacrificed herself in order that I might benefit from it. This was all horrible! And then she actually

53

proposed that I should not only keep silent about this, but offered to come forward and declare that it was her son who had the mole on his shoulder, so that I might get the whole and Rupert none. I don't want to say what I felt. I only told her I would think it over. I have been thinking it over, and I am going away. My dear father and mother, for I shall always think of you so, I thank you for all your love and kindness, which I have received through a horrible fraud. If it had all been an accident, and you had found out for yourselves by the likeness that Rupert was your son, I do not think that I should have minded, at least nothing like so much. I should, of course, have been very grieved that you were not my father and mother, and that Rupert and Madge were not my brother and sister; but it would have been nobody's fault, and I am sure that you would all still have loved me. But to know that it has been a wicked fraud, that I have been an impostor palmed upon you, that there has been a plot and conspiracy to rob you, and that I have a mother who not only did this, but who could propose to me to go on deceiving you, and even to join in a fresh fraud and to swindle Rupert, is so awful that there is nothing for me to do but to go away.

"I feel sure you will all be sorry, and that though I am not your son you would go on treating me as if I were a younger brother of Rupert's. But I could not bear it, father. I could not accept anything from you, for I should feel that it was the result of this wicked fraud, that it was what this woman, I cannot call her mother, had schemed for me to get. Some day when I have made my way, and when all this may not hurt me so horribly as it seems to do now, I will come and see you all if you will let me, to thank you all for the love and kindness that should never have been mine. But that will not be till I am in a position when I can want nothing, for I feel now that were I dying of hunger I could not accept a crust from your hands, for if I did so I should feel I was a party to this abominable fraud. God bless you, dearest father and mother and Rupert and Madge! – Your unhappy Edgar."

CHAPTER IV
BACK AT SCHOOL

IT was a long time after they had, with many breaks, read Edgar's letter to the end before Rupert and Madge could compose themselves sufficiently to accompany their father into the drawing-room. They again broke down when they met their mother; and it was not until Captain Clinton said, "Come, we must all pull ourselves together and see what is to be done, and talk the whole matter over calmly," that by a great effort they recovered their composure. "Now, in the first place, we must try to find Edgar. He has got twenty-four hours' start of us, but that is not very much. I suppose you think, Rupert, that there is no doubt that he went up to town by the night train."

"I have no doubt that he got away in time to do so, father; but of course he might have gone by the down train, which passes through Gloucester somewhere about the same time."

"I do not think it likely that he did that, Rupert. I should say he was sure to go to London; that is almost always the goal people make for, unless it is in the case of boys who want to go to sea, when they would make for Liverpool or some other port. But I don't think Edgar was likely to do that. I don't think he had any special fancy for the sea; so we may assume that he has gone to London. What money had he?"

"He had that five-pound note you sent three days ago, father, to clear off any ticks we had, and to pay our journey home. That is what he meant when he said, 'I have taken the note, but I know you won't grudge it me.' I think he had about a pound left – that is about what I had – and I know when the note came he said that the money he had was enough to last him to the end of the term. So he would have the five-pound note untouched when he got to London, and if driven to it he could get, I should think, six or seven pounds for his watch and chain."

"That would give him enough to keep him some little time. If he had been a couple of years older I should say that he would probably enlist at once, as you had both made up your minds to go into the army. But although lads do enlist under the proper age, no recruiting officer or doctor would pass him as being eighteen. The first thing to do will be to advertise for him – in the first place to advertise offering a reward for information as to his whereabouts, and in the second place advertising to him direct, begging him to come home."

"But he would never come, father," Rupert said, looking at the letter, which Captain Clinton still held in his hand.

"It would depend how we advertised. Suppose I were to say, 'Statement of woman not believed; we are in as much doubt as before.' "

The others looked up in intense surprise. "Oh, father, how could you say that?" Rupert exclaimed. "Oh, if we could but say so! I should be quite, quite content to know that either of us might be her son – that would not matter so much if we felt that you loved us both equally; but how could you say so!"

"Because, Rupert," Captain Clinton said gravely, "I still think there is great ground for doubt."

"Do you really, father? Oh, I am pleased! I think – yes, I am sure that I could bear now to know that Edgar is your real son, and not I. It would be so different to learn it from your lips, to know that you all love me still, instead of hearing it in the dreadful way Edgar did. But how do you doubt, father? It seemed to me from reading the letter so certain."

"Do you really doubt, Percy?" Mrs. Clinton asked.

BACK AT SCHOOL

"I do indeed, Lucy; and I will give you my reasons. In the first place, this woman left India a few weeks after the affair. She certainly could not have seen the children until we returned to England, and, so far as we know, has never seen them since. If she has seen them, she never can have spoken to them or come in any sort of contact with them, therefore she cannot possibly have known which is which. When she saw them at Cheltenham, and Rupert says that she was there more than a week, she met them upon every possible occasion and stared hard at them. It is evident, therefore, that she was for all that time doubtful. No doubt she was doing what we used to do, trying to detect a resemblance. Now, if we in all these years with the boys, constantly watching their ways and listening to their voices, could detect no resemblance, it is extremely improbable that she was able to do so from merely seeing them a score of times walking in the streets. I do not say that it is impossible she could have done so; I only say it is extremely improbable; and I think it much more likely that, finding she could see no resemblance whatever, she determined to speak to the first whom she might happen to find alone."

"But there is the mark, father," Rupert said.

"Yes, there is the mark," Mrs. Clinton repeated.

"I did not know you had a mark, Rupert. I wonder we never noticed it, Lucy."

"It is a very tiny one, father. I never noticed it myself – indeed I can hardly see it before a glass, for it is rather at the back of the shoulder – until Edgar noticed it one day. It is not larger than the head of a good-sized pin. It is a little dark-brown mole. Perhaps it was smaller and lighter when I was a baby; but it must have been there then, or she would not have known about it."

"That is so, Rupert; but the mere fact that it is there does not in any way prove that you are our son. Just see what Edgar says about it in his letter. Remember the woman could not have known which of you boys had the mark; and that she did not know, that is to say, that she had not recognized the likeness, appears from Edgar's letter. This is what he says: 'She said that one of us had a small mole on the shoulder. I knew that Rupert had a tiny mole there; and she said that was the mark by which she knew your son from hers.' Suppose Edgar had replied, 'Yes, I have such a mark on my shoulder,' might she not have said, 'that is the mark by which I can distinguish my son from that of Captain Clinton?'"

The others were silent. Then Mrs. Clinton said, "You know, Percy, I do not wish to prove that one more than the other of the boys is ours; but naturally the woman would wish to benefit her own boy, and if it had been her own boy who had the mark, why should she not have told Edgar that she had made a mistake, and that it was Rupert who was her son?"

"I do not suppose, Lucy, that she cared in the slightest which was her son; her main object, of course, was to extort money. Edgar does not say anything at all about that; and of course at first she would try and make out that she was ready to sacrifice herself for him, and would scarcely say that she expected him to make her a handsome allowance when he came into the property, but I have no doubt that was her motive. Well, you see, she had already begun with Edgar. Suppose she said that she had made a mistake, and Rupert was her son. Edgar would have gone in and told him, and would probably have telegraphed to me, so that I could get to Rupert before this woman saw him, and she would have known then that her story would have been upset altogether. No court of law would attach any weight to what she might say. She would have to stand confessed as having been concerned in a gross fraud, and with having lied at first; and unless she was in a position to produce corroborative evidence to prove that her child had this mark, her word would go for nothing.

"Now, I feel sure that she could produce no such evidence. The mark was almost an invisible one, for it was never afterwards noticed. Had she shown it to any of the women of her acquaintance, they would have come forward when the change of children took place, and have pointed out that the children could be easily distinguished, inasmuch as my child had a peculiar mark. I feel sure that even her husband knew nothing about this mark, for I don't believe he was a party to the fraud. He was terribly upset by the whole business, and took to drink afterwards. There were continual quarrels between his wife and himself, and she left him and went to England. I believe if he could have pointed out which was my child and which was his own, he would have done so.

"Certainly, I myself should have attached little or no weight to this woman's story if she had come here with it. I should have turned her out of the house, and have told her to go to a court if she dare and claim the custody of her son. She must have known the weakness of her own position, and as I say, having once opened the matter to Edgar, she determined to stick to it, knowing that a boy taken thus on a sudden would be likely to believe her, whereas if she said that you were her son she would find you already prepared and probably have to confront me too. So you see, Rupert, I can truthfully advertise – 'Woman's story not believed; we are in as much doubt as before; both are regarded by us as our sons.' "

"I am glad, father!" Rupert exclaimed excitedly. "Oh! if Edgar had but written to you first, instead of going straight away."

"It would have been better," Captain Clinton said, "but I cannot blame him. I think it was natural that he should go as he did. He would have thought that had he written to me it would have seemed as if he wanted something from me, and anything would have seemed better to him than that. However, we must set about doing something at once. I shall go by the nine o'clock local to Swindon, and on by the night mail to town. Then I shall set a detective at work. He may find out from the porters if anyone noticed a lad arrive by the night mail this morning, and shall draw up carefully-worded advertisements. I shall write to Mr. River-Smith before I start. What would you like, Rupert – to go back to-morrow, or to stay away until the end of the term? If you take my advice, you will go back; it would be a pity for you to miss your examinations."

"I don't think I could get through the examinations, father, with this on my mind; besides, what should I say to the fellows about Edgar's going away? You see, if we find him before next term begins, we need say nothing about it."

"You would have to account for his having run away, Rupert, anyhow. I think you had better go back, my boy, and tell the facts of the story. There is not the slightest discredit in it, and it would be better for Edgar himself that it should be known that he went under the influence of a mistake than that all sorts of reasons should be assigned for his absence. There will, of course, be no occasion to go into full details. You would tell the story of the confusion that arose as to the children, and say that Edgar had received some information which led him erroneously to conclude that the problem was solved, and that he was not my son, and that therefore he had run away so as to avoid receiving any further benefits from the mistake that had been made."

"Perhaps that would be best, father. Indeed I don't know what I should do if I were to stop here now with nothing to do but to worry about him."

"I am sure it will be best, Rupert. I will tell your master you will return to-morrow afternoon."

Captain Clinton went up to town by the night mail, and in the morning went to a private detective's office. After giving particulars of Edgar's age and appearance he went on: "As he had no luggage with him, and there was nothing particular about his personal appearance, I consider it altogether useless to search for him in London; but I think it possible that he may try to enlist."

"Sixteen is too young for them to take him, unless he looks a good deal older than he is."

"Yes, I quite see that. At the same time that is the only thing that occurs to us as likely for him to try."

"Not likely to take to the sea, sir?"

"Not at all likely from what we know of his fancies. Still he might do that for a couple of years with a view to enlisting afterwards."

"How about going to the States or Canada?"

"That again is quite possible."

"Had he money with him, sir?"

"He had about five pounds in his pocket, and a gold watch and chain that he had only had a few months, and could, I should think, get seven or eight pounds for; but I do not see what he could do to get his living if he went abroad."

"No, sir; but then young gents always have a sort of fancy that they can get on well out there, and if they do not mind what they turn to I fancy that most of them can. Is he in any trouble, sir? You will excuse my asking, but a young chap who gets into trouble generally acts in a different sort of way to one who has gone out what we may call venturesome."

"No, he has got into no trouble," Captain Clinton said. "He has gone away under a misunderstanding, but there is nothing whatever to make him wish to conceal himself beyond the fact that he will do all he can to prevent my tracing him at present. Here are half a dozen of his photos. If you want more I can get them struck off."

"I could do with another half-dozen," the man said. "I will send them down to men who act with me at Southampton, Hull, Liverpool, Glasgow, and Plymouth, and will send two or three abroad. He might cross over to Bremen or Hamburg, a good many go that way now. I will look after the recruiting offices here myself; but as he is only sixteen, and as you say does not look older, I do not think there is a chance of his trying that. No recruiting sergeant would take him up. No, sir; I should say that if he has no friends he can go to, the chances are he will try to ship for the States or Canada. But what are we to do if we find him?"

Captain Clinton had not thought of this.

"Of course," the man went on, "if you gave an authority for me to send down to each of my agents, they could take steps to stop him."

"No," Captain Clinton said after a pause, during which he had been thinking that as he could not swear that Edgar was his son, he was in fact powerless in the matter. "No, I do not wish that done. I have no idea whatever of coercing him. I want, if possible, to see him and converse with him before he goes. If that is not possible, and if he is not found until just as the ship is sailing, then I want your agent to wire to me the name of the steamer in which he goes and the port to which it sails. Then if there is a faster steamer going, I might be there as soon as he is; if not, I should wish you to telegraph to a private detective firm across the water, which I suppose you could do, to have somebody to meet the steamer as she came in, and without his knowing it to keep him under his eye until I arrive."

"I could manage all that, sir, easily enough. I will send off four of the photographs at once to the ports and the others as soon as I get them, and will go down with the other photograph to the recruiting office and arrange with one of the sergeants engaged there to let me know if he turns up, and will send a man down to the docks to watch the ships there. I will send off the other photos directly I get them."

There was nothing else for Captain Clinton to do, but before he returned home he wrote out a series of advertisements and left them at the offices of the principal papers. They ran as follows: – "If E. C., who left Cheltenham suddenly, will return home he will find that he has acted under a misapprehension. The woman's story was untrustworthy. He is still regarded as a son by P. C. and L. C." Having done this he drove to Paddington, and went down by an afternoon train.

Rupert arrived at Cheltenham just as the others had sat down to tea.

"Hullo, Clinton! Back again, eh? Glad to see you."

BACK AT SCHOOL

Rupert nodded a reply to the greeting. His heart was too full to speak, and he dropped into the seat he was accustomed to use, the others moving up closely to make room for him. A significant glance passed between the boys. They saw that Edgar was not with him, and guessed that there was something wrong. There had been a good deal of wonder among them at the Clintons' sudden disappearance, and although several of the boys had seen Rupert go into his brother's dormitory none had seen Edgar, and somehow or other it leaked out that Rupert had started in a cab to the station alone. There had been a good deal of quiet talk among the seniors about it. All agreed that there was something strange about the matter, especially as Robert, when questioned on the subject, had replied that Mr. River-Smith's orders were that he was to say nothing about it. As a precautionary measure orders were given to the juniors that no word about the Clintons' absence was to be said outside the house.

After tea was over Rupert went up to Pinkerton.

"Pinkerton, I should like to have a talk with you and Easton and two or three others – Skinner, and Mossop, and Templer – yes, and Scudamore."

"Just as you like, Clinton. Of course if you like to tell us anything we shall be glad to hear it, but we all know that your brother was not the sort of fellow to get into any dishonourable sort of scrape, and I can promise you we shall ask no questions if you would rather keep the matter altogether to yourself."

"No, I would rather tell you," Rupert said. "I know none of you would think that Edgar would have done anything wrong, but all sorts of stories are certain to go about, and I would rather that the truth of the matter were known. You are the six head fellows of the house, and when I have told you the story you can do as you like about its going further."

"Well, if you go up to my study," Pinkerton said, "I will bring the others up."

In three or four minutes the party were gathered there.

THE DASH FOR KHARTOUM

"Look here, Clinton," Easton said, "Pinkerton says he has told you that we are all sure that, whatever this is all about, your brother has done nothing he or you need be ashamed about. I should like to say the same thing, and if it is painful for you to tell it do not say anything about it. We shall be quite content to know that he has left, if he has left – although I hope we shall see him again next term for some good reason or other."

"No, I would rather tell it," Rupert said. "It is a curious story, and a very unpleasant one for us, but there is nothing at all for us to be ashamed about." And he went on to tell them the whole story, ending with "You see, whether Edgar or I am the son of Captain Clinton, or of this sergeant and his scheming wife, is more than we can say."

"It does not matter a bit to us," Easton said, breaking the silence of surprise with which they had listened to the story.

"We like you and your brother for yourselves, and it does not matter a rap to us, nor as far as I can see to anyone else, who your fathers and mothers were."

"I call it horribly hard lines for you both," Skinner put in; "deuced hard lines, especially for your brother."

Pinkerton said: "By what you say Captain Clinton and his wife don't care now which is their real son; one is real and the other adopted, and as they regard you in the same light they don't even want to know which is which. Well, now you know that, it seems to me you are all right anyhow. You see your brother didn't know that, and when this woman told him she was his mother, and that the whole thing had been a preconcerted plot on her part, I can quite understand his going straight away. I think we should all have done the same if we had had the same story told to us, and had seen we were intended to be parties to a fraud of that sort. Well, I am glad you told us, but I do not think there is any occasion for the story to go further."

"Certainly not," Easton agreed, "it would do no good whatever; and of course it would never be kept in the house, but would come to be the talk of the whole school. All that

64

need be said is that Clinton has told us the reason of his brother leaving so suddenly, that we are all of opinion that he acted perfectly rightly in doing so, and that nothing more is to be said about the matter. We will each give Clinton our word of honour not to give the slightest hint to anyone about it, or to say that it is a curious story or anything of that sort, but just to stick to it that we have heard all about it and are perfectly satisfied."

"That will certainly be the best plan," Pinkerton agreed; "but I think it would be as well for us to say he has left for family reasons, and that it is nothing in any way connected with himself, and that we hope that he will be back again next term."

"Yes, we might say that," Easton agreed; "family reasons mean all sorts of things, and anyone can take their choice out of them. Well, Clinton, I shouldn't worry over this more than you can help. I daresay Edgar will be found in a day or two. At any rate you may be sure that no harm has come to him, or is likely to come to him. If he emigrates, or anything of that sort, he is pretty safe to make his way, and I am sure that whatever he is doing he will always be a gentleman and a good fellow."

"That he will," Mossop said cordially. "I hope we should all have done as he has under the same circumstances, but it would be a big temptation to some fellows to have the alternative of a good fortune and a nice estate on one side, and of going out into the world and making your own living how you can on the other."

There was a chorus of assent.

"Yes," Easton said, "it is very easy to say 'Do what is right and never mind what comes of it;' but we should all find it very hard to follow it in practice if we had a choice like that before us. Well, you tell your brother when you hear of him, Clinton, that we all think better of him than before, and that whether he is a sergeant's son or a captain's we shall welcome him heartily back, and be proud to shake his hand."

THE DASH FOR KHARTOUM

And so it was settled, and to the great disappointment of the rest of the house no clue was forthcoming as to the cause of Edgar Clinton leaving so suddenly; but as the monitors and seniors all seemed perfectly satisfied with what they had heard, it was evident to the others that whatever the cause might be he was not to blame in the matter.

During the short time that remained of the term Rupert got on better than he had expected. While the examination was going on Easton invited him to do his work in his private study, gave him his advice as to the passages likely to be set, and coached him up in difficult points, and he came out higher in his form than he had expected to do.

Three days before the school broke up Easton said: "Clinton, I have had a letter from my father this morning, and he will be very glad if you will come down to spend the holidays at our place. And so shall I. There is very good hunting round us. My father has plenty of horses in his stables, and I expect we shall be rather gay, for my brother comes of age in the week after Christmas, and there is going to be a ball and so on. I don't know how you feel about it, but I should say that it would be better for you than being at home where everything will call your brother to your mind, and your being there will make it worse for the others."

"I am very much obliged to you, Easton; I should like it very much. I will write off to the governor at once and hear what he says. They might like to have me home, and possibly I might be useful in the search for Edgar. As I have told you, I feel sure that he has enlisted. He would be certain to change his name, and it would be no use to anyone who did not know him going to look at the recruits."

"But we agreed, Clinton, that no one would enlist him at his age, and he is altogether too old to go as a band-boy."

"Yes, I know that; and that is what worries me more than anything. Still I cannot help thinking that he will try somehow to get into the army. If he can't, I believe he will do anything he can to get a living until they enlist him."

BACK AT SCHOOL

"I don't think he can anyhow pass as eighteen, Clinton. If it was for anything else he might get up with false moustache or something; but you see he has got to pass a strict examination by a surgeon. I have heard that lots of fellows do enlist under age, but then some fellows look a good bit older than they are. I don't believe any doctor would be humbugged into believing that Edgar is anything like eighteen."

"Well, I will write to my father this afternoon and hear what he says. If he thinks I cannot do any good and they don't want me at home, I shall be very pleased to come to you."

Captain Clinton's letter came by return of post. He said that he was very pleased Rupert had had an invitation that would keep him away. "We have received no news whatever of Edgar, and I don't think that it would be of any use for you to join in the search for him. There is no saying where he may have gone or what he may be doing. I agree with you that he will most likely take any job that offers to keep him until he can enlist. Arrangements have been made with one of the staff sergeants at the head-quarters of recruiting in London to let us know if any young fellow answering to Edgar's description comes up to be medically examined. So we shall catch him if he presents himself there. Unfortunately there are such a number of recruiting depots all over the country, that there is no saying where he may try to enlist – that is, if he does try. However, at present there is certainly nothing you can do. I should like to have you home, and your mother says she should like you too, but I do think that for her sake it is better you should not come. As long as you are away there is nothing to recall at every moment the fact that Edgar has gone, whereas if you were here his absence would be constantly before her. She is quite ill with anxiety, and Dr. Wilkinson agrees with me that change is most desirable. I am sure she would not hear of going away if you were at home; it would give her a good excuse for staying here; but when she hears that you are not coming I think I may be able to persuade her to listen to Wilkinson's opinion, and in that case I shall take her and Madge down to Nice at once. If I can get her there by Christmas so much the better, for Christmas at home would be terribly trying to us all. Once we are there, we can wander about for two or three months in Italy or Spain, or across to Algeria or Egypt – anything to distract her mind."

Accordingly Rupert accepted Easton's invitation, and went with him to his father's in Leicestershire. Had it not been for the uncertainty about Edgar he would have enjoyed his holidays greatly. Although he had always joined to a certain extent in the chaff of his school-fellows at Easton's care about his dress and little peculiarities of manner, he had never shared in Skinner's prejudices against him, and always said that he could do anything well that he chose to turn his hand to, and had appreciated his readiness to do a kindness to anyone who really needed it. It had been his turn now, and the friendly companionship of the elder boy had been of the greatest value to him. Easton had never said much in the way of sympathy, which indeed would have jarred Rupert's feelings, but his kindness had said more than words could do; and Rupert, as he looked back, felt ashamed at the thought that he had often joined in a laugh about him.

At home the points that had seemed peculiar at school were unnoticeable. The scrupulous attention to dress that had there been in strong contrast to the general carelessness of the others in that respect, seemed but natural in his own house, where there were a good many guests staying. Rupert and Edgar had always been more particular at home than at school; but Easton was the same, indeed Rupert thought that he was if anything less particular now than he had been at River-Smith's.

A week after Christmas Rupert received a letter from his father, written at Nice, saying that a letter from Edgar had been forwarded on from home, and giving the brief words in which the lad said that he was well, and that they might be under no uneasiness respecting him. "This does not tell us much," Captain Clinton went on, "but we are very pleased, inasmuch as it seems that Edgar does not mean altogether to drop out of our sight, but will, we hope, write from time to time to let us know that at any rate he is well. The letter has the London post-mark, but of course that shows nothing; it may have been written anywhere and sent to anyone – perhaps to a waiter at an hotel at which he stopped in London, and with whom he had arranged to post any letters that he might inclose to him. The letter has greatly cheered your mother, who, in spite of all I could say, has hitherto had a dread that Edgar in his distress might have done something rash. I have never thought so for an instant. I trust that my two boys are not only too well principled, but too brave to act a coward's part, whatever might befall them. Your mother, of course, agreed with me in theory; but while she admitted that Edgar would never if in his senses do such a thing, urged that his distress might be so great that he would not be responsible for what he was doing. Happily this morbid idea has been dissipated by the arrival of the letter, and I have great hopes now that she will rouse herself, and will shake off the state of silent brooding which has been causing me so much anxiety. It was but this morning that we received the letter, and already she looks brighter and more like herself than she has done since you brought us the news of Edgar's disappearance."

This news enabled Rupert to enjoy the remainder of the holidays much more than he had done the first fortnight. He and Edgar had both been accustomed to ride since they had been children, and had in their Christmas holidays for years accompanied their father to the hunting field, at first upon ponies, but the previous winter on two light-weight carrying horses he had bought specially for them. Mr. Easton had several hunters, and Rupert, who was well mounted, thoroughly enjoyed the hunting, and returned to school with his nerves braced up, ready for work.

"I won't say anything against Easton again," Skinner said when he heard from Rupert how pleasant his holidays had been made for him. "I noticed how he took to you and made things smooth for you the last ten days of the term, and I fully meant to tell him that I was sorry I had not understood him better before; only, in the first place, I never happened to have a good opportunity, and in the second place I don't know that I ever tried to make one. However, I shall tell him now. It is not a pleasant thing to be obliged to own that you have behaved badly, but it is a good deal more unpleasant to feel it and not have the pluck to say so."

Accordingly the next time Easton came into the senior study, Skinner went up to him and said:

"Easton, I want to tell you that I am uncommonly sorry that I have set myself against you because you have been more particular about your dress and things than the rest of us, and because you did not seem as keen as we were about football and things. I know that I have behaved like a fool, and I should like to be friends now if you will let me."

"Certainly I will, Skinner," Easton said, taking the hand he held out. "I don't know that it was altogether your fault. My people at home are rather particular about our being tidy and that sort of thing, and when I came here and some of you rather made fun of me about it, I think that I stuck to it all the more because it annoyed you. I shall be going up for Sandhurst this term, and I am very glad to be on good terms with all you fellows before I leave; so don't let us say anything more about it."

And with another shake of the hands their agreement to be friends was ratified.

The term between Christmas and Easter was always the dullest of the year. The house matches at football were over. Although a game was sometimes played, there was but a languid interest in it. Paper-chases were the leading incident in the term, and there was a general looking forward to spring weather, when cricket could begin and the teams commence practice for the matches of the following term.

Easton was going up in the summer for the examination for the line. He was not troubling himself specially about it; and indeed his getting in was regarded as a certainty, for Mr. Southley had said that he would be safe for the Indian Civil if he chose to try, and considered it a great pity that he was going up for so comparatively an easy competition as that for the line. He occasionally went for a walk with Rupert, and while chatting with him frequently about Edgar, was continually urging him not to let his thoughts dwell too much upon it, but to stick to his work.

The watch at the various ports had long since been given up, for had Edgar intended to emigrate he would certainly have done so very shortly after his arrival in London, as his means would not have permitted him to make any stay there.

"I think it is very thoughtful of Edgar," Easton said one day when Rupert told him that he had heard from his father that another letter had arrived. "So many fellows when they run away or emigrate, or anything of that sort, drop writing altogether, and do not seem to give a thought to the anxiety those at home are feeling for them. He is evidently determined that he will go his own way and accept no help from your people, and under the circumstances I can quite enter into his feelings; but, you see, he does not wish them to be anxious or troubled about him, and I don't think there is anything for you to worry about, Clinton. He may be having a hardish time of it; still he is no doubt getting his living somehow or other, and I don't know that it will do him any harm.

"I think he is the sort of fellow to make his way in whatever line he takes up, and though what he has learnt here may not be of much use to him at the start, his having had a good education is sure to be of advantage to him afterwards. A fellow who could hold his own in a tussle such as we had with the Greenites last term can be trusted to make a good fight in anything. At any rate it is of no use your worrying yourself about him. You see, you will be going up in a year's time for your examination for the line, and you will have to stick to it pretty steadily if you are to get through at the first trial. It won't help matters your worrying about him, and wherever he is and whatever he is doing he is sure to keep his eye on the lists, and he will feel just as much pleasure in seeing your name there as he would have done if he had been here with you. So I should say, work steadily and play steadily. You have a good chance of being in the college boat next term; that and shooting will give you enough to do.

"It is no use sticking to it too hard. I was telling Skinner yesterday he will regularly addle his brain if he keeps on grinding as he is doing now. But it is of no use talking to Skinner; when his mind is set on a thing he can think of nothing else. Last term it was football, now it is reading. It must be an awful nuisance to be as energetic as he is. I cannot see why he should not take life comfortably."

"He would say," Rupert laughed, "he cannot see why he should do things by fits and starts as you do, Easton."

"Ah! but I do not do it on principle," Easton argued. "I am all for taking it quietly, only sometimes one gets stirred up and has to throw one's self into a thing. One does it, you know, but one feels it a nuisance – an unfair wear and tear of the system."

"Your system does not seem to suffer seriously, Easton."

"No; but it might if one were called upon to do these things often. But it is time for us to turn back, or we shall be late for tea."

CHAPTER V
ENLISTED

EDGAR had found but little difficulty in getting out from the house. He had timed himself so as to arrive at the station just before the train left for Gloucester, and taking his ticket, had slipped into an empty carriage. At Gloucester there was half an hour to wait before the up-train came in. This time he got into a carriage with several other people. He did not want to spend the night thinking, and as long as his fellow-passengers talked he resolutely kept his attention fixed on what they were saying. Then when one after the other composed themselves for a sleep, he sat with his eyes closed, thinking over his school-days. He had already, while he lay tossing on his bed, thought over the revelation he had heard from every point of view. He had exhausted the subject, and would not allow his thoughts to return to it.

He now fought the football match of the Greenites over again in fancy. It seemed to him that it was an event that had taken place a long time back, quite in the dim distance, and he was wondering vaguely over this when he too fell asleep, and did not wake up until the train arrived at Paddington. It was with a feeling of satisfaction that he stepped out on to the platform. Now there was something to do. It was too early yet to see about lodgings. He went to a little coffee-house that was already open for the use of the workmen, had some breakfast there, and then walked about for two or three hours until London was astir, leaving his things at the coffee-house. Then he went to a pawnbroker's and pawned his watch and chain. Then, having fetched his things from the coffee-house, he went into the Edgware Road and took an omnibus down to Victoria and then walked on across Vauxhall Bridge, and set to work to look for lodgings.

He was not long in finding a bed-room to let, and here he installed himself. He was convinced Captain Clinton would have a vigilant search made for him, but he thought that he was now fairly safe, however sharp the detectives might be in their hunt for him. He felt deeply the sorrow there would be at home, for he knew that up to now he and Rupert had been loved equally, and that even the discovery that he had had no right to the care and kindness he had received would make no great difference in their feeling towards him. Had the change of children been really the result of accident, he would not have acted as he had done.

He himself had had no hand in the fraud, but were he to accept anything now from Captain Clinton he felt that he would be an accessary to it. Had not his mother, his own mother, proposed that he should take part in the plot, that he should go on deceiving them, and even that he should rob Rupert altogether of his inheritance? It was too horrible to think of. There was nothing for it that he could see but for him to go out utterly from their lives, and to fight his way alone until he could, at any rate, show them that he needed nothing and would accept nothing. He was dimly conscious himself that he was acting unkindly and unfairly to them, and that after all they had done for him they had a right to have a say as to his future; but at present his pride was too hurt, he was too sore and humiliated to listen to the whisper of conscience, and his sole thought was to hide himself and to make his own way in the world.

Lest his resolution should be shaken he carefully abstained from a perusal of the papers, lest his eye might fall upon an advertisement begging him to return. His mind was made up that he would enlist. He knew that at present he could not do so as a private, but he thought that he might be accepted as a trumpeter. He thought it probable that they would guess that such was his intention, and would have given a description of him at the recruiting offices. It was for this reason that he determined to live as long as he could upon his money before trying to enlist, as if some time elapsed he would be less likely to be recognized as answering the description that might be given by Captain Clinton than if he made the attempt at once. From Vauxhall he often crossed to Westminster, and soon struck up an acquaintance with some of the recruiting sergeants.

"Want to enlist, eh?" one of them said.

"I am thinking of entering as a trumpeter."

"Well, you might do that. There are plenty of younger lads than you are trumpeters in the cavalry. I will look at the list and see what regiments have vacancies; but I doubt whether they will take you without a letter from your father saying that you are enlisting with his consent."

"I have no father that I know of," Edgar said.

"Well, then, it is likely they will want a certificate from a clergyman or your schoolmaster as to character; and I expect," the sergeant said shrewdly, "you would have a difficulty in getting such a paper."

Edgar nodded.

"Well, lad, if you have quite made up your mind about it, my advice would be, do not try here. In London they are a lot more particular than they are down in the country, and I should say you are a good deal more likely to rub through at Aldershot or Canterbury than you would be here. They are more particular here. You see, they have no great interest in filling up the ranks of a regiment, while when you go to the regiment itself, the doctors and officers and all of them like seeing it up to its full strength, so their interest is to pass a recruit if they can. I have known scores and hundreds of men rejected here tramp down to Aldershot, or take the train if they had money enough in their pockets to pay the fare, and get passed without a shadow of difficulty."

"I would rather not enlist for the next month or two," Edgar said; "there might be somebody asking after me."

"If you will take my advice, lad, you will go back to your friends. There are many young fellows run away from home, but most of them are precious sorry for it afterwards."

"I am not likely to be sorry for it, sergeant, and if I am I shall not go back. Do you think I could find anyone who would give me lessons on the trumpet?"

"I should say that there would not be any difficulty about that. There is nothing you cannot have in London if you have got money to pay for it. If you were to go up to the Albany Barracks and get hold of the trumpet-major, he would tell you who would teach you. He would not do it himself, I daresay, but some of the trumpeters would be glad to give you an hour a day if you can pay for it. Of course it would save you a lot of trouble afterwards if you could sound the trumpet before you joined."

Edgar took the advice, and found a trumpeter in the Blues who agreed to go out with him for an hour every day on to Primrose Hill, and there teach him to sound the trumpet. He accordingly gave up his room at Vauxhall, and moved across to the north side of Regent's Park. For six weeks he worked for an hour a day with his instructor, who, upon his depositing a pound with him as a guarantee for its return, borrowed a trumpet for him, and with this Edgar would start of a morning, and walking seven or eight miles into the country, spend hours in eliciting the most mournful and startling sounds from the instrument.

At the end of the six weeks his money was nearly gone, although he had lived most economically, and accordingly, after returning the trumpet to his instructor, who, although he had been by no means chary of abuse while the lessons were going on, now admitted that he had got on first-rate, he went down to Aldershot, where his friend the recruiting sergeant had told him that they were short of a trumpeter or two in the 1st Hussars.

It was as well that Edgar had allowed the two months to pass before endeavouring to enlist, for after a month had been vainly spent in the search for him, Rupert had suggested to his father that although too young to enlist in the ranks Edgar might have tried to go in as a trumpeter, and inquiries had been made at all the recruiting depots whether a lad answering to his description had so enlisted. The sergeant had given him a note to a sergeant of his acquaintance in the Hussars.

"I put it pretty strong, young un," his friend had said when he gave him the note; "mind you stick to what I say."

The sergeant had indeed – incited partly perhaps by a liking for the lad, partly by a desire to return an equivalent for the sovereign with which Edgar had presented him – drawn somewhat upon his imagination. "I have known the young chap for a very long time," he said; "his father and mother died years ago, and though I am no relation to him he looks upon me as his guardian as it were. He has learned the trumpet a bit, and will soon be able to sound all the calls. He will make a smart young soldier, and will, I expect, take his place in the ranks as soon as he is old enough. Do the best you can for him, and keep an eye on him."

"I will take you round to the trumpet-major," the sergeant said; "he had better go with you to the adjutant. You know what Sergeant M'Bride says in this letter?"

"No, I don't know exactly what he says. He told me he would introduce me to you, and that you would, he was sure, do your best to put me through."

"Well, you had better hear what he does say. It is always awkward to have misunderstandings. He says you have lost your father and mother; you understand that?"

"That's right," Edgar said quietly.

"And that he has known you for a very long time?"

Edgar nodded.

"It seems to me a very long time," he added.

"And that though he is no actual relation of yours he considers he stands in the light of your guardian. That is important, you know."

"I will remember that," Edgar said. "There is certainly no one as far as I know who has a better right than Sergeant M'Bride to advise me, or give me permission to enlist."

"Well, you stick to that and you are all right. Now, come along."

THE DASH FOR KHARTOUM

"I wonder who the young chap is," the sergeant said to himself as they crossed the barrack yard. "As to what M'Bride said, we know all about that; I have been on the recruiting staff myself. But I think the young un was speaking the truth. He has lost his father and mother, he has known M'Bride for some time, and he has got no one who has any right to interfere with him. Rum, too. The boy is a gentleman all over, though he has rigged himself out in those clothes. Well, we are short of trumpeters, and I don't suppose the adjutant will inquire very closely."

The trumpet-major was quite willing to do his share of the business. He was glad to fill up one of the vacancies, especially as it seemed that the new-comer would soon be able to take his place in the ranks; and after asking a few questions he went across with him to the adjutant. The latter looked at Edgar critically.

"Smart young fellow," he said to himself. "Got into some scrape at home, I suppose, and run away. Of course he has some got-up lie ready. Well, sergeant, what is it?"

"Lad wishes to enlist as a trumpeter, sir. Here is a letter from his next friend, Sergeant M'Bride of the 18th Hussars. Lad's father and mother dead. M'Bride stands in place of guardian."

"A likely story," the adjutant muttered to himself. "What is your name, lad?"

"I enlist as Edward Smith," Edgar said, "age sixteen."

"Parents dead?"

"I lost them when I was a child, sir."

"Who were they?"

"My father was a sergeant in the 30th Foot, sir."

The adjutant was watching him narrowly.

"Either he is telling the truth," he said to himself, "or he is one of the calmest young liars I have ever come across."

"And there is no one who has any legal right to control you or to object to your enlisting?"

"No one, sir."

"You cannot play, I suppose?"

ENLISTED

"I have been learning the trumpet for some little time, sir, and can sound a few of the calls."

"Well, I suppose that will do, sergeant. You had better take him across to the doctor. If he passes him put him up for the night, and bring him here to-morrow at twelve o'clock to be sworn in."

"Rather a tough case that," he said to himself as the trumpet-major left with the young recruit. "There is not a doubt the boy is lying, and yet I could have declared he was speaking the truth. Of course he may be the son of a non-commissioned officer, and have been brought up and educated by someone. He looks a gentleman all over, and speaks like one. Well, it is no business of mine;" and the adjutant gave the matter no further thought.

The next day Edgar was sworn in. The colonel, hearing from the adjutant that he had questioned the boy, and that there was no impediment to his enlisting, passed him without a remark, and Edgar was at once taken to the regimental tailor and measured for his uniform, and half an hour later was marched out with four or five of the other trumpeters beyond the confines of the camp, and was there set to work at the calls. His work was by no means light. He was at once sent into the riding-school, and he found it a very different thing to satisfy the riding-master and his sergeants than it had been to learn to sit a horse at home. However, his previous practice in that way rendered the work much easier for him than it would otherwise have been, and he was not very long in passing out from the squad of recruits. Then he had two or three hours a day of practice with the trumpet, an hour a day at gymnastics, and in the afternoon two hours of school. The last item was, however, but child's play, and as soon as the instructor saw that the lad could without difficulty take a first-class, he employed him in aiding to teach others.

The evening was the only time he had to himself; then, if he chose to take the trouble to dress, he could go out into the town or stroll through the camp or take a walk. If disinclined for this there was the cavalry canteen, with a large concert-room attached, where entertainments were given by music-hall singers brought down from London. The trumpeters and bandsmen had a barrack-room to themselves. Edgar, who had a healthy appetite, found the food of a very different description to that to which he had been accustomed. Although up at six o'clock in the morning, even in the winter, as it was, there was nothing to eat until eight. Then there was a mug of a weak fluid called tea, and an allowance of bread. The dinner, which was at one, consisted of an amount of meat scarcely sufficient for a growing boy; for although had the allowance consisted entirely of flesh, it would have been ample, it was so largely reduced by the amount of bone and fat that the meat was reduced to a minimum. However, when eked out with potatoes and bread it sufficed well enough.

Tea at six consisted, like breakfast, of a mug of tea and bread. Edgar found, however, that the Spartan breakfasts and teas could be supplemented by additions purchased at the canteen. Here pennyworths of butter, cheese, bacon, an egg, a herring, and many similar luxuries were obtainable, and two-pence of his pay was invariably spent on breakfast, a penny sufficing for the addition to his tea.

He found that he soon got on well with his comrades. It was like going to a fresh school. There was at first a good deal of rough chaff, but as soon as it was found that he could take this good-temperedly, and that if pushed beyond a fair limit he was not only ready to fight but was able to use his fists with much more science than any of the other trumpeters, he was soon left alone, and indeed became a favourite with the bandsmen. Two months after he joined he was appointed to a troop. He found, however, that he did not have to accompany them generally on parade. The regiment, like all others at home, was very short of its complement of horses, and only one trumpeter to each squadron was mounted. Edgar, however, cared little for this. He considered his first two years' work as merely a probation which had to be gone through before he could take his place in the ranks as a trooper.

ENLISTED

He found his pay sufficient for his needs. Although he had in the old days been in the habit of drinking beer, he had made a resolution to abstain from it altogether on joining the regiment. He determined to gain his stripes at the earliest possible opportunity, and knew well enough, from what he had heard Captain Clinton say, that drink was the curse of the army, and that men, although naturally sober and steady, were sometimes led into it, and thereby lost all chance of ever rising. He had never smoked, and it was no privation to him to abstain from tobacco, and he had therefore the whole of his pay, after the usual deduction for stoppages, at his disposal for food, and had always a little in his pocket to lend to any comrade who had the bad luck to be put on heavy stoppages by the loss of some of his necessaries.

In this respect he himself suffered somewhat heavily at first. Accustomed at school to leave his things carelessly about without the slightest doubt as to their safety, he was astonished and shocked to find that a very much laxer code of morality prevailed in the army, and that any necessaries left about instantly disappeared. The first week after joining he lost nearly half the articles that had been served out to him, and was for some months on heavy stoppages of pay to replace them. The lesson, however, had its effect, and he quickly learnt to keep a sharp look-out over his things. He was soon dismissed from school, obtaining his first-class at the examination, which took place two months after he joined, and this gave him time to attend the fencing-school, and to give more time to gymnastics.

When once accustomed to his work he found his life an easy and pleasant one, and had far more time at his disposal than had been the case at school. He resolutely avoided dwelling on the past, and whenever he found himself thinking of what had so long been home, he took up a book, or went out for a walk, or engaged in some occupation that served to distract his thoughts. He missed the games. Football was occasionally played, but there was no observance of rules, and after trying it once or twice he gave it up in disgust. He often joined in a game at fives, and practised running and jumping, so as to be able to take part in the regimental sports in the spring.

When Easter had passed and the weather became bright and pleasant he often took long walks alone, for it was seldom he could find anyone willing to accompany him. He had learnt drawing at Cheltenham, and as he found that it would be useful for him when he obtained the rank of a non-commissioned officer to make sketches and maps to send in with reports of any country reconnoitred, he accustomed himself to do this on his walks, jotting down the features of the country, noticing the spots where roads came in, the width of the bridges across the canals and the nature of their banks, and taking sketches of what appeared to him positions that would be occupied to check a pursuing force, or to be taken up by an advanced one.

At this time, too, he joined a class for signalling, and found it highly interesting, and before the end of the summer could send a message or read one with flags or flash-lights. As soon as the summer really began he took to cricket, and here he speedily attracted the attention of the officers. He had been the best bowler in the second eleven, and would have been in the first the next season at Cheltenham. But it was some little time before his proficiency as a bowler became known, although it was soon seen that his batting was far above the average.

"That youngster handles his bat well, Moffat," one of the lieutenants said to the captain, who was the most energetic cricketer among the officers, and who with one or two of the sergeants generally made up the team when the regimental eleven played against that of another corps.

"Yes, he plays in good form, doesn't he? Who is the young fellow at the wicket now, sergeant?"

"He is trumpeter of D troop, sir. He only joined three months ago, but he could play a bit when he came, and got posted to a troop before two others who joined four or five months before him."

"The man who is bowling now is not up to much, sergeant. Suppose you take the ball for an over or two; I should like to see how that young fellow would stand up to your bowling."

The sergeant, who was one of the regimental bowlers, took the ball. Edgar, who had been driving the previous bowler in all directions, at once played carefully, and for an over or two contented himself with blocking the balls, then one came a little wide and he cut it to leg for four.

Captain Moffat took off his coat and waistcoat and took the end facing the sergeant, and began to bowl some slow twisting balls, that were in strong contrast to the fast delivery of the sergeant. Edgar felt now that he was being tried, and played very cautiously. There were no runs to be made off such bowling until the bowler became careless or tired. At last a ball came rather farther than usual. Edgar stepped out to meet it, and drove it nearly straight forward and scored four, and it was not until his score ran up to thirty that he was at last caught.

"You will do, Smith," Captain Moffat said approvingly. "Where did you learn to play cricket?"

"I learned at school, sir."

"Ah! well, they taught you that well if they taught you nothing else. You go on practising, and I will give you a chance to play for the regiment the first time that there is a vacancy."

Two or three matches were played before the chance came. Then Sergeant Stokes, the bowler, hurt his hand the day before they were going to play the Rifle Brigade, which was considered the strongest team in camp.

"This is an unlucky business, sergeant," Captain Moffat said to him as they were talking over next day's play. "I thought if we had luck we might make a good fight with the Rifles. Bowling is never our strongest point, and now you are out of it we shall make a very poor show. Are there any of the men outside the eleven who show any bowling talent?"

The sergeant shook his head.

"Not one of them, sir. I hoped Corporal Holland would have made a bowler, but he seems to have gone off rather than come on. No; we must trust to the bowlers we have got. There are four or five of them who are not bad, though except yourself, sir, there is nothing, so to speak, to depend on."

"You cannot depend on me, sergeant; there is no certainty about my bowling. Sometimes I do pretty fairly, at other times I get hit all over the field. No; my proper place is wicket-keeping. I should never leave that if we had two or three bowlers we could depend upon. Well, we must go in for run making.

"I do not think that we can do better than put on that young trumpeter till you can play again. I have watched him several times at practice, and he always keeps his wickets up well, and hits freely whenever he gets a chance."

"Very well, sir. I will warn him that he will be wanted to-morrow. There can be no harm in trying him for once anyhow."

There was some little surprise among the men who played cricket at hearing that Trumpeter Smith was to play in the eleven against the Rifles, and some little grumbling among those who had hoped to be the next choice. However, all agreed that he was a very likely youngster. The Hussars won the toss, and went in first. The bowling of the Rifles was deadly, and the ten wickets fell for fifty-two runs. Edgar was the last to go in, and did not receive a single ball, his partner succumbing to the very first ball bowled after Edgar had gone out to the wicket. Then the Rifles went in, and the loss of the Hussars' fast bowler soon made itself felt. Two of the best bats of the Rifles were at the wicket, and in spite of several changes of bowling, seventy-four runs were scored without a separation being made. Captain Moffat looked round the field despairingly. He had tried all the men on whom he had any dependence. His own bowling had been very severely punished, and he had retired when thirty runs had been scored and was reluctant to take the ball again. As he was standing undecided after an over in which twelve runs had been scored, his eye fell on Edgar as he ran lightly across to take up his place on the opposite side.

"Smith!" Edgar ran up to him. "Do you bowl at all?"

"I have not bowled this season, sir, but I used to bowl pretty fairly."

"Very well, then, take the ball at this end after the next over. I am going to try Smith at this end," he said to the young lieutenant who was long-stop.

He shrugged his shoulders. "Well, there is one thing, he cannot make a worse mess of it than we are making already."

When the over was concluded, Edgar took the ball. The year that had elapsed since he had last played, and the gymnastics and hard exercise, had strengthened his muscles greatly, and as he tossed the ball from hand to hand while the field took their places he felt that he was more master of it than he had been before. He had then been a remarkably fast bowler for his age, and would have been in the eleven had it not happened that it already possessed three unusually good bowlers.

The first ball he sent up was a comparatively slow one; he wanted to try his hand. It was dead on the wicket, and was blocked; then he drew his breath, and sent the next ball in with all his force. A shout rose from the Hussars as two of the wickets went flying into the air. Another player came out, but at the fourth ball of the over his middle stump was levelled.

"What do you think of that, Langley?" Captain Moffat asked the long-stop as they walked together at the other end. "We have found a treasure. He bowls about as fast as any one I have ever seen, and every ball is dead on the wicket."

"He is first-class," the lieutenant, who was an old Etonian, said. "I wonder where he learnt to play cricket?"

The wickets fell fast, and the innings concluded for 98, Edgar taking seven wickets for twelve runs. Captain Moffat put him in third in the second innings, and he scored twenty-four before he was caught out, the total score of the innings amounting to 126. The Rifles had therefore eighty-one runs to get to win. They only succeeded in making seventy-six, eight of them being either bowled out by Edgar or caught off his bowling. After this he took his place regularly in the Hussar team, and it was generally acknowledged that it was owing to his bowling that the regiment that season stood at the head of the Aldershot teams.

CHAPTER VI
EGYPT

NATURALLY his prowess at cricket made Trumpeter Smith a popular figure in the regiment, and even at the officers' mess his name was frequently mentioned, and many guesses were ventured as to who he was and what school he came from.

That he was a gentleman by birth nobody doubted. There was nothing unusual in that, for all the cavalry regiments contain a considerable number of gentlemen in their ranks; men of this class generally enlisting in the cavalry in preference to the other arms of the service. It was, however, unusual for one to enlist at Edgar's age. Many young men, after having failed to gain a commission by competition, enlist in hopes of working up to one through the ranks. Another class are the men who having got into scrapes of one kind or another, run through their money, and tired out their friends, finally enlist as the only thing open to them.

The first class are among the steadiest men in the regiment, and speedily work their way up among the non-commissioned officers. The second class are, on the other hand, among the wildest and least reputable men in the ranks. They are good men in a campaign where pluck and endurance and high spirits are most valuable, but among the worst and most troublesome when there is little to do and time hangs heavily on hand.

There were two of the sergeants who had failed in the examination for commissions, and were hoping some day to obtain them. One had been five years in the regiment, the other three. Their attention had first been called to Edgar by his getting a first-class in the examination, which at once stamped him as having had an education greatly superior to that of the majority of recruits. His position in the regimental cricket team further attracted their attention, and they took an opportunity to speak to him when it happened they were walking together and met Edgar returning from an afternoon's ramble across the country.

"Well, Smith, how do you like soldiering?"

"I like it very well; I don't think that there is anything to complain of at all."

"It is better than grinding away at Latin and Greek and mathematics, and that sort of thing," the younger of the two sergeants said with a smile.

"There are advantages both ways, sergeant."

"So there are, lad. Of the two I like drill better than grinding at books, worse luck; if I had been fond of books I should not be wearing these stripes. I asked the band-master if you were learning an instrument. He said you were not. So I suppose you mean to give up your trumpet and join the ranks as soon as you get to eighteen?"

"Yes. I should not care about being in the band."

"Your cricket is not a bad thing for you," the elder of the two men said. "It brings you into notice, and will help you to get your stripes earlier than you otherwise would do; as a man who does his regiment credit either as a good shot or as a cricketer or in the sports is sure to attract notice, and to be pushed on if he is steady and a smart soldier. If you won't mind my giving you a bit of advice, I should say don't try to push yourself forward. Sometimes young fellows spoil their chances by doing so. Some of the old non-commissioned officers feel a bit jealous when they see a youngster likely to make his way up, and you know they can make it very hot for a fellow if they like. So be careful not to give them a chance. Even if you are blown up when you do not deserve it, it is better to hold your tongue than to kick against it. Cheeking a non-commissioned officer never pays."

"Thank you, sergeant," Edgar said quietly; "I am much obliged to you for your advice."

"An uncommonly good style of young fellow," Sergeant Netherton, who was the son of a colonel in the army, and had been educated at Harrow, said to his companion. "Comes from a good school, I should say. Must have got into some baddish scrape, or he never would be here at his age."

"It does not quite follow," the other replied. "His father may have died or burst up somehow, and seeing nothing before him but a place at a clerk's desk or enlisting he may have taken this alternative; and not a bad choice either. For, putting aside altogether the chance of getting a commission, which is a pretty slight one, there is no pleasanter life for a steady, well-conducted young fellow who has had a fair education than the army. He is sure of getting his stripes in a couple of years after enlisting. A non-commissioned officer has enough pay to live comfortably; he has no care or anxiety of any sort; he has more time to himself than a man in any other sort of business. There are no end of staff appointments open to him if he writes a good hand, and does not mind clerk work. If he goes in for long service he has every chance of being regimental sergeant-major before he has done, and can leave the service with a pension sufficient to keep him in a quiet way."

"Yes, that is all very well, Summers, but he cannot marry. That is to say, if he has, as we are supposing, been born and educated as a gentleman, he cannot marry the sort of woman he would like as a wife."

"No, there is that drawback," the other laughed. "But then, you see, if he had been obliged to take a small clerkship leading to nothing, he could hardly invite a young countess to share it with him."

As Edgar walked back to barracks he thought over the advice that had been given him, and recognized its value. He knew that the chances of his ever obtaining a commission were exceedingly small, and that even young men whose fathers were officers of high standing and considerable influence seldom obtain a commission under six or seven years' service, and that the majority of commissions from the ranks are given to old non-commissioned officers who were made quarter-masters or pay-masters. He had not entered the service, as had the two non-commissioned officers with whom he had been speaking, for the express purpose of gaining a commission, but simply because he had always had a fancy for soldiering, and because it seemed at the time he left Cheltenham the only thing open to him.

He had resolved from the first that he would regularly put by a portion of his pay, so that he could at any time purchase his discharge if he wished to, should he see any opening in which he could embark by the time he reached the age of three or four and twenty. He would have gained experience, and might then, if he liked, emigrate to one of the colonies. He resolved that when winter came he would go into one of the regimental workshops and learn a trade, either saddlery or farriery, which would enable him to earn his living for a time abroad until he saw something better to do. At school Edgar had held his place rather by steady work than by natural talent. Rupert was the more clever of the two, but Edgar's dogged perseverance had placed him in a more advanced position on the modern side than Rupert held on the classical, and in whatever position he might find himself his perseverance, power of work, and strong common sense were likely to carry him through.

Edgar was conscious himself that he had acted hastily and wrongly in leaving Cheltenham as he had done, and yet he felt that if again placed in the same circumstances he should do the same. Captain Clinton had certainly a right to have a voice in his future, and yet he felt so keenly the dishonour of the fraud in which he had been an unconscious accomplice, that he could not have brought himself to accept any assistance at Captain Clinton's hands. Still he knew that those at home – for he still thought of it as home – would be feeling much anxiety about him, and once a month he wrote a short letter to Captain Clinton saying that he was well and was keeping himself comfortably. These letters he gave in charge of comrades going up for a day's leave to London to post there for him.

EGYPT

One day Edgar had gone with a dozen others to bathe in the canal. After doing so they had returned to barracks, and he had gone for a walk by himself. On his return he was walking along a lane at a distance of about a mile from the town, when he heard a scream. He at once started off at the top of his speed, and at a turn of the lane he came upon a group of two tramps and two frightened ladies. One of these was in the act of handing over her purse to a tramp, while the second man was holding the other by the wrist, and was endeavouring to tear off her watch and chain, which she was struggling to retain. Just as Edgar turned the corner he struck her on the face, and she fell backward on to the bank.

Another moment and Edgar was up to them. The tramp turned with a savage oath. Edgar, who was carrying his riding-whip, struck him with it with all his strength across the eyes, and the man staggered back with a shriek of pain. The other stood on the defensive, but he was no match for Edgar, who was in hard exercise, and in regular practice with the gloves, and whose blood was thoroughly up. The fight lasted but a minute, at the end of which time the tramp was lying in the road roaring for mercy, and shouting to his comrade to come to his assistance.

The latter, however, was stamping with pain, and was still unable to use his eyes.

Edgar turned to the ladies. "If you will kindly walk on to the town," he said, "and send the first man you meet here to me, I will take care of these two fellows until he arrives, and then we will hand them over to the police. Do not be alarmed," he went on, seeing that they hesitated, "I think they have had enough of it."

The ladies hurried off, and before going many hundred yards came upon three infantry men, who, when they heard what had happened, set off at a run to Edgar's assistance. They arrived just in time. The man on the ground had recovered his feet, and he and his companion had attacked Edgar with fury, and it needed all the latter's skill and activity to defend himself. As soon as the soldiers arrived upon the scene the combat ceased. As a measure of precaution the

Edgar struck him with all his strength.

tramps were first knocked down; they were then dragged on to their feet and conducted by their captors into Aldershot, where they were lodged at the police station. They were followed by the two ladies, who after sending on the soldiers had waited until their return with the tramps. They waited outside the police station until a constable came out and asked them to sign the charge sheet, which they did. Edgar now looked at them fairly for the first time, and recognized one of them as being the wife of the major of his corps.

"You belong to my husband's regiment," she said as they came out from the police station. "What is your name?"

"Smith, madam. I am a trumpeter in D troop."

"Oh, yes! I remember your face now. I have often seen you in the cricket field. Miss Pearson and myself are greatly indebted to you. I should not mind so much being robbed of my purse, but I prized my watch very highly as it was a present from my father. Major Horsley will see you and thank you when he hears what you have done."

"I do not want any thanks," Edgar said; "it is a pleasure to punish such ruffians."

Half an hour later Major Horsley came across to Edgar's quarters, and the sergeant called the lad down.

"I am greatly indebted to you, Smith," he said, as Edgar saluted, "greatly indebted to you. You have behaved most gallantly, and have saved my wife from the loss of her watch and chain that she greatly valued, and perhaps from serious ill-treatment from those ruffians; as it was, one of them struck her a very severe blow on the face. I know enough of you, lad, to feel that I cannot offer you money for the service that you have rendered me; but be assured that I shall not forget it, and that when it is in my power to do you a good turn I will do so."

"Thank you, sir," Edgar said. "I am very glad to have been of service."

The major nodded kindly. Edgar saluted and turned away, well pleased at having made a friend who would have it in his power to be so useful to him, and still more pleased that the major had not offered him money as a reward for what he had done. An hour later he was sent for to the orderly-room, where the colonel in the presence of several of the officers thanked him for his gallant conduct.

"You are a credit to the regiment, Smith; and you may be sure that I shall keep my eye on you," he concluded.

The next day the tramps were brought up before the local magistrates and committed for trial for highway robbery with violence, and a month later they were brought up at the assizes at Winchester and sentenced to five years' penal servitude. Edgar gained a great deal of credit in the regiment from the affair, and came to be known by the nickname of "The Bantam." There were, of course, some men who were jealous of the young trumpeter's popularity, and two or three of the non-commissioned officers especially felt aggrieved at the notice taken of him. One of these was the corporal in charge of the barrack-room occupied by Edgar, for he had, since he had been regularly appointed to a troop, left the quarters he first occupied with the band for those allotted to troop D.

Corporals, however, have but little power in a barrack-room. They are in a sort of transitional state between a private and a sergeant, and are liable for even a comparatively small fault to be sent down again into the ranks. This being the case, they seldom venture to make themselves obnoxious to the men who were but lately their comrades, and may be their comrades again before a week is out. Corporal North, however, lost no opportunity of making himself disagreeable in a small way to Edgar. More than that he could not venture upon, for the men would at once have taken the lad's part.

The regiment had been for some little time first on the list for foreign service, and there was no surprise when the news ran round the barrack-rooms that the order had come to prepare for embarkation. It was supposed that as a matter of course India would be their destination; but it was soon known that the regiment was for the present to be stationed in Egypt. Most of the men would rather have gone direct to India, where soldiers are better off and better cared for than elsewhere. Edgar, however, was pleased at the thought of seeing something of Egypt, and it seemed to him, too, that there was a chance of active service there.

"It seems to me," he said, talking it over with several of his chums, "that sooner or later we must have some fighting in Egypt. I cannot understand how it is that some of the regiments there have not long ago been sent down to Suakim. We have smashed up the Egyptian army, and it seems to me that as we are really masters of the place we are bound to protect the natives from these savage tribes who are attacking them down on the Red Sea and up in the Soudan. The Egyptians always managed them well enough until we disbanded their army. If Hicks Pasha had had, as he asked for, an English regiment or two with him, he would never have been smashed up by the Mahdi's people; and it seems to me awful that the garrisons of Sinkat and Tokar should be deserted when we have a lot of troops lying idle at Cairo, while Baker is trying in vain to get up a native force to march to their relief. I wish, instead of going to Egypt, we were going straight down to Suakim to help him. There is one thing, if Baker fails and Sinkat and Tokar fall into the hands of the natives, there will be such indignation that government will have to do something. So I think there is a very good chance of our seeing some active service there, which will be a thousand times better than sweltering in hot barracks in Cairo."

"Right you are, Smith," one of the others said. "I don't go in for reading the papers, and I don't know anything about the chaps in Egypt; but if there is going to be a row, I say let us have our share in it. We are pretty well up in the pursuing drill; it would be a change to do it with somebody to pursue. Anyhow, wherever it is it will be a good job to get out of Aldershot, with its parades and its drills and its Long Valley, and the whole blooming lot of it."

Three days later the order came, and the regiment proceeded by rail to Southampton; they embarked as soon as they arrived there, and the transport started on the following morning. The weather was fine, and the voyage a pleasant one. They had but little to do, for they had left their horses behind them, as they were to take over the horses of the regiment they were going to relieve. The steamer was a fast one, and in twelve days after sailing they reached Alexandria. They were met when they arrived there by terrible news. General Baker's force had marched to the relief of Tokar, but on the way had been attacked by the natives and utterly defeated, half the force being killed; and the whole would have been annihilated had they not reached the sea-shore, where the guns of the vessels which had brought them down from Suakim checked the pursuit of the enemy. Sinkat had fallen.

The news had arrived only on the previous day, and the greatest excitement prevailed. The regiment at once proceeded to Cairo by train and took over the barracks and horses from the small detachment that had been left in charge of them, the main body of the regiment having crossed them on their journey from Alexandria, as they were to proceed to India in the same steamer that had brought out the Hussars. They were scarcely settled in their quarters before they heard that, now that it was too late, an expedition was to be sent down to Suakim. Two English regiments would have saved Baker's force from destruction, and would have rescued the garrisons of Sinkat and Tokar; now a large force would have to be employed. Some time would, of course, be needed for the organization of the expedition, and in the meantime the Hussars had plenty of opportunity for investigating Cairo.

To Edgar the town was delightful, with its bazaar and its varied population, and he and some of his comrades were never tired of wandering about examining the shops with their curious contents, their bright-coloured scarves, their wonderful pipes, their gaudy brasswork, and their oriental stuffs and carpets. But the population were even more amusing, with the mixture of Egyptians, Arabs, and Negroes clad in every variety of garb: from the Egyptian functionary in his neat blue uniform and fez, and the portly merchant in his oriental robes, to the Arabs muffled up in cotton cloths with turban and bernous, the lightly-clad Fellah, and the women shrouded in dark blue cottons with their faces almost entirely hidden by the yashmack. It needed some dexterity to avoid the strings of loaded camels that made their way through the narrow streets, the porters carrying heavy weights hanging from the centre of a thick bamboo pole resting on the shoulders of two or four men, and the diminutive donkeys with their high saddles, on the top of which were perched men who looked far more capable of carrying the donkeys than the donkeys of supporting their weight.

The men soon discovered that spirits were cheap in Cairo, and the result was a considerable addition to the number brought up at the orderly-room for drunkenness. Among these, to Edgar's satisfaction, was Corporal North, who was at once sent back to the ranks and sentenced to a week in the cells. On the day he came out Edgar went up to him.

"Now look here, North. You have made it pretty hot for me while you were corporal. If I had given you any cause for it I should bear no malice, but it has been simply persecution. As long as you were corporal I had to grin and bear it, but now that you are in the ranks we can settle matters; so I challenge you to meet me in the riding-school after we are dismissed from parade to-day."

"That will suit me exactly," North said. "You want a licking badly, young fellow, and now you will get it."

"Well, if I were you I would say nothing about it until it is over," Edgar replied; "for, you see, it is quite possible that it may be the other way."

As several of the men had heard the conversation there was a considerable gathering in the riding-school after they were dismissed from parade. The sympathies of the men were strongly with Edgar; but most of them thought that he was hardly a match for North, who had fought several times before he had got his stripes, and was a well-built young fellow of two-and-twenty.

THE DASH FOR KHARTOUM

The fight lasted upwards of an hour. North had some knowledge of boxing, but in this respect Edgar was his superior. He was far stronger and longer in the reach, while Edgar was the more active. In the early part of the fight the advantage lay all with the soldier, and Edgar was terribly knocked about, so much so that the general opinion was that he had better give in and say that he had had enough; but Edgar laughed at the suggestion.

"We have only begun yet," he said to the man who was acting as his second; "last tells in the long run. I have seen that before now, and I have double the last he has."

This was the fact. Edgar had been constantly at hard work since he joined the regiment, while North had had a comparatively easy time of it since he became a corporal. He had, too, spent no small portion of his pay in drink, and although he was seldom absolutely drunk, had had more than one narrow escape of his condition being observed on his return to barracks in the evening. As the fight went on, then, want of condition told upon him. Edgar, who had at one time seemed weak, gradually recovered his strength, while North became exhausted by the exertions he had made in the early part of the fight.

Edgar now took the offensive, and at the end of an hour and a quarter's fighting North was no longer able to come up to time, and a loud shout from the lookers-on proclaimed that Edgar was the victor. He went across to North and held out his hand.

"Let us shake hands, North," he said; "it has been a good tough fight. I owe you no malice now, and if you get your stripes again, as I daresay you will, I hope it will be a lesson to you not to drop unfairly upon anyone you may take a dislike to."

North took the hand held out to him.

"You have licked me fairly, Smith," he said. "I did not think you had it in you; but I don't think you would have thrashed me if I had been in as good a condition as you are."

"Very likely not," Edgar laughed. "Well, next time we fight I hope it will be against the Arabs, and not against each other."

This fight greatly added to Edgar's reputation in the regiment. North was not a popular character and had always been considered a bully, and the pluck with which Edgar had continued the fight was thoroughly appreciated. Neither of the combatants were able to take their place in the ranks for some days after the fight, being obliged to obtain an order from the surgeon dispensing them from appearing on parade, though they still did stable duty and inner guards. Through the surgeon the matter came to the ears of the officers, who, by quiet inquiry from the sergeants, learnt the particulars of the fight.

"Your friend Trumpeter Smith is reported as unfit for duty, my dear," Major Horsley said to his wife.

"Is he! I am sorry for that," the lady said. "Is there anything we can do for him in the way of sending him some soup, or anything of that sort? He is not seriously ill, I hope?"

"I am afraid he is beyond your skill, Emma," Major Horsley said; and then, seeing that his wife looked seriously grieved, went on, "don't be alarmed, he has only been fighting again."

"Oh! is that all? I was afraid it was fever, or something of that sort. Who has he been fighting with? He doesn't look quarrelsome at all."

"He has been fighting with a man named North, who was a corporal in his troop, and who, as I hear, has been persecuting him a good deal. The fellow got drunk the other day and was reduced to the ranks, and young Smith lost no time in challenging him to fight. I hear most of the men thought he was a fool for doing so, for North is five years older than he is, and a stiff-built young fellow too. I hear that it was a very hard fight, and lasted nearly an hour and a half. After the first half-hour it seemed to every one that Smith would have to give in, for the other man had all the best of it, knocking him down every round; but he stuck to it, and at last North was so beaten he could not come up to time. The sergeant says both of them are terribly knocked about, Smith worst. He can hardly see out of his eyes, and it will be fully a week before either of them can take their places in the ranks. I hear it was the longest fight that there has been in the regiment for years, and the sergeant-major tells me the men are quite enthusiastic over the pluck with which the young one fought. You see, he is not seventeen yet, and for a lad of that age to stand up against a man – and one too who, as I hear, is accustomed to use his fists – is a feather in his cap. It will do him good in the regiment. I have no doubt some of the men are rather jealous of the position he gained from his play at cricket, and from that affair of yours."

"It was very mean of them, then," Mrs. Horsley said warmly.

"Perhaps so, my dear; but favourites are not often popular. Anyhow, this will do him good, and will give him a better standing in the regiment than even his cricket could do; and, at anyrate, those who don't like him are likely after this to keep their opinion to themselves."

"I wish we could do something for him, Robert. You see, we have never done anything yet."

"I shall have a chance of giving him a helping hand some day," the major replied, "and you may be sure that when the opportunity comes I shall do what I can. I have not forgotten what I owe him, I can tell you."

The opportunity came sooner than the major had expected. In a short time it became known that four squadrons of the 10th Hussars and one squadron of the 1st were to accompany the expedition, and the greatest excitement prevailed in the corps as to which troops should be chosen. Two days later Edgar was delighted to hear that the A and D troops had been named for the service.

"Why have they chosen the D troop, Robert?" Mrs. Horsley asked her husband.

"Partly, my dear, because Atkinson is the senior captain."

"Oh, yes! I forgot that. And what is the other reason?"

"Well, Emma, that reason is known only to myself, but I do not mind your knowing it; but you must not whisper it to anyone."

"What is it?" his wife asked curiously.

"Because, my dear, Trumpeter Smith belongs to that troop, and I thought I would give him the chance of distinguishing himself. Some day, when it comes to a question of promotion, it will count in his favour that he has seen active service."

"Oh, I am glad, Robert! It was very good of you to think of it. I wish that he could know that you thought of him."

"That he certainly cannot know," the major said decidedly. "It would be a nice thing for it to be known by anyone that the arrangements as to which troop should go on service had been influenced by my desire to do a good turn to a trumpeter. The other reason is a good and sufficient one. Atkinson, as senior captain, has almost a right to the first chance that offers. He is pretty sure to get brevet rank if there is any hard fighting."

At this moment there was a knock at the door and an orderly entered, and saluting handed a note to Major Horsley. He glanced through it, and an expression of pleasure crossed his face.

"My compliments to the colonel. I will come across and see him at once."

"What is it, Robert?" his wife asked as the door closed behind the soldier.

"Well, my dear, it is news that I own gives me great pleasure, but which I am afraid you won't like."

"Not that you are to go with the detachment, Robert."

"Yes, Emma, that is it;" and he handed her the note.

"My dear Horsley, I have just received orders from the general that a field-officer is to go in command of the squadron. As senior major, you have, of course, the right to the chance. I congratulate you."

Mrs. Horsley turned a little pale as she read it, and her lip quivered as she said, "Well, Robert, no doubt you are glad of the opportunity, and as a soldier's wife I will not say anything to damp your pleasure. It is natural that you should wish to go. If I were a man I should wish so too. Anyhow, it will only last a very short time. You said you thought that they would be back again in a month, and surely there can be no very great danger in a fight with these savages."

"The smallest amount in the world, Emma. It is not like Baker's force, which was composed of these cowardly Egyptians; and it is ridiculous to suppose that these wild tribesmen, brave as they may be, can stand against British troops armed with breech-loaders. I am afraid that all our share of the business will be to do a little scouting before the fight begins, and a little pursuing practice afterwards, so there will be really no occasion whatever for you to be at all uneasy, child; and I must own that I am extremely glad of the opportunity of taking part in this little expedition against these fanatics. Well, I must go across and see the colonel."

Mrs. Horsley indulged in a quiet cry while he was away, for although she did not apprehend any real danger, the thought that her husband was going to run some risk of his life for the first time since she married him was a trial. However, she looked bright and cheerful when he returned, and at once set to work to pack up the kit required for the expedition.

The next morning the detachment of the 1st Hussars, eighty strong, marched down to the station with one hundred men of the 10th Hussars. They took train for Suez. Here they found another two hundred and twenty-eight men of the 10th who had come on by an earlier train, and the work of embarking the horses on board the steamer that was to take them down to Suakim at once began. It was continued until nightfall and recommenced again at daybreak, for the operation of getting horses on board a ship and slinging them down into the hold is necessarily a slow one; but by mid-day all was concluded, the baggage on board, and the troops in readiness for a start.

It was just sunset when the vessel steamed away from the wharf, the troops on board joining in a hearty cheer as she started. The ship was far more crowded than would have been the case had she been starting for a long voyage; but the run down to Suakim was so short that she was packed as full as she could hold, having in addition to the troops a number of mules for the transport. Every one was in high spirits. The change was a most welcome one after the monotony of barrack life in Egypt, and moreover all were burning to avenge the destruction of Baker's force and the massacre of the brave little garrison of Sinkat.

The voyage was a pleasant one. After passing out of the Gulf of Suez, with the lofty and rugged mountain of Sinai with its red rocks and patches of verdure rising almost from the water's edge, they entirely lost sight of land on the left. On the right, however, ran a range of steep hills, which became bolder and loftier as they made their way south. When night again fell the engines were slowed down, for it was not deemed advisable to arrive off Suakim before daylight, as the coast of the neighbourhood abounded with reefs, and the entrance to the harbour was intricate and difficult. As soon as day broke the engines were again put at full speed, and in an hour the masts of the shipping lying in the port could be made out. As they neared the port a small launch was seen coming out. An officer soon came on board.

"You are to go down the coast to Trinkitat," he said to the captain.

"The transports have gone down there; that is to be the base of operations."

The officers clustered round the new-comer to learn the news.

"You have been more lucky than the 19th," he said. "The *Neva* ran ashore on a shoal eighteen or nineteen miles away and has become a total wreck. Several steamers went out at once to help her, and got out the men and horses. A good deal of the baggage was lost, and fifty transport mules, which there was no time to take out before she went to pieces. It was a very close thing, and it was very lucky that aid came two or three hours after she struck. There has been trouble with the black regiments. The scoundrels mutinied as soon as they got on shore, and announced their intention of joining the rebels; so the marines have been kept here for the defence of the place, instead of going with the expedition, I am sorry to say that Tokar has fallen."

A groan broke from his hearers.

"It is a bad business," he went on; "but happily there has been no repetition of the Sinkat massacre. We heard the news yesterday morning. It was brought by five soldiers who made their way down the coast. They reported that the civil governor of the town had entered into negotiations with the enemy, and had agreed to surrender on the promise that the lives of the garrison should be spared. In the afternoon two of our spies came back and confirmed the intelligence. It seems that they could have held out some time longer, and that the governor has behaved like a traitor. They were annoyed by a distant fire from six Krupp guns taken at the defeat of Baker's force, and worked by some black artillerymen captured at the same time. The fire did no material harm, but it seems to have frightened what little courage was left among the officials, and the governor and a hundred and fifty of the townsmen went out and arranged the surrender, although they knew perfectly well that in a very few days help would arrive. There is one thing, the surrender will enable General Graham to choose his own time, and to wait until all the troops are up, instead of pushing forward, as he might otherwise have done, directly he thought he had men enough, to save Tokar."

In another five minutes the officer had taken his place in the launch and was steaming back into Suakim, and the transport was making her way south. By noon she was anchored off the landing-place, a low beach with a flat country extending behind it. The shore was alive with troops, and numbers of boats were plying backwards and forwards. The work of disembarking the horses began immediately, and the greater part of them were on shore before night.

There they found the Black Watch, Gordon Highlanders, Irish Fusiliers, 19th Hussars, and the Mounted Infantry, a corps of one hundred and twenty-six strong.

Edgar greatly enjoyed the bustle and excitement, and the troops were all in the highest spirits. The first comers were eagerly questioned. They said that during the day the 19th and Mounted Infantry had made a reconnaissance across a lagoon which lay between the beach and the country behind. The enemy had been seen there in force, but they retired at once upon seeing the cavalry advance. It was expected that by the following morning some of the infantry would cross the lagoon and occupy a battery which General Baker had thrown up there to cover his landing, for Trinkitat had been the spot from which he too had advanced to relieve Tokar, and the scene of the conflict in which his force had been destroyed would probably be crossed by the British in their advance.

No tents had been taken or were needed, for even in February the heat upon the shores of the Red Sea is very great; and as the evening went on the buzz of talk and laughter died out, and the troops lay down and slept under the starry sky.

CHAPTER VII
EL-TEB

THE next morning the Gordon Highlanders and Irish Fusiliers, accompanied by a squadron of Hussars and the Mounted Infantry, with a couple of small guns, crossed the lagoon and occupied the intrenchment. The cavalry went a little distance out; but the enemy were seen in considerable numbers, and as there might be a large force concealed among the low sand-hills, no attempt was made to attack them, as it was undesirable to bring on serious fighting until the whole force were in readiness to advance. In the evening the cavalry recrossed the lagoon, as there was no water obtainable on the other side, and the animals had to depend upon the supply landed from the steamers. All day the work of disembarkation had been going on, and in spite of the heat of the blazing sun, the men had worked enthusiastically in getting the horses and stores on shore.

The next day the Naval Brigade, one hundred and fifteen strong, all picked men from the crews of the gunboats, with ten officers, landed. The troops on the beach were most anxious to advance, but as those beyond the lagoon had to depend entirely upon food and water carried across to them, it was unadvisable to push a larger body of men forward, especially as the natives had clearly no intentions of attacking them, contenting themselves by keeping up a distant fire.

"I expect the beggars are gathering their forces just as we are gathering ours," one of the Hussars said, as they sat round a fire they had lighted with some drift-wood picked up on shore. The heat was in no way required, but the light was cheerful, and the smoke kept away troublesome insects.

"They reckon," another said, "upon falling upon us on the march as they did upon Baker's men, but they will find they have got into the wrong box."

"General Baker came down himself in the steamboat which arrived this afternoon. I heard one of the officers say so," Edgar put in. "It will be a satisfaction to him to see these fellows well licked on nearly the same ground where they cut up his force."

"Ah! I expect Baker would give his right hand to lead the cavalry in the charge. What a splendid officer he is! There is not a man in the army can handle cavalry as he can; and wouldn't the 10th fight with their old colonel at their head!"

There was a general chorus of assent.

"How splendidly he fought in Turkey!" another trooper said. "I am told the Turks he led would have done anything for him, and had just the same confidence in him our chaps used to have. If he had been in command of the whole army, instead of those rotten old pashas, the Russians would have found it a very different job. I wonder when we are going on. Now we have got all the stores ashore it will be precious slow work being stuck on this beach."

"We are waiting for the 65th," a sergeant said. "I hear the *Serapis* was expected this morning. It is great luck for them getting a fight without any trouble at all. How pleased they must have been when they heard at Aden that they were to be stopped on their way up, to have a share in the affair!"

"Yes, I call that a first-rate piece of luck," another agreed, "to have a good fight and then go straight home, while we have got nothing to look forward to afterwards but garrison duty in Cairo. I would rather be going on to India fifty times."

"Like enough we may see some service there," the sergeant said. "If this Mahdi fellow comes down, which they say he means to do, to invade Egypt, you may be sure we shall all have to go up to stop him."

"I don't call it 'fighting' against these savages," one of the troopers said. "What chance have they got against regular troops?"

"I don't know, Johnson. The Zulus were savages, and they made a pretty tough fight against us. I suppose you don't want anything much harder than that? These fellows have been every bit as brave as the Zulus. They cut Hicks Pasha's army into mincemeat, and they have licked two Egyptian armies down in this neighbourhood. If you think this is going to be no harder work than a field-day at Aldershot, I think you are likely to find you are mistaken."

"You don't suppose, sergeant, that these naked beggars are going to stand for a moment against a charge of eight hundred cavalry?"

"It did not seem as if naked savages could stand infantry armed with breech-loaders, but you see the Zulus did. It does not seem possible these Arabs can stand for a moment against our charge; but, you see, we do not understand these fellows. One knows what regular infantry can do against cavalry, and it may be we shall find that these Arabs are not to be ridden over as easily as we think. When you have got to reckon with men who don't care the snap of a finger whether they are killed or not, you never can count upon an easy victory however badly they may be armed, and however undisciplined they may be.

"There is nine o'clock," he broke off, as the bells on board the gun-boats rang out twice. A moment later a bugle sounded "lights out," and the call was repeated by the buglers and trumpeters of the various corps, and a few minutes later the men stretched themselves out on the sand, and silence reigned in the camp. The next morning Admiral Hewett sent on shore eight seven-pounder guns from the fleet, to take the place of the same number of little camel-guns, which had been found to be of no real utility. At noon the smoke of a steamer was made out in the distance, and a few hours later the *Serapis*, whose engines had gone wrong, arrived with the 65th, who were landed at once, and immediately crossed the lagoon to the intrenchment, and it was known that the advance would at once begin.

In addition to the guns sent on shore from the fleet the artillery had ten brass mountain-guns and four Krupps; the Naval Brigade had with them two nine-pounders, three Gatlings, and three Gardners. The troops were divided into two brigades, the first consisting of 610 men of the Rifles, 751 Gordon Highlanders, and 334 of the Irish regiment; the second brigade of 761 Royal Highlanders, 500 of the 65th, 361 Royal Marine Artillery and Infantry, and 100 Royal Engineers. There were 600 camels for the transport, 350 mules and 100 camels for the ambulance corps, while the camel battery was composed of 80 camels and 100 men.

In the course of the afternoon Major Harvey and Lieutenant-colonel Burnaby rode out two miles beyond the intrenchment and planted a white flag with a letter attached to the flagstaff, calling upon the enemy to retire and allow us to pass on to Tokar without opposition. They were fired at by the Arabs, and as the flag disappeared a short time after the officers had returned, there was no doubt that the letter would arrive at its destination. Before nightfall the whole of the force, with the exception of one hundred and fifty men left to defend the stores on the beach, had crossed the lagoon. Three hundred men were to remain in the intrenchment, when the rest marched, to defend the transport animals and stores left there against any attacks. Bivouac fires were lighted, and round these the troops sat smoking and chatting until the bugle-call ordered all to lie down in their ranks. They were bivouacked in the order in which they were to advance.

The formation was to be a sort of square, of which the Gordon Highlanders were to form the front face, the Royal Highlanders the rear line, the Irish Fusiliers the right face with the Rifles inside them; the 65th were on the outside of the left face, the Marines being inside them. The whole square was about 250 yards long by 150 deep. Between the Marines and Rifles in the centre were stationed the transport animals with the reserve ammunition and hospital appliances. The camel battery with the seven-pounders was to remain in reserve in the centre of the square, while the sailors with the six marine-guns were placed at the left front of the square, next to the Gordon Highlanders.

The bivouac fires were kept up all night, as it was considered probable that the enemy, who occasionally fired from a distance, might attempt an attack upon the sleeping force. The night, however, passed quietly, but towards morning rain fell heavily, soaking the troops as they lay, and there was a general feeling of gladness when the reveille called them to their feet. Fresh fuel was thrown on to the fires, and the men tried as best they could to dry themselves. The kettles were boiled and breakfast eaten, and the cavalry recrossed the lagoon to the beach to give their horses water at the tanks there. They then rejoined the infantry. Their place was to be in the rear of the square, but two squadrons were to move in extended order as scouts a mile in front of it and on both flanks.

Their orders were that if attacked they were not to charge the enemy, but to open right and left and to retire at once and rejoin the main body in the rear of the square, so as to allow a clear space for the sweep of the infantry fire. The infantry were to fire only in volleys on word of command, and were not to open fire until within three hundred yards of the enemy. Moving out from the camp the force was halted on open ground and a brief inspection made to see that all was in order, and soon after eight o'clock the advance began in earnest.

As soon as they moved forward the enemy could be seen retiring, evidently bent upon pursuing the same tactics that they had done upon the occasion of the advance of Baker Pasha's force from the same halting-place a month before. The officers with their glasses could make them out swarming along a slight ridge of ground in the neighbourhood of the wells; their flags extended along a front a mile in length, and guns could be made out in position. As the column advanced the enemy cleared off from the rising ground, but whether they had retired behind the ridge, and were there waiting in readiness to pour out to the attack, or whether they were moving round to fall upon the flank of the column, was uncertain. As the column neared the position it could be seen that a breastwork had been thrown up, and that the position of the guns had been well chosen, and the enemy could now be made out crowded among the bushes on the ridge.

It was now ten o'clock, the column was advancing briskly to the martial music of the pipes of the Royal Highlanders, the cavalry scouts had moved away from the front, and the square was within five hundred yards of the ridge. They were not, however, advancing directly against it, but were moving in a line almost parallel to its face, as General Graham had determined to pass it and then attack in flank, as it was evident that there would be serious loss in a front attack upon a position so strongly held and fortified. It was a trying moment, for all expected that the silence, so far preserved by the enemy, would be broken by the roar of cannon and the discharge of musketry, and that it would be followed by the tremendous rush that had proved fatal to Baker's force.

But the square kept its way for some distance across the face before the enemy opened fire. They had doubtless expected that a direct attack would be made upon their position, and the passage of the troops without the slightest attention to themselves surprised and disconcerted them. But at last they perceived that they must take the offensive, and suddenly a hot fire of musketry broke out from bush and earthwork, while the Krupp guns, manned by the soldiers who had formed part of the Tokar garrison, opened fire. The distance was but four hundred yards, and several of the men fell out from their places in the ranks wounded, but the greater part of the shot and bullets flew overhead.

No reply to the fire was made by the square, but its direction was changed a little more to the right so as to take it somewhat farther from the face of the enemy's position.

The artillery now opened fire upon the guns of the enemy, but the square kept on its course steadily, while a storm of bullets and fragments of shrapnel-shell flew around them. The enemy's gunners proved that their training had been good. They worked their guns quickly and their aim was accurate. General Baker, who was acting as head of the intelligence department, was struck in the face by a ball from one of the shrapnel-shells. This imbedded itself so deeply in his jaw that it could not be got out by the surgeons until after the conclusion of the fight. But the gallant officer, having had his face bandaged up, remounted his horse, and continued his duties throughout the day.

Upon getting to a position at the end of the ridge held by the enemy the men were ordered to lie down, while the artillery continued their fire against the enemy's batteries. At a quarter to twelve the Arab guns ceased to fire, and the men were ordered to their feet again, and with loud cheers continued the advance. The square moved on until well in rear of the enemy's position, and then marched straight towards it. Owing to this change in the direction of its march the left flank of the square now became its front, and it was the 65th with the Naval Brigade on one flank and the Royal Highlanders on the other, who were nearest to the enemy.

Fast and thick the flashes of musketry broke out from the bushes; but as the square approached the fire ceased, and then groups of black forms sprang to their feet, and with loud yells rushed towards the square, waving their spears and swords. It seemed incredible that these little groups of ten or twelve men each should intend to assail the solid lines of the British, but as fresh parties every moment sprang up and charged down, the order was given to fire. A flash of flame ran along the face of the great square, and then a continuous roar told that the breech-loading rifles were at work, while the machine-guns of the sailors added their rattle to the din of the musketry.

As if utterly heedless of death the Arabs rushed forward through the leaden storm, but were mowed down like grass before it. Not one of these intrepid warriors reached the face of the square, not one turned to fly; but of those who left their shelter to attack the square, every man fell with his face to the foe. Without halting for a moment the square kept on its way until the front line reached the bushes. Then with a wild yell a swarm of Arabs sprang to their feet, with so sudden and desperate a rush that they reached the sailors, and for a minute a hand-to-hand struggle took place – bayonet against spear. But the wild courage of the natives was of no avail against the steady discipline of the sailors. The assailants were swept away, and the square moved on.

But the ground was now so broken with bush and rock that the even line could no longer be preserved. From every bush, and from rifle-pits dug among them, and from behind rough intrenchments, parties of Arabs leapt to their feet and hurled themselves in vain upon the British bayonets. As the front of the square reached the ridge that had formed the Arab position the fight was most desperate, the enemy throwing themselves furiously on its flanks; and the Royal Highlanders and the sailors had to fight hard to win their way through them. But at last the ridge was won.

Two of the enemy's Krupp guns were captured, and as soon as the square had been formed up again in order these were turned against the position the Arabs had now taken up in rear of their first line of defence. In the centre of the position they now occupied was a brick building, where an engine for pumping up water for irrigation purposes had formerly stood. The Arabs had loopholed the walls and surrounded the building with rifle-pits. Here they made a desperate resistance, until at last the doors were burst in and the building stormed. Several mud huts were defended with equal obstinacy, and many of our men were wounded by Arabs who lay feigning death in the rifle-pits, and then when the first line of troops had passed leaped out and rushed in among them, cutting and slashing until bayoneted or shot down.

While the 65th were winning this position the Gordon Highlanders carried the village, while the Royal Highlanders captured the redoubt at the extreme right of the position the enemy had first held. The enemy now had been driven from their last line and fled in all directions, at a speed that rendered pursuit by the infantry impossible.

During the early portion of the battle the cavalry had been kept in the rear, out of the range of the enemy's fire, and the men had nothing to do but to sit quiet on their horses and watch the attack of the infantry square upon the enemy's position, fretting and fuming not a little that they were unable to take their part in what was evidently a desperate struggle. But at last bodies of the Arabs were seen streaming out from the position, and General Stewart, who was in command of the cavalry division, gave the order, and, wheeling far round to the right of the infantry, led them against a large body of Arabs in the plain beyond the ridge.

The enemy did not await their attack, but fled, hotly pursued by the first and second lines for some distance. The order to cease pursuing was sounded, when it was seen that the third line, composed of a hundred men, were attacked by a body of Arabs who had advanced from the left, and the main body wheeled round and advanced to assist them. But the ground between was already occupied by the Arabs; these as the cavalry advanced threw themselves down among the tufted hillocks and mounds which covered the whole plain. The horses in their course leaped the hillocks, swerving at the sight of the dark figures lying among them.

The Arabs sprang instantly to their feet in the intervals between the horsemen and hurled their spears at them, or as they lay thrust them into the horses, and as these fell sprang upon the riders and cut them down. At the same moment a small body of mounted Arabs dashed into the fray. Most of them were cut down, but some made their way through the line, and turning the instant they did so fell upon the rear of the charging squadron. Colonel Barrow who commanded it fell, but it still pressed forward, the opposition becoming every moment more severe. General Stewart led the second line to the assistance of the first, but these two were desperately opposed, and had to fight hard before they could reach them. One of the general's orderlies

EL-TEB

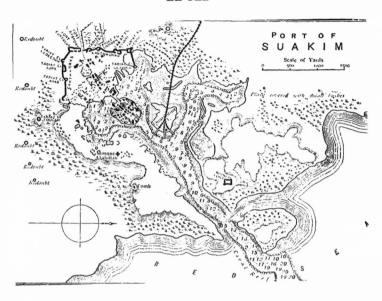

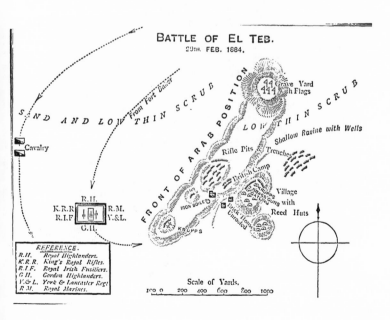

With a desperate rush they reached the sailors.

was killed and two others wounded. Major Slade of the 10th Hussars, Lieutenant Freeman of the 19th, and Lieutenant Probyn fell, and twenty men were killed and as many wounded before the enemy retired.

Colonel Webster's squadron, which made several brilliant charges at the enemy, now joined the rest of the cavalry. But the Arabs were momentarily reinforced, and after what had been seen of the desperation with which they fought it was deemed imprudent to pursue them further.

With the exception of the losses sustained by the cavalry the total loss at the battle of El-Teb was small, amounting to only thirty killed and one hundred and forty-two wounded. One infantry officer was killed, one mortally wounded, and one severely so, while many received slight wounds. The loss of the Arabs exceeded two thousand.

Edgar's squadron was among the first line when the charge was made to the assistance of Colonel Webster's squadron. He was in the rear rank and could not well see what was passing in front, and he was astounded upon seeing men spring up apparently from the earth and furiously attack the horsemen with spear and sword. He himself had a very narrow escape. His horse swerved as it leapt a low bush, and almost simultaneously a native sprang to his feet and lounged at him with his spear. Instinctively he threw himself forward on the neck of his horse, and as he did so felt the spear graze his back below the shoulders. The next moment his horse had taken him beyond the Arab's reach; but at that instant he heard a cry and saw Corporal North's horse fall with him, pierced by a spear thrust given by a native lying on the ground.

Before the corporal could rise the Arab was upon him with his sword, and struck him down with a sweeping cut upon the shoulder. Edgar had wheeled his horse round instantly, and before the blow was repeated was within striking distance of the man and his sword fell upon the uplifted wrist. Dropping his sword the Arab sprang upon the horse and strove to tear Edgar from the saddle, while at the same instant the Arab who had first thrust at him ran up.

Fortunately he came up at the side on which his comrade was clinging to Edgar, and was therefore unable to use his spear against him; but after a moment's hesitation he plunged it into the horse, which reared high in the air and then fell. Edgar had at the moment rid himself of the man who was grasping him, by shortening his sword and plunging it into his body, and as the horse reared he drew his feet from the stirrups and dropped off over his tail, coming down upon his feet just as the animal rolled over dead. The other Arab rushed at him with his spear. Edgar cut at it with his sword and severed the iron head from the staff, and then springing forward ran the Arab through before he could take to his sword. But several others were running up, and Edgar felt that his case was desperate. By this time the corporal, though badly wounded, had freed himself from his fallen horse, and drawing his carbine from the bucket shot the Arab nearest to him. The others, however, came on without a pause. Edgar and his wounded companion made a desperate defence; but both received several sword-cuts, and Edgar felt the end was at hand, when with a roar like thunder the second line burst down upon them, and the Arabs were instantly cut down.

"Take those two men up behind you!" an officer shouted.

Two of the troopers reined in their horses and assisted Edgar and his companion to climb up behind them, and then riding at full speed soon regained the line. In another minute the trumpet sounded for a halt. Edgar and his companion now slipped from the horses and joined their own squadron. The corporal was scarce able to stand, and Edgar was not in a better plight. Major Horsley rode up to them.

"Not badly wounded, I hope?" he asked. "It is a miracle your getting in when once dismounted."

"I think I am pretty nearly done for, sir," the corporal said. "But I wish to report that Trumpeter Smith has saved my life by coming back to my assistance when my horse was stabbed and fell with me. He killed the two men who attacked

118

me, and so gave me time to free myself and to aid him in making a fight of it until the second line came up." As Corporal North concluded he fell insensible from loss of blood.

At that moment the surgeon came up. "Are we going to charge again, major? because if so, these men, with the others badly wounded, had better be sent across at once to the infantry. There are too many of these Arab scoundrels about for them to be left behind here. But if we are not going to charge I will give their wounds a first dressing at once."

"I don't know," the major said. "I will ride to the general and ask him, and speak to him about the wounded. Sergeant Meekings, if the order comes to charge before I return, tell off a trooper to take up each man too badly wounded to ride, and let them carry them straight across to the infantry."

After giving this order he rode rapidly away, but returned in two or three minutes. "We are not going to charge again, doctor," he said; "they are mustering too strongly for us to attempt it. The general says he will halt where we are until the worst cases of the wounded are attended to. Here, two of you men, dismount and assist the surgeon."

"Get their jackets off, lads," the doctor said. "Take this corporal first; he is the worst case."

The other wounded men were now brought up, and their wounds were all bandaged. Those who could sit a horse then mounted behind other troopers, while a number of soldiers were ordered to dismount and to lay the others upon blankets and carry them in.

Edgar was one of these. He had received one cut on the top of his head, and his helmet had alone saved his skull from being cleft. He had another gash on the right cheek. His side was laid open with a spear thrust, the weapon having fortunately glanced from his ribs, and he had another sword-cut on the hip. He was unable to walk from loss of blood, but he felt that none of his wounds were very serious; and the surgeon said to him cheerfully, "You will do, lad. Your wounds are ugly to look at, but they are not serious. You will be on horseback again in another ten days."

Major Horsley had not spoken to him, but he had given him a little nod of satisfaction when the corporal gave his report. The cavalry moved across at a walk towards the wells of El-Teb, the wounded being carried between the lines, as there was no saying how many Arabs might be lurking among the bushes. On reaching the wells they were taken to the field hospital, which had already been organized. There their wounds were more carefully examined and re-dressed; and after a drink of lime-juice and water, with a little brandy in it, Edgar soon dropped off to sleep. In the morning Major Horsley and Captain Atkinson came round to see how the men of their regiment were getting on. The surgeon's report was favourable except in the case of Corporal North.

"I think he will pull round, major; but I am sure he will never be fit for service again. That wound on the shoulder, which he tells me is the first he got, has cut clean through the collar-bone and penetrated almost to the upper rib. I doubt whether he will ever have the use of his arm again; but that I cannot say. Anyhow, it will be long before it is fit for hard work. Trumpeter Smith? There is nothing serious the matter with him, but he has had a marvellous escape. If his helmet had not saved his head, the blow would have cleft right through his skull; if the wound in his cheek had been a couple of inches higher, it would have opened the temporal artery; and if the spear had penetrated instead of gliding off his ribs, that alone would have been sufficient to have done his business. As it is, he is not much the worse except for loss of blood, and with luck will be fit to take his place again in the ranks in a fortnight."

"I am glad to hear so good an account of you, Smith," the major said as he went up to his bedside. "I have reported your conduct to General Stewart, and your name will be sent in among those recommended for the Victoria Cross. Mind, I don't say that you will get it, lad,– I don't think you will; for so many men distinguished themselves yesterday in that hand-to-hand fight that the names sent in will be very much larger than the number of crosses given. Still, your having been recommended will count in your favour when the time comes." So saying, with a kindly nod he moved on to the next bed.

At nine o'clock the force moved out towards Tokar, half the Gordon Highlanders being left at El-Teb for the protection of the hospital and stores, and with orders to find and bury the Europeans that had fallen. During the day many of the Egyptian garrison of Tokar came into the camp from the surrounding villages. In the afternoon a mounted orderly brought in the news that the force had met with no resistance whatever on their way. Several parties of the enemy had been seen, but these fled as soon as they saw the troops advancing. In Tokar seventy of the Egyptian garrison were found in a half-starved condition. While their comrades had consented to join the Arabs they had steadily refused to do so, and had been very badly treated in consequence by them and by the inhabitants of the town. The arrival of the troops was hailed with great joy. The inhabitants had had a terrible time during the occupation of the place by the Arabs, and the whole population were preparing to accompany the troops on their march back to the coast. The cavalry had ridden out to Debbah, where the camp of the force besieging Tokar had been established.

In the afternoon Edgar was so far recovered that he was able to sit up. His wounds were sore and painful, and the strapping of plaster in which they were enveloped rendered him very stiff and uncomfortable. But, as he said to another soldier, he had been just as stiff and sore after a football match, and felt confident that in a few days he should be as well as ever.

The next evening the force returned from Tokar, and Edgar and the other troopers who were well enough to go outside the hospital tent to see them come in were amused at their appearance, for they had before starting armed themselves with spears taken from the fallen Arabs; for the fight on the previous day had shown them that their swords were of little avail against the tactics of the Arabs in throwing themselves flat upon the ground, and that spears were much better suited for warfare against savages. They were accompanied by the greater portion of the population of Tokar, who were to be conveyed in the ships up to Suakim. The cavalry had found that the Arabs had left the camp at Debbah before they arrived.

The expedition there was, however, by no means useless, for they found an immense quantity of rifles and ammunition, together with a Gatling and mountain gun, all of which had been captured by the Arabs at the rout of Baker Pasha's army, or at the destruction of the force under Colonel Moncrieff some months before. The guns captured in the intrenchments made up the complete number of those that had fallen into the hands of the natives on those two occasions, and so left them without artillery. The work of burying the dead had been carried on by the force left in camp, and by the aid of those who now returned was completed in a short time.

No less than a thousand Arabs were found to have fallen in and around their intrenchments, and numbers must have got away only to die subsequently from their wounds. It was learned from prisoners that Osman Digma had not himself been present at the battle, but had sent a thousand men to reinforce those engaged in the siege of Tokar.

The force now moved down to Trinkitat with three hundred men of the garrison of Tokar who had rejoined them, and four or five hundred men, women, and children from that town. The re-embarkation was speedily effected, and a few hours later the ships entered Suakim harbour. It was found that the natives of that town had received the news of the victory of El-Teb with absolute incredulity, but the arrival of the Tokar fugitives convinced them that the Arabs had really been defeated. One of the prisoners taken at Sinkat came in a day or two later, having made his escape from Osman Digma's camp. He reported that the news of the battle of El-Teb had arrived there before he left, and that it had been given out that seven thousand of the English had been killed, and that it was only nightfall that saved them all from destruction.

The first step of Admiral Hewett and General Graham on their arrival at Suakim was to issue a proclamation calling upon all the tribesmen to leave Osman Digma and to come in and make their submission, promising protection and pardon to all who surrendered. This proclamation was backed by a letter by the Sheik Morghani, who was held in the highest estimation for his holiness. He told them that God had sent the English to destroy them because they had forsaken the old religion for a new one, and entreated them to come in and make their peace.

A fortnight had now passed since the fight at El-Teb. Edgar, who had remained on board the hospital-ship, had made rapid progress towards convalescence, and was now reported by the surgeons as fit to return to duty, which he was most anxious to do, as it was daily expected that the force would move out against Osman Digma, who was at Tamai, a place sixteen miles to the south-west of Suakim. The troops had been disembarked, and he was delighted when he was again able to join his squadron. Spies came and went daily, and they were unanimous in saying that Osman would fight another battle. The news that El-Teb was a disastrous defeat was by this time known, but his explanation that the misfortunes were solely due to his orders having been disobeyed, perfectly satisfied his followers, and their belief that he was invincible was wholly unshaken.

The most fanatical of the coast tribes still held to him, and on the 9th of March twenty-one of their sheiks sent in a defiant reply to the proclamation, saying that the ten thousand men they commanded would meet us in the field. It was therefore evident that the struggle to come would be much more serious and determined than that of El-Teb.

THE DASH FOR KHARTOUM

Edgar received quite an ovation upon rejoining his troop. The manner in which he had defended his wounded comrade had awakened their lively admiration, the more so since the man for whom he had so imperilled his life had but lately been his personal antagonist.

"Well, young un, you are getting on," a sergeant said to him. "I won't say you are getting all the luck, for luck has nothing to do with it this time, anyhow. You are doing well, Smith, and it won't be many months before you are in our mess, and it needs no prophet to see that you have every chance of going higher if you keep on as you began. Here you are only about seventeen years old, and you have made a big mark in the regiment already. You have got the major and the rest of the officers on your side from that affair at Aldershot, then the fact that you are the best cricketer in the regiment counts for a lot, and now you have got wounded and have been recommended for the Victoria Cross.

"If you don't mount up after all that it will be your own fault. You have every advantage. The fact that you have been a gentleman is in your favour, for naturally men are picked out for promotion who are best fitted for the position of officers; and your having been able to take a first-class certificate in the school in itself brings you into notice. Be careful with yourself, lad. I know you don't drink, so I need not warn you about that. Don't get cocky. I don't think you will, for you haven't done so at present, and the notice you have had from your cricket and that Aldershot affair would have turned a good many lads' heads. But it is a thing to be careful about. You know there are a good many old soldiers who are inclined to feel a little jealous when they see a young fellow pushing forward, but if they see he is quiet, and gives himself no airs and is pleasant with every one, they get over it in time; and in your case every one will acknowledge that you deserve all the luck that may fall to you. So be careful on that head, Smith.

"You will find very little jealousy among us sergeants when you once get into our mess, for there are very few of us who have any idea whatever of ever getting a commission, or would take one if it were offered. A sensible man knows when he is well off, and except for a man who has had the education you have had one is much more comfortable as a sergeant, and better off too, than one would be as an officer. When one is with other men one wants to do as they do, and an officer who has got to live on his pay finds it hard work and painful work. Of course most men promoted from the ranks – I mean my class of men – get quarter-masterships, but there is no great pull in that. Quarter-masters are neither one thing nor the other. The officers may try to put him at his ease, but his ways are not their ways; and I have known many a quarter-master who, if he had his choice, would gladly come back to the sergeant's mess again."

"Thank you for your advice, sergeant," Edgar said quietly. "I will follow it to the best of my power. I don't think there is anything to be cocky about; for the thing at Aldershot was pure luck, and so it was the other day. I happened to be next to North when his horse fell, and of course I turned round to help him without thinking who he was or anything about him. It was just instinct, and it hasn't done him any good after all, for I hear he is not likely to live many days."

CHAPTER VIII
TAMANIEB

A RE you sure you feel fit for active work again, Smith?"
Major Horsley said as he met Edgar in camp.

"Yes, sir," the lad said saluting. "I am a little stiff, and it hurts me if I move suddenly, but I am sure I should not feel it if we were engaged again."

"Well, do not do anything rash, lad; these fellows are not to be trifled with." That, indeed, was the general opinion in camp. The men were ready and eager for another fight with the enemy, but there was little of the light-hearted gaiety with which the contest had been anticipated before they had met the Arabs at El-Teb. The idea that savages, however brave, could cope with British troops with breech-loaders had then seemed absurd; but the extraordinary bravery with which the Arabs had fought, the recklessness with which they threw away their lives, and the determination with which they had charged through a fire in which it seemed impossible that any human being could live, had created a feeling of respect. There was nothing contemptible about these foes, and it was expected that not only would the force be very much larger than that met at El-Teb, but as it would be composed of Osman Digma's best men, and would be fighting under his eye, the battle would be much more hardly contested than before. The cavalry were particularly impressed with the formidable nature of these strange foemen. While they would have hurled themselves fearlessly against far superior forces of the best cavalry of Europe, they felt that here their discipline and mastery of their horses went for little. They could charge through any number of the enemy, but the danger lay not in the charge but after it. The Arab tactics of throwing themselves down only to stab the horses as they rode over them, and then rising up cutting and thrusting in their midst, were strange and bewildering to them.

"I am game to charge a dozen squadrons of cavalry one after the other," a trooper said as they sat round the fire on the night of the 9th of March, "and if we had orders to go at a square of infantry I should be ready to go, although I might not like the job; but as for these slippery black beggars, the less we have to do with them the better I shall be pleased. You go at them, and you think you have got it all your own way, and then before you can say knife there they are yelling and shouting and sticking those ugly spears into you and your horses, and dancing round until you don't fairly know what you are up to. There ain't nothing natural or decent about it."

There was a general murmur of assent.

"We shall know more about their ways next time," another said. "But lancers would be the best for this sort of work. There is no getting at these beggars on the ground with our swords, for the horses will always leap over a body, and so you cannot reach them with your swords; but a lance would do the business well. I don't care much for lances for regular work, but for this sort of fighting there is no doubt they are the real thing. Well, there is one thing, if we get among the niggers this time we know what we have got to deal with, and up or down there will be no mercy shown."

On the 10th the Royal Highlanders marched out six miles towards Tamai and formed an encampment there, defending it with bushes interlaced with wire, this kind of defence being known among the natives as a zareba. The next afternoon the rest of the infantry marched out and joined them. Next morning the cavalry moved out, and in the afternoon the whole force started, the cavalry thrown out ahead. A few shots were exchanged with parties of the enemy, but there was no serious fighting. The march was slow, for the ground was thickly covered with bushes, through which the troops with the ambulance and commissariat camels moved but slowly. The sailors had very hard work dragging their guns through the deep sand, and it took four hours before they reached a spot suitable for encampment, within two miles of the enemy's position.

The spot selected for the halt was a space free from bushes, and large enough to afford room for the encampment and to leave a clear margin of some fifty yards wide between it and the bushes. As soon as the column halted the cavalry and part of the infantry took up their position as outposts to prevent a surprise on the part of the enemy, and the rest set to work to cut down bushes and drag them across the sand to form a fresh zareba. When this was completed the cavalry trotted back to the post held on the previous night, as they would be useless in case of a night attack, and their horses might suffer from a distant fire of the enemy.

Inside the zareba the greatest vigilance was observed. Fully ten thousand determined enemies lay but a short distance away, and might creep up through the bushes and make a sudden onslaught at any time. The moon was full, and its light would show any object advancing across the open space. Had it not been for this the general would not have been justified in encamping at so short a distance from the enemy. The march had been a short one, but the heat had been great and the dust terrible, and the troops threw themselves down on the ground exhausted when the work of constructing the zareba was completed; but after a short rest they took up their posts in readiness to repel an attack.

During the early part of the night all remained under arms. But Commander Rolfe of the Royal Navy crept out at the rear of the camp, gained the bushes, and crawled among them until he came within sight of the enemy. He saw them in great numbers sitting round their fires or stretched upon the ground, and returned to camp with the news that whatever might be the case later on, certainly no attack was meditated at present. The greater part of the troops were thereupon allowed to lie down and get what sleep they could.

TAMANIEB

The cavalry felt much anxiety respecting those they had left behind them; but the moon was sufficiently bright to permit signals to be flashed to them from the camp, and they learnt to their satisfaction that all was quiet.

Soon after one o'clock in the morning the stillness round the zareba was suddenly broken. A roar of musketry burst from the bushes all round, and it was evident that the enemy were assembled there in great force. The troops were ordered to lie down; and fortunately here, as at El-Teb, the Arab fire was far too high, and the storm of bullets swept for the most part overhead. Many of the camels, mules, and horses were, however, hit, but only one man was killed and an officer and two men wounded. Grasping their rifles the troops lay ready to spring to their feet and repel the attack should it be made; but the hours passed on slowly without the expected movement taking place, and there was a general feeling of relief when morning at last broke. As the Arabs continued their fire, a nine-pounder and Gatling gun were brought into play upon the bushes, and the fire of the enemy soon died out and they fell back to their camp.

The troops now had breakfast, and soon after they had finished the cavalry arrived from the other zareba. At eight o'clock the Mounted Infantry moved out, accompanied by a party of Abyssinian scouts. They had gone but a short distance when a very heavy fire was opened upon them, and the officer in command sent back to the general to say that there was a broad ravine stretching across the country a few hundred yards ahead, although hidden by the bushes from observation until closely approached, and that this ravine was held by the enemy in great force. The infantry now moved out from the zareba, formed in two squares. The second brigade, composed of the Royal Highlanders, the 65th, and the Marines, led the way. It was commanded by General Davis, and in its centre rode General Graham with his staff. As soon as this had marched out the first brigade followed, taking its place in echelon a hundred yards on its right rear, so that its fire commanded its right flank and protected it from an attack in the rear. It consisted of the

89th, 75th, and 60th Rifles, under General Buller. The camels and baggage animals remained under a guard at the zareba.

The Mounted Infantry and Abyssinians fell back as the first brigade advanced, and as soon as they had moved clear of the face of the square the machine-guns at its angles opened fire. The enemy's fire soon ceased, and the brigade again advanced. But the Arabs had simply thrown themselves down and had not retreated, and their fire broke out again as soon as that of the machine-guns ceased.

General Graham now gave the order for the Highlanders, who formed the front face of the square, to charge. With a cheer they went forward at the double, and sweeping the enemy before them soon reached the head of the ravine. The result of the order was, however, that the square was broken up. Its front face had moved on at a run, while the flanks and rear had continued their march at the same pace as before, and there was consequently a wide gap between the 65th on the right flank and the Highlanders in front. Orders were given to the 65th to hurry up; but as they did so, masses of the enemy were seen coming on at a run and making for the gap in the square.

The right companies of the 65th tried to form up to meet them, while Lieutenant Graham, R. N., with the men of the Naval Brigade working the three machine-guns under his command, threw himself into the gap. But the yells of the enemy and the roar of musketry rendered it impossible for the men to hear the orders given, and before the 65th had formed up the enemy were close at hand. Their fire and that of the Gatlings mowed down the Arabs in hundreds, but the wild mob charged on. Some hurled themselves on to the 65th, others poured like a wave over the little group of sailors, while the rest, dashing through the gap, flung themselves on the rear of the 42d.

The sergeants, whose place is in rear of the men, were cut down almost to a man; and the rear rank, facing round, were at once engaged in a desperate hand-to-hand fight with the natives. All was now confusion. Fresh masses of the enemy poured down with exulting shouts, and in a confused crowd the brigade retreated. Had not help been at hand they would probably have met with the same fate that befell Baker's force, and none would have reached Suakim to tell the news of the massacre. The sailors, in vain trying to drag off their guns, were almost all killed, and the guns fell into the hands of the enemy.

But a check was given to the advance of the Arabs by the cavalry, who had moved forward to the left of the square. The officer in command saw that were he to charge across the broken ground his little force would be lost among the throng of Arabs. He therefore dismounted them, and they poured volley after volley with their carbines into the thick of the enemy. In the meantime General Buller's square was advancing. It had been attacked as desperately as had that of General Davis; but it was well handled, and its formation had not been broken up by any order such as that which had destroyed the formation of the other brigade. So steady and terrible a fire was opened upon the advancing enemy that not one of the assailants reached the face of the square; and having repulsed the attacks, it advanced rapidly to the relief of the shattered brigade ahead, pouring incessant volleys into the ranks of the Arabs as they swept down to its assault.

Thus, as they advanced, the first brigade cleared the right face of the second from its foes, and as soon as they came up with the retreating force these halted and reformed their ranks. Both brigades were now formed in line, and advanced steadily towards the ravine. Upon their way they came upon the abandoned guns, which the enemy had in vain tried to carry off. Sweeping the Arabs before them, the British force reached the edge of the ravine. It was filled by the flying Arabs, and into these a terrible fire was poured by the musketry and guns until the Arabs had gained the opposite side and were concealed among the bushes. The fighting was now over, although the enemy still maintained a distant fire. It was necessary, however, to keep the troops

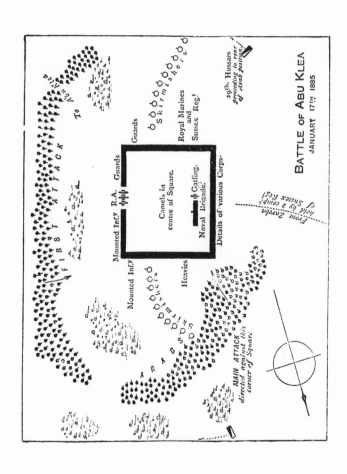

BATTLE OF ABU KLEA
JANUARY 17TH 1885

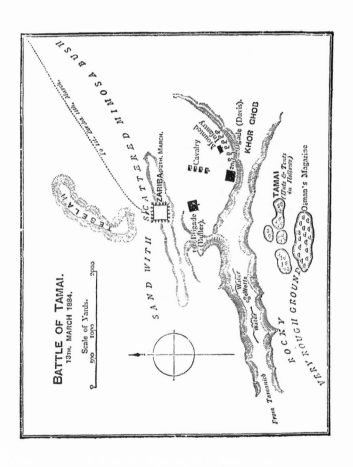

BATTLE OF TAMAI.
13TH, MARCH 1884.

Scale of Yards.

together, for numbers of the Arabs still lay hidden among the bushes, leaping up and flinging themselves desperately upon any who approached them.

The scene of the conflict was terrible. A hundred and twenty of the British lay dead, of whom more than half belonged to the 42d. Three naval officers and ten sailors were killed, while a large number of officers and men of the 42d and 65th were seriously wounded. The slaughter among the natives had been very great – no less than four thousand of them strewing the ground in all directions. The British wounded were sent back to the zareba, and the force again advanced. Crossing the ravine they made towards three villages in its rear. Here was Osman Digma's camp, and the Arabs mustering in strength again opened a heavy fire. They were, however, unable to withstand the British guns and the heavy volleys of the infantry, and the troops advanced into the camp.

It was found filled with property of all kinds; for the Arabs had removed nothing, making perfectly sure that they should be able to repel the English advance. Bags of money, bundles of clothing, Korans, great quantities of grain, and plunder of all kinds were found in the huts. Osman Digma himself had taken no part whatever in the fight. He had looked on from a distant eminence, and when he saw the repulse of the Arab attack and the flight of his men he at once made off.

The next day the cavalry went on to a village two or three miles distant. Here they found a great quantity of ammunition for Krupp cannon and other loot, which had been captured from the forces of Baker and Moncrieff. The village was burnt and the ammunition blown up.

The next day the force started on its return march, after burning and destroying Osman's camp and the three adjoining villages. No attempt was made to pursue Osman Digma or his Arabs. The country beyond was steep and mountainous, and there would have been no chance whatever of overtaking and capturing him, while the troops might have been attacked in difficult positions and have suffered heavily.

It was supposed that after the two crushing defeats that had been inflicted on the enemy, and the proof so afforded of the falsehood of Osman Digma's pretensions, the tribesmen would no longer believe in him, and that his authority would have been altogether destroyed. The expectation was not, however, justified by events, for two years later the Arabs again mustered under him in such formidable numbers, that another expedition was necessary to protect Suakim against the gathering of fanatics reassembled under Osman's banner.

The cavalry had suffered no loss during the operations, and as they had had some share in the fighting, and had materially aided the shattered brigade by their fire upon the Arabs, they were not ill satisfied that they had not been called upon to take a more prominent part in the operations. But little time was lost at Suakim. The greater part of the troops were at once embarked on the transports and taken up to Suez, a small body only being left to protect the town should the Arabs again gather in force. The policy was a short-sighted one. Had a protectorate been established over the country to the foot of the hills, and a force sufficient to maintain it left there, the great hulk of the tribesmen would have willingly given in their allegiance, and no further hostile movement upon the part of Osman Digma would have been possible; but the fact that we hastened away after fighting, and afforded no protection whatever to the friendly natives, effectually deterred others from throwing in their lot with us, and enabled Osman Digma gradually to restore his power and influence among them.

Short though the campaign had been it had the effect of causing some inflammation in Edgar's wounds, and as soon as the expedition returned to the coast the surgeon ordered him into hospital, and it was six weeks before he again took his place in the ranks. By this time the regiment was re-united at Cairo, and there was for some months nothing to break the even tenor of their way.

Long ere this Edgar had learnt that his recommendation for the Victoria Cross had not been acceded to. This, however, was no surprise, for after what he had heard from Major Horsley he had entertained but little hope that he would be among the favoured recipients of the cross.

"Never mind, Ned," a comrade said to him when the list was published and his name was found to be absent. "It is not always those that most deserve the cross who get it. We know that you ought to have had it, if any fellow ever did, and we shall think just as much of you as if you had got it on your breast."

In spite of the heat cricket matches were got up at Cairo, and the Hussars distinguished themselves here as they had done at Aldershot. The chief topic of interest, however, was the question of the safety of Khartoum, and especially that of General Gordon. He had been sent out by the British government in hopes that the great influence he possessed among the natives might enable him to put a stop to the disorder that prevailed in the Soudan. At the time that he had been in the service of the Egyptian government he had ruled so wisely and well in the Soudan that his prestige among the natives was enormous. He had suppressed slave-trading, and restored order throughout the wide province, and by mingling mercy with justice he was at once admired and feared even by those whose profits had been annihilated by the abolition of the slave-trade.

But although Gordon had been rapturously received by the inhabitants of Khartoum, the tribes of the Soudan had not rallied, as it was hoped they would do, in opposition to the Mahdi, whose armies had gradually advanced and had besieged the city. General Gordon with the troops there had made expeditions up the river in the steamers, and brought in provisions for the besieged town; he had fought several battles with the Mahdists, in which he had not always been successful, and it was known that unless help arrived the city must finally surrender. Many letters had been received from him asking urgently for aid, but weeks and months passed, and the government who had sent him out were unable to make up their minds to incur the cost necessary for the despatch of so distant an expedition.

In Cairo public feeling ran very high, and among the troops there the indignation at this base desertion of one of England's noblest soldiers was intense and general. At last the news came that public feeling in England had become so strong that government could no longer resist it, and that orders had been issued to prepare an expedition with all haste. A number of flat-boats were to be built for conveying the troops up the Nile. Canadian boatmen had been sent for to aid in the navigation of the river. Camels were to be purchased in Egypt, a mounted infantry corps organized, and stores of all kinds hastily collected.

People who knew the river shook their heads, and said that the decision had been delayed too long. The Nile would have fallen to a point so low that it would be difficult if not impossible to pass up the cataracts, and long before help could reach Khartoum the city and its noble governor would have fallen into the hands of the Mahdi.

There was much disgust among the troops when it was known that many of them would remain in lower Egypt, and that of the cavalry especially but a very small force would be taken, while three regiments mounted on camels, two of them consisting of cavalry men from England, would take part in the expedition.

Some of the soldiers, however, looked at the matter more philosophically. "We have had our share," they argued, "and if the Mahdi's men fight as well as Osman Digma's we are quite willing that others should have their whack. There will be no end of hard work, and what fighting they get won't be all one way. Sand and heat, and preserved meat and dirty water out of wells, are not very pleasant when you have to stick to them for months together. Like enough, too, there will be another rumpus down at Suakim while the expedition is away, and then those who are left here now will get some more of it."

But although these arguments were loudly uttered, there was no doubt that there was considerable soreness, and that the men felt the hardship of favoured troops from England being employed in their stead in a service that, if dangerous, was likely to offer abundant opportunities for the display of courage and for gaining credit and honour.

CHAPTER IX
THE CAMEL CORPS

TRUMPETER Smith! Trumpeter Smith!" The shout ran through the arched corridor of the barracks, and a soldier putting his head through one of the windows repeated the cry at the top of his voice, for Trumpeter Smith was not in his barrack-room. Edgar, in fact, was walking on the shady side of the great court-yard chatting with two other troopers when his name was shouted.

"Hullo! What is it?"

"You are to go to Major Horsley's quarters."

Edgar buttoned up his jacket, ran to the washing-place, plunged his head and hands in water and hastily dried them, smoothed down his hair with his pocket-comb at a piece of looking-glass that had been stuck up against the wall above the basins, and adjusting his cap to the correct angle made his way to Major Horsley's quarters, wondering much what he could be wanted for, but supposing that he was to be sent on some message into the town.

The soldier-servant showed him into the room where Major Horsley and his wife were sitting.

After a word or two of kindly greeting from the lady, Major Horsley went on: "I told you a long time back, Smith, that I should not forget the service you did my wife and her sister, and that I would do you a good turn if I ever got the chance. Is there anything you particularly want at present?"

"No, sir, except that I have been thinking that I should be glad to give up my trumpet. I am just eighteen now, and it would be better for me, I think, to take my regular place in the ranks. I should be more likely to be promoted there than I am as a trumpeter."

"Yes, you would be sergeant in a very short time, Smith; after your behaviour at El-Teb you would be sure of your stripes as soon as you were eligible for them. But I should not advise you to give up your trumpet just at the present moment."

"Very well, sir," Edgar said, somewhat surprised.

"But there is something else you are wishing for, is there not? I fancy every officer and man in the regiment is wishing for it."

"To go up the Nile, sir?" Edgar said eagerly. "Yes; I do wish that, indeed. Is there any chance of the regiment going, sir?"

"No, I am sorry to say there is not," the major said.

"And a very good thing too, Richard," his wife put in.

"I do not think so at all. It is the hardest thing ever heard of that the regiments here that have had all the heat and hard work, and everything else of this beastly place, are to be left behind, while fellows from England go on. Well, Smith," he went on, turning to Edgar, "I am glad to say I have been able to do you a good turn. When I was in the orderly-room just now a letter came to the colonel from the general, saying that a trumpeter of the Heavy Camel Corps is down with sunstroke and will not be able to go, and requesting him to detail a trumpeter to take his place. I at once seized the opportunity and begged that you might be chosen, saying that I owed you a good turn for your plucky conduct at Aldershot. The adjutant, I am glad to say, backed me up, saying that you have done a lot of credit to the regiment with your cricket, and that the affair at El-Teb alone ought to single you out when there was a chance like this going. The colonel rather thought that you were too young, but we urged that as you had stood the climate at Suakim you could stand it anywhere on the face of the globe. So you are to go, and the whole regiment will envy you."

"I am obliged to you indeed, sir," Edgar said in delight. "I do not know how to thank you, sir."

"I do not want any thanks, Smith, for a service that has cost me nothing. Now you are to go straight to Sergeant Edmonds. I have sent him a note already, and he is to set the tailors at work at once to rig you out in the karkee uniform. We cannot get you the helmet they are fitted out with. But no doubt they have got a spare one or two; probably they will let you have the helmet of the man whose place you are to take. You will be in orders to-morrow morning, and I have asked Edmonds to get your things all finished by that time. Come in and say good-bye before you start in the morning."

There was no slight feeling of envy when Edgar's good fortune became known, and the other trumpeters were unanimous in declaring that it was a shame his being chosen.

"Well, you see, you could not all go," the trumpet-major said, "and if Smith had not been chosen it would have been long odds against each of you."

"But he is the last joined of the lot," one of the men urged.

"He can blow a trumpet as well as any of you," the sergeant said, "and that is what he is wanted for. I think that it is natural enough the colonel should give him the pull. The officers think a good deal of a fellow who helped the regiment to win a dozen matches at cricket, and who carried off the long-distance running prize at Aldershot; besides, he behaved uncommonly well in that fight, and has as good a right to the V. C. as any man there. I think that a fellow like that ought to have the pull if only one is to get it, and I am sure the whole regiment will be of opinion that he has deserved the chance he has got."

THE DASH FOR KHARTOUM

By the next morning the suit of karkee was ready, and Edgar was sent for early to the orderly-room and officially informed by the colonel that he had been detailed for service in the Heavy Camel Corps.

"I need not tell you, Smith, to behave yourself well – to be a credit to the regiment. I should not have chosen you for the service unless I felt perfectly content that you would do that. I hope that you will come back again safe and sound with the regiment. Good-bye, lad!"

Edgar saluted and left the room. Several of the officers followed him out and bade him a cheery farewell, for he was a general favourite. All knew that he was a gentleman, and hoped that he would some day win a commission. He then accompanied Major Horsley to his quarters, and there the officer and his wife both shook hands with him warmly.

"You will be a sergeant three months after you come back," Major Horsley said; "and your having been on this Nile expedition, and your conduct at El-Teb, will help you on when the time comes, and I hope you will be one of us before many years are over."

Edgar then went up to his barrack-room to say good-bye to his friends, and took off his smart Hussar uniform and put on the karkee suit, amid much laughter and friendly chaff at the change in his appearance. The adjutant had ordered a trooper to accompany him to the camp of the Camel Corps, which was pitched close by the Pyramids, and to bring back his horse. He therefore mounted and rode out of the barracks, amid many a friendly farewell from his comrades. He rode with his companion into the town and down to the river, crossed in a ferry-boat, and then rode on to the camp. Inquiring for the adjutant's tent Edgar dismounted and walked up to that officer, and presented a note from the colonel.

The officer glanced at it. "Oh, you have come to accompany us!" he said. "You look very young for the work, lad; but I suppose your colonel would not have chosen you unless he thought you could stand it. I see you have got our uniform, but you want a helmet. We can manage that for

THE CAMEL CORPS

you. Sergeant Jepherson, see if Trumpeter Johnson's helmet will fit this man; he is going with us in his place. Fit him out with water-bottle and accoutrements, and tell him off to a tent."

The helmet fitted fairly, and only needed a little padding to suit Edgar, who, after putting it on, ran out to where his comrade was waiting for him and fastened his own head-gear to the pummel of his saddle.

"Good-bye, young un!" the trooper said. "Hold your own with these heavies for the honour of the regiment. They mean well, you know, so don't be too hard upon them."

Edgar laughed as he shook the man by the hand, and as he rode off turned to look at the scene around him.

There were two camps at a short distance from each other, that of the Heavy Camel Corps to which he now belonged, composed of men of the 1s and 2d Life Guards, Blues, Bays, 4th and 5th Dragoon Guards, Royals, Scots Greys, 5th and 16th Lancers. The other was the Guards Corps, composed of men of the three regiments of foot guards. Edgar's first feeling as he looked at the men who were standing about or lying in the shade of the little triangular Indian mountain-service tents, was that he had suddenly grown smaller. He was fully up to the average height of the men of his own regiment, but he felt small indeed by the side of the big men of the heavy cavalry regiments.

"This way, lad," the sergeant into whose charge he had been given, said. "What is your name?"

"I am down as Ned Smith."

The sergeant smiled at the answer, for no inconsiderable number of men enlist under false names. He led the way through the little tents until he stopped before one where a tall soldier was lying at full length on the sand. "Willcox, this man has come to take the place of Trumpeter Johnson. He is detached for duty with us from the Hussars. He will, of course, share your tent."

"All right, sergeant! I will put him up to the ropes. What's your name, mate?"

143

THE DASH FOR KHARTOUM

"I go as Ned Smith," Edgar said.

"So you are going in for being a heavy at present."

"I don't care whether I am a heavy or a light, so that I can go up the river."

"Have you been out here long?"

"About a year; we were through the fighting at Suakim, you know. It was pretty hot down there, I can tell you."

"It is hot enough here for me – a good deal too hot, in fact; and as for the dust, it is awful!"

"Yes, it is pretty dusty out here," Edgar agreed; "and of course, with these little tents, the wind and dust sweep right through them. Over there in Cairo we have comfortable barracks, and as we keep close during the day we don't feel the heat. Besides, it is getting cooler now. In August it was really hot for a bit even there."

"Where are we going to get these camels, do you know?"

"Up the river at Assouan, I believe; but I don't know very much about it. It was only yesterday afternoon I got orders that I was to go with you, to take the place of one of your men who had fallen sick, so I have not paid much attention as to what was going on. It has been rather a sore subject with us, you see. It did seem very hard that the regiments here that have stood the heat and dust of this climate all along should be left behind now that there is something exciting to do, and that fresh troops from England should go up."

"Well, I should not like it myself, lad. Still I am precious glad I got the chance. I am one of the 5th Dragoon Guards, and you know we don't take a turn of foreign service – though why we shouldn't I am sure I don't know – and we are precious glad to get a change from Aldershot and Birmingham and Brighton, and all those home stations. You are a lot younger than any of us here. The orders were that no one under twenty-two was to come."

"So I heard; but of course as we are out here, and we have got accustomed to it, age makes no difference."

"What do they send us out here for?"

THE CAMEL CORPS

"There are no barracks empty in the town, no open spaces where you could be comfortably encamped nearer. Besides, this gives you the chance of seeing the Pyramids."

"It is a big lump of stone, isn't it?" Willcox said, staring at the Great Pyramid. "The chaps who built that must have been very hard up for a job. When I first saw it I was downright disappointed. Of course I had heard a lot about it, and when we got here it wasn't half as big as I expected. After we had pitched our tents and got straight, two or three of us thought we would climb up to the top, as we had half an hour to spare. Just as we set off one of the officers came along and said, 'Where are you going, lads?' and I said, 'The cooks won't have tea ready for half an hour, sir, so we thought we would just get up to the top and look round.' And he said, 'If you do you will be late for tea.'

"Well, it didn't seem to us as if it would take more than five minutes to get to the top and as much to get down again, so off we went. But directly we began to climb we found the job was not as easy as we had expected. It looked to us as if there was but a hundred steps to go up; but each step turned out to be about five feet high, and we hadn't got up above twenty of them when the trumpet sounded, and we pretty near broke our necks in coming down again. After that I got more respect for that lump of stones. Most of the officers went up next day, and a few of us did manage it, but I wasn't one of them. I did try again; but I concluded that if I wanted to go up the Nile, and to be of any good when I got there, I had best give it up, for there would not be anything left of me to speak of by the time I got to the top. Then those Arab fellows got round, and shrieked and jabbered and wanted to pull us up; and the way they go up and down those stones is wonderful. But of course they have no weight to carry. No, I never should try that job again, not if we were to be camped here for the next ten years."

THE DASH FOR KHARTOUM

"I have been up to the top," Edgar said, "but it is certainly a hard pull, and there is nothing much to see when you do get there – only so much more sand in all directions. The view from the great mosque at Cairo is much finer. Do you have much drill?"

"Morning and evening we work away pretty stiff. It is infantry drill we have. They say we are not going to fight on the camels, but only to be carried along by them and to get off and fight if we see the enemy, and as we are all new to each other there is a good bit of work to be done to get us down to work as one battalion. We and the 4th make a troop together. We have drill in the afternoon, too, for a bit. Of a morning those that like can go across and have a look at the town. I went yesterday. Rum old place, isn't it? The rummiest thing is the way those little donkeys get about with a fat chap perched on the top of a saddle two feet above them. Never saw such mokes in my life. They ain't bigger than good-sized dogs some of them, and yet they go along with fifteen or sixteen stone on their backs as if they did not feel it. Those and the camels pleased me most. Rum beasts those camels. I can't think what it must feel like to be stuck up on top of them, and if one does fall off it must be like coming off a church. Have you tried one?"

"No. I have never been on a camel. Of course we always have had our horses."

"Why didn't they get us horses?"

"I don't know. They could have bought a couple of thousand, no doubt, if they had tried; besides, they could have got some from the Egyptian cavalry. But if they had they would never have sent out you and the Guards; though the horses would have done very well to carry light cavalry. I fancy the idea is that in the first place we have to go long distances without water. Camels can stand thirst for three or four days together, and each camel can carry water for its rider. Then, too, we may perhaps march sometimes, and the camels could carry water and food. So, you see, they will be useful both ways."

"Well, I suppose it is all right," Willcox said; "and as you say, if they had gone in for horses they could not have carried us heavies. I am precious glad to come. So are we all; though why they wanted to bring us and the Guards – the biggest and heaviest men they could pick out in the army – on a job like this, is more than I can say."

"It is more than anyone can say, I should think," Edgar said; and indeed no reason has ever been assigned for the singular choice of the heaviest men that could be collected in the service for duty on a campaign such as this was to be, and for which light, active, wiry men were especially suitable.

"There is the dinner call."

"What troop are we in?" Edgar asked, seizing his trumpet, and on learning at once gave the troop call.

"We are in messes of eight," Willcox replied. "We and the three tents to the right have one mess. It is our turn to go over and get the grub."

Accordingly Willcox and Edgar went across to the field-kitchen and received the rations for their mess, consisting of beef and vegetables – the bread for the day had been served out early. Returning to the tents the rations were divided between the party of eight, and Edgar was introduced by Willcox to his new messmates.

"Your regiment was at Aldershot with us eighteen months ago."

"Yes; but I did not know any of your men. I was over one or two evenings at your canteen, which was by a long way the best in the camp."

"Yes, we used to have some good singing there and no mistake," one of the men said.

"The Long Valley is not bad in the way of dust, but this place beats it hollow," another put in.

"This is a cleaner dust," Edgar said. "The Long Valley dust blackened one; this does not seem to have any dirt in it. As far as the uniforms go there is not much difference, but one doesn't feel so grimy after a charge over this Egyptian sand as one did in the Long Valley."

"We played you fellows at cricket, I remember," the man said. "I was in our eleven. You beat us, for you had a youngster we could not stand up against, he was a beggar to bowl."

Edgar laughed. "I rather think I am the fellow," he said, "Trumpeter Smith."

"It was Trumpeter Smith, sure enough. Well, you can bowl and no mistake, young un. It is rum meeting out here like this. And how have you been getting on since? You fellows were in the thick of it at El-Teb, I saw; and got cut up a bit by those niggers, didn't you?"

"That we did," Edgar replied. "I am not sorry that we are going to fight as infantry this time, for I can tell you it is not pleasant charging among fellows who throw themselves down and hamstring your horse or drive a spear into him as he passes over them; and once down it is likely to go pretty hard with you."

"The infantry had it pretty hot too at Tamanieb?"

"Yes, they got into one of our squares, and I don't think many of our fellows would have ever got away if it had not been that Buller's square came up to their assistance. Still, I don't suppose that will ever happen again. If the infantry stand firm and shoot straight they ought never to be broken, while that cavalry business was a thing nothing could guard against. The best horseman in the world may go down if a fellow shams dead and then suddenly stabs your horse."

"There is no doubt the beggars can fight," Willcox said; "and I expect we shall get some tough work before we get to Khartoum. I only hope they won't catch us suddenly before we have time to get off those camels. Fancy being stuck up on one of those long-legged beasts with half a dozen niggers making a cock-shy of you with their spears."

"I don't think that will happen," Edgar replied. "We shall have the 19th to acts as scouts, and as there will be no woods or thick scrub, from what I have heard of the country, as there was on the plains round Suakim, we ought not to be surprised."

THE CAMEL CORPS

"This meat is horribly tough," Willcox remarked. "It strikes me they ought to have examined every one's mouth before they sent them out, and to have chosen men with good sets of grinders, for I am sure they will want them for this stuff."

"The meat is tough out here. You see, it won't keep and has to be cooked pretty nearly warm, but it is better by a long way than that tinned meat which is all we shall get, I expect, when we once start."

"When are we going to start?"

"In a few days, I should think. The boats are being taken up fast, and I believe a lot of the Canadians went up yesterday. There are two or three infantry regiments up there ready to go on as soon as the boats for them get up; and as most of the camels are up there too, I should think they will push us up as soon as they can, as I suppose we are intended to go ahead of the boats and clear the banks."

Then they began to talk about the route, and Edgar, who had studied the maps and knew all that was known on the subject of the journey, drew on the sand the course of the Nile with its windings and turnings.

"You see the river makes a tremendous bend here," he said, "round by Berber. The general idea is that when we get to this spot, where there is a place called Ambukol, if there is news that Gordon is hard pressed and cannot hold out long, a column will march across this neck to Metemmeh, where there are some of Gordon's steamers. I expect that is the work that will fall to the Camel Corps, and that it is specially for this that we have been got up. You see, the rest of the journey is along the water side, and horses would have done just as well as camels, and would be much more useful, for, of course, the infantry will do the main fighting, and the cavalry are only wanted for scouting and pursuit. Camels are no good for either one work or the other, for nothing will persuade the beggars to move out of their regular pace, which is just about two and three-quarter miles an hour. If they did not intend to cut across this neck, I don't see what they wanted more than the boats with the infantry and a

149

regiment or two of light cavalry on these country horses, which are wonderfully hardy and can stand work that would knock English horses to pieces in no time."

"Well, then, all that I can say is," Willcox put in, "that it is very lucky for us that the river makes that big twist, otherwise we might be all kicking our heels at Aldershot or the Curragh, or in some garrison town. But I thought camels were fast beasts. I am sure I have seen pictures of Arabs riding about in the desert at a tremendous pace."

"There are some sort of camels called riding camels that are faster than the others, and there are dromedaries, which can trot as fast as a horse and keep it up for a long time; but the riding camels and dromedaries are both scarce and expensive, and you may be sure we shall not have many of them with us."

"They are beastly ill-tempered looking brutes," Willcox said. "When I was walking in the streets there the other day a string of them came along, and they grumbled and growled like wild beasts, and one showed his teeth and made as if he was going right at me. If I had not jumped into a shop I believe he would have had my ear off."

"They can bite, and bite very hard too; but it is very seldom they do, though they do make a wonderful pretence of being fierce. They call them the patient camel, but from what I have seen of them I should say that they are the most impatient, grumbling beasts in creation. It makes no difference what you do for them – whether you load them or unload them, or tell them to get up or lie down, or to go on or stop – they always seem equally disgusted, and grumble and growl as if what you wanted them to do was the hardest thing in the world. Still, they can do a tremendous lot of work, and keep on any number of hours, and I don't know what the people of this country would do without them."

In the afternoon Edgar paraded with his troop and fell into the usual routine of duty. As he had had a year's campaigning in Egypt he was regarded as an authority, and after three or four days was as much at home with the troop as he had been in his own regiment. He found these big men very pleasant and cheery companions. All had been picked for the service as being men of exemplary character; they were in high spirits at the prospect of the expedition before them, and were like a party of great school-boys out on a holiday. They took to Edgar kindly; belonging, as he did, to the light cavalry, they regarded him as a sort of guest among them, and from his being so much younger and smaller than themselves they looked upon him as a boy, and he quickly got the nickname of "The Kid." Many questions were asked him as to the fighting powers of the wild natives.

"How they could break right into a square beats me altogether," one of the big troopers said. "They always tell us that cavalry have no chance nowadays of breaking into a square, for they would all be shot down by the breech-loaders before they could reach it, and yet these niggers, with nothing but spears, manage to do it. I cannot make head or tail of it; no more I can of you chaps getting cut up by them."

"You will understand it when you see it," Edgar said. "They run pretty nearly as fast as a horse can gallop, and they don't seem to fear death in the slightest, for they believe that if they are killed they go straight to heaven. It seems to me that savages must be braver than civilized soldiers. It was the same thing with the Zulus, you know, they came right down on our men at Isandula, and the fire of the breech-loaders did not stop them in the slightest."

"No more it would stop us, young un, if we got orders to charge. It did not at Balaclava."

"No, that is true enough," Edgar agreed; "but then we have got discipline. The order is given, and the whole regiment goes off together; one could not hold back if one would. But that is a different thing from rushing forward each man on his own account, as they did against us, and running up to what seemed certain death. I know the feeling among our fellows was that they would not have believed it had they not seen it."

"Well, I hope we shall get a chance of seeing it," the man said, "only I hope that we shall not be atop of them camels when they try it. I have been looking at the beasts over there in the city, and there does not seem to me to be any go about them. Beastly-tempered brutes! I don't believe you could get a charge out of them if you tried ever so much."

"No, I don't think you could," Edgar laughed. "But, you see, we are intended to fight on foot. We shall be like the old dragoons, who used their horses only to carry them to the place where they were to fight."

"No chance of any loot?" another put in.

"No chance in the world. At the best of times they wear a sort of dirty cotton sheet round their shoulders, but when they go into battle they leave that behind them, and fight only in their loin-cloths."

"I have heard," an old soldier said, "from some of our chaps who fought in the Indian mutiny, that they often found a lot of money and jewels and things in those loin-cloths of the Sepoys."

"Ah, that was because they had been plundering treasuries and capturing booty of all sorts. But I do not suppose many of these Arabs ever saw a gold coin in their lives. They don't see many silver ones. What wealth they have is in sheep and cattle and horses, and with these they barter for such things as they require. No; if you are fighting out here for a year you will get nothing except a few worthless charms, of no value whatever except as curios."

"Well, I wish they would let us be off," another said. "I am sick already of these sands and that big lump of stone. I hear the boats are going up every day, and if they do not move us soon the infantry will be there before us."

"I think we shall travel a good deal faster than they do when we are once off," Edgar said. "They will have rapids and all sorts of difficulties to contend with, while we shall go on steadily, five and twenty miles a day perhaps. You may be sure we shall be well in front when the time for work comes. They would never go to the expense of sending you all out, and mounting you on camels, and then keep you behind."

"Have you heard the news, lads?" a sergeant asked, joining the group.

"No! What is it?"

THE CAMEL CORPS

"We are to strike tents at four o'clock this afternoon, march down to the river, embark in a steamer, and start to-night."

"Hooray!" the men shouted. "That is the best news we have had since we landed." In a short time most of the men were at work giving a final polish to their arms. By four o'clock the tents were levelled and rolled up, the baggage was packed and sent forward on camels, and the regiment was formed up awaiting the orders to march. The heat of the day had somewhat abated, but the march, short as it was, was a trying one, from the clouds of light sand that rose from beneath the feet of the column, and the men were heartily glad when they embarked, two troops on board the steamer and the rest on large flats which she was to tow up the stream. Kits and belts were taken off, and the men made themselves as comfortable as the crowded state of the flats would permit. The officers were on board the steamer. As they started a loud cheer broke from the men. They were fairly off at last. There was no thought of the dangers and difficulties before them. It was enough for them that they were fairly on their way up the Nile to relieve, as they hoped, Khartoum, and to rescue Gordon.

"If this is campaigning I don't care how much we have of it," the soldier who was sitting next to Edgar said, looking up at the deep blue sky studded with stars. "This suits me down to the ground."

"You had better make the most of it," Edgar laughed, "it won't last long; and you will have nothing like it again. I own that, at any rate until we reach the highest point to which the boats can go, I think the infantry have got the best of it. Of course they will have hard work in hauling the boats past the rapids, and they will have some rowing to do when the wind is too light for the sails to carry them up, but I would rather sit in a boat and row than sit on the back of a camel."

"But the boats will go all the way, won't they?"

"It is not known yet. It is possible that when we get to a place named Korti, where the river makes a tremendous bend, some of us may cross the desert to Metemmeh, where

153

Gordon's steamers will meet us. If we do I expect that will be the work of the three Camel Corps, and all the boats will go right round the river and join us there; that is, if they can get up the cataracts. I know the Egyptians say the water will be too low for the boats to go up. That may be true enough as to the native boats, but ours draw so little water that I believe there must always be depth enough for them, for there is always a good lot of water coming down here even at the driest season."

The regiment was disembarked at Assouan, and the next day four companies went up in two steamers to Wady Halfa, a hundred and eighty miles higher up the river. Edgar's troop formed part of the detachment. They had expected to see a place of some size, but found that it consisted only of a few mud huts and some sheds of the unfinished railway. Here for some days the men practised infantry drill and received their equipments and saddles, and then they were marched to the camel depot a mile away.

The soldiers were immensely amused at the sight of their chargers. These animals had been collected from all parts of Egypt, from Aden and Arabia. As soon as the proper number had been received and told off to the men, the work of fitting on the saddles commenced. This was by no means easy, as the camel humps differed greatly from each other, and a good deal of padding and altering was necessary before the saddles were comfortably fitted. When the men mounted they formed in line, and found that the animals were docile and obedient to the rein, and manœuvred together without difficulty. Several days were spent in learning to sit the animals, and there were many spills, but as the sand was deep no harm came of them, and they caused great amusement to all except the victims themselves.

The greatest difficulty was the mounting and dismounting, both of which performances had to be done when the camel was kneeling. In order to make him kneel it was necessary to tug at the head-rope, at the same time making a sound like clearing the throat. Then the rope was pulled at until his head was brought round to his shoulder.

This prevented him from getting up again. The rifle, which was slung in a bucket on one side behind the rider, was found to render it impossible to get the leg over, and it consequently became necessary for the man to mount with his rifle in his hand, and to drop it into the bucket afterwards. As the camel always rose and lay down with great suddenness, men were, until accustomed to it, constantly pitched over his head.

"I never want to see a camel again," Edgar grumbled, after one or two days' exercise diversified by numerous falls; "they are the most discontented beasts I ever saw."

"I don't mind their growling," a trooper said; "it is the twistiness of the brutes I hate. When you are looking after a horse you know what he can do and where he can reach you. Of course if you get behind him he can kick, but when you are standing beside him all that you have got to look after is his head, and he cannot bring that round to bite very far. These brutes can reach all over the place; they can kick at you any way. They can scratch their ears with their hind legs, and even rub the top of their humps with it if they are disposed, or scratch themselves under the chin. Their necks are the same, they can twist them anywhere. They can bite the root of their tails, and lay their heads back and give them a rub on the top of their humps. There is no safety with them at all; and when they come at you growling and roaring with their mouths open and showing their teeth it is enough to scare you."

"It is fortunate that their hoofs are soft and spongy, so that they cannot hurt like the kick of a horse," Edgar said.

"Spongy, be blowed!" the trooper replied. "Mine kicked me in the chest yesterday and I went flying about ten yards, and the breath was knocked out of my body for a quarter of an hour."

"That was bad, no doubt," Edgar laughed; "but if it had been a horse you would be in the hospital-tent now with some of your ribs broken, if you hadn't been smashed up altogether."

THE DASH FOR KHARTOUM

"They are up to all sorts of tricks," the trooper went on, looking savagely at his growling camel. "There was Rogers, this morning, he was just passing a camel who was kneeling down. Well, who would think that a kneeling camel could do anything except with his head. Rogers swore that he did not go within four yards of him, and the brute suddenly shot out his hind leg and caught him on the knee and cut him clean over, and he thought for some time that his leg was broken. Blow all camels, I say!"

As the camels were not to be used for fighting from, in the presence of an enemy the troopers were to dismount and fight on foot. When down the camels were to be knee-haltered, one of the fore-legs being doubled up and strapped, which prevented the animal from rising. Each camel received about five pounds of grain night and morning, and the whole were taken down to the river every other day to drink. The conduct of many of them was exasperating in the extreme to their riders. When taken down into the stream they would stand and look about in an aimless way as if wondering what on earth they had been brought there for, and would be sometimes ten minutes or a quarter of an hour before the idea seemed to occur to them that they might as well have a drink.

Once on the march they went steadily and well, obeying the slightest motion of the halter, and keeping up their regular pace without intermission from the time they started until they were ordered to halt.

After a week's drill and practice the men became accustomed to the ways of their animals, and were glad when the order came for them to start. By this time the leading regiments of the infantry had begun to go up in their boats. These were broad, flat crafts, which had been specially built in England for the purpose. Each carried twelve men and three months' supply of provisions and stores for them. They were provided with sails and oars, and as the direction of the wind was up the river the sails were of great assistance.

Towing the boat up the Nile.

THE DASH FOR KHARTOUM

As the cavalry passed the Great Cataract they had an opportunity of seeing the process of getting the boats up. The rush of waters was tremendous, and it seemed well-nigh impossible to force the boats against them. It would indeed have been impossible to row them, and they were dragged up by towropes by the united strength of the troops and a large number of natives. At times, in spite of all the efforts of the men at the ropes, the boats made no progress whatever, while if the steersman allowed the stream for a moment to take the boat's head it would be whirled round and carried down to the foot of the rapid, when the work had to be recommenced.

The troopers thought, as they watched the exertions of the infantry, that, rough as was the action of the camels, they had decidedly the best of it, but such was not their opinion on the following day when, as they were jogging wearily along, several of the boats passed them running before a strong wind, with the soldiers on board reclining in comfortable positions in the bottom or on the thwarts. Again their opinions changed when, the wind having dropped, they saw the men labouring at the oars in the blazing sun.

"There are pulls both ways," one of the troopers said philosophically, "and take it all round I don't know which has got the best of it. If there are many of these cataracts I should say we are best off, and they say there are lots of them between this and Khartoum."

"I think we have got the best of it, certainly," Edgar said; "for if it comes to leaving the river and pushing on we are sure to be in it."

The journey from Wady Halfa to Dongola was 235 miles. The day's march was generally about twenty miles, the halting-places being made at spots previously settled upon, where there were depots of provisions formed for them. The start was made about five o'clock in the morning. For the first two hours the men walked, leading their camels; then when the sun became hot they mounted and rode the rest of the distance.

THE CAMEL CORPS

At first they found the monotonous motion very trying, but became accustomed to it in time, and would even go off to sleep in the saddles, with the result, however, that they were probably shot off if the camel came upon a sudden irregularity of the ground.

In the cool of the evening the men bathed in the river, and the officers often went out in search of game, which was found, however, to be very scarce. There were many regrets among the men that they had brought no fish-hooks or lines with them, for these would have furnished not only amusement during their halts, but might have afforded a welcome change to the monotony of their diet.

The country bordering the Nile was composed of low rocky hills and hard gravel, with occasional tufts of dry grass and scrub. Sometimes the troops marched four abreast, at other times they had to go in single file across the rocky ground. The fun of the camel-riding very soon passed off, and the men found the marches extremely dull and monotonous, and were heartily glad when they got to Dongola.

Here the rest of the regiment joined them. Marching twenty miles up the river they crossed the Nile in boats, and another day's march took them to Shabadud; and after a stay there of some days, drilling with other corps, they moved on to Korti, four days' march. The site chosen for the camp delighted the men. Groves of palms grew along the steep banks of the river; beyond were fields of grass and broad patches of cultivated land. Here they were to wait until the rest of the mounted troops came up, and a portion, at any rate, of the infantry arrived in the boats.

CHAPTER X
AN UNEXPECTED MEETING

I T is a nice place for a camp, isn't it, youngster?"

"Very nice, sergeant; but it will soon be spoiled with all these troops arriving. It is very pretty now with that grove of palm-trees, and the low green bushes that hide the sand, and the river with all the boats with white sails. I have just been counting them; there are thirty-two in sight. But when we get three or four regiments here they will soon cut down the scrub and spoil its appearance altogether."

"That is so, lad; troops make a pretty clear sweep of everything where they settle down."

Edgar had taken a good deal to Sergeant Bowen, who had shown him many little kindnesses on the way up. He was an older man than most of those engaged in the expedition, and Edgar judged him to be thirty-two or thirty-three years old. He was a fine, tall, soldierly-looking fellow, and had served in various parts of the world.

"Let us sit down," the sergeant said; "this bush will give us a little shade. How long have you been in the army, lad?"

"Better than two years. Directly the campaign is over I shall give up my trumpet, and hope I shall get my stripes soon."

"How old are you – nineteen?"

"Not for some months yet, sergeant."

"Hope to get your commission some day?" the sergeant said. "I suppose that is what you entered the army for."

"Yes, partly, sergeant; partly because I saw no other way of keeping myself."

"But what are your friends doing?"

AN UNEXPECTED MEETING

"I have not any friends; at least none that I care to apply to," Edgar answered shortly.

"No friends, lad? That is bad. But I do not want to know your story if you do not choose to tell it. It is easy to see that you have had a good education. Keep steady, lad, and you will get on. I might have been a quarter-master years ago if it hadn't been for that. Drink and other things have kept me down; but when I was twenty I was a smart young fellow. Ah! that is a long time back."

"Why, one would think that you were an old man, sergeant," Edgar said, and smiled.

"Older than you would think by a good bit. How old do you take me to be?"

"Something past thirty."

"A good deal past that. I am just forty, though they don't know it, or I should not be here."

"Why, then, if you enlisted when you were my age, sergeant, you must have done over twenty years' service."

"It's twenty-two since I first enlisted. I served eight years in the infantry. I don't know why I am telling you this, but somehow I have taken a fancy to you. I was uncomfortable in the regiment. It does not matter why. I got my stripes twice, and had to give them up or I should have been put back for drinking. Then I left the regiment without asking leave. I was three or four years knocking about at home; but I had no trade and found it hard to get work, so at last I enlisted again. I was thirty then, but looked years younger than I was. Of course I had shaved off my moustache and put on a smock-frock when I went to enlist, and I gave my age as twenty-two. No one questioned it. I chose the cavalry this time, because I knew that if I entered an infantry regiment again they would spot me as an old soldier at once; but as it was all new in the cavalry I managed to pass it off, and now I have had ten years' service, the last six of them as sergeant. And as I gave up drink years ago I have a good character in the regiment, and when a steady non-commissioned officer was wanted for this business I had the luck to be chosen. Officers coming, lad!"

They rose to their feet and saluted as three officers passed. They were talking eagerly together, and returned the salute mechanically without glancing at the two soldiers.

"It is a rum chance, Clinton, our meeting here. I ran against Skinner at Assouan quite accidentally. I had seen his name in the list of the officers of the Marines going up; but we met quite by chance, and only forgathered here yesterday, and now here you are turning up as one of Stewart's A. D. C.'s. Who would have thought that we three should meet here, when we have never seen each other since we left Cheltenham?"

The sergeant stood looking after them with an air of interest till their voices died away. Then he turned to his companion.

"Hullo, lad, what is the matter? Are you ill?"

"No, I am all right," Edgar said huskily.

"Nonsense! Your colour has all gone, and you are shaking like a leaf. What! Did you know any of those officers?"

"I knew them all once," Edgar said. "We were at school together. I did not know that any of them were out here. I would not have them recognize me for anything."

"Oh, that is it! I thought you must have run away from school; got into some scrape, I suppose. Well, my lad, as you have made your bed you must lie in it. But it is not likely that any of them would know you even if they ran up against you. Two years' service under this sun changes a lad of your age wonderfully. By the way, one of them called the other Clinton; do you happen to know whether he is the son of a Captain Clinton – Captain Percy Clinton?"

"Yes, he is."

"He was captain of my company when I was a young sergeant. Well, well, time flies fast, to be sure. Do you know whether this young fellow has a brother, and, if so, what he is doing?"

"No, he has no brother," Edgar said shortly.

AN UNEXPECTED MEETING

"There were two of them," the sergeant said positively. "Perhaps one has died. I wonder which it was," he muttered to himself.

"Do you know the story?" Edgar asked suddenly. "Do I know the story!" the sergeant repeated slowly. "What story do you mean?"

"The story of Captain Clinton's baby being confused with another."

"Oh, you know about that, do you?" Sergeant Bowen asked in turn. "So they made no secret of it. Ay, lad, I know it; every man in the regiment knew it. And good cause I had to know it, it was that that ruined me."

"Are you Sergeant Humphreys?" Edgar asked, putting his hand on the man's shoulder.

The sergeant started in surprise.

"Why, lad, how come you to know all the ins and outs of that story? Ay, I was Sergeant Humphreys, and for aught I know that young fellow who has just passed, whom they call Clinton, is my son."

"No, he is not, sergeant; I am your son!"

The sergeant looked at the young trumpeter in bewilderment, then his expression changed.

"You have got a touch of fever, lad. Come along with me to the hospital; I will report you sick. The sooner you are out of the sun the better."

"I am as sensible as I ever was in my life," Edgar said quietly. "I was brought up by Captain Clinton as his son. I was at Cheltenham with Rupert Clinton, who has just passed us. We believed that we were twins until the day came when a woman came down there and told me the story, and told me that I was her son and yours; then I ran away, and here I am."

"My wife!" the sergeant exclaimed passionately. "I have not seen or heard of her for fifteen years. So she came down and told you that. She is a bad lot, if ever there was one. And so she told you you were my son? You may be, lad, for aught I know; and I should be well content to know that it was so. But what did she come and tell you that for? What

163

game is she up to now? I always knew she was up to some mischief. What was her motive in coming down to tell you that? Just let me know what she said."

"She said she had deliberately changed me as an infant for my good, and she proposed to me to continue the fraud, and offered, if I liked, to swear to Rupert's being her child, so that I might get all the property."

"And that she might share in it!" the sergeant laughed bitterly. "A bold stroke, that of Jane Humphreys. And how did she pretend to recognize you as her child more than the other?"

"She told me that Captain Clinton's child had a tiny mole on his shoulder, and as Rupert has such a mark, that settled the question."

"Jane Humphreys told you more than she knew herself. Whether she intended to make the change of babies or not I don't know, but I believe she did; but whether it was done by chance, or whether she purposely mixed them up together, one thing I am certain of, and that is, that she confused herself as well as every one else, and that she did not know which was which. When I came into the room first she was like a woman dazed, and, clever as she was, I am sure she was not putting it on. She had thought, I fancy, that she could easily distinguish one from the other, and had never fancied that she could have been confused as well as other people. She undressed them, and looked them over and over, and it was then she noticed the little mole on the shoulder, and she turned to me and said, 'If I had but noticed this before I should always have told them apart.'

"We had a pretty bad time of it afterwards, for it made me the laugh of the whole regiment, and caused no end of talk and worry, and we had frightful rows together. She taunted me with being a fool for not seeing that there was money to be made out of it. She acknowledged to me over and over again that she had intended to change the children, and had dressed them both alike; and when I asked her what good had come out of her scheming, she said that in the first place we had got rid of the bother of bringing up the boy, and that if I were not a fool we might make a good thing out of it yet. But she was vexed and angry with herself for not having seen this little mark, and for having herself lost all clue as to which was her child. I told her that as she had intended to change them she could have cared nothing for her own boy, and that her only object could have been to make money.

"She did not deny it, but simply jeered at me for being content to remain all my life a non-commissioned officer when there might be a fortune made out of this. I do not say that if she had been able to tell one child from the other she would have told me, for if she had I should certainly have gone to Captain Clinton and told him; but she did not know. A woman can act well, but she cannot make herself as white as a sheet and put such a wild look into her eyes as she had when I found her turning those children over and over, and trying to make out which was which. I could take the Bible in my hand and swear in court that Jane Humphreys knew no more than I did which was her child, that she had never noticed the mark until after the change was made, and that to this day she does not know.

"One of the points we quarrelled on was that I made her start for the captain's quarters in such a hurry. She afterwards said that when it first came across her that she did not know which child was which, her blood seemed to go up into her head, and she lost her power of judgment altogether. She said over and over again that if I hadn't hurried her so, and had let matters be for a day or two, so that she could have slept on it and had looked at them quiet, she would have known which was her child. So that is how it is, lad. You may be Jane Humphreys' child and mine, or you may be Captain Clinton's, but no living soul can decide which. As to Jane Humphreys, she is a liar and a thorough bad un, and if it is only on her word that you have run away you have made a bad mistake of it. Still it is not too late to put that right. My word is as good as hers; and as she swore before she did not know which was which, her swearing now that she does, after all these years, will go for nothing at all."

165

Edgar was silent for some time, then he said, "I have thought a good many times since I ran away that I was wrong in not waiting to hear what Captain Clinton said. But I had no reason to doubt the story she told me, and when she proposed that I should go on with this fraud and cheat Rupert out of his position as heir, it was too horrible, and the thought that such a woman was my mother was altogether too much to bear. I will not make such a mistake again, or act in a hurry. My present thought is that as I have chosen my way I will go on in it. Before, Captain Clinton and his wife did not know which was their child and loved us both equally, now that they believe that Rupert is their son and that I was a fraud, they will have come to give him all their love, and I am not going to unsettle things again. That is my present idea, and I do not think that I am likely to change it.

"I shall be glad to know that I need not consider myself that woman's child, though it would not grieve me, now that I know you, to be sure that you were my father. But Captain Clinton and his wife were a father and mother to me up to the day when I ran away, and I could never think of anyone else in that light."

"Quite natural, quite natural, lad! You have never seen me or heard of me, and it would be a rum thing if you could all of a sudden come to care a lot about me. I know that you may be my son, but I don't know that at present I like you any the more for that than I did before. So we are quite of one mind over that. But we will be friends, lad, stout friends!"

"That we will," Edgar said, clasping warmly the hand the other held out to him. "You have been very kind to me up to now, and now that at any rate we may be father and son we shall be drawn very close together. When this campaign is over it will be time to talk again about the future. I do not think now that I am at all likely to change my mind, or to let the Clintons know what you have told me; but I need not trouble about it in any way until then. I was contented before, and I am contented now. If I had made a fool of myself, as I think I have, I must pay the penalty. I have much to be thankful for. I had a very happy time of it until the day I left Cheltenham. I have had a good education, and I have a first-rate chance of making my way up. I have made friends of some of the officers of my regiment, and they have promised to push me on. I had the luck to attract the colonel's attention at El-Teb, and was among the names sent in for the Victoria Cross; and although I did not get it, the fact that I was recommended will count in my favour."

"You are the right stuff, lad," the sergeant said, putting his hand on his shoulder, "whether I or the captain was your father. I reckon that it was he – I don't see where you can have got what there is in you from our side. And now it is time to be going back to camp. Who would have thought, when we strolled out together, that so much was to come out of our walk?"

While this conversation had been going on, Rupert Clinton and his two old school-fellows were sitting on the ground in the tent which Easton shared with another of General Stewart's aides-de-camp.

"The scene has changed," Easton said as he handed them each a tumbler of weak rum and water, "otherwise one might imagine that we were in my study at River-Smith's, and that Skinner was about to lay down the law about the next football match."

"Ah! if we had but Edgar here!" Rupert sighed.

"I did not like to ask whether you had found him, Clinton; but I guessed you had not by your keeping silence."

"No, we have heard nothing of him beyond the fact that we have occasionally a letter saying that he is well and comfortable. They were all posted in London, but I still believe that he is in the army. My father is as convinced as ever that the statement of that woman I told you of was a false one, and that Edgar is just as likely to be his son as I am. I know I would gladly give up my share of the heirship to find him. However, unless I run against him by pure chance I am not likely to do that. We still put in advertisements occasionally, but my people at home are as convinced as I am that we shall not hear from him until he has made his way in some line or other, and he is in an independent position."

"He always was a sticker," Skinner said, "and if he took a thing in hand would carry it through. You remember his rush in our last match with Green's, how he carried the ball right down through them all. I should not worry about it, Clinton; it will all come right in time. He will turn up some day or other; and when he finds that matters are just as they were before, and that your people believe him to be just as likely to be their son as you are, he will fall into his old place again – at least that is my opinion of it."

"Yes, that is what I hope and believe," Rupert said. "Well, Easton, how do you like the Guards, and how do you like campaigning? I see that you have given up white shirts, like the rest of us. I rather expected that if we did meet I should find that, in some miraculous way, you still contrived to get up immaculately."

Easton laughed. "No, I left my last white shirt at Cairo, Clinton. I consulted my soldier-servant about it. He was ready to guarantee the washing, but he did not see his way to starching and ironing; so I had to give them up and take to flannels. They were awful at first, and irritated my skin until they brought on prickly heat, and I was almost out of my mind for a few days. However, I have got over it now. What made you go into the Marines, Skinner?"

"Well, just before the exam came off an uncle of mine, who is a great friend of the first lord, wrote to say that he could get me a commission. Well, in the first place I did not feel very sure of passing for the line; in the second place I had a liking for the sea; and in the third place, as my governor's living is not a very large one and I have a lot of sisters, and I thought I had had more than my share already in being sent to Cheltenham – and one can live a good deal cheaper in the Marines than in the line – I concluded the best thing I could do was to accept the offer; and I have not been sorry that I did it. It was awful luck my coming out in the Naval Brigade here; it was just a fluke. The man who was going was chucked off a horse and broke his arm the day before the brigade sailed from Suakim, and I was sent up in his place. Well, what is the last news, Clinton? You ought to know, as you are on the staff."

"They don't intrust aides-de-camp with their secrets," Rupert replied; "but I think it likely there will be a move in a day or two, and that the Camel Corps will push across to Metemmeh and wait there till the boats get round."

"Yes, that is what every one is talking about," Easton said. "The question that is agitating us is whether all the Camel Corps will go; and if not, which will be chosen?"

"Ah, that I know nothing about, Easton; but I should think if any go, the Guards would be sure to be in it. But whether the Heavies or the Lights will go, if only two are chosen, I cannot say. I should fancy one will go with the boats anyhow, so as to keep along parallel with them and protect them against any sudden attack while they are afloat."

"Will the chief go on, do you think?"

"Not if only a small body cross the desert. At least I should think not. I should say he would stay here until Metemmeh is occupied and the boat column is well on its way, and that then he will go on to Metemmeh, and take the command there when the whole force is assembled. In that case Stewart would of course command the desert column, and I should be all right."

"The great question is, will the beggars fight?" Skinner remarked; "and if so, where?"

"They are sure to fight," Easton said. "I don't think there is the least doubt about that, but I should not think there will be any fighting this side of Metemmeh; it will be somewhere between that and Khartoum. The Mahdi cannot help fighting after smashing up Hicks and giving himself out as invincible. He would lose his hold altogether of the people if he did not come down and fight. Of course there is no doubt about the result; but, judging from the way those fellows fought down by the Red Sea, it is likely to be pretty tough work. I shall be sorry for the poor beggars with their spears against our breech-loaders, but it has got to be done."

Skinner and Rupert both laughed, for Easton spoke exactly as he used to do with regard to football.

"It will be a nuisance your having to exert yourself, won't it, Easton?"

"Yes, that is always a nuisance, and in a climate like this!" Easton said seriously. "Why nature made a place so hot, I cannot make out. I am sure if I were to be weighed I should find I had lost nearly a stone since I came out."

"You have quite enough flesh on you," Skinner said critically. "If you have lost a stone you must have been getting beastly fat. You fellows in the Guards do not take enough exercise. The time was when the Guards used to row and had a very good eight, but they never do that sort of thing now. It would do you all a lot of good if, instead of wandering between London and Windsor and Dublin, you were to take your turn for foreign service."

"But then we should not be Guards, Skinner."

"Well, you would be none the worse for that," Skinner retorted.

"He is just as bad as he used to be, Clinton," Easton laughed; "just the same aggressive, pugnacious beggar that he was at River-Smith's."

"He means well, Easton. We never expected more than that from him. He must make himself fearfully obnoxious to the fellows who have the misfortune to be shut up on board ship with him."

"I shall make myself obnoxious to you, Clinton, if you don't look out. It is only the heat that protects you. Have you met any others of our fellows out here?"

"Not from our house, but I know there are seven or eight fellows of about our own standing out here altogether."

"If we are up here in the cold weather," Skinner said, "that is, if there ever is any cold weather, we will get a football made and challenge a team from any other school."

"Don't talk about it," Easton said plaintively. "It throws me into a perspiration even to think about it. The dust would be something awful. Possibly if we are up here through the winter, or through the period they are pleased to call winter, we might get up cricket; but as for football, it is out of the question. Of course if we were stationed at Dongola, or Berber, or Khartoum, we could get the bats and stumps and things sent up to us. It would be fun if it were only to see how these lazy, squatting beggars would stare when they saw us at it."

"But you were never enthusiastic about cricket."

"No. But then, you see, I do not propose to play on our side. My idea is that I should sit down on the sands in the shade of the scrub and smoke my pipe quietly. That is the oriental idea of taking exercise; pay somebody to dance for you, and sit and watch them, but do not think of attempting to take a hand yourself. It would be fatal to any respect that these Egyptians may feel for us if they were to see us rushing about the sand like maniacs in pursuit of a ball. However, though I should not play myself, I should take a lively interest, Skinner, in seeing you and Clinton working hard. But I must be going, it is near time for us to parade. Come across to my tent at nine o'clock this evening. I cannot ask you to dinner – that must be deferred until we get home again – but we can smoke a pipe and talk over old days; and I can give you a glass of good brandy and water, which is a change from the commissariat rum. I managed to smuggle up half a dozen bottles."

Edgar was much disturbed by the story he had heard so unexpectedly from the sergeant. He regretted now that he had acted so hastily. Certainly the story put a completely new complexion on the case, and his chance of being Captain Clinton's son was just the same as it had ever been. He wondered whether his father and mother – for so in his thoughts he always named them – had doubted the truth of this woman's statement to him, or whether they had believed it as he had done, and had put him out of their hearts as one with whom they had nothing to do, and who had been already too long imposed upon them. But he felt that this was an unjust view, and that however they might now be confident that Rupert was their son and heir they still cherished an affection towards him. "However," he said, "this will make

171

no difference to me. The die is cast, and I cannot go back now. Still I shall be happier than I was before. Then I considered that I had been an impostor who had received affection and care and kindness to which I had no shadow of right. Now I know that this is not so, and that it is just as likely that I am their son as it is that Rupert is; and I stay away for my own choice, and because, having made them believe that Rupert was their son, I am not going to disturb and make them unhappy again by showing them that this was a mistake, and that everything is as unsettled as before.

"I told them that they would never hear of me until I had made my own way, and I shall stick to that. Who would have thought of meeting Rupert here? It has been a great piece of luck for him getting out here as General Stewart's aide-de-camp, but I know the general is a friend of my father, and that accounts for it. Perhaps this sergeant is my father. I did not seem to mind the thought before. I did not even know whether he was alive, and never really faced it; and yet, if Sergeant Bowen is to be my father, he is as good as another. He seems a fine fellow, and has had no hand in this fraud. I ought, indeed, to think myself lucky; for he is steady and respectable, a good soldier, and, I can see, liked by the officers as well as the men. It was curious that he should have taken a fancy to me.

"Still it does go against the grain, though I can see he has no intention of claiming me openly as his son. If he had, I think I should have kicked against it; but as it is, I am sure we shall be very good friends."

After drill was over next morning, and the camels had been seen to and the men dismissed, Sergeant Bowen came up to him –

"Let us take another turn together, lad. I have been thinking a lot," he went on when they were beyond the lines, "of our talk yesterday. Now, lad, you have been brought up as a gentleman, and to consider yourself as Captain Clinton's son; remember, I don't want you to think that I expect you to make any change about that. I have done nothing for you as a father; and whether I am your father or not you do

172

not owe me anything, and I want to tell you again that I don't expect in the least that because it is possible you are my son you should regard me in the light of your father.

"I can understand that after all your life looking at the captain as your father, and after he and his wife being everything to you, you would find it mighty hard to regard me in that way. I don't expect it, and I don't want it. If he is not your father by blood, he is your father in right of bringing you up and caring for you and educating you, and it is quite right and quite proper that you should always regard him so. You can look upon me, lad, just as a foster-father – as the husband of the woman who was for a time your nurse, and who would gladly repair the wrongs he did to you. I just say this, lad, to make things straight between us. I want us to be friends. I am an old soldier, and you a young one. We are comrades in this expedition. We have taken to each other, and would do each other a good turn if we had a chance. I don't want more than that, lad, and I don't expect you to give more. If I can lend you a helping hand on or off duty, you know I shall do so. So let us shake hands on it, and agree to let the matter drop altogether until this campaign is over. Then we will talk over together what had best be done. A few months longer of this life will do you no harm, and you will make all the better officer for having had two or three years in the ranks. But I will say at once that I think that you are wrong, now you know how the matter stands, in not writing at once to the captain and letting him know the truth. Still there is no harm in its standing over for the present. You must go through the expedition as you are now, and they would be no easier for knowing that you are exposed to danger out here than they are at present when they know nothing of your whereabouts."

Edgar shook the sergeant heartily by the hand, and the bargain was sealed.

Every day troops kept on arriving, and by the 27th of December there were already at Korti a considerable portion of the Sussex, the Duke of Cornwall's Light Infantry, the Essex, Gordon Highlanders, Black Watch, and Staffordshire, all of whom had come up in the whale-boats; a large number of the commissariat, transport, hospital, and engineer train in native boats; the whole of the Guards' Camel Corps, and the greater portion of the Heavy and Light Camel Corps, a hundred men of the Marines, who were provided with camels, and appointed to form part of the Guards' Camel Corps, two squadrons of the 19th Hussars, and the Mounted Infantry.

In the few days that had passed since the troops to which Edgar was attached had arrived at Korti the change in the appearance of the place was great. The grove of palm-trees still stood near the bend of the river, but the green fields of grass and the broad patches of growing crops had been either levelled or trampled down, and the neighbourhood of the camp presented the appearance of the sandy wastes of Aldershot.

On the evening of that day Skinner rushed into Easton's tent.

"I have just seen Clinton," he said, "and the rumours are going to be fulfilled at last. They did not inspect our water-skins, arms, and accoutrements for nothing to-day. We are to start on the 30th across the desert. There is no secret about it, or of course Clinton wouldn't have told me. There are to be our regiment, a squadron of Hussars, the Mounted Infantry, and engineers. We are to take with us baggage-camels and the camels of the heavy and light regiments. We are going to Gakdul, about a hundred miles off. There all the stores are to be left, and the camels and Mounted Infantry to come back here. We are to remain to guard the stores. As soon as the camels return here, the Heavies are to take their own beasts, and, with the Mounted Infantry, escort every baggage animal that can be got up here, when we shall all go on together. Sir Herbert Stewart commands."

"What about baggage?" Easton asked, after expressing his deep satisfaction that the advance was about to begin.

"Only what we can carry ourselves on our camels, and the weight is limited to forty pounds, which is abundant even for sybarites like you guardsmen. A quarter of that would be amply sufficient for me. A couple of blankets, a waterproof sheet, half a dozen flannel shirts, ditto socks, pair of slippers, and a spare karkee suit; sponge, tooth-brush, and a comb. What can anyone want more?"

"I should like to take my waterproof bath," Easton said.

"Pooh! nonsense, man! Where are you going to get your water from?"

"There is water at Gakdul, and there will be plenty when we get to Metemmeh," Easton said.

"Well, I will grant that," Skinner said; "but anyhow you can manage very well as we do. Make a hole in the sand and put your waterproof sheet into it, and there you have got as good a bath as anyone can want. What is the use of lumbering yourself up with things you do not want? Much better take those three bottles of brandy you have got left and a couple of pounds of tobacco. That is the utmost allowance I should give. The camels will have to go a long time without water, and the less you put on their backs the better. You know what a difference a few pounds makes to a horse; and I suppose it must be the same thing with them."

At three o'clock on the afternoon of the 30th the force intended for the desert march paraded, and after marching past Lord Wolseley moved off in solid formation, thirty camels abreast. The total force consisted of 73 officers, 1212 men and natives, and 2091 camels. The whole camp had turned out to see the departure of the column, and Edgar, with his helmet pressed down low over his eyes, watched Rupert as he rode after Sir Herbert Stewart, and Easton and Skinner with the Guards' Camel Corps. The Heavies had been much disappointed at not forming part of the first advance, and especially at their camels being taken for baggage animals; but they consoled themselves by the fact that the native spies all reported that there were no bodies of the enemy between Korti and Gakdul, and it was not likely therefore that there would be any fighting until the whole force moved forward together from Gakdul to Metemmeh.

THE DASH FOR KHARTOUM

In front of the column were half a dozen natives on camels. These acted as the guides of the party. They had been extremely unwilling to go, and it was only when the general offered them the alternative of going willingly and receiving good pay for their work, or being lashed to their camels and forced to go without any pay whatever, that they elected the first. The Hussars scouted in front of the column, riding far ahead and scouring the country in search of lurking foes. Two hours after starting there was a halt, fires were lighted from the dry grass and mimosa bushes, and tea was made and served out. By this time it was five o'clock, and the sun had set. In an hour or two the moon, which was nearly full, rose, and afforded ample light for the journey.

For a time the silence of the desert was broken by the laughter and talk of the men, but as the time went on the sounds were hushed as sleepiness fell upon them. Short halts were of frequent occurrence, as the baggage animals in the rear lagged behind, or their loads slipped, and had to be readjusted. Then a trumpet was sounded by the rearguard, and it was repeated by the trumpeters along the column, and all came to a halt until the trumpet in the rear told that the camels there were ready to advance again. So the march continued throughout the whole night.

The ground was of hard sand or gravel, with round smooth hills of dark stone rising from it. Near the hills the ground was covered with low mimosa bushes and long yellow grass, and in some places the mimosa trees rose to a length of ten or twelve feet. At five o'clock day broke, and at half-past eight the column halted at a spot where there were a good many trees. Here they dismounted, breakfasted, and slept for some hours. At three in the afternoon they started again, and at half-past eight arrived at the first wells, those of Hambok; but as they were found to contain very little water, the march was continued to the El Howeiyat Wells, thirteen miles further. Before they got there the watches told that midnight had arrived, and the commencement of the new year was hailed with a burst of cheering, and singing broke out all along the line, and was continued for an hour, until they reached the wells.

There was but little water here, but the men carried theirs in skins. The horses of the 19th Hussars received a bucketful apiece, which exhausted the supply of the wells. At six o'clock in the morning they again advanced, and after a rest of three hours at mid-day continued their way until midnight, when a light being seen at a distance the column was halted, and the Hussars went out and captured a caravan loaded with dates for the use of the Mahdi troops. It was not until eight o'clock in the morning that the weary troops and animals reached the wells of Gakdul.

CHAPTER XI
ABU KLEA

WHERE on earth are the wells?" Skinner said to the officer who was riding next to him; and a similar question was asked by scores of others.

They had advanced through a narrow pass, and were now in a small flat surrounded apparently on all sides by hills. However, as Major Kitchener, the head of the intelligence department, and the native guides were there, every one supposed it was all right, and set to work to unload the camels. It was not such easy work as usual, for the ground was strewn with large stones, upon which the camels objected strongly to kneel. For a time there was a prodigious din – the camels grumbling and complaining, the natives screaming, the soldiers laughing, shouting, and using strong language. At last the loads were all off, the stores piled, and the din quieted down.

"Where on earth is this water, Skinner?" Easton asked as the two young officers met after the work was done.

"I cannot make out, Easton. I hope it is not far, for my water-skin has leaked itself empty and my throat is like a furnace."

"I have some water in mine," Easton said, "but it tastes of leather so strongly that it is next to undrinkable. Oh, here is Clinton. Where is the water, Clinton?"

"By that rock at the end of the valley. I am just going to have a look at it. Can you come?"

"Yes; there is nothing to do here at present."

ABU KLEA

They hurried towards the rock that Clinton pointed out, and when they reached it they still saw no signs of water, but on going round it burst into a shout of delight. Before them lay a pool some sixty feet wide by a hundred long. The rocks rose precipitously on each side; it was evident that the water was deep.

"There are two more pools further up," an officer who had got there before them said.

"Let us climb up and have a look," Clinton said; and with some difficulty they climbed up to the top of the rock. Going along for some little distance they looked down. Eighty feet below them lay two beautiful pools. They were evidently very deep, for at the edge the water was green, but nearly black in the centre of the pools.

"This is something like it," Skinner said. "There is no fear of running short of water. Come on, let us clamber down and get a drink. Look there, at the rows of camels coming along to the lower pool. I suppose that will be kept for them, and that we shall get our water from these."

With a good deal of difficulty they got down, but were unable to reach the edge. However they tied a string round one of their water-bottles, and soon brought it up full. The water was deliciously clear and cool, the high rock completely sheltering the pools from the heat of the sun. They indulged in several long draughts before their thirst was satisfied.

"I shall never say anything against water again," Skinner remarked. "I have always allowed its utility for washing purposes, but have considered it a distinct failure as a drink. I recant. While considering that at home beer is good enough for me, I am prepared to maintain that, in the middle of the Bayuda Desert, clear cold water and plenty of it is good enough for anyone. But how in the world are we going to get at this water? Oh, here come the Engineers; they are going to do it somehow."

A party of Engineers arrived with some pumps and a hundred yards of hose.

"How are you going to take it down?"

THE DASH FOR KHARTOUM

"We are going to lead the hose right through the lower pool, letting it lie at the bottom. That is the only way we can do it. There is no way of fixing it against that wall of rocks."

The pumps were fixed in a very short time and the hose laid, and in less than an hour the stream of pure water was being poured into a large trough placed near the lower pool, and from this the cooks of the various companies filled their kettles and boilers.

Some of the men, in spite of their long and fatiguing journey, had followed the example of the young officers and filled their water-bottles as they had done, but the majority had thrown themselves on the ground and were fast asleep a few minutes after the work of unloading the camels had been completed. For hours the work of watering the camels went on, slowly at first, as only a few could drink at a time, but more rapidly when large troughs were erected, at which thirty could be watered at once.

As soon as dinner was over the Guards set to work to erect two forts that the Engineers had already marked out. One of these was at the mouth of the pass leading into the little valley, the other was placed just above the pools. The baggage was piled close to the wells. By evening the work was well advanced, and at eight o'clock the Mounted Infantry and the whole of the camels started on their return journey, leaving the Guards, with fifteen Engineers and six Hussars, to hold the wells and guard the great pile of stores that had been brought up. As soon as work was over there was a general movement to the wells, and there were few who did not indulge in the luxury of a bathe in the lower pool.

Rupert Clinton returned with the column to Korti, as General Stewart went back with them to bring out the main body of troops. It was calculated that ten days must elapse before these would arrive at Gakdul, and the Guards and Marines set to work in earnest the next morning to get things into order. The work was very heavy, but as the men had plenty to eat and no lack of excellent water they did not mind it, congratulating themselves heartily upon the fact that they had not to make the long and wearisome journey to Korti and back. In the course of the ten days the walls of the forts rose to a height of over five feet – a very laborious piece of work, for one fort measured twenty yards by twenty-three; the other thirty yards by fifteen, and the stones had all to be picked up and carried considerable distances, or loosened out of the solid rock by aid of the six pickaxes and four crowbars that were alone available.

In addition to this the site of a camp was marked out, roads were formed by clearing away the stones, and paths made up to the forts and picket stations. The outpost duty was very severe, two officers and sixty-five men being always on duty, as it was possible that at any time, night or day, an attack might be made.

"This is awful!" Easton said to Skinner, as, sitting down on the ground, he mournfully contemplated his boots. "These boots that I relied upon to last me through the campaign are hopelessly done for."

"They do look bad," Skinner agreed, "but no worse than mine, or in fact than any one else's. These rocks are awful. If Nature had scattered ten million knives broadcast about this valley they could not have been more destructive to boots than these rocks. I used to think that, although the camels were well enough for taking up the baggage or as a means of conveyance for men, they were a mistake, and that it would be much pleasanter to march than to sit upon these wearisome beasts; but my opinion has been changed by our experience here. If we had to march many miles over such a country as this the whole force would be barefooted. I had a frightful job of it last night. I went the rounds with the field-officer, and how it was I didn't break my neck I cannot imagine. I had a dozen tremendous croppers down the rocks. The lantern went out the first time, and got smashed the second. The major seemed to think that it was my duty to have kept it alight whatever happened to myself, and was as savage as a bear. We lost our way a dozen times, and once came up to a picket on the wrong side, and deuced near got potted."

THE DASH FOR KHARTOUM

"I know all about it," Easton said. "I did it three nights ago, and have no skin at present on my knees or my elbows or my hips, and mighty little on my back. I went down one place fifty or sixty feet deep head-foremost, bumping from rock to rock, and it flashed through my mind as I did so what a fool I was to be going through all this when I might be comfortably in bed at home. They don't tell one of these things," he said plaintively, "when they talk of the advantages of the army."

"Bosh!" Skinner said wrathfully. "I don't suppose you were a bit more hurt than you would be in a good close rally at football. It is a thousand times better after all than mooning about Windsor, or being mewed on board a ship at Suakim. However, I shall be precious glad when the others arrive, and we have done with this fatigue work. The men's hands are pretty well cut to pieces getting up and carrying those sharp rocks, and I am heartily tired of acting as a sort of amateur mason."

On the 11th of January a convoy of a thousand camels with stores and ammunition arrived, and the next day the troops were delighted at seeing the main body approaching. In addition to the Mounted Infantry and Heavy Camel Corps, 400 men of the Sussex Regiment came up on the camels. They were intended to garrison the forts and protect the wells when the rest of the force moved forward, but a hundred of them were to go forward with the troops. With the new-comers were 30 sailors with a Gardner gun, 30 men of the Royal Artillery with three 7-pounder guns, 45 of the Medical and Commissariat Staff, and 120 native drivers for the baggage camels. As the Heavy Camel Regiment numbered 380 and the Guards 367, the Mounted Infantry 360, and there were 90 men of the 19th Hussars and 100 of the Sussex, the total force which was to advance was about 1500 men, 90 horses, and 2200 camels.

All the men with the exception of the natives, who were on foot, were mounted on camels, the Hussars of course excepted, as they rode sturdy little Egyptian horses, which, although little larger than ponies, were capable of enduring an amount of fatigue, hardship, and privation, that would in the course of a few days have rendered English horses useless.

Those who had left Gakdul but ten days before were astonished at the change which the labours of the Guards' Camel Corps had effected in it, and great commendation was given them by the general for the zeal with which they had worked.

Large as was the number of animals to be watered, the work was conducted with far greater speed and ease than had been the case on their former arrival. The arrangements were all excellent, and in a comparatively short time the whole were watered and fed. The troops, however, were dismayed at the change which had come over the camels. These animals are capable of enduring great fatigue and scarcity of water and food, but the authorities had acted as if there were no limits whatever to those powers, and for a fortnight the camels had been kept at work with only three or four hours' rest out of each twenty-four, with a very scanty supply of food, and a sufficient allowance of water but twice, namely, at Gakdul and Korti. The natural result had followed: the animals were weak and exhausted, the majority were suffering from sore backs, some had already succumbed, others were absolutely incapable of further work until they had had a rest. In this respect none of the three corps had any advantage over the other, as the camels had all performed the three journeys.

"If we are only going to Metemmeh, and are to halt there until the boats come round, the poor beasts will have time to recover before we want them again," Easton said to Skinner as they were looking ruefully at the condition of the camels who had carried them so well ten days before; "but they certainly won't be fit to advance for some time. I am afraid, Skinner, that they must have very bad news from Khartoum, and that every day is of extreme importance. If the matter hadn't been most urgent they would never have ruined the whole of our transport as they have done in this way. If the camels had had a couple of days' rest here before

At the wells of Gakdul.

starting to go back again, and four or five days' good feeding at Korti before they started up again, it would have made all the difference in the world to them. A camel is not a steam-engine, that can take in fuel and water, and be off again an hour after it comes in from a journey."

"I don't like these night marches," Skinner said. "I consider them to be a mistake altogether."

"So do I, Skinner. It was bad enough when we had the moon, but it will be ten times worse now. As to the heat, that is all rot. We travelled in the daytime coming up by the banks of the Nile, and it is cooler now than it was then. It is all very well for men to march at night if they have no animals or baggage-train with them, but it is a different thing altogether on such an expedition as this. To begin with, the delays from falling behind and readjusting baggage are far greater at night than at day; there is much greater difficulty in keeping the column together; the men are in a state of drowsiness the whole time, if they were marching they would keep awake, but sitting on the camels there is nothing to rouse them. Then when they get in camp the heat of the day has just begun, and what with that and the flies it is next to impossible to sleep. What sleep they get does not refresh them. I quite dread this march on to Metemmeh. However, it has got to be done; but certainly I should not mind it half so much if we were going to travel by daylight."

It was soon known that there was to be no delay at Gakdul, and orders were issued that the start was to be made on the 13th; the intervening day being devoted to seeing to the arms and ammunition, issuing stores, and replenishing the water supply. The water-skins were extremely defective, leaking freely, the only exception being the India-rubber bags with which the sailors had been supplied. Every effort was made during the halt to sew up holes and stop leaks, but with poor success. Each man carried on his camel one of these skins in addition to his water-bottle. Strict orders were given that upon the march he was to rely upon the latter alone; the supply in the skins being for general purposes, such as cooking and making tea.

THE DASH FOR KHARTOUM

During the halt Edgar applied himself steadily to the work of repairing the water-skins. The camp of the Heavies joined that of the Guards, and he felt that his danger of being recognized by Easton or Skinner was great; but sitting with a group of others sewing, with his face shaded by his helmet, the risk was very much less than if standing up or moving about the camp. At two o'clock in the afternoon the force paraded and moved off in columns of companies. The Heavy Camel Corps led, the Guards followed, the baggage and stores were in the centre, and the Mounted Infantry in the rear.

Many of the camels had to be left behind, and those that remained were only sufficient to carry the absolutely necessary stores, the rations for the men, and a quantity of corn that would suffice but to give two feeds of eight pounds each to the animals, who were, therefore, obliged to depend almost entirely on such sustenance as they could pluck from the mimosa shrubs and the dry yellow grass. The men carried a hundred and seventy rounds each. There were a hundred rounds per gun for the artillery, but only a thousand rounds were brought for the Gardner gun, a quantity sufficient but for five minutes' work when in action.

The journey was over a gravelly plain, and the halt was made at six o'clock in the evening. Fires were lit of the shrubs and dry grass; the camels were unloaded and fed, and were ranged in such order that in case of attack the troops could form square at the angles of the mass, and thus support each other and protect the convoy. At three in the morning the trumpets and bugles sounded. The fires were soon blazing again, and at half-past four breakfast had been eaten, the camels loaded, and the column on its march again. At ten o'clock there was a halt for two hours for dinner and a short rest; and it was not until just as they were going to start that the rear-guard arrived, having been delayed by the breaking down of numbers of the camels, many of which had fallen dead as they walked, while others incapable of movement had to be left behind to take their chance of recovering sufficiently to browse upon the bushes and make their way back to the wells. As the loads of those that fell had to be distributed among their already exhausted companions the prospect was far from cheerful.

Starting at twelve, the column passed a conical hill known as Gebel El Nur an hour later, and entered a broad valley covered with grass and trees twenty feet high, and where, doubtless, water could be obtained had the force been provided with little Abyssinian pumps. At five o'clock the column halted, and as the ground was sandy passed a more comfortable night than the one before. Every one was in good spirits. The men found the journeys by day far less fatiguing than those at night, and were able to obtain refreshing sleep in the cool night air.

Before daybreak they again started over a gravelly plain, hoping to reach the wells of Abu Klea that evening. They halted at eleven in a valley flanked by hills. The track, according to the maps, lay over a steep hill in front and then along a pass between two hills, the wells lying some three miles beyond the pass. Dinner was cooked, and as soon as they had finished their meal the Hussars started for the wells, as their horses had had no water since leaving Gakdul. The rest of the force were stretched upon the ground taking it quietly when two of the Hussars returned at full gallop with a message to the general, and the order was immediately issued for the men to fall in and for the officers to examine their arms and ammunition. Then the news spread through the force that the enemy had been discovered in large numbers upon the hill, and were evidently prepared to bar the way to the wells.

The change effected by the news was wonderful. It had been generally supposed that Metemmeh would be reached without fighting, all the spies agreeing in saying that there was no force of the enemy near the line of march. In a moment fatigue and thirst were forgotten, and the quiet was exchanged for bustle and animation. Men laughed and joked with each other in the highest spirits, and all prepared for the fray with the most absolute confidence as to the result. As the troops fell in the general with his staff galloped ahead to some rising ground, and with their field-glasses reconnoitred the hills surrounding the pass, upon which numbers of white-robed Arabs could be made out.

The Hussars speedily reported that there was a considerable force in the pass below. With the fighting men in front and the baggage behind, the troops moved slowly forward up the hill in front, and finally took up their position on a piece of flat ground whence they could see down the pass by which the Arabs expected the advance would be made. On the side of the hills commanding it they had thrown up small stone walls from which to fire. On the hilltops out of range large numbers of Arabs could be seen in constant motion, gesticulating and waving their arms. It was now four o'clock in the afternoon, and the general decided that as the real force of the enemy was unknown it would be imprudent to attempt to force the passage with only an hour and a half of daylight before him, consequently a halt for the night was ordered.

A strong detachment of Mounted Infantry and sailors with their Gardner ascended a hill on the other side of the pass and set to work to build a small fort and mount the gun there. A company from each of the camel regiments extended to cover the front. The camels were all made to kneel, their legs being lashed at the knee so that they could not rise. This done, the whole of the troops were set to work to build a wall. There were, however, but few loose stones lying about, and though officers and men alike worked hard the wall in front was but two feet high when the sun went down. A hedge of thorny bushes and wire was raised to protect the flanks as much as possible.

As twilight fell a number of the enemy took possession of the top of a hill some twelve hundred yards away on the right and opened fire, to which the three guns of the artillery replied with shrapnel-shell. The guns ceased firing when darkness came on, but the enemy kept up an occasional fire all night. A drink of lime-juice and water was served out to all the men, who then lay down, with their arms in readiness to repel an attack, by the little wall. All night the enemy kept on beating tom-toms and occasionally yelling, approaching at times comparatively close to the position. Knowing, however, that the sentries were out in front, the men for the most part slept quietly in spite of the noise and firing. As the Arabs could fire only at random but two men were hit during the night.

In the morning it was found that the number of the enemy on the hilltops had largely increased during the night, and the bullets now flew incessantly round and over the inclosure. Lying under such shelter as the wall afforded, the men ate their breakfast of the tinned meat and biscuits they carried in their haversacks.

"I must admit, Skinner," Easton said to his comrade, who had come across from his own company to have a chat with him, "that this is more unpleasant than I had expected. This lying here listening to the angry hiss of the bullets is certainly trying; at least I own that I feel it so."

"It is nasty," Skinner agreed. "I sha'n't mind it as soon as we go at the beggars, but this doing nothing is, as you say, trying. I wish they would make up their minds and come out to us, or if they cannot get up their pluck enough to do it, that we should sally out and attack them."

"You may be sure we shall before long, Skinner. They know well enough that we cannot stop here, but must move on to the water sooner or later; and knowing that, they would be fools if they were to give up their strong position to attack us here. At any rate I would rather be lying behind this wall than moving about as the general and his staff are doing. Major Dickson has just been shot through the knee, I hear. There! Look! there is another officer down. I wonder who he is. I do hope they won't pot Clinton."

A few minutes later an officer passing by told them that Major Gough of the Mounted Infantry had been knocked senseless by a bullet which had grazed his forehead, and that an officer of the artillery had been hit in the back.

"What do you think of it, sergeant?" Edgar asked, as he and Sergeant Bowen were eating their breakfast together under shelter of the wall.

"I think that it is going to be a hot job, lad. If they had attacked us out in the plain we should have made short work of them, but it is a different thing altogether among these hills. The beggars can run three feet to our one, and if we were to climb one of these hills to attack them, they would be on the top of the next before we got there. I see nothing for it but to move straight for the wells, and let them do their worst as we go. It would be all right if we hadn't this tremendous train of camels; but if they come pouring down while we are on the march we shall have difficulty in protecting them all."

"I wish Rupert were lying here with us," Edgar said, looking anxiously at his brother, whose figure he could perceive among those near the general. "It is horrid lying here in safety while he is exposed to their bullets."

"We must all take our chances," the sergeant said. "Maybe presently you will be in more danger than he is."

Half an hour later orders were issued that the men were to prepare for action, and it became known among the officers that the general had determined to leave a small garrison to protect the baggage and camels in the zareba, and to push forward with the rest of the force and capture the wells, and then send back and fetch in the camels and baggage. But the movement was delayed until ten o'clock in hopes that the enemy would attack. As they did not do so, orders were given and the square formed up. The Guards' Camel Corps formed half the front of the square, and the right flank. The Mounted Infantry filled up the other half of the front, and half the left flank. The rest of the left flank and the rear were formed by the Heavy Camel Corps and the Naval Brigade; the hundred men of the Sussex taking the right rear corner between them and the Guards, while the Naval Brigade with their Gardner gun were in the centre of the rear line, between the troop of the 4th and 5th Dragoon Guards and that of the 1st and 2d Life Guards and Blues.

In the centre behind the fighting line were two guns of the Royal Artillery, the other having been left in the zareba, while the centre of the square was filled with camels carrying water, ammunition, and cacolets or swinging beds for the carriage of the wounded.

The instant the square was formed and moved out the fire of the enemy redoubled. Swarms of natives appeared on the top of the hills, moving parallel with the advance of the square. The march was taken in slow time to allow the guns and camels to keep up. The ground was extremely difficult and broken, deep water-ruts and rocky hillocks having to be crossed, and the whole very undulating and broken. Men fell fast, and frequent halts had to be made to enable the doctors to attend to the wounded, and place them in the cacolets. The front face and sides of the square advanced in fair order, but there was much confusion in the rear face, caused by the lagging camels. Skirmishers were thrown out on either side, and these did their best to keep down the fire of the enemy. For an hour the square proceeded, and had nearly emerged from the pass on to the plain beyond, when a number of green and white flags were seen at some distance on the left front. As the firing had principally come from the right, and as it was from that side that an attack was expected, there was considerable curiosity as to the meaning of these seemingly deserted flags; and a small party were about to go out to investigate them, when a great number of other flags suddenly appeared at the same spot, and a moment later a vast mass of Arabs who had been concealed in a gully sprang to their feet.

They were about five hundred yards distant from the square, which was at the moment halted at the foot of a stony knoll. It was moved at once on to the rising ground, and the skirmishers were called in. The Arabs with wild yells moved across the left front, disappeared for a minute behind some rocks and high grass, and then reappeared close to the left rear, when they wheeled into line, and with wild yells charged

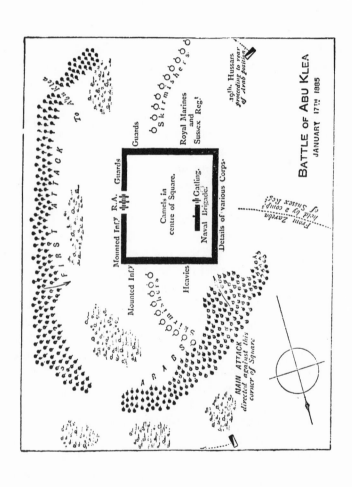

BATTLE OF ABU KLEA

JANUARY 17TH 1885

19th. Hussars *proceeding to rear of Arab position*

From Zareba *held by 2 comp.s of Sussex Reg.t*

Guards

Skirmishers

Royal Marines and Sussex Reg.t

R.A. Guards

Mounted Inf.y

Camels in centre of Square.

Gatling.

Naval Brigade.

Details of various Corps.

Heavies

Mounted Inf.y

Skirmishers

To Abu Klea

FIRST ATTACK

ARABS

MAIN ATTACK *directed against this corner of Square.*

192

down upon the square. So quick were their movements that the skirmishers had hardly time to reach the square, and one man was overtaken and speared before he reached it.

Several of the exhausted camels with their loads of wounded had been left outside, lying down at the foot of the slope when the square moved up it. Their native drivers rushed into shelter, and the wounded would have fallen into the hands of the enemy had not an officer of the Guards' Camel Corps and several privates of the Heavies rushed out, seized the camels, and by main force dragged them into the square. In the square itself there was a din of voices, the officers shouting to the men to stand steady and reserve their fire until the skirmishers, who were between them and the enemy, had run in. The instant they had done this a roar of musketry broke out from the left and rear faces of the square, at first in volleys, then in independent fire as fast as the men could load; but though scores of the enemy fell, their rush was not checked for a moment, and with wild yells they fell upon the left corner of the square.

The men were but two deep, and were unable to stand the pressure of the mass of the enemy, and in a moment the rear face of the square was driven in, and a hand-to-hand fight was going on between the soldiers, mixed up with the struggling camels and the Arabs. All order was for a time lost; the voices of the officers were drowned by the din of musketry, the yells of the Arabs, and the shouts of the men. Each man fought for himself; but their bayonets were no match for the long spears of the Arabs, and they were pressed back until the throng of camels pushed hard against the Guards in front of the square.

The rear ranks of the Mounted Infantry on the left and the Marines on the right were faced round, and opened a terrible fire into the crowded mass of natives, while the Heavies with bayonets and clubbed muskets fought singly, man to man, with their foes. The combat did not last long. Mowed down by the fire on both flanks the assailants withered away, and it was not long before silence succeeded the terrible din of battle. In the interior of the square the last Arab of

The Arabs, with wild yells, charged upon the square.

those who had pierced the square had fallen, and the fire of the outside faces of the square had prevented them from receiving any reinforcement from their friends, and these now fell back sullenly before the leaden hail. As soon as they had done so there was time to investigate what had taken place in the centre of the square.

A terrible sight presented itself. The ground was strewn with bodies of the natives, mingled with those of men of the corps that had formed the rear face of the square, the 4th and 5th Dragoon Guards, Naval Brigade, 1st and 2d Life Guards, and the Sussex. Among them lay camels which had been hamstrung or speared by the natives, broken cacolets, and water tanks and skins, medical stores, and a confusion of articles of all kinds.

Although forced back by the sheer weight of the native attack, the Heavies had never been completely broken up. They maintained their resistance to the end, jammed up as they were against and among the camels, and thus enabled the men on the two sides of the square to concentrate their fire on the Arabs.

A loud cheer had broken from the square as the enemy retreated, and they were prepared to resist another onslaught; for only a portion of their foes had yet been engaged with them. However, the enemy contented themselves with keeping up a distant fire from the hills, and then, doubtless as the news spread how terrible had been the loss of those who had charged the square, they gradually drew off and all became quiet. The square now moved off from the rocky knoll upon which they were crowded, and the work of seeing who had fallen and of assisting the wounded began. No less than nine officers had been killed and nine wounded, the greater portion of them belonging to the Heavy Camel Regiment. Two officers of the Naval Brigade were also among the killed. Eighty of the rank and file were killed, and upwards of a hundred wounded. Among the whites lay hundreds of dead Arabs, while arms of all sorts – spears, javelins, muskets, clubs, hatchets, swords, and knives, banners and banner-staffs – were everywhere scattered thickly.

Among the killed were Colonel Burnaby, Majors Gough, Carmichael, and Atherton, Captain Darley, and Lieutenants Law and Wolfe – all belonging to the Heavies.

To the survivors of those corps who had formed the rear face of the square, the scene they had gone through seemed a wild and confused dream. Sergeant Bowen and Edgar had been among those who rushed out and hauled in the camels with the wounded just before the Arabs came up. As they got them inside the ranks the roar of fire broke out and they fell into their places. "Independent firing!" the officer shouted as the first volley had been discharged, but scarcely had the roll of musketry begun than through the smoke a dense mass of black figures appeared. A storm of spears and javelins were poured in upon them, and in an instant there was a crash as club, spear, and sword struck the muskets, and then the Heavies were hurled back.

Edgar scarce knew what had happened, but the instant the square was broken Sergeant Bowen threw himself beside him.

"Steady, lad, steady," he said, "don't throw away a shot; load and stand ready to shoot the first man who falls on you. That is good!" he said as Edgar shot a tall Arab who was rushing at him with uplifted spear; "load again. Now it is my turn," and he brought down a man; and so firing alternately, sometimes defending themselves with their bayonets, but always keeping together, they fell back. Once Edgar stumbled and fell over the body of one of his comrades, but the sergeant seized him by the shoulder and jerked him on to his feet again, and the next moment ran an Arab through who was rushing at them with uplifted hatchet. When they were back among the crowd of camels the fighting became more even. Stubbornly the men made a stand here, for the natives could no longer attack them except in front, while the roar of fire from the troops on the flanks told with terrible effect upon the Arabs.

"Thank God that is over!" the sergeant said as the fight ended. "Are you badly hurt, lad?"

"I am not hurt at all," Edgar said.

The sergeant pointed to Edgar's left arm. The latter uttered an exclamation of surprise. He had bayoneted an Arab in the act of striking at him, and in the wild excitement had for the moment been unconscious that the blow of the native had taken effect. It had missed his shoulder, but had cut a deep gash in the arm, almost severing a strip of flesh down to the elbow.

"I had not the least idea I had been touched," he said. "I don't think there is any great harm done; the principal arteries are on the other side of the arm."

"We must stop the bleeding, anyhow," the sergeant said. "I will soon find a bandage. There are sure to be plenty about, for the surgeons were at work when they broke in."

He was not long in finding one, and then assisting Edgar off with his coat he bandaged up his arm.

"You have got a wound on the side, sergeant!" Edgar exclaimed suddenly.

"It is of no consequence, lad. A fellow threw a spear at me. I tried to dodge it, but was not quite quick enough, and it has grazed my side."

"It is more than a graze – it looks like a deep cut. Just undo your belt."

"Well, give me your handkerchief. I will roll that and mine into a pad and shove it in, and put a bandage tightly round my waist to keep it there. That will do for the present.

"That will do nicely," he said as Edgar fastened the bandage round him. "Now we shall both do very well until the surgeons have time to tie us up properly. I am afraid they will have serious cases enough to last them all night. Now, what is the next move, I wonder? I am horribly thirsty."

"So am I," Edgar agreed.

"Are you both wounded?" an officer asked, coming up with two men carrying a water-skin.

"Yes, sir, but not seriously; but we are awfully thirsty."

"Then you can have a drink of water," the officer said. "There is little enough of it, and it is kept strictly for the wounded."

Many of the men standing near looked on with envious eyes, for all were suffering horribly from thirst. Several fainted, and the men's lips were black and swollen, and in some cases the tongue swelled so that the mouth could not be closed. The 19th were out searching for the wells, but for a long while their search was in vain. The general was about to give the word to retire to the zareba where there was a little water still left, when the Hussars fortunately hit upon the wells. The wounded who were unable to walk were at once carried there, and the troops followed and halted near them, and in a short time the thirst of all was satisfied. Although the water was not to be compared with that at Gakdul, being found in shallow pools one or two feet deep, and stirred up by the Arabs till it was almost of the consistency of thin cream, nevertheless it was water, and was enjoyable indeed.

CHAPTER XII
METEMMEH

AS soon as the thirst of the men was satisfied the troops formed up for the night on some rising ground near the wells, where it was probable that the natives might renew their attack. Volunteers were called for, and three hundred men from the various corps started to march back to the zareba to bring in the baggage before daylight. It was a heavy duty after such a day's work, but those who remained behind had reason almost to envy those engaged in active work, for the night was terribly cold. The men had left everything behind as they advanced prepared for action, and had no blankets, and nothing but their shirts and their suits of thin serge to protect them from the cold.

The surgeons were at work all night attending to the wounded. No alarm was given by the outposts during the night, and as when morning broke there were no signs of the enemy, the men were allowed to fall out. A herd of lean cattle left by the Arabs was discovered not far off, and the Hussars went out in pursuit of them; the tired horses were, however, no match in point of speed for the cattle, but a few of them were shot, cut up, and a supply of fresh meat for the day secured. At seven o'clock the baggage train came up. The camels were quickly unloaded, and the men set to work to prepare breakfast, having had nothing to eat since the meal they had taken the previous morning under fire in the zareba.

During the day the dead were buried, the arms left by the natives collected and destroyed, and a stone inclosure commenced near the wells, for here the wounded were to remain under the protection of a small force of the Sussex. Both Edgar and the sergeant protested that they were perfectly capable of continuing the march, and were permitted to take their place in the ranks again. At four o'clock the force formed up, and half an hour later set out. It was given out that the march would be a short one and they would presently halt for the night, but as the hours went on it became evident that the general had determined to keep straight on for the river, a distance of twenty-six miles from the wells. It was known that there was a considerable force of the enemy at Metemmeh, and as this would be augmented by the addition of the thousands of Arabs who had been engaged on the previous day, it was probable that, were the enemy aware of the advance of the force, a battle even more serious and desperate than the first would have to be fought before reaching the Nile. The object of the night march, then, was to reach the river before they were aware that the column had started from the wells. The Nile once gained, and a supply of water ensured, the force would be able to withstand any attack made on it. Nevertheless it would have been far better to have risked another battle in the open than to have made a night march across an unknown country.

The guides differed among themselves as to the route to be pursued, and more than once the column marched in a complete circle, the advance guard coming up to the rear. Thick groves of mimosa were passed through, causing the greatest confusion among the baggage animals. Great numbers of these lay down to die, unable to proceed a step further, and the transport of all kinds got mixed up together in the most utter confusion. The men, who had had but little sleep for two nights, were unable to keep awake on their camels, and in their passage through the bushes many of the animals straggled away from the main body.

Sergeant Bowen had managed to place Edgar next to himself upon the plea that being wounded he wanted to keep his eye upon him. Both being weakened by loss of blood, they were less able to resist the pressure of sleep than the others, and when their animals got separated in the passage through the mimosa grove from the main body, and stopped to crop the leaves, they were unconscious of what had happened until Edgar woke with a start as one of the boughs his camel had pushed aside struck him smartly in the face. His exclamation roused the sergeant. "Hullo! what has happened?"

"I don't know what has happened," Edgar said. "But it seems to me that we are alone here. We must both have been asleep, and these brutes must have separated from the column."

"This is a pretty mess, this is!" the sergeant said. "I cannot hear anything of them, and there was row enough in the rear with the baggage to be heard miles away. What on earth are we to do, lad?"

"Well, we were marching nearly south. The Southern Cross was almost dead ahead of us. We had better steer by that, and go on ahead until morning."

The camels were at once set in motion, and for hours they plodded on. All desire for sleep had been completely dissipated by the excitement of the situation, and they talked in low tones as to what they were to do if they could make out no signs of the column when day broke. They agreed that their only plan was to keep on until they got to the river, and that when they arrived there they would water the camels and give them a feed, and after a rest start on foot along the bank one way or the other until they found the column.

"There is sure to be a lot of firing," the sergeant said; "for even if the Arabs don't discover the force in the morning before they get to the river, they are certain to turn out to attack them as soon as they get there. Judging by the pace we were going, and the constant halts for the baggage to come up, there is very little chance of the column getting to the river before daylight; and as we have nothing to delay us, I expect we shall be there before they are."

"In one respect that will be all the better," Edgar said; "for as soon as the natives make out the column they will be swarming all over the country to look for stragglers, whereas if we are ahead of them we may get through to the river without being noticed. I don't think that it will be very long before morning breaks, and, do you know, sergeant, I think our camels are going faster than they were."

"I think so too, lad. That looks as if we were getting near the water, and they smell it."

Just as the first signs of daybreak were apparent in the east the character of the country changed, and they could make out clumps of trees, and, as the light grew brighter, cultivated ground. Ten minutes later they both gave a shout of joy as on mounting a slight ascent the river lay before them. A few minutes later they were on its bank. The camels rushing down put their noses into the water; their riders slipped from their backs regardless of the fact that the water was knee-deep, and wading back to the shore threw themselves down by the edge, and took long draughts of the clear water. Then throwing off their clothes they rushed in and indulged in a bathe.

The camels, after filling themselves nearly to bursting, lay down in the stream until the sergeant and Edgar went out and compelled them to return to shore, when they set to work cropping the long grass that grew abundantly there, while their riders sat down and made a meal from the contents of their haversacks.

"Well, at any rate," the sergeant said, "we can do nothing just at present. The troops may be within a mile, and they may be ten miles off; there is no saying. There is nothing for us to do but to wait until we hear something of them. If we do not hear anything of them we shall know that they either have not struck the river, or have struck it so far off that we cannot hear the guns. In that case my opinion is that we may as well rest here for to-day. Before we move I think it will be decidedly better to take the saddles off the camels and hide them in the bushes, and then move away some distance and hide up ourselves. This is evidently a cultivated country, and if there are any natives about they will be sure to see the camels, so we had better not be near them. There is no fear of the animals straying; they will be eating and drinking all day."

The saddles were accordingly removed from the camels' backs and hidden; the two men went back a few hundred yards from the river and lay down amongst some bushes. Edgar was just dropping off to sleep, when the sergeant exclaimed, "Listen! they are at it."

Edgar at once roused himself, and distinctly heard the boom of a distant gun.

"That is one of the seven-pounders," the sergeant said; "and I think I can hear the sound of musketry, but I am not sure about that."

Presently, however, the wind brought down distinctly the sound of dropping shots.

"Skirmishing, lad! I suppose the enemy are hovering about them, but haven't come to close quarters yet."

"It is horrible being here instead of with them!" Edgar exclaimed as he rose to his feet.

"It is no use thinking of moving, lad; they are four or five miles away, certainly, and as the Arabs are probably all round them, there wouldn't be the slightest chance of our joining them. There is nothing to do but to wait here. The sound comes from inland, so it is certain they have not got to the river yet. As far as I can judge it is pretty nearly behind us, so when they lick those fellows they are likely to come down on the river somewhere near this point. They will be down before evening. You may be sure they had not got water enough to last them through the day, so they must move forward however many of the natives may be in their way. It is not like the last business; then they were on us almost before we knew they were coming, but in this flat country we shall have plenty of warning; and I will bet a year's pay they don't get up to our square again. I think, lad, I will get you to set my bandages right again."

Edgar uttered an exclamation of alarm. There was a large dark patch on the sergeant's trousers. In dressing after their bathe the bandages had shifted a little, and the bleeding had recommenced. It was evident at once to Edgar that a great deal of blood had been lost, for Sergeant Bowen lay faint and exhausted upon the ground. Unknown to himself the action of the camel had set the wound off bleeding during the night, and although he had said nothing to Edgar about it, he had with difficulty walked up from the river to their hiding-place. Edgar ran down to the river with the two water-bottles; when he returned he found his companion insensible. He unbuttoned his tunic and got at the wound, from which blood was still flowing. He washed it, made a plug of wet linen, and with some difficulty bandaged it tightly. After some time the sergeant opened his eyes.

"Don't try to move," Edgar said. "I have staunched and bandaged the wound, and you will be better soon."

"It is a bad job, lad; just at present when we want to be up and doing."

"There is nothing to do at present, sergeant. We have only to wait quietly until our fellows come down to the river, and then I will soon get you assistance."

"Do you hear the firing still?"

"It is just as it was," Edgar replied, after listening attentively for a minute.

"Then I expect they have formed another zareba, as they did at Abu Klea, and that they will leave the camels there and march straight down to the river."

"I will steal up to the edge of the desert, if you don't mind being left alone a bit. I shall be able to judge then how far they are off."

"Do so, lad; I am all right here. But do not be too long away or I shall be anxious."

Edgar made his way a quarter of a mile back. Some cultivated fields stretched before him, and beyond them the rolling hillocks of the desert. He could see men on horseback and foot moving about, and looking to the right saw about half a mile distant a place of some extent, which was, he felt sure, Metemmeh. Numbers of men were pouring out from the town. The firing was not straight ahead, but somewhat to the left. "If they attack Metemmeh at once we shall be all right," he said to himself. "If they march straight down to the river we shall be all right still. We shall only have to move along to them. It is lucky we did not strike the river above the town, for it would have been next to impossible to get round to them without being observed."

He went back to his companion, and told him what he had seen.

"There is evidently going to be another tough fight before they get down to the water," the sergeant said. "It is very hard our being cut off here. Not that I should be good for any fighting if I were with them."

"I have no great desire to be in another fight like the last," Edgar said. "One go at that sort of thing is quite enough for me."

The hours passed slowly. The sergeant slept a good deal, and anxious as Edgar was he too several times dozed off.

Presently he exclaimed, "The fire is become much heavier, sergeant; and it is nearer too. Listen!"

"It is the Arabs, lad," the sergeant said, raising himself on his elbow. "It is heavy, but it is nothing like the roll of musketry you hear when our fellows begin. But, as you say, it is much nearer; the column, or part of it, is on its march towards the river."

Five minutes later a dull continuous rattle came to their ears.

"They are at it now. They have stopped!" he said a minute later when the roar suddenly ceased. "What has happened now, I wonder? Ah! there they are again. That is more like it – steady and even."

The musketry came in sudden crashes. "Volleys!" the sergeant said. "They are near them."

For three or four minutes the sounds continued, and then there was silence.

"They have beaten them off," the sergeant said. "They didn't let them get near them this time, I expect. If they had there would have been independent firing. As long as you hear volleys you may be sure our fellows are not pressed."

THE DASH FOR KHARTOUM

Beyond an occasional shot the firing had ceased.

"How far do you think they are away now, sergeant?"

"If they were four miles before I don't think they are more than two now, and a good bit more away to the left. They are making to the river, so as to establish themselves there before they tackle Metemmeh."

"Then in half an hour they will be down on the river," Edgar said. "I will wait that time, and then start and get a party to bring you in."

"You had better wait until to-morrow morning, lad. We can do very well until then. I may be able to crawl by that time. Anyhow, they will have their hands full this afternoon. They will have to make a zareba by the river, attend to the wounded, and perhaps send back a force to bring in the camels and baggage, who were no doubt left behind at the spot where they were firing this morning. There is grub enough in the haversacks to last us until to-morrow, and plenty of water for the fetching."

"Just as you think best, sergeant. My shoulder is smarting a good deal, and I shall be all the better for a few more hours' rest myself. It will soon be getting dusk, so I will go down and get another supply of water at once, and then we can do a good twelve hours' sleep without fear of being called up for outpost duty. We have got three or four nights' sleep to make up." It was broad daylight before they awoke. The sergeant got on to his feet, but it was evident to Edgar that he was altogether unfit for walking.

"Shall I saddle your camel for you, sergeant?"

"No, lad; I will stay where I am. Like enough the Arabs will be swarming about just within gun-shot of our camp. They are obstinate beggars, and do not know when they are fairly beaten. If I were as active as you are we might manage to get through on foot, but a man on a camel would be sure to be seen. Be very careful, lad, how you go. Remember, if you are seen you are lost; for these fellows could run you down to a certainty, and your only chance is to get through without being noticed."

"I don't like leaving you, sergeant."

METEMMEH

"But you must leave me, lad. We have no food to speak of left, and it will be just as dangerous to-morrow or next day as it is to-day. Besides, your duty is with the corps. Every musket may be needed, and the sooner you go the sooner I shall be fetched in."

"Very well, then, I will start at once," Edgar said.

He first went down to the river, filled the two water-bottles and placed them both by the sergeant's side, and emptied what little food remained in his haversack.

"Now you will do for a couple of days if anything should occur to prevent them from sending out."

"I shall do very well, lad. It is not of myself I shall be thinking, but of you. The gladdest sound that ever fell on my ears will be the tramp of infantry, for then I shall know that you have got safely through. Good-bye, lad, and God bless you!"

Edgar wrung the sergeant's hand, and, unable to trust himself to speak, turned and started through the wood. He had not gone very far when he found that the grove was by no means a large one, for the trees opened before him. He bore to his left, hoping that they would extend along the river bank; but it was not so. The grove was isolated, and a large patch of cultivated land stretched down to the river. Half a mile further there was another grove; but whether this was more extensive than that in which he now was he had no means of telling. Standing at the edge of the trees he could see several figures on horseback moving about, and saw at once that they were natives.

"The Hussars will want two or three days' rest, I expect," he said, "before their horses are fit to go out and drive these fellows into the town. Well, here goes!" and he descended the bank of the river, which was now low, and kept along under its shelter until he reached the next grove. It seemed so much safer where he was than it would be above that he determined to keep under shelter of the bank until he reached the camp. He had gone a hundred yards farther when there was a sudden exclamation on the bank above him, and almost at the same instant a spear struck his helmet

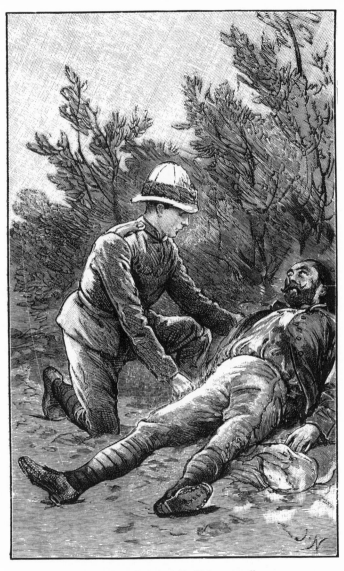

"Good-bye, lad, and God bless you."

from his head. He turned round and brought his rifle to his shoulder, but in a moment the Arab on the bank was joined by a score of others, who with loud yells rushed down upon him.

He saw that to fire was to ensure his death, and that resistance was worse than useless. He therefore threw down his gun and held up his arms. The Arabs rushed upon him in a body with uplifted spears and swords, but on an order sharply given by one who seemed to be their leader they lowered these. Edgar was, however, knocked down, kicked, and beaten, then some cords were placed round his body and arms, and he felt himself lifted up and carried away.

He was thrown down again in the wood, and an animated and, as it seemed to him, angry discussion was carried on some time. He had picked up a good many Arabic words, but not enough to enable him to understand the discussion; but he had no doubt that the subject of dispute was whether he should be killed at once or carried away prisoner. As after a time he was lifted up, the cords round his legs taken off, and he was hurried along with many curses and an occasional sharp prick with a spear, he judged that those in favour of sparing his life for the present had won the day.

His own prospects seemed desperate, but for the time he was more concerned at the thought that the man who was perhaps his father was lying helpless in the wood vainly expecting his return. But he did not consider his case altogether hopeless. As soon as the troops were all assembled on the river bank they would be sure to move forward against Metemmeh; and even if they did not pass through the wood the sergeant might gain sufficient strength to reach its edge, get sight of them, and join them. Unless one or other of these alternatives took place, he was lost. As to himself, he could not blame himself for the misfortune that had befallen him. He had taken what seemed far the safest course, and had it not been for the accident that one of the Arabs had been standing at the moment at the edge of the river, he would have got through safely.

THE DASH FOR KHARTOUM

His captors had evidently no fear of being attacked. Probably the column that had gone out to fetch in the baggage had not yet returned, and the small force left at the zareba on the river bank would certainly not undertake any offensive operation until it came back. He was sorry now that he had not persisted in his own opinion and remained with the sergeant, as in another day or two some scouting party might have passed near the grove in which they were concealed. However, it might have made no difference. The Arabs were evidently swarming about the country, and parties would be likely to occupy that wood just as they occupied the one nearer to the English camp.

As they approached the village the Arabs raised shouts of triumph, and a crowd gathered as they entered the street, gesticulating and screaming so furiously that Edgar thought he would be torn to pieces. However, his captors forced their way through the crowd, turned off from the street, and entered a court-yard, in the centre of which stood a house of larger size than the majority of those that composed the town. Edgar's legs were again tied, and he was thrown into an outhouse, where he lay for hours. He could hear almost continuous talking in the house, and the voices occasionally rose into angry altercation.

He was surprised that he had not been killed as he entered the place, for the Arabs, if they fought with the same courage as those engaged at Abu Klea, must have suffered very heavily before they fell back, and the friends and relatives of those who had fallen would be thirsty for vengeance upon any European who fell into their power. Then he considered that it was probable that the people of Metemmeh itself, who lived by the passage of caravans and the river traffic, would at heart be as much opposed to the Mahdi as were those of Khartoum and other cities.

The force with which the British had fought at Abu Klea was composed partly of the Mahdi's regular followers, partly of wild tribesmen, animated alike by Mahommedan fanaticism and the hope of plunder; and although these might unite in an attack against Christians, they had little love for each other. The band into whose hands he had fallen might be townspeople, but more probably were members of some tribe that had been summoned to arrest the progress of the troops going up to the relief of Khartoum.

Now that he was detained a prisoner instead of being at once killed, Edgar felt that there was a strong chance for him. In a couple of days the force might attack Metemmeh, and in that case he might be rescued. It was, however, a place of considerable size, and containing at present a very large number of fighting men; and after the losses the column had suffered in the first fight and during its subsequent encounters, General Stewart might well hesitate to risk still greater loss than he had already suffered by an attack upon the place.

It was probable that the Madhi would send down a large body of troops from those besieging Khartoum, as soon as he heard of the arrival of the small British force on the river, and every gun might be needed to maintain the position and repel attacks until the arrival of reinforcements across the desert.

Thus Edgar felt it to be very doubtful whether any attack would be made for the present. Of course as soon as reinforcements arrived, or the boat column came up the river, Metemmeh would be captured; but by that time he might be hundreds of miles away. The boat column might not get round for six weeks, while all reinforcements coming across the desert from Korti would have to march, for Edgar felt sure that it would be a long time before the camels were in a condition for work again.

It was well that when he filled the two water-bottles for the use of the sergeant Edgar had taken a long drink, for no one came near him until after dark, and he suffered a good deal from thirst, and from the pain caused by the tightness with which he was bound. He began to think that he had been altogether forgotten, when the door of the outhouse opened and two Arabs came in, and seizing him as if he had been a package dragged him out into the court-yard. Then he received two or three kicks as an intimation that he could sit up; but this, roped as he was, he was unable to accomplish, and seeing this the men pulled him against a wall and raised him into a sitting position against it.

A fire was burning in the centre of the court-yard. On some cushions in front of it sat a man, whom he recognized as the leader of the party who seized him. Other Arabs were squatted on the ground or standing round. The chief was past the prime of life, but still a powerful and sinewy man. His features were not prepossessing; but Edgar, looking round, thought that the expression of his face was less savage than that of the majority of his followers.

"Does the Christian dog speak the language of the Prophet?" he asked.

"I speak a little Arabic," Edgar replied, inwardly congratulating himself upon the trouble he had taken to pick up a little of the language during the time he had been in Egypt.

The answer was evidently satisfactory. The chief bowed his head.

"It is good!" he said. "The Kaffir is henceforth a slave in the tents of the Sheik Bakhat of the Jahrin tribe."

As he pointed to himself, Edgar understood that his captor intended to keep him as his own property, at any rate for the present, and bowed his head to signify that he understood.

"Why are the English foolish enough to come here?" the sheik asked. "They must know that they cannot stand against the power of the Mahdi."

"They did not come to interfere with the Mahdi, but to bring back their countryman Gordon and his friends from Khartoum."

"They will never reach Khartoum," the sheik said. "Their bones will whiten in the desert."

Edgar did not reply, partly because his knowledge of Arabic was insufficient for a discussion, partly because it was not worth while to run the risk of exciting the anger of the chief by pointing out that as they had failed to prevent a thousand men crossing the desert to Metemmeh, they might similarly fail in preventing a force of seven or eight times that amount marching up the banks of the river to Khartoum. He therefore remained silent.

"The Madhi is invincible," the sheik went on after a pause. "He will conquer Egypt, and after that will destroy the Kaffirs and take their city of Rome, and will capture Constantinople if the Turks deny his authority."

"The Madhi is a great man!" Edgar said gravely, although with difficulty repressing a smile. "Who can say what may happen?" Then seeing that this answer was also considered satisfactory he went on: "Your slave is hungry and thirsty. He has been wounded, and his bonds hurt him greatly. If he is to be of use to you, will you order that food and drink be given him?"

The chief nodded, and at a motion of his hand two of his followers freed Edgar from his bonds, and a dish containing some boiled meal and a jug of water were placed beside him. Edgar drank deeply, but was only able to take a few mouthfuls of food, as he was feverish and in considerable pain, for the wound in his arm, which would have been comparatively slight had proper attention been paid to it, was inflamed and angry, and the arm greatly swollen.

As no further attention was paid to him he returned to the outhouse, took off his karkee tunic, and tearing some strips from it, wetted them and laid them on his shoulder. Presently the door was closed, and he heard a heap of brushwood thrown against it, an effectual way of preventing an attempt to escape, for as the door opened outwards the slightest movement would cause a rustling of the bushes and arouse the Arabs who were sleeping in the court-yard. There was no window. Edgar, seeing that escape was out of the question, laid himself down and tried to sleep, but the pain of his arm was so great that it was some hours before he succeeded in doing so. The next morning he was allowed to go out into the yard, and for some time no attention was paid to him. Then a considerable hubbub was heard in the town, with much shouting and yelling. An Arab ran in at the gate with some news. Edgar could not understand his hurried words, but the effect was evident. The men seized their arms, and then at the sheik's order Edgar was again securely bound and fastened in the outhouse.

In the course of an hour he heard firing, first dropping shots and then two or three sharp volleys, and knew that the British were advancing against the town, and that the Arabs had gone out to skirmish with them. Then there was a long pause, and he heard the sound of the English field-pieces. He listened for musketry, but in vain.

"It is only a reconnaissance," he said to himself. "Those little guns would not batter down the mud walls round the town without an expense of ammunition that could not be afforded. No doubt the troops could take it by storm, but surely the general would not risk the heavy loss they would suffer before they got in, especially as the place would be of no use to them when they took it, and must fall as a matter of course when the rest of the force arrives."

Such being his opinion, he was but little disappointed when the firing ceased, and he knew by the triumphant yells of the Arabs that the British force were retiring. In a short time he heard a clamour of voices in the court-yard, and he was presently unbound and released.

"The Kaffirs did not dare to attack the place," the Arab said exultantly. "They have gone back to their camp. In a day or two there will be forces here from Khartoum and Berber, and then we will destroy or make slaves of them all."

Four days later there was a great firing of muskets and triumphant yelling in the streets. Edgar felt very anxious, fearing that the expected reinforcements had arrived, and that a tremendous attack was about to be made upon the camp. He did not believe that it had already taken place, for he felt confident that every pains had been taken to strengthen the position, and that in whatever numbers the assault might be made it would be repulsed. Presently, however, the sheik himself deigned to tell him the cause of the rejoicing.

METEMMEH

"There is news from Khartoum," he said. "The city has been taken, and the Englishman Gordon and all his followers have been killed. The news is certain. It has been brought down to us by tribesmen on both sides of the river. I told you that the Mahdi was irresistible."

The blow was a terrible one to Edgar. In the first place it was grievous to think that the expedition had been made in vain, and that, owing to those in authority at home delaying for months before making up their minds to rescue Gordon, it had failed in its object, and that the noblest of Englishmen had been left to die, unaided by those who had sent him out. He thought of the intense disappointment that would be felt by the troops, of the grief that there would be in England when the news was known, and then he wondered what would be done next. It was evident to him at once that his own position was altogether changed. He had before felt confident that unless his captors moved away from the town before the arrival of the main body of the expedition he should be rescued, but now it seemed altogether uncertain whether the expedition would come at all.

So long as Gordon was alive England was bound to make every effort to rescue him; but now that he and his companions were dead, and Khartoum had fallen, she might not feel herself called upon to attempt the reconquest of the Soudan. It was probable, however, that this would be the best, and in the end the cheapest way out of the difficulty. Here was a force that had at an enormous expense been brought up almost to within striking distance of Khartoum, and which could be relied upon to make its way thither to defeat the armies of the Mahdi, and to recapture Khartoum without any very great difficulty. The provisions and stores had all been purchased and brought up, and scarce any outlay additional to that already incurred would be entailed by the operation.

Upon the other hand, to retire now would be to leave the whole Soudan in the hands of the Mahdi and his fanatics. It would mean the destruction of the settled government established by the Egyptians, and it would expose Egypt to incessant invasions, which we should be bound to repel. Common sense, humanity, and even economy seemed to favour the advance of the force to Khartoum. The British people, roused to anger by the fate of Gordon, would probably call loudly for the vindication of the national honour, and for an act of retribution on the murderers of Gordon.

But Edgar felt that another way out of the difficulty might present itself to the authorities at home. It was not unlikely that the counsels of those who, from the first, had been against the expedition would prevail, and that it would retire to Egypt without striking another blow. In that case it seemed that there was nothing before him but lifelong slavery. Edgar, however, was at an age when hope is not easily relinquished.

"I may be a slave a long time," he said, "but sooner or later I will escape. I will get to speak the language like a native. I am already almost burnt to their colour, and shall ere long be able to pass as one of themselves. It is hard indeed if after a time I cannot manage to escape, and to make my way either back to Egypt or down to the Red Sea, or into Abyssinia. If I did not feel sure that I could do either one or the other, I would do something that would make them kill me at once."

CHAPTER XIII
ABU KRU

SERGEANT Bowen and Edgar were by no means the only men who straggled away from the main body during that terrible night's march from the wells of Abu Klea. Many straggled; some managed to rejoin the column in the morning, others wandered away and were never heard of again. Morning found the exhausted and worn-out men and animals still at a distance from the Nile. Some miles away a long line of verdure showed where the river lay, but the general felt that at present the men could do no more, and that a halt for some hours was absolutely necessary. Parties of the enemy's horse and foot men could be seen among the sand-hills, and distant shots had already been fired.

The object of the terrible march had failed; it was no longer possible to reach the river without fighting again, and to fight as they were, encumbered with the baggage train and overpowered with fatigue, was but to court disaster. Therefore a halt was ordered. To the soldiers the order was unwelcome; tired as they were, they would rather, now that the river was but some four miles away, have pushed straight on and have done with it. But the condition of the animals positively forbade this. A camping ground was chosen on a bare gravelly place on the scrub where the ground rose slightly. The work of unloading and arranging the camels at once began, but before it was concluded a dropping fire was opened by the natives from the long grass and bush in the distance.

THE DASH FOR KHARTOUM

The troops were set to work to erect a zareba with the saddles, biscuit-boxes, and other stores, while parties of skirmishers endeavoured to keep down the fire of the enemy. This, however, was a difficult task, as the natives were entirely concealed, and the men could only fire at the puffs of smoke arising from the grass and bushes. To the Arabs, however, the camp presented a clear mark, and the sharp rap of the musket-balls as they struck the wall, or the thud with which they buried themselves among the crowd of kneeling camels, was very frequent. Several men were hit, and soon after nine o'clock the report spread through the camp that Sir Herbert Stewart had received a very dangerous if not mortal wound. The news caused deep sorrow throughout the troops. The general was most popular both with officers and men, and there was not one but felt that his loss would be a personal one. It was, moreover, most unfortunate for the expedition itself at such a moment to be deprived of its leader. Before starting, Colonel Burnaby had been designated to assume the command in case of any accident happening to the general; but Burnaby had fallen at Abu Klea, and it therefore devolved upon Sir Charles Wilson, who was accompanying the force solely in a diplomatic capacity, and who was to push up the river in one of the steamers and communicate with General Gordon as soon as the force reached the Nile.

Soon afterwards orders were given that a ridge of ground sixty yards distant on the right front should be occupied, as from that point the ground beyond was commanded to a considerable distance, and the enemy thus prevented from gathering for a sudden rush from that direction. Skinner and Easton were lying down together under cover of the wall when the order was given. Skinner was energetically denouncing the night march and the present halt. Easton was smiling quietly, and occasionally pointing out the difficulties which would have ensued had his companion's view of the matter been adopted.

"It is beastly lying here doing nothing," Skinner finally grumbled.

"Well, there is no occasion for you to do so," Easton said as an officer passed along saying that volunteers were required to carry boxes to build a small work on the ridge.

Skinner at once jumped to his feet, ran to the pile of biscuit-boxes, seized two of them, swung them on to his shoulders and started for the ridge. Easton followed in more leisurely fashion, and a number of other officers and men at once set about the work. It was not pleasant. As soon as the concealed enemy saw what was being done they directed their fire upon the party, and the bullets flew fast across the ground that had to be passed over. Several men dropped, but the work was continued vigorously, and in the course of an hour a small work was raised upon the ridge, and a half-company placed there as its garrison. Hour after hour went on, the fire of the enemy getting heavier and heavier, the men dropping fast.

"Well, Easton, what do you think of it now?" Skinner asked.

"I think it is most annoying," Easton said. "I cannot think why we don't do something. I suppose the general being hit has upset the arrangements. If we are going to move I don't see what advantage there is in putting it off; it isn't as if we were getting any rest here. I hope to goodness we are not going to wait here until dark; every hour we stop adds to the casualties. I hear two of the special correspondents have been killed, Cameron of the *Standard* and St. Leger Herbert of the *Post*. The camels are being killed in scores. Another four-and-twenty hours of this work there won't be enough men left to fight our way down to the river. It has got to be done, and we might just as well do it at once."

It was not until half-past three that the welcome order was given to prepare to move forward. A portion of the Heavy Camel Regiment, the Hussars, and Naval Brigade were left behind with the three guns to hold the inclosure, while the rest, formed in square as at Abu Klea, advanced.

THE DASH FOR KHARTOUM

The camels with the wounded were in the centre. The Marines and Grenadiers formed the front of the square, the Coldstream and Scots Guards were on the right, the Mounted Infantry on the left, the Sussex and the remainder of the Heavies in the rear. The fire of the enemy redoubled as the square set out on its way. Halting occasionally to fire a few volleys at the spots where the enemy's fire was thickest the square made its way gradually onward, keeping as much as possible on ridges so as to avoid being surrounded by the enemy placed in commanding positions. At last the fire of the Arabs suddenly ceased, and a great crowd, several thousand strong, headed by many horsemen, charged down upon the face and left flank of the square. They were some five hundred yards away, and a cheer broke from the British square when it was evident that the long suspense was over and the supreme moment at hand. Volley after volley was fired, and then, seeing that the fire was taking but little effect, and knowing that nothing discourages men so much as seeing their fire fail to stop the rush of an enemy, Sir Charles Wilson ordered the bugle to sound "Cease firing!"

The order was obeyed; the men stood steady until the enemy were within three hundred yards; then the bugle-call "Commence firing!" sounded, and from the front and left face of the square sweeping volleys were poured into the crowded mass.

"Aim low and fire steadily, men!" was the shout of the officers; and so well were they obeyed that the front ranks of the Arabs were mown down like grass. For a time they still pushed forward, but the fire was too terrible to be withstood; and although a few of the leaders arrived within fifty yards of the square, their followers hesitated when still at a distance of a hundred. Hesitation in the case of a charge is fatal. The storm of bullets still tore its way through the mass; the Arabs wavered, turned, and were soon in full flight. The battle had lasted but a few minutes, but the victory was complete, and three hearty cheers broke from the victors. There was a halt for a few minutes for the men to fill up their pouches from the reserve ammunition and to have a drink of water. They then moved forward again, confidently expecting that the attack would be renewed; but the Arabs had had enough of it, and the square moved on without interruption until, half an hour after sunset, they reached the river. The wounded were at once carried forward to the water, and then the troops were marched up by companies, and each in turn were permitted to drink their fill. Then guards were posted, and the exhausted troops threw themselves down on the ground. The object of their long march was attained, the Nile was reached, and thenceforth there would be no further suffering from want of water. The next day communication would be opened with Gordon's steamers, their friends would in the morning be fetched in from the zareba, and then there would be a long rest until the boat column arrived and the remainder of the force from Korti marched across to join them. In the morning Easton went across from his own company to the Marines.

"Where is Mr. Skinner?" he asked a sergeant.

"He is down with the wounded at the river, sir. He had his left arm broken by a bullet just as we left the zareba. He was just in front of me at the time, and I made a shift to bandage his arm and tied it up to his body, and then he took his place in the ranks again and kept on with them until we got here; then when we halted he fainted right off, and we carried him down to the hospital camp by the water."

Easton at once went down to visit his friend. He was lying on a stretcher.

"Well, Skinner, I am awfully sorry to hear that you got hit. How are you feeling, old man?"

"I cannot say much for myself just at present; it is only about half an hour since they finished bandaging me up and putting on splints; they just stopped the bleeding last night, and then I asked them to leave me alone until this morning. They had lots of serious cases to attend to, and mine would keep well enough; besides, I was so weak with loss of blood, and so really done up, that I felt that I could not stand any more then, and I was asleep in a very few minutes. However, my arm woke me up before daylight, and I was glad enough to have it put in proper shape, though it hurt me deucedly, I can tell you. However, it is comparatively easy now, and I hope I shall be all right by the time the advance begins. What a blessing it is having shade and water here!"

"It is, indeed," Easton agreed. "Now I must say good-bye, for I don't know what is to be done, and we are sure to be under arms directly."

The troops moved off in a few minutes after Easton returned to his company, and after carefully examining the ground, a small village named Abu Kru, a few yards from the river on rising ground, entirely deserted by the natives, was selected for a camp. The wounded were at once carried up there and were left in charge of the Heavies, while the Guards and Mounted Infantry started for the zareba, the Sussex being sent out on the right to watch Metemmeh and keep the enemy in check should they advance against the village. The water-skins and camel-tanks were all filled, for but little water had been left at the zareba; and the men, although they had scarcely eaten any food for the last forty-eight hours, started in good spirits, perfectly ready for another fight should the enemy try to stop them. But although large numbers of them gathered on a hill near the town they abstained from any attack, and the column reached the zareba, where they were received with hearty cheers by its little garrison.

These had not been attacked during their absence, although a scattered musketry fire had been kept up upon them until dark. To this they replied vigorously, and the guns had done good service to the square while on its march by keeping up a shell fire upon any bodies of the enemy that could be made out on the eminences near it. The garrison had suffered great suspense after the square had disappeared from their sight, for they could see large bodies of men hurrying in that direction, and their anxiety was great when the sudden outburst of musketry told them that the square was attacked. What the issue of the fight had been they knew not, but their hopes that the Arabs had been defeated

222

increased as time went on and no attack was made upon themselves, for had the enemy been successful they would speedily have poured down to the attack of the feebly-defended baggage.

As soon as the column arrived the work of pulling down the walls of boxes and saddles, getting the camels to their feet and loading them, began. So many of the camels had been killed that the number surviving was insufficient to carry down the stores, therefore the smaller redoubt was left untouched and a stronger garrison than before placed in it, and the rest moved down to the river. The troops all partook of a hearty meal before the start was made. Sir Herbert Stewart and the rest of the wounded were taken down in the cacolets with the column.

Rupert Clinton had remained in the zareba when the square had marched forward. He had been greatly exhausted by the night march and had had a slight sunstroke before the square moved out; the doctors had therefore ordered him not to accompany it, but to stay at the zareba and assist the general and other wounded.

"You are looking very shaky, Clinton," Easton said when he joined him.

"I am all right, to-day," he replied; "rather heavy about the head; but a bath and a long night's rest will set me up again. Skinner is all right, I hope?"

"No, I am sorry to say he has got his left arm broken. I saw him for a moment before we started. He got hit just after he left here, but stuck to his company all through. I asked one of the surgeons, and he said that unless fever or anything of that sort came on he was likely to go on all right, and that he did not think that there was much chance of his losing his arm. He has plenty of pluck, Skinner has."

"I should think so," Rupert said. "A fellow who could play an uphill game of football as he could can be trusted to keep his courage up under any circumstances. Do you know what we are going to do, Easton? Are we going to attack Metemmeh?"

"I have not the least idea. It is a big place, a lot bigger than we expected, and there are a tremendous lot of fighting men there. It is fortunate they did not all make a rush at us together yesterday, although I don't think it would have made any difference. But it would be a very risky thing to attack such a place as that, swarming with fanatics, with our present force. It would be too big to hold if we took it, and we might lose two or three hundred men in the attack and street fighting; and as it is said that a big force is coming down the river to attack us, it would certainly be a risk, and a big one, to lose a lot of men in an attack on this place, which we shall be able to take without any difficulty as soon as the rest of the force comes up. I expect we shall try a reconnaissance. If the Arabs bolt, and we find that we can take the place without hard fighting, we shall take it; but if they show a determination to stick there and defend it to the last I think we shall leave it alone."

The column returned to the river without meeting with any opposition; but it was evident from the number of Arabs who were seen moving about in the direction of Metemmeh that the check of the previous day had by no means disheartened them, and that they were still in very considerable force in and around the town.

Late at night the orders were issued for the troops to parade at half-past four in the morning; and leaving a small force to guard Abu Kru, or, as it was sometimes called, Gubat, the rest of the troops marched towards Metemmeh. Two villages deserted by the inhabitants were passed, and then a view was obtained of the town. Crowds of Arabs were seen outside its walls.

The officer in command of the company of Grenadiers that was marching in extended order in front of the column picked out twenty of the best shots and ordered them to elevate their sights to two thousand yards and fire five volleys. Great as the distance was, the effect was considerable. With the aid of glasses two or three of the enemy were seen to fall, and the rest scattered in all directions and speedily took shelter within the walls. The seven-pounders then opened fire, but the shot produced little or no result, simply punching holes in the mud walls. The troops then moved nearer, marching along the southern side to see if any place suitable for an assault could be discovered; but everywhere the wall was loopholed, and the incessant fire showed that it was strongly manned.

A Krupp gun on the walls presently opened fire with so accurate an aim that the column fell back a short distance. At this moment a cheer rose as four steamers were seen coming along the river flying the Egyptian flag. They ran towards the shore and landed two hundred negro soldiers with some small brass guns. These were speedily placed into position beside the seven-pounders, and the negro infantry, advancing in skirmishing order, opened fire at once. They brought news that Gordon was still holding out, and also that three thousand of the enemy were on their way down and were but two days' march away.

This news decided Sir Chas. Wilson against running the risk of materially weakening his force by an assault on the town, and the column fell back to Abu Kru. On their way a portion of the Guards' Regiment was told off to search the groves and plantations to see that there were no Arabs lurking there.

Presently they came upon two camels grazing in a grove.

"Search about well, men," the officer in command said; "their owners may be hidden somewhere close."

In a minute or two one of the men called out, "Here are two saddles, sir, hidden in the bushes; they are scarlet, and belong to one of our regiments."

The officers speedily gathered to the spot. "They are certainly our saddles," the officer in command said; "how in the world did the camels get here? I suppose they must have wandered away during the night march and been picked up by some of the Arabs and driven on here."

"But they are riding camels," one of the others put in; "they must have belonged to some of the men who were missing on the night march; the poor fellows were killed, no doubt."

"They may have ridden them on here," Easton suggested. "After they got separated from the column the camels may have smelt the water and come on here before daylight broke."

"That is true, Easton. You see one of these saddles has blood stains on it; perhaps its rider was wounded. We will search the grove thoroughly."

The search was renewed, and in a few minutes a sergeant ran up to the group of officers. "We have found a man, sir; he belongs to the Heavies; he is insensible."

The officers hurried to the spot. "Yes, the poor fellow is a sergeant of the Heavies. No doubt you were right, Easton. You see he has been wounded in the side. He looks in a bad way."

"There are two water-bottles by him," Easton said; "one is empty and the other is half full," he added as he took them up and shook them. "He must have a comrade somewhere."

"No doubt he has, Easton; he could scarcely have been in a condition when he arrived here to take off the saddles and hide them away. What can have become of the other?"

The grove was searched thoroughly from end to end, but no sign found of the missing man. Some boughs were cut down and a rough stretcher made, and upon this the sergeant was laid and the force then moved on, the camels being saddled and mounted by two of the men, and on arriving at the camp the sergeant was taken to the hospital.

As soon as dinner was eaten the men were paraded again. A council had been held to decide upon the best course to be taken, and it was decided that a fort should be built down by the river, and that the whole force should establish itself there with the exception of the Guards' Camel Regiment, which should remain at Gubat so as to prevent any body of the enemy posting themselves there and keeping up an annoying fire upon the fort down by the river.

Gubat had already been roughly fortified, and the whole force was therefore set at work to erect with camel-saddles and boxes a defence for the position by the river. When this was done the wounded were all carried down to the new fort. After the work was over Rupert strolled up through the village to have a chat with Easton. As he was sitting there an orderly came up.

"Mr. Clinton, the surgeon has sent me up with two letters that were found inside the jacket of the wounded sergeant who was brought in this afternoon. One is directed to you and the other to Captain Percy Clinton."

"That is very curious," Rupert said, taking the letters and turning them over in his hand. "How is the man going on, orderly?"

"He is insensible still, sir. I believe the doctors say that it is fever, and that his wound is not serious. One of the men of his regiment who is in the hospital says he got it at Abu Klea, and that it was attended to there."

"Thank you, orderly, that will do. What in the world can the man be writing to me about, and to my father, which is still more curious?"

"I should say the best way of finding out, Clinton, will be to open the letter."

"Well, I suppose it will be," Rupert replied. "Still, it is always interesting to guess at a mystery before you find the key."

"Well, guess away," Easton said, stretching himself out on his back. "I never was a good hand at riddles."

It was some little time before Rupert, finding himself unable to find any solution whatever to the mystery, opened the letter. As he did so he stirred the fire by which they were sitting into a fresh blaze. He read a few lines and uttered an exclamation of such intense surprise that Easton sat up with a start.

"What is it, Clinton?"

"It is the most extraordinary thing I ever came across, Easton. You know the story about Edgar and myself. Well, this wounded sergeant is either his father or mine."

"Impossible!" Easton exclaimed; "he did not look much above thirty; besides, no soldier of twenty-one years' service – and he must have had fully that – would be out here."

Rupert made no reply; he was running his eyes rapidly through the letter.

"Good heavens!" he exclaimed; "Edgar is out here; he is a trumpeter in the Heavies."

"That is news, Rupert. I congratulate you heartily, old fellow. You are sure that there is no mistake?"

"No; there cannot be any mistake about that," Rupert said, thrusting the letter into his tunic. "Come along, Easton, let us be off. He goes by the name of Ned Smith."

"Wait a moment, old man," Easton said, laying his hand kindly on Rupert's shoulder. "Where was the letter written?"

"At Korti."

"Well, Clinton, don't be too sanguine. You know how terribly the Heavies suffered at Abu Klea. Don't make up your mind too warmly to see your brother; he may be among the wounded we left behind at Abu Klea; he may –"and he stopped.

"I won't think it," Rupert said; "it would be too hard, after our searching for him for all these years, to find out that but four or five days since he was in camp with us, and to learn it only too late. I won't think it."

"I hope to God that it is not so, Clinton, only I thought it best to prepare you for what may be possible. Which troop did he belong to?"

"The Dragoon troop."

Easton was silent, for it was upon this troop that the heaviest loss had fallen.

"Well," Rupert went on, "let us go down and learn the best or the worst."

They walked down the slope to the new fort by the river, and finding out where the Heavies were bivouacked soon discovered the Dragoons.

"You go and ask, Easton," Rupert said nervously; "I dare not."

Easton went on alone and presently accosted a sergeant.

"Sergeant, can you tell me whether the trumpeter of your troop was wounded at Abu Klea? Is he here now?"

"He was wounded at Abu Klea, sir, though not seriously; but he is not here now, he was one of those missing on the night march, he and Sergeant Bowen. I hear the sergeant was found and brought in this morning very bad, but I have heard nothing of Smith; but I expect that one of the camels brought in this afternoon was his; in fact I know it was, for it has got Smith's number on the saddle. It is likely that they would be together, for the sergeant had taken a great fancy to the lad. We all liked him. He joined us at Cairo from the Hussars, as our own trumpeter was taken ill; he was a general favourite, but Sergeant Bowen took to him specially."

"Thank you, sergeant;" and Easton turned and walked slowly back to where Rupert was awaiting him.

"You have bad news, Easton," Rupert said huskily. "I could see it as you stood talking to that man."

"Yes, I have bad news," Easton said, "but hardly the worst, Clinton."

"He is badly wounded then," Rupert groaned.

"I am afraid it is worse than that, Clinton; he is missing. It was he who was the rider of the second camel that we found in the grove this morning. He and the sergeant were both missing on the night march, and evidently found their way down to the river where we discovered the sergeant. What can have become of your brother since I know not. Evidently he left his water-bottle by his comrade and went somewhere, probably to join us. As I was saying to you when we were chatting about it before you opened that letter, he was probably either making his way towards the square on the day of the fight or coming towards our camp after we got in, and was seized by the Arabs. That was the conclusion at which we all arrived, though I had little thought when we were talking it over that the missing man was your brother."

"Then you think he has been killed?" Rupert said hoarsely.

"I don't know that, Clinton. He may have been made a prisoner. You see, we have searched the ground between that grove and our camp thoroughly to-day, and had he been killed there I think we should certainly have found him. Of course it may have happened further out on the plain if he was making his way out to join our square; but I should think he would never have done that, for the Arabs were swarming all round it. Besides, the Hussars were scouting about all over the plains this morning, and if they had seen the body of any of our men would certainly have reported it. The Arabs in fight never show mercy, but if they came upon him by himself they might very well have carried him off as a prisoner, especially if he made no resistance. You see, they are all slave-dealers at heart; besides, they might think that a white prisoner would be an acceptable present to the Mahdi. Of course I know no more about it than you do, but I should say that the chances are quite as great of his being taken prisoner as of his having been killed."

"One is as bad as the other," Rupert said in a broken voice. "This is awful, Easton. I will walk up to your camp again. Would you mind seeing the colonel of his regiment or the officer of his troop, and find out what you can about him?"

Easton soon found one of the few surviving officers of Edgar's troop.

"Can you tell me anything about Trumpeter Smith?" he asked. "I have reason to believe that he was a relative of a friend of mine, and that he ran away and enlisted under a false name."

"He bore an excellent character," the officer said. "He came to us from the Hussars at Cairo, and no one could behave better than he has done from the time he joined us. They would not have sent him to us if he hadn't been a thoroughly well-conducted young fellow. I was chatting with one of the officers of his regiment on the day we left Cairo; he spoke in very high terms of him, and said that he was quite a popular character in the regiment. It seems that he was a first-rate cricketer, and especially brought himself into notice by some exceedingly lucky conduct when two ladies belonging to the regiment were attacked by a couple of tramps at Aldershot; and besides that he had greatly distinguished himself at El-Teb, where the Hussars got badly mauled. His name was amongst those sent in for the Victoria Cross, and he was specially chosen to go with us to give him another chance. I never heard a young fellow more warmly spoken of. We were awfully sorry when we heard that he was missing. There is no doubt he was with Sergeant Bowen whom your men brought in this morning. One of the two camels was the one he rode. We have been talking that over to-day, and the general opinion is that he was caught by the Arabs as he was trying to rejoin the regiment. It is a thousand pities he did not wait a little longer in that grove, but I have no doubt he was anxious to get assistance as soon as possible for the sergeant. I intend as soon as we are settled here to ask the colonel to let me go out with a party to search the plains to see if we can find his body."

"I am more inclined to think that he has been taken prisoner," Easton said; "he would hardly have gone out to meet the square, as he must have seen the plains swarming with Arabs and that he had no chance whatever of getting through. He would have known that we were making for the water, and that he would have a far better chance of reaching us by waiting until we got there. My own idea is that he did wait, and that the Arabs came upon him somewhere between that grove and our camp; if so, they did not kill him, for if they had done so we must have found his body to-day, for we searched every foot of the ground. I think that he is a prisoner in their hands."

"He had better have been killed at once," the officer said.

"I agree with you, except that it is just possible that a slave may escape. You see, on our way up to Khartoum if we defeat the Mahdi's troops – which we certainly shall do – all the country will no doubt submit, and there would be in the first place the chance of his being given up to us, and in the second of his escape."

THE DASH FOR KHARTOUM

"It is possible," the officer agreed, "but I certainly would not build on that. The probability is that if he is taken prisoner he will be sent to the Mahdi, and if he isn't killed at once when he gets there, he will be when the Mahdi sees that his game is up."

Easton nodded, and then, thanking the officer for his information, took his way up to the village, where he repeated to Rupert what he had heard. His own voice faltered as he told the story, while Rupert sobbed unrestrainedly. When he had finished Rupert rose, pressed his hand silently, and then returning to his own bivouac threw himself down and thought sadly for hours over the loss of his brother.

The next day Rupert was busy from morning until night. A portion of the force was employed in strengthening the fortifications of the two posts, and a strong body was at work cutting wood for the use of the steamer in which Sir Charles Wilson was to start next morning for Khartoum. While at work they were guarded by another strong party, lest the enemy should make a sudden attack. All, however, passed off quietly, and on the following morning Sir Charles started with two steamers, taking with him twenty men of the Sussex regiment and one hundred and fifty of the black troops. On the same day three hundred troops selected from the various regiments started on camels, with four hundred baggage camels under their convoy, for Gakdul, in accordance with the orders given to General Stewart by Lord Wolseley at starting, that as soon as he had established himself upon the river he was to send back a convoy for some more stores.

The convoy was, however, but a small one, for of over two thousand camels which had left Korti, this number alone survived, and most of these were in such a state from exhaustion, starvation, and sore backs, that they were wholly unfit to travel. The force on the river was now reduced to some fifty officers and eight hundred and seventy men, including medical staff; commissariat, natives of all kinds, and the remainder of the black troops and one hundred and twenty wounded. The defences were greatly strengthened, officers and men both sharing in the work.

ABU KRU

During the day the Hussars scouted round the camp, frequently exchanging shots with the enemy. At night strong lines of sentries were posted round the forts. No attack was, however, made, although the natives sometimes showed in considerable force during the day, and the beating of tom-toms went on day and night round Metemmeh. The hard work upon which the troops were engaged kept them for the most part in good health, and the wounded did extremely well, the doctors themselves being surprised at the rapidity with which wounds healed and the men recovered their strength, an effect doubtless due to the clear dry air. The troops in the village enjoyed better health than those down by the river, as they obtained the benefit of the air from the desert, while down near the stream heavy dews fell at night and there were several slight cases of fever. All looked eagerly for the return of the steamers from Khartoum with news how things were going on there. As for their own position, no one had the slightest anxiety. No news had been received of the approach of the three thousand troops which had been reported as on their way down against them, and they felt confident in their power to repulse any attack that the enemy at Metemmeh could make against them. They were, too, in hourly expectation of the arrival across the desert of reinforcements from Korti.

CHAPTER XIV
A SLAVE

ALTHOUGH Edgar had felt disappointed when the sounds of the firing round Metemmeh died away, and he knew by the triumphant shouts of the Arabs that the British had retired, he had hardly expected that an attack would be made upon the town until reinforcements came up, and he consoled himself with the idea that within a few weeks at the utmost the reinforcements would arrive, and that if the Arabs remained in the town until that time he would be rescued. Two or three days later he heard a great hubbub just after nightfall in the streets outside. The Arabs who were in the court-yard snatched up their guns, and the din became louder than before. Above the uproar Edgar could catch the words, "Death to the Kaffir!" and "Send him to the Mahdi!" and guessed that his own fate was the subject of dispute. Picking up one of the Arab swords he determined at least to sell his life as dearly as he could. For an hour his fate trembled in the balance. At times there were lulls in the tumult, while a few voices only, raised in furious argument, were heard. Then the crowd joined in again and the yells became deafening, and every moment Edgar expected to hear the clash of weapons, and to see the little party to which he belonged driven headlong into the house followed by the Mahdi's men. But he had before witnessed many Arab disputes, and knew that however furious the words and gestures might be they comparatively seldom came to blows, and though greatly relieved he was not altogether surprised when at last the uproar quieted down, and his captors returned into the court-yard and barred the door behind them.

In a short time an argument broke out, almost as furious and no less loud than that which had taken place outside. The sheik had evidently his own opinion and was determined to maintain it. Two or three of his followers sided with him, but the rest were evidently opposed to it. From the few words Edgar could catch in the din he gathered that the sheik was determined to carry him off as his own particular slave, while the bulk of his followers were in favour of handing him over to the Mahdi's officers. All Arabs are obstinate, but the sheik happened to be exceptionally obstinate and determined even for an Arab. Had the Mahdi's officers recognized his right to the captive, and offered him some small present in return for his slave, he would probably have handed him over willingly enough; but that they should threaten him, and insist on his handing over his property, was, he considered, an outrage to his dignity and independence.

Was he, an independent sheik, to be treated as if he were a nameless slave, and ordered to surrender his own to the Mahdi or anyone else? Never! He would slay the slave and stab himself to the heart rather than submit to be thus trampled on. If his followers did not like it they were free to leave him and to put on white shirts and follow the Mahdi; he could do without such men well enough. What would the Mahdi do for them? He would send them to be shot down by the Kaffirs, as they had been shot down at Abu Klea and outside the town, and someone else would possess their wives and their camels and their fields. If they liked that they could go, and he went to the gate, unbarred and threw it open, and pointed to the street. The effect was instantaneous. The Arabs had no desire whatever to become soldiers of the Mahdi, and they at once changed their tone and assured the sheik that they had no idea of opposing his wishes, and that whatever he said should be done, pointing out, however, that in the morning the Mahdists would assuredly come and take the prisoner by force.

The sheik was mollified by their submission, and ordering Edgar to close and bar the gate again seated himself by the fire.

"By to-morrow," he said, "we will be far away. I am not a fool; I am not going to fight the Mahdi's army. As soon as the town is still we will make our way down to the river, take a boat, and cross. Two days' journey on foot will take us to the village where we sent our camels with the plunder and came on here to fight, believing, like fools, that the Mahdi was going to eat them up. We have seen what came of that, and they say that there are crowds more of them on the way. I am ready to fight; you have all seen me fight over and over again, and all men know that Sheik El Bakhat is no coward; but to fight against men who fire without stopping is more than I care for. They are Kaffirs, but they have done me no harm, and I have no vengeance to repay them. Fortunately we did not arrive till an hour after the fighting was over, or our bones might be bleaching out there in the desert with those of hundreds of others. It is the Mahdi's quarrel and not mine. Let him fight if he wants to, I have no objection. Why should I throw away my life in his service when even the slave we have captured is not to be my own."

As these sentiments commended themselves to his followers the sheik's plans were carried out. The unfortunate trader and his wife, who had been cowering in a little chamber since the sheik and his party had unceremoniously taken possession of the rest of the house, were called in and informed that their guests were about to leave them, and were ordered to close the gate after them and on no account to open it until morning. The party then set to work to cook a large supply of cakes for the journey. A little before midnight they sallied out, and making their way noiselessly through the streets issued out near the river at a point where the walls that surrounded the other sides of the town were wanting.

There were several boats moored against the banks, and choosing one of them they allowed it to drift quietly down the river until some distance below the town, and then getting out the oars rowed to the other side of the river and landed below the large town of Shendy. They made a wide detour to get round the town, travelling at a long swinging trot that soon tried Edgar's wind and muscles to the utmost. He was not encumbered by much clothing, as before leaving he had been made to strip and to wrap himself up in a native cloth. Before he did so, however, he had been rubbed from head to foot with charcoal from the fire, for his captors saw that the whiteness of his skin, which greatly surprised them, for his face and hands were tanned to a colour as dark as that of many of the Arabs, would instantly betray him.

The perspiration was soon streaming from him at every pore, but he well knew that any display of weakness would only excite the contempt of his captors, and although he was several times well-nigh falling from fatigue he kept on until, when many miles away from Metemmeh, the natives slackened their pace, and broke into a walk.

"I thought," Edgar muttered to himself, "that a good long run with the hares and hounds at Cheltenham was pretty hard work, but it was nothing to this. This climate does take it out of one and no mistake. There is one thing, I have got to get accustomed to it, and am not likely to try any other for some time."

They continued the journey until morning broke, and then turned off to the left, and after miles of walking halted among some sand-hills outside the zone of cultivated land. Edgar was ordered to go and find some fuel, for the morning was cold, and even the Arabs felt the keen air after their exertions. Edgar at once hurried away, and was fortunate enough to find some dried stalks of maize in a field not far off. Pulling it up by the roots he collected a large bundle and carried it on his shoulder to the point where he had left the Arabs. An exclamation of satisfaction greeted his arrival. The sheik produced a box of matches from a corner of his cloth, for European goods were obtainable in Metemmeh, and they had found several boxes in the house that they had occupied. A fire was soon blazing, and the Arabs squatted closely around it, while Edgar, tired out with his journey, threw himself on the ground some distance away.

The sheik was in high spirits; he was, in the first place, glad that he had had his way, and carried off his captive; and in the second, he felt assured by the manner in which Edgar had kept up with them by the way, and by the speed with which he had collected the materials for a fire, that he would turn out a very useful slave. Before starting they had partaken of a good meal, and each of them had carried off a bag of five or six pounds in weight of dry dates from the merchant's store. A few of these were eaten, and then the whole party lay down to sleep, the sheik first rousing Edgar, and ordering him to lie down between him and another Arab, tying a cord from his wrists to theirs, so that he could not move without disturbing one or other of them.

A few hours' rest was taken, and then, with the sun blazing overhead, the journey was recommenced. They now kept among the sand-hills so as to avoid the villages near the river, in case a party should be sent out from Metemmeh in pursuit of them. Edgar had difficulty in keeping up with the rest, for the hot sand burned his naked feet, and he had to avoid the prickly grass through which his companions walked unconcernedly.

They continued their journey until nightfall, and then went down to the river for a drink. Edgar had suffered greatly from thirst, which he had in vain endeavoured to assuage by chewing dry dates. His feet were causing him agony, and after satisfying his thirst he sat with them in the water until his companions again moved back into the desert.

Edgar could not obtain a wink of sleep for the pain of his feet, and in the morning he showed them to the sheik, who only laughed at their raw and swollen condition. As, however, he was desirous that his slave should continue in good condition, he told him to tear off a strip from his cotton cloth, and himself walked down to the river with Edgar. There he allowed him to again bathe his feet, and showed him some broad smooth leaves which he bade him gather; these were placed under his feet, which were then bandaged with the strip of cotton.

As soon as this was done they returned to the party, and again set out. Edgar found the application greatly relieved the pain, and as the leaves and bandages kept the feet from contact with the sand, he was able to get on fairly. He felt, too, the benefit from the drink of water he had obtained from the river, and was able to keep up with the party until, late in the afternoon, they approached the village where the natives had sent their camels.

Edgar was left in charge of two of the Arabs half a mile from the village when the others went on, the sheik saying that in the morning they were to await him half a mile on the other side of the village. There was a good deal of grumbling on the part of the men who were left with Edgar, and he saw that nothing would please them better than to cut his throat; but when they looked threatening towards him, he simply laughed, knowing that they dare not use their weapons, and that, did they venture to strike him with hand or stick, he was a match for both of them.

It was nearly two years now since he had stood up against the two tramps at Aldershot, and in that time he had grown from a lad to a powerful young fellow, with every muscle hardened by exercise. Perhaps the men concluded that the experiment was not worth trying, and presently left him to himself, and entered into an animated conversation together.

When it became dark they insisted on tying Edgar's legs, and to this he made no objection, for he understood that here they were only obeying the orders of the sheik. A few minutes later he was sound asleep, and did not wake once until he was roused by the Arabs stirring; they untied his feet, and at once started on their way. In less than half an hour they were at the spot the sheik had named; in a few minutes he came up with six of his men mounted on camels and four spare animals. The two Arabs and Edgar mounted three of these, and the journey was continued. They struck off from the river and journeyed all day among sand-hills, among which they camped for the night. They had brought water-skins with them, and Edgar received his share. They started at daybreak again, and travelling the whole day came down at night upon a small village at a short distance from the river. Here the sheik had evidently friends, for he was warmly greeted as they entered. By the conversation at the camp on the previous evening Edgar had gathered that the rest of the party had gone off to villages to which they belonged in that neighbourhood, and that those with the sheik belonged to the village of Bisagra, near Khartoum, that word being frequently repeated. Before entering the village a short stay had been made, while some pieces of wood were burned, and Edgar was again rubbed over with charcoal.

When they arrived at the house at which the sheik intended to stop, Edgar was directed to follow him, while the rest looked after the camels. On entering the house he was told by the sheik to go into a little court-yard, where a negro presently brought him a dish of boiled meal and some water. He heard a great talk inside the house, but could understand nothing of what had been said. Half an hour later two of the Arabs came in, and lay down beside him as before, and in addition his feet were firmly tied. The next morning the party still further divided, the sheik with two men and Edgar starting alone.

He felt sure that they were now some distance above Khartoum, as the city lay less than eighty miles from Metemmeh; they had made, he calculated, fully fifteen the first night. They had walked at least five-and-twenty on the second, and had ridden thirty, he calculated, on each of the last two days. On these they had not, as he noticed by the sun, followed a straight course, going far to the east of south on the first day, and to the west of south on the second, having doubtless made a large detour to avoid the city. During the whole time they had been travelling over a trackless country, and had met no parties of natives on the way. They started again before day-break, and now travelled along the bank of the river.

A SLAVE

Here the country had been cultivated for some distance back, and villages were scattered here and there. Nevertheless they passed but few natives, and Edgar saw that many of the houses were roofless, and that there were signs of fire and destruction everywhere, and understood that this ruin had been wrought by the hosts of the Mahdi. About mid-day they arrived at a village on the bank. Its name, Edgar learned by the exclamations of the Arabs when they caught sight of it, was Gerada. Here a large native boat was lying moored. Bidding Edgar remain among the camels the sheik alighted, and was for half an hour engaged in bargaining with two men, who were apparently owners of the boat.

Terms were at last agreed to, the camels were led down and placed on board, and the boat pushed off. The sheik made a peremptory sign to Edgar to lie down and cover his head with his cloth, and Edgar heard him say to the boatman, "My slave is ill." The river was now at its shallowest, and the men were able to pole the boat across. Edgar was hurried ashore with the camels, while the sheik remained behind settling with the boatman. They were now, he knew, between the two Niles, which joined their waters at Khartoum. The country here had evidently been rich and prosperous before the host of the Mahdi passed like a blight over it. They halted a few miles from the river, near a ruined and deserted village. Edgar was told to watch the camels while they plucked heads of corn from the deserted fields, while the Arabs lit a fire and baked some cakes. None of these were offered to Edgar, who had to content himself with some heads of dried maize that he picked from the field.

Two days later they arrived at the bank of the White Nile. They followed it for upwards of a mile, and then the sheik, who evidently knew the way, turned off the bank into the river, the others following. The ford, for such it was, was shallow, the water scarcely coming up to the girths of the camels. Although the journey had been a short one, they halted again for the night in cultivated ground, a mile from the river, and Edgar was ordered to pick corn. The fields had already been ransacked, and it was only here and there that he found a head of maize hidden in its brown cases.

After a time the two Arabs joined in the search, and by nightfall a good-sized sackful had been collected. At daybreak the camels were taken to a well, where the apparatus for drawing the water still stood, with a trough beside it. When Edgar had filled the trough the camels were urged to drink their fill, being taken back once or twice to the trough, until they could drink no more. The water-skins were filled, the Arabs took long draughts from a bucket, and the sheik ordered Edgar to do the same. Then the bag with their maize was fastened on the back of the spare camel, which was already laden with a miscellaneous collection of goods, and the party started.

Edgar understood by the preparations that had been made that they had still a serious journey before them, and it proved to be so. For eight days they travelled across a desert, their course being to the north of west, marching from early dawn until sunset. The moment the day's journey was over he was set to work to gather tufts of coarse grass growing among the rocks, which cropped out here and there from the sand. Other vegetation there was none, save some low stunted bushes, which he also gathered whenever he came across them. With these and the grass a fire was lighted, and the sheik and two followers roasted a few heads of maize for their own eating, and with these and a handful of dry dates appeared perfectly satisfied.

After they had done Edgar was permitted to roast some maize for his own use. The camels had each a dozen heads given to them. Except at one halting-place, where there was a muddy well, they received no water; the Arabs themselves drank sparingly, and Edgar received but a mouthful or two of the precious fluid. Towards the end of the eighth day the Arabs began to hasten their camels, and soon afterwards, on mounting an eminence, Edgar saw some tents standing in a small green valley ahead. The Arabs fired their guns and uttered loud yells, and at once some figures appeared at the entrances of the tents and hastened towards them. In five minutes the two parties met. There were a few men among those that came out, but the majority were women and children. All uttered shouts of welcome, and a babel of questions arose.

The sheik did not alight from his camel, but with his followers continued his way until he reached the encampment. Here dismounting he entered one of the largest of the tents. The other two Arabs were surrounded by the natives, and Edgar stood by the camels doubtful as to what he was expected to do next. He was not left undisturbed long. The Arabs had evidently told the news that their black comrade was a white slave whom the sheik had captured, and all crowded round him examining him with the greatest curiosity. There was nothing to them remarkable about his colour, for he was darker than any of them; but his hair, closely cropped like that of all engaged in the expedition, evidently amused them much.

One of the women quickly fetched a large gourd full of water, and made signs to him to wash himself, which he was glad enough to do after his four days' dusty journey, but before commencing he plunged his face into the bowl and took a long drink. Shouts of surprise and amusement arose as with diligent rubbing he gradually got rid of the thickest part of the charcoal, and his skin began to show through.

"I wish to goodness," he muttered to himself, "I had got a cake or two of soap here, but I suppose it is a thing that they never heard of; even a scrubbing-brush would be a comfort. I shall be weeks before I get myself thoroughly white again; it is completely ground into my skin."

He had, however, managed to get rid of the greater part of the charcoal, and was from the waist upward a dingy white, when the sheik came out from his tent. He was followed by a good looking Arab woman. He called Edgar to him and said, "This is your mistress." Edgar had during the journey guessed that he was intended as a special present for the sheik's wife, and that his lot would depend in no slight degree upon her, and resolved to do his utmost to earn her good opinion. He therefore bent on one knee, and taking her hand placed it on his head. The woman laughed good-naturedly, and said something to the sheik which by its tone Edgar felt was an expression of approval.

The camels had all this time remained kneeling, and the sheik now ordered them to be unloaded. Edgar had wondered what the various bundles might contain, and looked with almost as much curiosity as the expectant Arabs at the process of opening them.

As their contents were gradually brought to light, he understood at once why the sheik and his followers had taken no part in the fight outside Metemmeh. They had evidently been far out in the desert, on the track the column had followed, on the search for loot. The collection was a singular one, and it appeared to Edgar that they must either have got hold of three or four of the camels that had strayed away from the column, or had followed the troops and rifled boxes and cases that had fallen from the backs of the animals on their way through the trees, or that had been left behind when the camels fell.

Here were articles of clothing of all sorts – shirts, socks, karkee suits, boots, ivory-backed brushes (the property, no doubt, of some officer of the Guards or Heavies), a hand-glass, a case of writing materials and paper, a small medicine-chest, some camp-kettles, two or three dozen tins of cocoa and milk and as many of arrow-root, scores of small tins of Liebig (these three lots clearly forming part of the burden of one of the hospital camels), a handsome field-glass, an officer's sword without a scabbard, a large bundle of hospital rugs, a tin-box marked "tea, 10 lbs.," a number of tin drinking-cups, plates, knives, forks, and spoons, and a strange collection of odds and ends of all sorts.

Each article that was taken out caused fresh excitement, its uses were warmly discussed, and Edgar was presently dragged forward and ordered to explain. The various articles of clothing particularly puzzled the Arabs, and Edgar had to put on a shirt and pair of trousers to show how they should be worn. The chocolate and arrow-root had apparently been brought chiefly for the sake of their tins, and one of the Arabs illustrated their use by putting one of them down on a rock, chopping it in two with his sword, cleaning out the contents, and then restoring as well as he could the two halves to the original shape. Some of the children were about to taste the arrow-root scattered about the ground, but the sheik sharply forbade them to touch it, evidently thinking that it might be poison. Edgar was consulted, and said that the contents of all the tins were good.

As they were evidently anxious to know their uses, he took one of the tin pots, filled it with water, and placed it over the fire. Then with one of the Arabs' knives he opened a tin of chocolate, cutting it carefully round the edge so that it should make a good drinking tin when empty. When the water boiled he took out some of the contents of the tin with the spoon and stirred them into the pot, and poured the contents into a dozen of the cups. The sheik still looked a little suspicious, and ordered him to drink one first, which he did with deep satisfaction. The others then followed his example, and evidently approved very highly of the compound, and another pot of water was at once placed on the fire. Edgar was then requested to show what were the virtues of the white powder, and of the little tins. He said that both these were good for people who were ill. The Arabs, however, were not satisfied without making the experiment.

The arrow-root was not approved of, and the chief would have ordered the tins to be all opened and the contents thrown away, but on Edgar continuing to insist that they were good for illness, he told his wife to put them away in the tent. The Liebig was warmly approved of. Edgar explained that it was good for sickness, and good for a journey. The Arabs, seeing how small a quantity was required for making a tin of broth, at once recognized this, and the sheik ordered his wife to take great care of them, and said they were to be used only on a journey. The medicine-chest, with its bottles of various sizes, was also the subject of great curiosity, and one of the women, going into a tent, brought out a girl seven or eight years old, and requested Edgar to say which was the medicines that were suitable for her case.

Edgar felt the child's pulse, and found that she was in a high state of fever. Quinine was, he knew, a good thing for fever, but whether it ought to be administered to a patient in that stage he did not know. He told the sheik that he was not a Hakim, but that if he wished he would give the child the medicine that he thought was best suited to it, but he could not say for certain whether it would do it good. The sheik, who, like all the rest, was deeply interested in the contents of the chest, said he must do his best. He accordingly gave the child a dose of quinine, and told the mother to give her a cup of the arrow-root, and that in two hours she must take another dose of the quinine.

The last subject of investigation was the tea. There was a small sliding trap at the top of the tin, and when Edgar poured out half a cup of the contents, these were examined with great curiosity. The men took a few grains in their fingers, smelt them, and then tasted them. The result was unsatisfactory, and they were content to watch Edgar's proceedings before they went further. When he had the water boiling, he put the tea into a tin pot and poured the water over it, and when it had stood a few minutes served it out. The verdict was universally unfavourable, and the chief, in disgust at having brought tin of useless stuff so far, kicked it over and over. Seeing that Edgar had drunk up his portion with satisfaction, the sheik's wife told him that if he liked the nasty stuff he might keep it for himself, a permission of which he very thankfully availed himself.

The uses of all the articles being explained, the sheik proceeded to a distribution. He took the lion's share for himself, gave a good portion to the two men who had followed him, and a very small one to each of the other grown-up men and women in the camp. He ordered Edgar to carry his portion into the tent, where, under the instructions of the sheik's wife, the articles were all stowed away. The tent, which was a large one, was constructed of black blanketing woven by the women from camels' hair, and was divided into two portions by a hanging of the same materials. The one next to the entrance was the general living and reception room, that behind being for the use of the sheik's wife and children.

There were two female slaves who slept in a tiny tent constructed of a blanket in the rear of that of the sheik, and two negro slaves who looked after the camels, tilled the ground, and slept where they could.

The sheik's wife was evidently pleased with Edgar, and regarded him as her special property. Darkness had fallen long before the examination of the booty had concluded, and as soon as he had carried the sheik's share into the tent, she gave him a bowl of camel's milk and some meal in a gourd, and also bestowed on him one of the black blankets, and pointed out to him a place where he was to sleep just outside the tent.

"It might be a great deal worse," Edgar said to himself as he ate his supper; "the sheik himself does not seem to be a bad fellow; and at any rate I owe him my life for his obstinacy in sticking to me, instead of handing me over to the Mahdi's people. His wife is evidently disposed to be kind, and my work will be no harder than an agricultural labourer's, at any rate as long as we stay here. This is an out-of-the-way sort of place, and if it does not lie on the route between any two places, it is not likely to be much visited. It certainly looks as if the sheik regarded it as his private property, which he would not do if it were a regular caravan halting-place.

"It is likely enough that there are very few people who know of its existence. We travelled something like fifty miles a day, and must be three hundred miles to the west of the Nile. What I have got to do now is to work willingly, so as to keep in the good graces of the sheik and his wife, and to learn the language so as to speak it fluently. It is no use my thinking about escaping until I can pass as a native, unless, of course, I hear that we have gone up and taken Khartoum. I wonder how they are getting on at Metemmeh, and whether they have found the sergeant. If they have, it is likely enough when he finds that I have never reached the camp he will go to Rupert and tell him who the trumpeter of his troop was. I hope he won't; it is much better that they should wonder for some years what has become of me, and at last gradually forget me, than know that I am a slave among the Arabs. I am sure that would be a great grief to them all, and I hope they will not know anything about it until I return some day and tell them."

He was very glad of his blanket, for the nights were cold; and when he had finished his supper he wrapped himself up in it and was soon asleep. He was awoke at daylight by voices inside the tent, and a few minutes later the sheik and his wife came out, and seeing Edgar standing there the sheik ordered him to go and assist the other slaves; but Amina pouted: "I thought you had brought him home as a present to me; what use will he be to me if he is to work in the field all day with the others?"

"But the Kaffir must do some work, Amina; he cannot have his food for nothing."

"Of course he shall work when I don't want him," the woman said, "but I shall find much for him to do. He will draw the water, he will fetch the fuel, he will grind the meal when I have anything else for the women to do. When he has done all I require of him, then he can go and work in the fields. It is no use your giving me a slave and then taking him away again."

"Well, well!" the sheik said, "do with him as you will; women are always pleased with novelties. You will soon get tired of having this Kaffir about the tent, but keep him if you will."

Amina took one of the large hospital kettles, and putting it into Edgar's hands pointed to the well which lay a hundred yards away and told him to fetch water. When he returned with it she bade him go out and gather fuel. The last order was by no means easy to execute. The Arab fuel consisted almost entirely of dried camels' dung, as the scrub very speedily becomes exhausted for a considerable distance from a camp. Edgar took a rough basket to which Amina pointed and was away for some hours, following the track by which he had arrived and making a circuit of the oasis, and returned with the basket piled up with the fuel.

Amina was evidently well satisfied with the result of his work, for fuel is one of the great difficulties of Arab life in the desert. She rewarded him with a calabash of meal.

"Has my lady anything more for me to do?" he asked when he had finished his food.

"Not now," she replied.

"Then I will go out and help the others in the field;" and he walked off to where the negroes were engaged in watering a plantation of maize. The process consisted of drawing water from the well in leathern buckets and pouring it into channels by which it was conducted to the plantation. The negroes looked at him sourly as he took hold of the rope attached to the long swinging beam that acted as a lever to bring the bucket to the surface, and one of them muttered in Arabic, "Kaffir dog!" Slaves as they were they despised this white Christian.

"Well, look here," Edgar said in English, letting go the rope, "the sooner we come to an understanding the better. I am not going to stand any nonsense from you fellows; and if you don't keep a civil tongue in your heads I will give you such a licking as will teach you to do so in future."

Although they did not understand his words they guessed the import of them, and the biggest of the men, a powerful negro, repeated the word "Kaffir" and spat upon him. Edgar's right arm flew out from his shoulder, the blow struck the negro on the nose, and in an instant he was upon his back upon the ground. His comrade stood for a moment stupefied, and then with loud yells ran towards the tents, leaving the negro to pick himself up at his leisure. Edgar continued the work of raising and emptying the bucket until the negro returned, followed by the sheik, his wife, and all the inhabitants of the village. By this time the negro who had been knocked down had risen to his feet and was roaring like a bull at the top of his voice, while the blood was streaming from his nose.

"What is this?" the sheik shouted in great anger.

The negro volubly explained that the Kaffir slave had struck down their comrade.

"Why is this?" the sheik demanded of Edgar.

"I am my lord's slave," Edgar said; "but this fellow is a slave also. He called me a Kaffir dog and spat upon me. I knocked him down; and if any other slave does the same I will punish him also."

As the woman whose child had been ill had a short time before reported that the fever had left her, and that having drunk two basins of the arrow-root she was much better, the sheik had been greatly pleased with the idea that he had made a far more valuable capture than he had anticipated; he therefore received Edgar's explanation in his broken Arabic favourably.

"The white slave has done right," he said. "Who are you that you are to insult him? He came to work on my business, and you would have interfered with and hindered him. Hamish has been rightly punished, though truly the white man must have hit hard, for his nose is flattened to his face. Mashallah! It must have been a wonderful blow. The white men are Kaffirs, but they have marvellous powers. Now go to work again and let me hear of no more quarrels."

"The white man is my slave," Amina said, stepping forward and addressing the negroes, "and if anyone insults him I will have him flogged until he cannot stand. He is a Hakim, and his medicines have saved the life of Hamid's child. He is worth a hundred of you." And bestowing a vigorous and unexpected box on the ears to the negro standing next to her she turned and walked back to her tent, accompanied by her husband, while the rest of the villagers remained for some time staring at the negro, and commenting upon the wonderful effect of the white man's blow.

CHAPTER XV
BAD NEWS

NO sooner was work over in the afternoon of the day after that on which Rupert had heard of his brother's loss than Skinner came across with Easton to see him.

"My dear Skinner, surely you are not fit to be walking about," he said as he saw them approaching.

"Oh, it won't do me any harm, Clinton; my arm is all in splints, and, as you see, bandaged tightly to my side. The doctor seemed to say that I had better not move, but I promised to take care of myself. I should have come, old man, if I had been ten times as bad. Easton has just been telling me of this horrible business, so of course I came over to see you. I think from what he says you take too dark a view of it. There is no doubt in my mind that he is a prisoner, and that is bad enough; but these Arabs don't slaughter their prisoners in cold blood, they are not such fools as that, they make them useful. I own it must be disgusting to be a slave, especially to these Arabs, and of many fellows I should say they would never stand it any time. Easton wouldn't, for example. In the first place he wouldn't work, and in the next place, if they tried to make him he would be knocking his master down, and then of course he would get speared. But I have great hopes of your brother; he was always as hard as nails, and I should have no fear of his breaking down in health. Then he is a chap that can look after himself. Look how well he has been going on since he bolted from Cheltenham. Then he is a beggar to stick to a thing, and I should say the first thing he will make up his mind to do will be to escape some day, and he will be content to wait any time till the opportunity occurs. You see he has learnt a lot since he left school. He has been roughing it pretty severely. He has had over a year in this beastly hot climate, and will be able to make himself at home pretty near anywhere. I tell you, Clinton, I would lay odds on his turning up again even if he is left to himself. Besides that, if we go on to Khartoum and thrash the Mahdi, these Arabs will all be coming in and swearing that they are most grateful to us for freeing them from him, and you may be sure that any slaves they have will be given up at once. I don't say your brother is not in a hole; but I do say that he is just the fellow to get out of it."

"I have thought of everything you say, Skinner, and I do think that Edgar is as likely to make his escape some day as anyone would be under the circumstances; but I doubt whether anyone could do it."

"Why not?" Skinner asked, almost indignantly. "I don't suppose he could make his way down the Nile, although he might do that; but there are several caravan routes down to the Red Sea, and then there is Abyssinia. The people are Christians there, and, they say, fighting against the Mahdi's Arabs now; so if he got there he would be pretty sure to be treated well. I should say that there were lots of ways that he could escape. I don't mean now; but when he has got accustomed to the country, it seems to me a fellow with pluck and energy such as he has got ought to find no great difficulty in giving the people he is with the slip, and making his way somewhere. I do think, Clinton, there is no occasion to feel hopeless about your brother. It may be a long time before you see him again, but I do honestly believe he will turn up some time or other."

"I begin to hope he will," Rupert said. "At first I did not think so for a moment; but now I have had time to look at it calmly I think that there is a chance of his getting off some day; besides, when we are once at Khartoum and have scattered the Mahdi's army, I have no doubt General Gordon will send orders through the land for all Egyptian and European slaves to be brought in. You know it is still hoped that some of Hicks' officers may be alive, and there is such a feeling for Gordon throughout the country that his orders will be sure to be obeyed."

"That is right, Clinton," Easton said; "that is the view I take of it myself, and I am very glad to see that you have come to see it in that light. And now will you tell us what there was in that letter that gave us the news of your brother's being out here? How came the sergeant to write you? How did he know you were his brother? It seems an unaccountable business all through."

"I have not looked at the letter since," Rupert said. "It would have been very important if it had not been for Edgar's loss. As it is, it does not seem to matter one way or the other. Still, as you say, it is very singular altogether its coming into my hands;" and he took out the letter. It began:

"Sir, two days ago I was with the trumpeter of my troop when you passed by with two other officers. One of them called you Clinton, and as I had an interest in the name it attracted my attention, and I found that it also attracted the attention of the young fellow with me. I questioned him, and he acknowledged that he had been to school with you and the two officers with you."

"Good heavens!" Skinner broke in; "to think that we three should have passed close to your brother and that none of us should have recognized him! How awfully unfortunate!"

"It is terrible to think of now," Rupert agreed, and then continued reading the letter: "I then told Smith, which is the name the trumpeter went by, that my interest in you consisted of the fact that for aught I knew I was your father. He exclaimed, that in that case it was probable that I was his father, as he had been brought up with you. He then told me how he came to enlist, namely, that my wife, whom I have not seen since she left India, and who was, I thought, dead long ago, had been to him and had told him all about the change of infants, and said that she had done it on purpose for his good, and that she knew that he was her son because you had a mole on your shoulder; and she wanted him to go on pretending to be Captain Clinton's son, and offered to swear that the other one was hers, so that he might get all the money.

"That is why I write this. My name is Humphreys. I was a sergeant in the 30th, and it was at Agra, when we were stationed there, that the change of infants took place. My wife went over to England. I took to drink and disgraced myself, and five years afterwards deserted. I stayed in England for some years and then enlisted again in the Dragoon Guards, and being young looking gave my age as eight years younger than I was. I now go by the name of Bowen, and am a sergeant and bear a good character in the regiment. The lad did not wish me to say anything about this, at any rate until the campaign was over; but as we shall be marching in a day or two, and it may be that I shall be killed, I write a letter to you and one to Captain Clinton, so that in case I am killed the truth may be known.

"I affirm most solemnly that the statement made by my wife was a lie. Whether she did intend to change the children or not is more than I can say. Sometimes she said she did, sometimes she said she didn't; but at any rate, she herself did not now which child was which, and did not discover the little mark on the shoulder until after the babies got mixed up. Over and over again I have seen her cry and wring her hands because she could not say which was which. She acknowledged that she meant to make money out of it, and lamented that she had lost her chance because she could never herself tell which was which. Of this I am ready to take my oath in any court of justice, and if she says she knows now she is a liar. I have read this letter over to Troop-sergeant Matthews, and have in his presence sworn on a Bible to its truth. He will place his name by the side of mine as witness to that and to my signature. I remain, your obedient servant, John Humphreys, now known as John Bowen. The letter to your father is word for word the same as this. I have written it in duplicate in case you should be killed before I am."

BAD NEWS

"Well, that is plain enough," Easton said when Rupert had finished. "It is just what you said all along. The woman did not know which was her son, and you and Edgar stand in the same relation to Captain Clinton that you always did."

"Thank God for that!" Rupert said. "We want no change, and my father has said, talking it over with me again and again, he has two sons and loves us both equally, and it would be a deep grief to him now to know for certain that one of us is not his son. I will walk across to the hospital and ask how the sergeant is going on. I am strangely placed towards him now."

"It is a curious position," Easton said; "but in any case you do but stand towards him as a son would do towards a father who had given him up in infancy to be adopted by someone else."

Rupert did not reply, but, saying, "Wait here until I come back," walked over to the hospital lines. He returned in a few minutes.

"The doctor says he is sinking," he said gravely. "I shall go over there and remain until all is over."

"Will he be sensible at the last?" he asked the surgeon as he stood by the litter.

"Possibly," the surgeon said.

"I have a great interest in asking, doctor; I am most anxious to have a few words with him if possible before he dies."

"If you will call me if he opens his eyes," the surgeon said, "I will do what I can to rouse him. His pulse is getting weaker and weaker; I do not think the end is far off."

Half an hour later the dying man opened his eyes. Rupert beckoned to the surgeon, who came across at once and poured a few drops of spirits between his lips, and moistened his forehead with a sponge dipped in vinegar and water.

"Do you know me, Humphreys?" Rupert asked. "I am Rupert Clinton."

The dying man's face brightened. Then his lips moved. "Where is Smith? He left me to get help; he never returned."

"He is away now," Rupert said, anxious not to disturb the dying man. "When we got to you you were insensible, that was two days ago. Edgar is not in camp at present."

"There is a letter for you."

"Yes, it was found on you and I have read it, and I know how we stand towards each other, and that perhaps you are my father; here is the letter."

"I will swear to it; get a witness."

Rupert called the surgeon. "Doctor, the sergeant wishes you to hear him swear that this letter was written by him and that its contents are true."

"Bible," the sergeant said faintly. A Bible was brought and the dying man's hand placed upon it. "I swear," he said in a firmer voice than that in which he had hitherto spoken, "that this letter was written by me and that every word in it is true, and that neither I nor my wife, nor anyone save God, knows whether Trumpeter Smith or Lieutenant Clinton is my son."

The effort was made and he closed his eyes. Rupert took his hand and knelt beside him. Once again the sergeant opened his eyes and spoke. "Good lads both," he said; "better as things are."

A few minutes later he ceased to breathe. The surgeon had retired after hearing the sergeant's declaration. When he saw Rupert rise to his feet he came up to him. "I have just written down the words," he said, "and have signed my name as a witness to the fact that it was a declaration sworn on the Bible by one who knew that he was dying."

"Thank you," Rupert said; "it is a strange story, I will tell you it some day."

After leaving the hospital Rupert went to Easton, in whose judgment he had a great deal of confidence, and after stating what had occurred asked him if in his opinion he could take any steps to learn more about Edgar.

"I think, Clinton, that were I in your place I should go to the commanding officer and tell him you have learnt that the trumpeter who was with the wounded sergeant of the Heavies found in the grove, and who left him to fetch aid from our camp, was your brother. You can say that on account of a misunderstanding he left home and enlisted under a false name, and beg that a search be instituted for his body, and also that the politicals who are in communication with the natives should make inquiries whether any white captive had been brought into Metemmeh. If you like I will say as much to our colonel, and I am sure that he will give orders that whenever detachments go out strict search will be made of all ground over which they pass. I am afraid that if we do learn from the natives that he is at Metemmeh our chance of getting him back before we take the place is small, for even if the people into whose hands he fell were willing to part with him for a ransom, the fanatical dervishes would not allow it; however, there would be no harm in trying. I know that to-day half a dozen natives came in with some cattle and grain, and no doubt some others will be in to-morrow."

Rupert took the advice, and at once went over to the quarters of the officer in command and made the statement that Easton had suggested. The colonel expressed great regret, and promised that every step should be taken to ascertain the fate of his brother and to endeavour to recover him if alive. Another party was sent out in the morning, and a further and most minute search made of the ground between the camp and the grove where the sergeant had been found, and the 19th Hussars were directed while scouring the plain to search every depression and to examine every clump of bushes to discover if possible the body of a missing soldier or any signs of his clothes or accoutrements. The political officer closely questioned all the natives who came in, but these came from villages higher up the river, and no news was obtained of what was going on at Metemmeh. The next day there was a great outburst of firing in Metemmeh, guns and cannon being discharged incessantly for two or three hours. At first it was thought that some dispute might have arisen between the various tribes now occupying the place, but this idea was abandoned when it was seen that the cannon on the walls were discharged not into the town but towards the open country, and it was then concluded that some great festival of the Mahdi was being celebrated. The following day was Sunday. Just as the troops were being formed up for a church parade a staff-officer came up to Rupert and his fellow aide-de-camp as they were buckling on their swords.

"Is anything wrong, major?" Rupert asked, as he saw that the officer was much agitated.

"Yes, we have terrible news. A boat has just come down from Wilson with the news that he arrived too late; that Khartoum has fallen, and that Gordon is murdered."

An exclamation of horror broke from the two young officers.

"Do you think it is true, major?"

"I fear there is no doubt of it. The steamers got up to the town, and the Mahdi's flags were flying everywhere, and the vessels were peppered with shot from all the batteries. There is other bad news. Wilson's steamers both ran aground, and cannot be got off. Beresford is to go up and bring the party off, that is, if he can fight his way past the batteries. You see, that is what the firing in Metemmeh yesterday was about. No doubt a messenger had arrived from the Mahdi with the news of the fall of Khartoum. Don't say anything about it. Of course the news will not be kept from the officers, but it is to be kept from the men as far as possible."

Feeling almost stunned with the news, Rupert and his companions joined the rest of the staff and proceeded to the parade-ground. An hour after the service had concluded the terrible intelligence was known to all the officers. The feelings of grief, indignation, and rage were universal. All their efforts and suffering had been in vain, all the money spent upon the expedition entirely wasted. Gordon and his Egyptian garrison at Khartoum had perished, and it seemed not unnatural that the authorities at home should be blamed for the hesitation they had displayed in sending out the expedition to rescue the heroic defenders. Even at the last moment, they had countermanded their orders for the purchase of camels, which, had they been available, would have enabled General Stewart's desert column to march straight across, instead of being obliged to send the camels backwards and forwards; and in that case the steamers would have arrived in time to save Gordon, for it was but two days before they reached Khartoum that the town had fallen.

Never was an expedition so utterly useless, never did brave men who had fought their way through all difficulties find their efforts so completely vain!

The news could not long be kept from the men. The words of passionate grief and indignation that burst from their officers were soon caught up and carried through the camp, and the rank and file joined with their officers in a wholesale denunciation of those who were responsible for this disaster which had suddenly overtaken the expedition. The future was warmly debated among the officers. Some maintained that the expedition having come so far, the money having been laid out, it would be allowed to finish its work, to proceed to Khartoum, to recover the city, crush the Mahdi, and restore peace and order to the Soudan.

Others asserted that after this failure to carry out the main object of the expedition, the authorities at home might now hasten to withdraw an expedition which they had only with apparent reluctance sent out at all. Rupert feared that the latter alternative was the most probable, and with it his hopes of seeing his brother before long were dashed to the ground.

It was maddening to think that he was lying a helpless prisoner in the hands of the Arabs in the mud-walled town but two miles away; for it was now probable that the force would march back, and Edgar be left to his fate. Easton and Skinner in vain attempted to cheer him. They had, however, no arguments to combat his conviction that the expedition would be abandoned, and could only fall back upon their belief that sooner or later Edgar would manage to make his escape from the hands of the Arabs. To Rupert's distressed mind this was poor consolation.

THE DASH FOR KHARTOUM

Lord Charles Beresford at once started up the river in a small steamer to rescue Sir Charles Wilson's party. As it was known that there was a strong battery below the spot where the steamers had been lost, and that Beresford would have to run the gauntlet of this on his way up, much anxiety was felt as to the result, and a constant and eager watch was kept up for a sight of the steamer on her return. When the time came that she was expected to make her appearance, and no signs were visible of her, the anxiety heightened; and when another day passed, and still she did not return, grave fears were entertained for her safety. At last the welcome news came that smoke could be seen ascending from the river higher up, and loud cheers burst from the men when the flag at the masthead was seen above the trees.

There was a general rush down to the shore of all who were not on duty to hear the news when she arrived; and when she drew up near the bank and the first party landed, it was found that her escape had been a narrow one indeed. In passing the battery she had had a sharp engagement with the artillery there, and a shot had passed through her boiler and disabled her, and she had been obliged to anchor. Fortunately she was a little above the battery when this took place. The guns could not well be brought to bear upon her; and although assailed by a constant fire of musketry, her own guns, her Gardner, and the rifles of the troops had kept the enemy at a distance and prevented them from shifting any of their guns so as to play upon her, until an officer of the Naval Brigade, who was acting as her engineer, had managed to repair the boiler.

While the fight was going on Sir Charles Wilson's party were upon an island, near which the second steamer had sunk, two miles higher up the river, and were hotly engaged with a force upon the bank. They were able to see that the rescuing steamer was disabled, and at night had crossed to the river bank, and marching down it to a point opposite the steamer, opened communication with her by signals, and then did what they could to divert the attention of the enemy from her by opening fire upon the battery with one of their

A shot had been passed through her boiler.

guns, causing the enemy to turn two or three of his pieces of artillery against them. At nightfall they marched down the river to a point where the steamer had signalled she would pick them up. The steamer ran past the battery in the morning and fortunately escaped without serious injury, and then picking up the whole of Sir Charles Wilson's party came down the river without further molestation.

All this time no despatch of any kind had been received from Korti, although a small reinforcement consisting of a company of the Naval Brigade and half a battery of artillery had arrived, and the camels – or rather a portion of them, for nearly half had died upon the journey – had returned from Gakdul with a supply of stores. The days passed heavily until, on the 10th of February, General Buller and the 18th Royal Irish arrived; hopes were entertained, as they were seen approaching, that the appearance of the infantry signified that the expedition was still to continue to advance; but it was very soon known that the Royal Irish had merely arrived to cover the retreat. The next morning the whole of the wounded were sent off under a strong escort; then the work of destroying all the stores that had been brought up by the last convoy, except what were needed for the march down to Gakdul, was carried out, and two days later the forts that had been built with so much labour were evacuated, and the whole force set out upon their march down to Korti.

This time the journey was performed on foot. The camels of the three corps and of the vast baggage train with which they had started were bleaching on the desert, and scarce enough animals remained for the service of carrying down the sick and wounded. Rupert Clinton was among them. His strength had failed rapidly, and a sort of low fever had seized him, and he had for some days before the convoy started been lying prostrate in the hospital lines. Skinner was, at his own request, carried by the same camel that conveyed Rupert, the beds being swung one on each side of it. He had protested that he was perfectly capable of marching, but the doctors would not hear of it; and when he found that he could accompany Rupert he was glad that they decided against him, as he was able to look after his friend and to keep up his spirits to a certain extent by his talk.

Several of the wounded died on their way down, among them Sir Herbert Stewart, who had survived his wound a much longer time than the surgeons had at first believed possible. One piece of news that they had learned the day before they left the neighbourhood of Metemmeh had some slight effect in cheering Rupert, a native of that town having reported that a white prisoner had been brought in on the day after the battle near the town; he had been captured by some men of the Jahrin tribe and not by the regular troops of the Mahdi; three or four days later there had been a quarrel, the Mahdi's people wanting to take the prisoner and send him up to Khartoum; his captors had objected, claiming him as their private property; but as they were only a small party he would doubtless have been taken from them by force had they not, during the night, stolen out of the town with him, taken a boat, crossed the river, and made off.

Thus there was evidence that Edgar was still alive, and Skinner endeavoured to impress upon Rupert that in every respect the intelligence was favourable.

"You see, Clinton, if your brother had been sent up to the Mahdi, the villain would have endeavoured to force him to change his religion. Edgar would never have done that, and in that case it is pretty certain that they would have chopped his head off. As it is, the chief of these Arabs who took him evidently means to keep him as a slave for himself. Of course it is not pleasant to be a slave, but it is better than having the choice between worshipping a greasy Arab or having your head chopped off, and it will give him time to learn the language, to make his plans of escape, and to carry them out."

Rupert was too weak and ill to fully enter into the question, but he did see that Edgar's position was certainly better under an Arab master than it would have been had he been sent up to Khartoum, and the knowledge that he was alive and was in no immediate danger of his life did much to revive him, and enable him to bear the weary journey down to Korti better than he would otherwise have done. Once there the comparatively cool air of the hospital tents, the quiet, and the supply of every luxury soon had their effect, and in the course of three weeks he was up and about, though it would be some time before he would be fit for active duty. It was still altogether uncertain what decision would be finally arrived at at home respecting the expedition, but for the present the troops were stationed at various points on the river as far down as Dongola, and it was hoped that later on the advance against Khartoum would be recommenced.

Rupert, as soon as he was able to get about, had a long conversation with Major Kitchener, the political officer who was in charge of all communications with the natives. He related to him the circumstances of his brother's capture, and how he was a prisoner of some men belonging to the Jahrin tribe. Major Kitchener promised that his spies should make every inquiry, and held out hopes that by the offer of a large reward his captors might be induced to bring him down to the camp.

The time passed very slowly, the heat increased in intensity and became intolerable from nine in the morning until five in the afternoon. Between those hours there was nothing to do but to lie still in the mud huts that had now been erected, for it would have been well-nigh impossible to exist in the little tents that the troops had brought with them.

In the early morning and in the evening every one bathed in the Nile. Then the officers, each of whom had picked up some sort of pony from the natives, went for a ride, chased the wild dogs, or wandered gun on shoulder in search of such game as was to be found. After sunset was the only really pleasant time of day, and when the moon was up both officers and men enjoyed themselves; but on dark nights neither walking nor riding could be indulged in, so broken was the ground, and there was nothing to do but to talk, sing, and vary the tedium by a game of cards.

BAD NEWS

The Guards' Camel Regiment were posted close to Dongola. Rupert, who since the death of General Stewart had no longer any staff duties, was attached to the transport corps and spent a considerable portion of his time going up or down the river in boats. He did not, therefore, see much of his friends, although he never passed Dongola without managing to make it a halting-place so as to have a few hours' talk with them.

"You have thoroughly picked up again, Clinton," Skinner said as he arrived upon one of these visits. "No one would know you to be the same fellow who was brought down to Korti with me on that wretched camel's back. I think you are very lucky to have got put on to that transport work."

"So do I, Skinner; it gives me little time to sit and think, and though it is terrifically hot in the middle of the day I can always manage to get up some sort of shelter with straw or matting of some kind, and at any rate it is cooler there than on shore."

"I wish they would give me a turn at it," Skinner said. "I cannot offer to take an oar, for although my arm is going on very well the doctor says it may be months before I can venture to use it in anything like hard work. We get up jolly horse-races here once a week in the evening. The natives enter their animals. Of course we have no chance with them on our little tats, but we sometimes manage to requisition two or three horses from the Hussars. I dare not ride myself, for though the horses and ponies are both very sure-footed these natives ride in the wildest way and one might get cannoned over. Still it is an amusement to look on and make small bets and watch the natives; crowds of them come out to see it, and they get tremendously excited over it. I wish we could get up a good football match, the Guards against Dongola; it would be awful fun. As far as running goes we should not be in it, and if one of them got the ball he would carry it right through us up to the goal, for they are as active and slippery as eels. Of course when it came to a good close fight we should have it our own way."

THE DASH FOR KHARTOUM

"Have you managed to get up football on board ship, Skinner?" Easton, who was stretched at full length on the ground, asked lazily.

"Not yet," Skinner laughed. "If we played at all we should have to use a cannon-ball, so that it should not be kicked over the sides; but then, unless we got iron shoes made for the purpose, we should all be laid up. But I have got a football in my cabin, and once or twice we have had games at Suakim, and very good fun it was too."

"No news, I suppose, Clinton?" Easton asked, sitting up.

Rupert shook his head. "Not a word. We hear very little of what is going on above us, and the natives who do come in lie so, there's no believing a word they say. I have been thinking that if one could trust them I would pay one of the sheiks to dress me up and stain my skin and take me with him on a wandering expedition to Khartoum and over the country on both sides of the river."

"It would be madness," Easton said. "Of course if you could talk their language perfectly it might be possible to manage it, for I suppose that with dye and false hair one might be got up to pass as far as appearances go, but not being able to speak the language would be fatal."

"Of course I should have to go as a dumb man. I was asking the surgeon the other day if there would be any great difficulty in cutting a fellow's tongue out."

"In doing what?" Easton and Skinner asked in astonishment.

"Cutting my tongue out," Rupert said seriously. "You see, if my tongue was cut out anyone could see at once that I was dumb. Of course it wouldn't be pleasant, but I believe it would be possible to get to talk after some time. If there were no other objections I should not hesitate for a moment; but unfortunately I should have to pass for deaf as well as dumb, for of course I should not understand anything that was said to me. I have been thinking it over in every light, and really the only great objection I see to the plan is that though one might depend upon the chief's being faithful if he were well paid, it would be very doubtful as to his followers."

"And are you really serious in saying that you would have your tongue cut out, Clinton?"

"Of course I am serious," Rupert said, almost angrily. "What is one's tongue in comparison to one's brother? What do you think, Easton? Do you think the idea is at all feasible? I may say that for the last two months I have been working almost night and day at the language. I engaged a fellow the day I came out of hospital. He was working for one of those Greek shopkeepers. He is a native of Dongola, but has been down in Egypt and picked up a certain amount of French. He goes about with me in the boat, and we talk all day and as long as I can keep him awake at night. Of course I don't think for a moment that I could learn enough to pass as a native for at least a couple of years; but it would be of no use my going up with a party of Arabs if I could not make out what they say and learn what news they pick up, and make arrangements to get Edgar away if we find him."

"It would be a fearfully risky business, Clinton," Easton said gravely. "The betting would be tremendously against you, but I don't say that it is absolutely impossible that you should be successful. I don't think it would be necessary to carry out the idea of having your tongue cut out. As you say, a tongue is nothing in comparison to a brother, and if I thought that the loss of your tongue would ensure your success I should say nothing against it, it would be a matter for you and you only to decide; but I should think it might be managed in some other way. The fellow you would be with would naturally avoid all large encampments, and would send you off to look after camels or something if other natives arrived at the same encampment."

"You don't really mean, Easton," Skinner said, "that you seriously think that it might be done; that is, that the betting is not more than ten to one against it?"

"No; I don't think the odds are longer than that, Skinner. You know Burton went to Mecca in disguise, and I believe that it has been done since by somebody else. I grant that Burton could talk the language well, and that having to play the part of a dumb man adds to the risk. Still, I do not think, as I said, that the chances are more than ten to one against it."

"Well, I shall think it over," Rupert said; "but I must be going now, for the boat will be loaded by this time."

"Why did you encourage Clinton in this mad idea, Easton?" Skinner asked after Rupert had left them.

"I don't think I did encourage him. I told him the betting was ten to one against his coming back alive, and I don't call that encouraging; but I believe it is possible, and I am not at all sure that if I were in his place, and the idea had occurred to me, that I shouldn't try to carry it out."

CHAPTER XVI
IN DISGUISE

A S long as there was a chance that the expedition might
again advance Rupert did nothing farther, and indeed
was unable to come to any decision as to his course.
He had long since received an answer from Captain Clinton
to his letter written as soon as he was well enough to sit up
after arriving at Korti, with the news that Edgar had been
present with the expedition, and was now a prisoner in the
hands of the Arabs.

Captain Clinton wrote in great distress himself, and said
that his wife was completely prostrated with the news. He
said: "I know I need not urge you, Rupert, to use every
means to obtain some news of Edgar. Draw upon me for
any amount, however large, that may be necessary for bribing
natives to find, and if possible rescue, him. I fear that the
latter is hopeless. Still, if you see even the most remote
chance of it, let no question of expense stand in the way."

But even the promises of rewards that seemed to them
to be fabulous failed in eliciting from the spies any
information as to Edgar's whereabouts. He certainly was
neither at Berber nor at Khartoum, nor had the people he
was with returned to Metemmeh; but beyond this negative
information Rupert could learn nothing. He continued to
work assiduously with his interpreter, and by the middle of
May he had, after three months' work, made such progress
that he was able to converse in simple phrases and to
understand what was being said by the natives around him.

THE DASH FOR KHARTOUM

In the third week in May, on his arrival at Korti, he learned that orders had that day been received that the whole force was to at once retire, that even Dongola was to be abandoned, and that Wady Halfa was to be the highest point on the river occupied. That evening he went up to General Buller's tent. The general was still at mess, and Rupert waited outside his tent until he returned. He had several times spoken to the general on matters of duty.

"Who is that?" General Buller asked as he saw a figure standing in front of his tent.

"Clinton, sir. I am particularly anxious to speak to you if you can spare me a short time."

"Come in," the general said. "What can I do for you? Take a seat there."

"You have perhaps heard, sir, that I made the discovery at Metemmeh that a brother of mine, who had two years and a half ago run away from school and enlisted, was the trumpeter of the Heavies who was carried off by the Arabs close to Metemmeh."

"Yes, I heard that, Clinton, and was very sorry for you. I cannot imagine a more distressing affair."

"It was really no fault of his that he ran away, general; he was under a misconception altogether, and neither my father nor mother blamed him in the slightest. I only say that to show that he did not run away from wildness. No one could have been steadier than he was. It was a frightful mistake connected with his birth which I need not trouble you about. We were greatly attached to each other, and my father and mother are completely broken down at the thought of his being a slave for life in the hands of the Arabs. Now, sir, for the last three months I have been working almost day and night at the language, and can get on fairly in it."

"Yes?" General Buller put in, wondering what was coming next.

"I have come to ask you if you would be good enough to ask Lord Wolseley to let me have six months' leave. My intention is to disguise myself, and to go up the country with one or two friendly natives. I should pass as being dumb; as although I can make myself understood in simple matters I should, of course, be detected were any native to enter into a long conversation with me. I have seen Major Kitchener to-day, and he says that he has no doubt he could arrange with one of the sheiks for me to go with him, and to travel about the country with him until we found my brother. My father has authorized me to spend any money that may be required, and I could pay high enough to make it well worth the while of any of these natives to be faithful. I do not see any reasons why I should not succeed. I have been speaking to one of the surgeons, and he says that if at any time it is suspected that I am not really dumb, I can in half a minute burn my tongue so with caustic that if I open my mouth anyone would think I have got some disease of the tongue which prevents my speaking. As to the disguise, I got Captain Hunter, who sketches capitally, to make sketches of the heads of some of these Arabs. I sent these down to a man at Cairo, and I have got up from him a wig that will, I think, deceive anyone."

"It is a tremendous risk, Clinton," General Buller said when he concluded; "a tremendous risk, and I don't know that Lord Wolseley would consider himself justified in allowing you to attempt it. The idea does you honour, but upon my word I do not know what to say to it. It seems a mad scheme, and yet I cannot say that it might not succeed. You seem to have worked it all out in your own mind. To carry it through will require not only pluck but unfailing watchfulness and presence of mind. A simple word or a gesture might betray you."

"I have thought of all that, sir; but I don't see any reason why it shouldn't be done. I am quite sure, general, that if you had a brother a slave among the Arabs you would not hesitate a moment about attempting it."

General Buller did not reply, but rising put on his helmet. "I will go to the chief and ask him," he said; "but I don't think he will feel authorized in letting you go."

THE DASH FOR KHARTOUM

"I don't ask him to authorize it officially, sir. I only ask for six months' leave of absence, or even for a month's leave of absence. At the end of that time of course my name would be removed from the Army List, but I think, if I ever return, I should be reinstated, or if not, I might get a fresh commission granted me."

"Oh, that would be all right! the general would see to that. Wait here until I come back."

In a quarter of an hour General Buller returned.

"Come with me to the chief's tent," he said. "I think that if you can convince him that you have thought the matter out thoroughly, and are prepared at all points, he will give you three months' leave, and will get it renewed as long as there is a chance of your turning up alive."

Rupert was most kindly received by Lord Wolseley, who asked him many questions as to his plans. After he had again explained them Rupert said: "Major Kitchener has kindly promised that if you give me leave he will buy for me two of the fast camels. He said there was a party came in yesterday with two exceptionally good ones, and that no doubt they would sell if a sufficient price were offered. Of course I should not think of riding on either of these unless I had to run for my life, or until I found my brother, for they would at once attract attention. The natives could ride on them, and I should have an ordinary camel until the time came to use the fleet ones. I have a letter from my father authorizing me to draw to any extent; therefore no question of money would interfere with my carrying out the plan thoroughly."

"I do not know what your father would say to me on my return to England should you never get back, Clinton."

"I am sure that if my father were here he would approve, sir. Of course I shall write him a long letter explaining the whole circumstances, and I am as sure as if he stood here that he would say that I was perfectly right in making an effort to rescue Edgar. I should never be happy again were I to turn my face down the river now and leave him to slavery for life among the Arabs."

IN DISGUISE

"Well, I will strain a point and let you go," Lord Wolseley said. "I don't know whether I am right in doing so, but I cannot resist your desire to carry out your scheme for your brother's rescue. It is a noble attempt, Clinton, and I honour you for undertaking it. When your preparations are complete let me see you again. Consider yourself relieved of all duty at once."

Thanking Lord Wolseley and General Buller for their kindness Rupert left the tent and returned to his quarters. The next morning he went the first thing to Major Kitchener's camp and told him that the question of his leave was settled, and that he should start as soon as the camels were procured and an arrangement could be made with one of the sheiks.

"Very well, Clinton, I will manage that for you. I expect a sheik down in three days who has worked faithfully with us since the beginning of the campaign. He is the man I had in my eye, he has made journeys to Wady Halfa, and to points on the Red Sea, and will know that our promises as to payments will be kept, and that whatever sum is agreed upon would be handed him over at any place to which he may take you. In order to prevent any difficulty on that score, I will, before you start, give you letters to merchants at Wady Halfa and all the ports requesting them to pay the sum we may agree upon, upon the presentation of my letter with your signature attached. I put it in that way because it is possible that you may have to make your way alone into Abyssinia, and in that case if you are satisfied with your guide you will put your name to the letter and he may then obtain the money at whichever port he may go to. All this of course I will explain to him. I will get the two camels this morning. They are exceptionally good beasts, and the owner will want a very long price for them. Camels like these are very rare, but they may be the means of saving your life."

"I will pay whatever he wants me to, sir; I quite see the importance of getting them. I am off duty now, and as the sheik is not to arrive for three days I will go down to Dongola. There is one of the transport boats starting in half an hour.

I shall want to lay in a stock of dye. Fortunately, the exact colour is not material, for the natives are any shade between yellow and black."

When Skinner and Easton came in from an evening ride they got off their ponies, and Skinner entered his hut. He was astonished at seeing a native calmly sitting there with the usual wild tangled hair and a dirty cotton cloth wrapped round him. For a moment Skinner stood astonished.

"Well, this is cheek!" he exclaimed. "Easton, look here; here is a beast of a native squatting in my hut. Sentry, what the deuce do you mean by letting a nigger come into my hut? Now, then, who are you? What do you want? What do you mean by it? Out you go sharp or I will break your neck!"

The two young officers, for Easton had joined his friend, stood astounded when the native broke into a yell of laughter.

"He is mad, Easton; he is a mad nigger who has escaped from a lunatic asylum!" Skinner exclaimed. "Don't go near him; perhaps he bites, and you might get hydrophobia. How is this, sentry?" he asked, turning to the soldier, who had come up to the door. "How is it you let this mad nigger come in here?"

"I did not see him come in, sir," the sentry said; "he must have slipped in when my back was turned. I saw an officer come in half an hour ago, but I haven't seen anyone else."

"Well, move him out, sentry; prod him up with your bayonet if he won't go."

The sentry was about to enter the tent when Rupert gasped, "That is enough, Skinner; order him out. You will kill me with laughing."

"Clinton!" The word broke from the lips of Easton and Skinner simultaneously, while the sentry almost dropped his rifle in surprise at hearing his officer thus addressed in pure English by the native.

IN DISGUISE

"It is all right, sentry, you can go," Easton said, recovering himself first from his astonishment; and then saying as soon as they were alone: "What on earth does this masquerade mean, Clinton? Have you gone out of your mind?"

"Then you think I shall do, Easton?"

"Do!" Easton repeated, the truth dawning upon him. "You don't mean to say that you are going to carry out that scheme you talked about a month since?"

"Indeed I do, Easton. I have obtained the chief's permission. Major Kitchener is making the arrangements for me, and I hope in another three days to be out on the desert again. At any rate you will allow that as far as appearances go I can pass fairly as a native."

Skinner had not yet spoken. He now walked round and round Rupert two or three times, and at last gave vent to his feelings: "Well, I am jiggered! There is no doubt about your disguise, Clinton, at least if you are Clinton and not a nigger who has stolen his voice. Did you ever see such a head of hair, Easton?"

"Never mind that," Easton said impatiently; "don't you understand, man, that Clinton is going away among those Arabs to search for his brother?"

"No, I did not understand; in fact I did not hear a word that was said. I was too much stunned to do anything but stare. And you are really going, Clinton, old fellow?"

"Yes, I am off to-morrow at daybreak for Korti. There is a good strong breeze blowing, and I shall go up as quickly as I came down. There was a delay of three or four days before we could get hold of the man I am to go with, if he will take me, so I ran down here partly to get some dyes for my skin in the bazaar here, but principally to say good-bye to you both. My wig, that so astonishes you, Skinner, I had made at Cairo and sent up."

"Well, there is no fear, Clinton, of anyone recognizing you as an Englishman. You may ride in the middle of them from here to Khartoum, and they would never suspect you as far as looks go. You have abandoned that idea about your tongue, I hope?"

"Yes. I have got a bottle of caustic from one of the surgeons. He put me up to it. He says if I see that I am suspected, if I slip aside and rub one of these little sticks of caustic over my tongue it will make such a sight of it that I have only to open my mouth and let them look at it, and they will believe readily enough that I have got some frightful disease in my tongue and cannot use it. In case of necessity I can mumble out a few words, and the state of my mouth will quite account for any difficulty they may have in understanding me."

"Will that stuff you have got on your skin wash off?" Easton asked.

"Yes, this will with a little difficulty; but I have got some other stuff that my interpreter tells me will only want renewing once a week or ten days."

"Then for goodness' sake set to and get it off, Clinton, and put on your own clothes and let us see you again as you are. I don't seem to be able to talk to you naturally in that disguise, and it will be a long time before we get another talk together."

Rupert at once set to work with soap, water, and a nailbrush, and in a quarter of an hour got his face and hands tolerably white. Then he put on his uniform.

"Now you are yourself again, Clinton. Sit down and tell us all about it. What are your plans?"

Rupert told him the arrangements that Major Kitchener was making for him, and both his companions greatly approved of the purchase of the fast camels. "That is a capital idea, and if you can get a good start with them you may laugh at Arabs who are mounted on ordinary camels or on foot; but you must mind that there are no fellows with horses about when you make your bolt. You see, all these fellows who led the attacks were mounted, and I suppose you will find that a few of the principal men in every large village have horses. Now a horse will go faster than the fastest camel for a bit, although the camel will beat him in a long-distance race. What are you going to do about arms?"

"I cannot take any arms, Easton; they would betray me at once."

"You cannot show any, I grant, but there is no reason in the world why you shouldn't take a brace of revolvers. They could be stowed away easily enough, with a couple of boxes of cartridges, somewhere in the saddle. There is room to hide anything in one of these great clumsy contrivances. Of course pistols would be of no use to you if you are discovered in the middle of a tribe or a big town; but if you find your brother, and you make a bolt for it together on these camels and are pursued, you could make a pretty good fight against half a dozen mounted men, and the betting is against more than that getting together, if you had a revolver apiece. I should advise you most strongly to take them."

"I think you are right, Easton: I will certainly do so."

"Have you got a brace?"

"No, I have only one."

"Then you shall have mine, old fellow. What calibre is yours?"

"·45."

"Ah! that is the same as mine. I have got a couple of boxes of cartridges, and as they are done up in India-rubber they are sure to be all right. By the way, is it true that we are all going down? There was a rumour last night that orders had come."

"Yes, we are to retire to Wady Halfa."

"What! And abandon Dongola?"

Rupert nodded.

"Then I call it a beastly shame. More than that, I call it a downright dishonourable action!" Easton said hotly. "Here we are going to abandon a town of some twenty thousand inhabitants to these fanatics. Not only that, but to give up to their vengeance all the tribes between Wady Halfa and Metemmeh who have trusted in our promises, have thrown in their lot with us, and have for the last four months been doing all our transport. Our fathers used to be proud to call themselves Englishmen, but, by Jove, there is very little reason for us to be. That Boer business was shameful and humiliating enough, but this is worse still. I don't say that we are bound to go on to Khartoum, although it would be the best and cheapest and most satisfactory mode in every way of settling this Mahdi and ensuring order in the Soudan; but I do think that we are bound to hold the river from Korti downwards to protect the tribes that have been friendly to us, and to save this town from ruin and desolation. Not only this town, but all the peacefull villages down the river. Besides, so long as we are here the Arabs will see that the Mahdi is not all-powerful, and may sooner or later rise against his tyranny. Well, I never thought this campaign was going to end in the disgraceful abandonment of the Nile Valley from Korti to Wady Halfa. However," he went on, checking himself suddenly, "it is of no use talking of that now; we have got to think about your expedition, which to us three is a far more important business. How does your Arabic get on?"

"Fairly well. I don't say that I can talk a great deal, but as I have learnt it by ear I speak with a fair accent, at least so Ibrahim says. I have taken particular pains with what you may call salutations, such as one man gives another as they pass each other on a journey, or what one says on entering a house or a village. I can ask for food all right, return thanks for hospitality, ask the way, and all that sort of thing; and Ibrahim said that in all these things I could pass very well as a native, especially as there are slight distinctions and differences between the language of the various tribes. They are a very mixed people of Arab, Egyptian, and Negro blood. So that as far as it goes my language will pass, and of course every day I travel I shall improve. I intend, as I have said, to pretend to be dumb whenever we come across strong parties of strangers, and my sheik will shield me as much as possible by sending me out to look after the camels and to gather wood and to fetch water, or on other business, whenever we are with strangers. I really think, Easton, I have a very fair chance of getting through it without being found out. Major Kitchener tells me that the sheik only has two or three of his tribesmen with him, and that he has no doubt picked men he can trust to hold their tongues, otherwise he would get into a mess when he went back again among his people. Of course the men will be promised a reward also if I get safely through. The trouble on my mind is more the difficulty there will be in finding Edgar and getting him off than about myself. In the first place there is no saying as to the direction in which the men who have got him have gone. They have probably gone to some out-of-the-way place, so as to be out of the way of the Mahdi's people.

"Ibrahim tells me that there are no people more pig-headed than these Arabs, and if they once make up their mind to a thing nothing will turn them. That is all the better, as far as the risk of Edgar falling into the hands of the Mahdi is concerned, only it makes it all the more difficult to find him. There is no saying where he may have moved to; he may have gone far south of Khartoum, he may have pushed away near the borders of Abyssinia, he may be within a few miles of Suakim, he may be in the desert we crossed. I don't disguise from myself that it is likely to be a long search; but that is nothing if I am but successful at last. Of course the great thing will be to endeavour to pick up a clue near Metemmeh.

"The tribe is a very scattered one, and is to be found dispersed among other tribes all the way from Berber to Khartoum on the eastern side of the river, and I hear that there is a branch of it who live in the desert to the west. Well, it is likely that Edgar's master will have stopped in some of these villages among his own people, if only for a few hours, and it is from them I hope to get some clue as to the general direction at least in which they were travelling. Unless they disguised Edgar, and wrapped him up as a woman, or something of that sort, the fact of a white prisoner passing through is certain to have caused talk. However, it is impossible to say where or how I may find a clue.

"At any rate I shall stick to it. I shall tell my father, that as it may take me a year to find Edgar he need not even begin to feel anxious until the end of that time, and that as I shall be continually improving in my knowledge of the language, the risk of detection will become less and less every month, and that I anticipate no difficulty whatever when the time comes in passing down to Suakim or Massowah, or should any difficulty arise in that direction, in either working down to Wady Halfa or through Abyssinia."

They sat and talked until far into the night, and then lay down for a few hours' sleep, and at daybreak Rupert said good-bye to his friends and took his place in the boat, which, spreading its sails, rapidly made its way up stream. The two friends stood for a long time looking after it.

"By Jove, Clinton has turned out a fine fellow," Skinner said; "a grand fellow! I hardly thought he had it in him. Of course I knew he was plucky, and all that sort of thing; but this is a tremendous undertaking."

"It is," Easton said. "Of course now the die is cast I would not say a word last night to discourage him; but the risk is tremendous. However he is going about it in the right spirit, and somehow I feel almost confident that he will pull through it, and that we shall shake his hand in England again. May God protect him on his journey!"

Skinner responded with an earnest Amen, and then they walked slowly back to the camp.

As soon as he arrived at Korti Rupert made his way to Major Kitchener's, and was greeted with a cheery welcome by that officer.

"Things are going well, Clinton. I have bought the two riding camels. I was a whole day haggling over the price with the chief. I had to pay a stiff price after all, but that I expected. But it won't come quite so heavy, because he wanted to take it out in goods, and as we don't mean to take all the things back to the coast again, I got an order from the chief for our quarter-master's department to sell me a lot of rugs, cooking pots, and tin goods, and also some powder and ball and a dozen muskets. As I got them cheap the camels won't cost you more than half what they would if you had had to pay in silver for them. In the next place, the sheik arrived yesterday afternoon and I had a long talk with him. He is willing enough to undertake the business and to wander about with you for as many months as you may choose, and to assist you in getting off your brother if you find him, if he thinks that you can disguise yourself well enough to pass as a native, but of that he is to be the judge. He won't take you at any price unless you satisfy him in that respect."

"I think I can do that, major," Rupert said. "I will go back to my tent and dress now. I took in my two friends of the Guards, and I think I can pass inspection even by a native."

In half an hour Rupert returned in his native get-up, carrying as usual a spear and a sword and two or three knives stuck into his girdle. Major Kitchener was inside his tent, and Rupert squatted down outside and awaited his coming out. When the major issued from his tent his eye fell upon him.

"Hullo!" he said in Arabic, "what do you want? Where do you come from?"

"I am my lord's servant," Rupert replied in the same language.

"Yes, that is all very well; but I suppose you want something."

"I am ready to go for my lord to Khartoum, and to bring him news."

Major Kitchener shook his head. "I don't want to send anyone up at present," he said; "we know all about it."

"Then you think I shall do, major?" Rupert said in English.

"Bless me!" the officer exclaimed. "Is it you, Clinton? I did not suspect you for a moment. You will do, lad, you will do. The sheik himself won't know you to be white with that wonderful head of hair of yours. It is a splendid imitation.

One would think you had scalped one of these natives and put his hair on. Come along with me. You will see how we shall take in the sheik."

He went across to a small group of camels by the side of which a sheik and two natives were seated talking and gesticulating violently. The sheik rose to his feet as they came up and began to talk volubly; he was evidently in a rage with his followers, for he pointed to them with open hand and was complaining of their conduct. Presently they began to interject angry denials, and then sprang to their feet and excitedly poured out their view of the question. Rupert could not catch a word, and had no idea of the subject of the dispute, although he saw that Major Kitchener was listening with some amusement. The combat rose higher and higher. At last, with a sudden gesture, the sheik, who had looked furtively at this disguised stranger several times, seized the two men by the arm and whirled them round until they faced Rupert, who was leaning on his spear. "There!" he shouted. "Where are the eyes you boast of? You say that anyone could in a moment detect a white man through his disguises. What! are you then blind or idiots that you do not see that this is a white man standing here?" The Arabs stood motionless, wondering and incredulous, while the chief broke into a triumphant laugh at his own superior sagacity.

"Is he white?" one of the men asked, turning to the major.

"Yes, this is the officer who is to travel with you."

"What is it all about, major?" Rupert asked as the three natives proceeded to walk round him and examine him from every point.

"The sheik was declaiming against the obstinacy of his followers. He really wants to take you, and was in vain trying to persuade his men that such clever people as the whites could disguise themselves so that they would not be known. The two men protested against the risk, and maintained that anyone could tell a white from a native a mile off. Really the sheik did not suspect you in the slightest, but I thought it was well to let him have a triumph over his followers, and so as he was going on I gave a little nod towards you and he caught it at once; but I could see at first he thought he was mistaken, and while the others were having their say I nodded to him and said, 'Yes, it is he.' "

With many interjections: "It is wonderful! Can such things be! Eyes have never seen it!" the three Arabs had continued to gaze at Rupert while the officer was speaking.

"It is a white man," the sheik said at last; "there is more flesh on his limbs than on those of a young Arab. But who ever saw such hair on a white man; by what miracle did it grow thus?"

"It is what is called a wig," Major Kitchener explained. "It was made for him at Cairo; he can take it off and on. Take it off, Clinton."

Rupert pulled off his wig and stood before them in his closely-cropped head. The natives made a step or two backwards in astonishment and awe.

"The whites are great people," the sheik said; "they can turn a white man into a black. They can put an Arab's hair on to their heads, so that they can take it on and off like a turban. It is well, my lord; we will take the young officer with us; but he must remember that though when he is standing still he may look so like an Arab that no eyes could detect him, it is the movements and the ways and the tongue, and not the skin and hair only, that make a man. He will have to keep a watch always over himself and be ever careful and prudent, for were he discovered it would cost him his life, and would go hard with us also for bringing him as a spy into the land."

"We know that, sheik," Major Kitchener said; "and all that has, you know, been considered in the handsome terms we have offered you."

"If he spoke the language as you do, my lord, it would be easy."

"It will not be long before he does so, sheik; you will see that he speaks with a fair accent already. Just suppose that you are the sheik of a village and that he has come in to get something. Now, Clinton, begin with the usual Arabic salutations."

Rupert at once addressed the sheik, and the usual ceremonial salutations which precede all conversation were exchanged between them.

"I have wandered from my camp," Rupert went on; "my camel has travelled far, and I am hungry and athirst. I would buy meal and dates for my further journey, and a feed of grain for the camel," he continued, with a dozen other sentences that he had committed to heart and gone over scores of times with Ibrahim.

The sheik nodded his approval. "It is good," he said. "For a time, as you have said, he will not talk, but will go as an afflicted one who has lost his speech; but even now he could pass through a village with us without exciting suspicion. We will take him. What say you?" he asked his followers, who replied together, "We will take him."

Then there was a long discussion in Arabic between the sheik and Major Kitchener. "He has seen your camels," the major said, turning to Rupert, "and wants them thrown into the bargain when it is all over. I have told him that this is quite out of the question. The terms I have already agreed upon are ten times as high as he could earn with his camels in any other way; besides it is, as I pointed out to him, probable that you and your brother may have to ride away alone on the camels. But I have said that if you should arrive together at any port or place where the sum agreed upon can be paid to him, and if you are thoroughly satisfied with the way in which you have been treated, you will let him have them, deducting from the amount to be paid half the sum that you have just given for them, and as you paid for them in goods that will really be about the price they cost you."

IN DISGUISE

"That will be an excellent arrangement," Rupert said; "the hope of getting the camels at the end of the journey will certainly be a great inducement to him to be faithful. I know that the Arabs think as much of these fast camels as we do of race-horses at home. And will you tell him too that if we have to leave him and take the camels, I will see that they are left, to be given up to him on his arrival, at some place he may name. I think that it would be as well that he should feel that he will get the camels anyhow in addition to payment; otherwise the temptation to seize them might be so great that he might get rid of me on the first opportunity."

"Yes, that would be as well, Clinton. A pair of such camels as these are certainly a great temptation to an Arab. I have great faith in this man, for he was very highly recommended to me by some Egyptian merchants at Cairo who had travelled with him right down to the great lakes. At the same time it is always better to throw no temptation in people's way. He wanted a portion of the money down, but I would not hear of this. I said that he knew he was certain of it when the duty was performed, and that therefore there was no reason whatever for his making any demand beforehand, except that he should have a sum just sufficient and no more to enable him to pay any expenses he might incur for his own food and that of the camels. That is little enough: dates, meal, a kid sometimes for the men, and an occasional feed of grain for the camels, who as a rule pick up their own living except when engaged on hard work."

What Rupert had said was explained to the sheik, who, although he showed little outward satisfaction, was evidently pleased with the prospect of some day owning the two fast camels. There was now a long discussion between Major Kitchener and the sheik as to the best route to be pursued, and the probabilities as to the course that Edgar's captors had followed, and then the conference broke up, the sheik saying his camels required another two days' rest, and that on the third day at daybreak he should be ready to start. At the last moment Rupert suggested, that as the Arabs had, they said, two spare camels before, and would now have three, he should present them with a sufficient load of rugs, powder, and other things they valued to form light loads for the three spare animals. There would be nothing suspicious in their possessing such goods, as many of the loaded camels had, especially on the night march to Metemmeh, strayed away or fallen, and their loads had been plundered by the Arabs. For twenty pounds he could get from the quarter-master's stores plenty of goods for the purpose, and as these could be used for barter it would obviate the necessity of carrying silver. The offer added to the good temper of the sheik and his followers, and as Rupert walked back to Major Kitchener's tent with him the latter said, "I think, Clinton, you have won your fellows fairly over. I could see by the way they discussed the routes to be followed, that they have got thoroughly interested in the matter themselves, and will throw themselves heartily into it. I really think you have a very fair chance of getting through this business safely. I did not think so when you first proposed it to me, but the difficulties seem to have disappeared as we have gone on; and now that I have seen you in disguise, I think that, unless from some unforeseen accident, or some forgetfulness on your own part, there is no reason why you should not travel with those Arabs from end to end of the Soudan."

CHAPTER XVII
A RUNAWAY SLAVE

NEGROES have an immense respect for strength, and the, to him, astounding manner in which Edgar had struck down his comrade as by a stroke of lightning completely cowed the other negro, and he resumed his work with Edgar with an air of timidity; but he soon recovered from this, and before long was laughing and joking at the speed with which the bucket was being raised and emptied, the water pouring out at a rate vastly exceeding that usually achieved by their leisurely movements. Indeed, he entered heartily into the fun of the thing, repeating Edgar's English words of "Now, then, up she goes!" "Over with her!" and working until the perspiration rolled down his black skin as fast as it did down Edgar's white one. The other man had thrown himself down by the trough, and lay there bathing his face with water till at an angry shout from the sheik he rose to his feet and joined in the work sullenly and silently.

"There is no great harm done," Edgar said cheeringly to him. "You had no beauty to spoil, so you will be none the worse that way. You have had a lesson, and it will do you good. I daresay we shall get on very well together in future." Hamish gave an angry growl; he was in no mood for a reconciliation, and continued to work silently until the sun went down. As soon as it sunk below the sand-hills the negroes ceased work, and signified to Edgar that their time of labour was over.

The sheik had several times looked out from his tent to see how the work was getting on. "My capture was indeed a fortunate one, Amina," he said. "Never did I see men work as they have done this afternoon. Three times the usual amount of water has been poured over the field; truly he is a treasure."

When the slaves had ceased work they went to the lower end of the valley, where, on some ground covered with coarse grass, separated from the growing crops by a thorn hedge, a herd of goats and some twenty camels were grazing, and proceeded to milk the females. Edgar was a passive spectator, for the animals all showed their aversion to his white skin, and would not let him approach them. When the work was over they returned to the tents with the calabashes of milk, and were rewarded for their extra work with large platefuls of meal. Before eating his share Edgar filled a tin pannikin Amina had given him for his special use with water, boiled it over the fire, and dropped in a spoonful of tea, and going up to Amina asked for a little milk, which she readily gave him, surprised that a spoonful or two was all that he required.

"If I use it sparingly," he said to himself as he sat down to his meal, "that ten pounds of tea will last me over a year, and before it is gone I hope I shall see some way of getting off." As soon as he had finished it the woman whose child was ill came to him and took him off to see her. She was, as even Edgar could see, better; her skin was soft and her pulse was quieter, but she was evidently very weak. The woman held out a bowl of the arrow-root, and signified that she would not eat it, which Edgar was not surprised at, for it was thick and lumpy.

"I suppose the water didn't boil," he said to himself. "No wonder the poor little beggar cannot eat that stuff. I should think the Liebig would be the best for her, at any rate better than this stuff. I will get a tin or two from Amina, or rather she had better get it; I don't want to be always asking for things."

He had noticed where he had thrown the little pot the evening before, brought it to the woman, and then pointing to the sheik's tent said, "You fetch."

A RUNAWAY SLAVE

The woman understood and went off, and presently returned with two of the pots. Boiling water was required. This is not an item to be found in an Arab tent. Edgar therefore boiled some in his own tin over the fire in front of the sheik's tent, and showed the woman how much of the paste was to be used and how much water. When this was made he asked her for milk; this also he boiled and made some arrow-root, and told the woman to give that and the Liebig alternately every three or four hours. The benefit the child had received had created a most favourable impression towards Edgar in the community, and several of them came round him as he left the tent to ask for medicine. Edgar was sorely puzzled, and determined that if he could do no good he would certainly do no harm. He thought it likely that most of the illnesses were imaginary, "For why," he said to himself as he looked at three of them who were all placing their hands on their stomachs and twisting about to show that they were suffering great pain, "should they be all bad together?" There was in the chest a large bottle of pills marked "blue-pills," and of these he gave two to each applicant.

One case of those who applied was of a very different character. It was a boy some fifteen years old. He crawled up on his hands and knees, and sitting down took off some bandages and showed him his leg. It was terribly inflamed from the instep up to the knee, with a great sloughing wound that showed the bone for two or three inches. It was evidently the result of a serious graze, perhaps caused by falling on to a sharp rock. Had it been attended to at first it would have been trifling, but doubtless the boy thought nothing of it and had continued to get about as usual. The sand and dirt had got into the wound, inflammation had set in, and the leg was now in a very serious state.

Edgar felt a little more certain of his ground this time, for he remembered that one of the fellows at River-Smith's house had had a bad leg after a severe kick in the shin at football, and he knew what had been done for it. The lad's father, who was one of the elderly men who had remained in

289

camp, had accompanied him. Edgar told him that in the first place he wanted a good deal of water made hot. The chest contained a half-gallon bottle of carbolic acid, and searching among the smaller bottles Edgar found one containing caustic. When the lad's father returned with the hot water, Edgar bathed the wound for a long time; then he poured a little of the acid into a calabash of cold water, dipped a piece of cotton cloth into it, folded it several times, and laid it on the wound, then wrapped another cloth soaked in water round and round the limb, and explained as well as he could to the father that as often as the bandage became dry the one must be dipped in the calabash with the lotion, the other in water, and applied again. For two or three days this treatment was continued, and then Edgar burned the unhealthy surfaces with caustic, continuing the carbolic poultices.

In a week the inflammation had greatly abated, and the sore assumed a healthy aspect. The process of healing would in England have been a long and tedious work, but in the dry air of the desert it healed with a rapidity that surprised Edgar, and in a fortnight the boy was able to walk again. The girl too had gained strength rapidly, and Edgar was regarded in the encampment as a Hakim of extraordinary skill; and even the children who had at first shouted Kaffir after him, and thrown stones at him whenever they could do so unobserved, now regarded him with something like awe, while the friends of the boy and girl showed him many little kindnesses, often giving him a bowl of camels' milk, a handful of dates, or a freshly-baked cake of meal. With one of the negro slaves he got on very well. He could not be persuaded to continue to work with the energy which he had displayed the first afternoon, but he seconded Edgar's efforts fairly, and his merry talk and laughter, although he could understand but a small portion of what he said, cheered Edgar at his toil. The other negro remained sullen and hostile. For some days after his encounter with Edgar his face was so swollen up that he was scarcely able to see. He would have been compelled to work as usual, for humanity is not a characteristic of the Arabs; but Edgar told the sheik's wife that if the man was forced to work at present he would be very ill, and that he must for a time remain quiet and apply bandages soaked in hot water to his face. Under this treatment the swelling gradually abated, but the nose did not resume its normal shape, the bridge having been broken by Edgar's blow. Any presents that the latter received in the way of milk or other articles of food he shared with the negroes, the allowance of food served out being very scanty and of the coarsest description.

"Kaffirs are dogs," the sheik said to his wife as he one day saw Edgar dividing some milk and dates with the others; "but there is good in them. That Muley," for so they had named Edgar, "divides all that is given him with the others, even giving Hamish a share. I could understand his giving it to the other, so that he might do some of his work for him, but not to Hamish, who I can see has not forgiven him that blow."

"I don't think the other does his work for him," Amina said. "He works for me of a morning and then goes into the fields; and when I watch them to see that they are doing their work it seems to me that he does more than any of them."

"He does," the sheik agreed; "he is a willing slave. I am glad I did not give him up to the Mahdi. Kaffir as he is, I think he brings good luck to the village. If he would change his religion and follow the Prophet I would adopt him as my son, seeing that you have only girls."

Edgar made very rapid progress with the language. It was well for him that he had picked up a few words and sentences at Suakim and Cairo, for this enabled him to make far more rapid progress than he would have done had he been ignorant of the language. He attempted to keep up a constant conversation with the negro, and although the latter often went into screams of laughter at his mistakes he was ready to help him, correcting his errors and repeating sentences over and over again until he was able to pronounce them with a proper accent. In two months he was able to converse with tolerable fluency, and the sheik was meditating broaching the subject of his conversion to him when an event occurred that for a time gave him other matters to think of.

One morning when the encampment woke, Hamish was found to be missing, and it was ere long discovered that the best camel in the encampment had been stolen, and that two water-skins had been taken from the sheik's tent, and a perfect hubbub arose in the village when this became known. The sheik seizing a stick fell upon the other negro and showered blows upon him, exclaiming that he must have known of and aided his companion in his flight, although he declared he had not the least idea of his intentions. As soon as his first burst of rage was over the sheik ordered four of the best camels to be saddled and water-bottles to be filled.

"The fellow must be mad," he said as he walked up and down before his tent; "he must know that he cannot escape; he would be known as a slave by the first people he comes upon, and it would only be a change of masters, and he would be long before he finds one so gentle as I have been with him."

"I do not think he has gone away to make a change in masters," Amina said. "It is worse than that, I fear."

"What is it, Amina? What do you mean?"

"I fear that he has made for Khartoum to report that you have a white slave here. He hates Muley, and I think that it is to obtain vengeance on him that he has fled."

"You are right, Amina; that is what the son of Sheitan intends to do. Quick! bring up those camels," he roared.

Three of the men were ordered to accompany him. Then he gave orders that the rest of the camels should be loaded at once with his goods, the valuables of the village, and a portion of the crops, and that they should start without delay to the oasis of Wady El Bahr Nile, or the valley of the Dry River, two days' journey to the west, driving with them the herd of goats.

A RUNAWAY SLAVE

"If I do not catch him we must break up the douar," he said, "and all who do not wish to be found here by the Mahdi's men had best be in readiness to start when we return. Let half a dozen men and women go to the wady to look after the goats and guard the property. The camels must be brought back as soon as they get there."

Ten minutes later he and his three companions had disappeared from sight over the brow of the nearest sand-hill, while all in the encampment were busy in preparing for their departure. A camel was allotted to each of the ten tents of which the camp consisted; three camels were claimed by Amina for the sheik's possessions; the remaining six were to carry the food. All who were not engaged were at once set to work gathering the maize that was fit to pluck and cutting and tying up into bundles the forage for the camels. In three hours a great change had been effected in the appearance of the little valley. The sheik's tent and three others remained standing, but the rest were levelled to the ground, their occupants preferring to start at once rather than risk being caught by the Mahdists. It was mid-day when the party started. Edgar could hardly help smiling at the appearance the camels presented, each animal being almost hidden by the pile of baggage, bundles, cooking-pots, and articles of all kinds, at the top of which were perched a woman and two or three children. The men walked, as did many of the younger women and boys and girls.

It would be a fatiguing journey, for they would travel without a halt until morning, then rest until the sun was low again, and again journey all night, when they would reach the wells soon after daybreak. As it was but a two days' journey the camels carried far heavier loads than would have been placed upon them had it been one of longer duration. Amina took the lead in the whole matter. She gave orders to the men, scolded the women, and saw that everything was done in order.

"Do you think that the sheik has any chance of catching Hamish?" Edgar asked her as they stood together watching the retreating line of camels.

She shook her head.

"Very little," she said, "unless the camel breaks down, which is not likely, or he misses the track. When he once gains the cultivated land he will turn the camel adrift and will make his way on foot to Khartoum. He will avoid all villages where he might be stopped and go straight to the city, where he will tell his story to the first officer of the Mahdi he meets. If the sheik does not overtake him before he gets beyond the limit of the desert he will pursue no further. It would be useless. He would never find him in the fields, where he might lie down among the crops. It would only be a waste of time to search for him."

"Does Hamish know of the other wady?"

She nodded. "It may be that the Mahdists will not follow further. It will depend upon the orders they have received. Of course we shall leave someone here to watch, and if they start for the wady he will bring us news before they get there."

"Are there any other wells?"

"None nearer than six days' journey to the south. Then there is a great cultivated country with many villages and towns, but the journey would be terrible. I do not know what we shall do. But do not be afraid, Muley; whatever we do you will not be given up until the last thing. When my lord once sets his face one way he never turns it. He has said the Mahdi shall not have you, for you are his captive and none other's, and he will never go back from that."

"You have been very good to me," Edgar said, "and I would rather run my own risk than that suffering and perhaps death should fall upon the women and children of the douar."

"My lord will never hear of it," she said. "When he has said a thing he has said it. There is nothing to do now but to wait until we learn what force is coming against us. There is another encampment of the tribe in a wady two days' journey to the north, and we may summon help from there if the party is not too strong. The great thing will be to kill Hamish, for the Wady El Bahr Nile is known only to a few of our own tribe, and were he not with them they would not be able to find their way there. Even this wady is known to few, for it

294

lies altogether beyond the track of caravans. But now there is nothing to do but to wait until my lord returns. It will be I think on the fourteenth day. You were eight days coming across the desert. They will do it in six but will be eight on their return, for there will be no occasion for haste. Hamish will take two more days to get to Khartoum; it may be a day or two before a party is sent out from there, and they will take ten days getting here, so that it should be some days at least after my lord's return before they appear."

"I am sorry, indeed, to have been the cause of so much trouble falling upon you," Edgar said.

"It is not your fault. It was the will of Allah that you should be brought here. But anyhow we should not have stopped here much longer. We have been here six months now, and my lord was saying but a few days since that as soon as the rest of the crops were gathered he should send those who are not fit to travel to El Bahr Nile, and should leave you there and should start with the camels to Khartoum, sell our crops there, and then carry merchandise to El-Obeid or some other distant place. He has been waiting for things to settle down; we have only been stopping here so long because trade has been stopped by the siege of Khartoum, and since then he has not ventured to go there lest his camels should be seized by the Mahdi; but, as he said, he must risk something. Of what use is it to have camels if you do not employ them. They are getting fat and lazy; never have they had so long a rest before. It matters nothing our having to leave this wady. The worst is that the Mahdi will be set against us, and that we shall have to move away far from here to get trade."

"It is possible that at the present time Khartoum is in the hands of the English," Edgar said. "We have heard no news from without since I came here three months ago now, and by this time our expedition may have arrived there and the Mahdi's power may be altogether broken."

"I hope it may be so," the woman said; "before the Mahdi came the country was peaceful and prosperous; there was employment and trade for our camels, and all went about their occupations unmolested. Now everything is changed; trade is at an end, the villages are destroyed, and the fields deserted. I know not how it will end. If the tribes would all turn together against them they would soon drive them out of the land. But there is no hope of this; we have our own quarrels, and cannot unite even when everything is at stake. The Mahdi may be the Mahdi, but what is that to us? He tells his followers that he will lead them to conquer Egypt, and to go to Jerusalem and Roum (Constantinople). But how is he to do it when a handful of white soldiers defeated thousands of his men in the desert? What would it be were he to meet a great army of them? It is one thing to fight the Egyptians as they did at El-Obeid, but another when it is your soldiers. I hear that multitudes of Osman Digma's men were slain down by the sea, and yet they say they fought well."

"They did fight well," Edgar said. "I was there and saw it; no men could have been braver; but we have terrible weapons, and it was impossible for them to stand against them. The Mahdi may say what he likes, but there is no more chance of his taking Egypt as long as we stay there than there is of his flying."

"Well, well!" the woman said. "It will be as Allah chooses. You do not believe in Allah, Muley, you are a Kaffir."

"I beg your pardon," Edgar said; "we and you worship the same God. We call him God, and you call him Allah; but it is the same. Your Prophet acknowledges Moses and Christ to be prophets. The only difference between us is that you believe that Mohammed was also a prophet, and the greatest of all, while we do not acknowledge that, but in other respects there is no great difference between us."

"My lord will talk to you, Muley; I am but a woman, and these things are not for us."

Each morning one of the boys remaining at the douar was sent up to the crest of the sand-hills, and there remained all day on watch. At the end of the thirteenth day the sheik's wife gave orders that everything should be in readiness for instant departure. The camels had returned on the previous day from El Bahr Nile, having made two journeys there and back, and were now ready for a fresh departure. There was a further cutting of the crops until as much was gathered as would, with the remaining tents and goods, make up a full load for the camels, for as the party had not arrived it was almost certain that they had not succeeded in overtaking the fugitive. On the evening of the thirteenth day a shout from the boy on the hill proclaimed that he saw figures coming.

"How many of them?" one of the men shouted to him.

"There are five camels, but only four of them are ridden."

There was a shout of satisfaction. This looked as if the party had overtaken the fugitive, in which case they would have brought the camel back and left the body of Hamish in the desert.

A shout of welcome greeted the chief as he rode up. "You have overtaken him, El Bakhat, I see; Bishmillah, God be praised, we are safe from the trouble the treacherous dog would have brought upon us!"

The sheik shook his head. "The son of Sheitan has escaped. We caught sight of him just at the edge of the desert, having ridden with scarce an hour's rest from the time we started. As soon as we did so Aboo and myself dismounted and started in pursuit; but he must have seen us as soon as we caught sight of him, for when we came up to his camel it was alone. We followed him to the edge of the cultivated lands, but the grass was long and the crops stood in some places as high as our heads, and it would have been useless searching for him, so we brought the camels on, gave them water and a night's halt to fill themselves in the fields, and then started back. Has all been well?"

"All has been well," his wife replied. "The camels made three journeys, have rested, and are ready to start afresh. We have cut down as much as they can carry, and have indeed left but little remaining."

"We will start the day after to-morrow," the sheik said. "Our camels need a rest, and time does not press. Before we leave the wady we will set fire to the dry stalks and grass.

There is little that will not burn. We must destroy all that we can, so that when they arrive here in search of us they shall not be able to sit down here, but must turn and travel back with all speed, unless they decide to push on in pursuit of us to Wady El Bahr Nile."

Two days later the tents were struck and the camels loaded up; then when they had moved away, the dried grass and corn stalks were fired at the windward end of the valley and in a few minutes the flames swept along in a broad sheet, and in a quarter of an hour a coating of gray ashes covered the soil where lately the encampment with its surroundings of cultivation stood. Two of the men were left behind with fast camels. They were to leave the animals a mile from the camp on its northern side, so that they would neither be on the line by which the enemy would come or that leading to the wady. They had forage for their camels and food for themselves for a fortnight. One was to remain by the camels, the other to keep watch concealed among the sand-hills near the well.

If an enemy was seen approaching the watcher was to return at once to the camels, take his own animal, and ride to the wady with news as to their strength; the other was to remain on watch until they either retired or set out on the track of the fugitives, when he was to push forward with all speed with the news. A messenger was also sent off to the douar to the north saying that an expedition of the Mahdi's men was on its way out to plunder and destroy the encampments of the tribe, and begging them to send to El Bahr Nile all their fighting men in order that the dervishes should have such a lesson that they would be well content to leave the tribes alone in future.

As before, the women and children were perched on the summit of their household goods on the top of the camels. Contrary to their usual custom most of the men walked, as the camels were loaded to the full extent of their powers.

Edgar had manufactured for himself, soon after his arrival at the camp, a pair of sandals from the skin of a goat that had been killed for food, and he was therefore able to keep up with the camels with comfort. As it was considered that there was no occasion for hurry, and as the camels were very heavily laden, three days instead of two were devoted to the journey, and even then it was a very fatiguing one for those on foot. On arriving at El Bahr Nile Edgar found that the oasis was much smaller than that they had quitted. The soil was rocky, and although there were two large pools of clear water there was but little ground round them in any way suitable for cultivation. Acacias and other shrubs, however, grew thickly down the valley, showing that there was a certain amount of moisture below the surface. The tents were soon erected by the side of those of the first party, and when the fires were lighted and the camels unloaded, taken to the water and then turned loose to browse among the trees, the place assumed a home-like appearance.

"You can shoot, Muley," the sheik said to Edgar. "If I give you a gun will you fight against these dervishes?"

"Certainly I will, sheik."

"Your guns carry a long way; they are wonderful weapons. At Metemmeh men were killed two miles away."

"Yes, they are good weapons, sheik, and I wish I had one of them here, for I am afraid I should not be able to do much with your guns."

The sheik turned to his wife: "Fetch out that Kaffir gun, Amina." And to Edgar's surprise she brought out from the tent a Martini rifle and a pouch filled with cartridges. This gun had been found strapped on to one of the camels that had been captured, and the sheik had appropriated it for his own use, concealing it in one of the bales, so that Edgar had not noticed it when the camels were unloaded.

"I do not understand it," the sheik said; "it is much stranger to me than our guns would be to you. I tried to put these brass things with the bullet sticking out into it, but they would not go into the barrel. You shall show me how to use it, but if the dervishes come I will hand it to you, for you understand it and will do much better with it than I should; but show me how it works."

The sheik's astonishment was great when Edgar pushed the lever, opened the breech, inserted a cartridge, and closing the breech said that it was now loaded and could be fired at once.

"Fire at that rock," he said, "and then load again as quickly as you can."

Edgar did so, and in a few seconds was again ready to fire.

"Inshallah!" the sheik exclaimed. "But it is wonderful. No wonder that they tell me that the roar of the guns was like never-ceasing thunder, and that the sound of one shot could not be heard from another. Can you take out the cartridge without firing?"

Edgar showed him how this was done, and the sheik then repeatedly loaded and unloaded the gun until he could manipulate it quickly. "And what is this thing?" he asked, touching the back sight.

Edgar explained to him that the sight was raised or lowered according to the distance of the object to be aimed at.

"The Franks are wonderful men," the sheik said gravely; "if they had but the true faith, and Allah was with them, no one could stand against them. When the ammunition is used up can you make more?"

Edgar shook his head.

"If I had caps to fit in here and a mould for the bullets I could refill these cases two or three times, but after that they would be useless. Powerful machinery is used for making these cases. It might be possible to have them made by hand by a skilled worker in brass in Khartoum, but it would be very expensive, and I am afraid, sheik, when the ammunition is gone the gun would be useless unless you can procure some more cartridges from traders in Egypt; unless, indeed, my countrymen have retaken Khartoum, in which case I could obtain for you any quantity of cartridges."

"Your countrymen have retired to Korti," the sheik said.

Edgar gave a cry of disappointment. He had feared that when the news of Gordon's death was known the expedition might be abandoned; but he had still retained some hope that it might advance to Khartoum. The news that they had already fallen back to Korti came as a shock.

"How did you learn the news, sheik?" he asked presently. "You did not say that you had spoken to anyone."

"Yes, we went a little way into the fields in hopes of catching sight of Hamish, and came upon two peasants who were gathering the crop. They had seen nothing of the negro. Upon questioning them as to what was going on at Khartoum they said that the Mahdi was still all-powerful; that the Kaffirs had fallen back from Metemmeh and were scattered along the river between Korti and Dongola; and that the Mahdi had announced that his forces would ere long advance, conquer Egypt, and destroy the Kaffirs."

"Do you mean to wait for the attack of the Mahdi's men here or to go to meet them?" Edgar asked after a long pause.

"If they come here too numerous to fight we must fly; but if they are not too strong we will give them battle here. Why should we go to meet them?"

"It is for you to decide," Edgar said. "I know nothing of your Arab ways of fighting. But it seemed to me that it might be better, if they are not altogether too strong, to meet them as near the other wells as we can."

"But why so, Muley? They would have water close to them and we should have none. If one was wounded he would have to be carried a long distance. Why do you advise that we should fight them there?"

"You told me, sheik, that the existence of this well was only known to you and your people and a small section of the tribe."

"That is so, Muley. It is a secret that has been well guarded. The wady has served as a retreat many times in our history."

301

"If they come on and any of them go back again the secret will be a secret no longer," Edgar said. "It is for this reason that I thought that we had better go out and meet them. There is but one man with them who knows the way hither, and against him our balls should be all directed. If we kill him they would be without a guide and would be unable to find the way, for they would never venture into this desert knowing that if they failed to find our well they might all perish for want of water."

"You speak well," the sheik said. "I had not thought of this; but I see that your plan is a good one. As soon as I learn that they have arrived at the wells we will set out to meet them unless their force is altogether too strong for us."

On the seventh day after their arrival at the wady the messenger who had been despatched for aid returned. His news was that the greater part of the men were away; they were expected in a few days, but it might be a week or more before they came back. The sheik was unwilling to send off the few men at the douar, but promised that as soon as his main force returned he would set out with the whole strength of his fighting men to their assistance.

Upon the following morning one of the men left to watch the wells also returned. He had come through without stopping, and reported that late in the evening before he left he and his companions had seen a line of camels with some horsemen coming towards the wells. He had waited until morning in order to discover their force; he put it down as forty men.

"That is very bad news," the sheik said. "We can only muster eighteen fighting men, and some of these are old and others mere lads. They are two to one against us, and if we were beaten and forced to fly their horsemen would overtake us and destroy us. Think it over, Muley; you are full of expedients."

"How many men do you expect to get from the other douar?"

"Their encampment is the same size as ours; they are sure to leave some of the old men to guard it, perhaps fifteen will come. That will make our force nearly equal to theirs, and we might defend this wady, though I doubt it, but I am sure that they would beat us easily in the desert. They are almost all armed with the rifles that they took at El-Obeid from Hicks Pasha's men, and will have found an abundance of arms at Khartoum; besides, these dervishes fight desperately. The faith they have in the Mahdi gives them strength and courage; they do not care whether they die or live, and doubtless picked men have been sent on the expedition. I fear there is nought before us but flight, unless you with your knowledge of the Frank method of war can hit upon some plan."

"I will think it over, sheik, but at present I see no way in which we can withstand them. We might, of course, cut down trees and make so strong a fort here that we might beat them off; but in that case they might return in much greater numbers, therefore it seems to me that if we fight we must fight at the other wady."

"Then we cannot fight at all," the sheik said decisively. "There are two to one against us, and it would be madness to attack them when they could with their horsemen cut off all retreat."

"I will think, sheik," Edgar said, rising and walking away. In half an hour he returned. "I have thought of a plan, sheik, but it is not without great danger."

"I care not for danger," the sheik said, "so that it be but possible."

"My idea is this: that we should load up all your camels with closely-pressed bundles of forage; then that we should advance a day's march across the desert; and there that we should form a zareba. With the forage we should, of course, take water-skins with us, with sufficient to last for at least a week. I should send the camels back again as soon as they are unloaded, and should order those who remained behind to load all their goods upon them and to set out either for the other douar of your tribe or for the villages to the south.

I should send a messenger to the other douar to say that we are going to defend the zareba to the last and praying them to come at once to our rescue, promising the moment they appear to sally out and fall upon the dervishes while they attack them in rear. Your messenger should point out that before they arrive a number of the enemy will certainly have fallen in their attack upon us, and we shall, therefore, be decidedly superior to them in point of numbers."

"The plan is a bold one," the sheik said; "but do you think that it would be possible for us to defend the zareba?"

"I think so, sheik. It need be but a small one some twelve feet square inside. They will have to cross the open to attack us, and outside we can protect it by a facing of prickly shrubs."

"We will do it!" the sheik said in a tone of determination, springing to his feet. "One can but die once, and if we succeed it will be a tale for the women of our tribe to tell for all time."

CHAPTER XVIII
THE ZAREBA

NO sooner had the sheik decided to carry out Edgar's plan than he rapidly issued his orders. In five minutes the whole of the inhabitants of the douar were at work, the boys going out to fetch the camels, the men cutting down the long grass near the well and laying it in great bundles very tightly pressed together, the women cooking a large supply of flat cakes for the party. In two hours the preparations were completed and the twenty men moved off from the oasis. They travelled until ten o'clock in the evening. By the light of the moon which was four days short of full, the sheik and Edgar selected a point for the erection of the zareba. It was a patch of rock cropping up from the summit of a sand-hill that fell away from it on all sides, and was just about the size required for the zareba. The camels were unloaded and the bundles of forage laid down side by side and formed into a square, the wall being some four feet thick and two feet high. The whole party, including the boys who were to take back the camels, then set to work to cut thorny bushes. These were piled thickly at the foot of the rock all round, being kept in their places by stakes driven into the sand and by ropes interlacing them. The work was only completed just as daylight broke.

"I don't think," Edgar said, walking round the little fort, "that any men can get through this hedge of thorns until they have pulled it away piece by piece, and that, with us lying in shelter above and firing down upon them, will be a difficult task indeed."

THE DASH FOR KHARTOUM

The Arabs, who had obeyed the chief's orders with reluctance and had been very silent upon the journey out, were now jubilant, feeling convinced that they could beat off the attack of such a force as that which they heard was advancing. The camels were now sent off, and they had scarcely disappeared among the sand-hills when an Arab was seen approaching on a camel.

"It is our scout," the sheik said; "he brings us news."

He tied a cloth to the end of a spear and waved it. A minute later the camel's course was changed and the rider soon arrived outside the fort.

"What is your news, Yussuf?"

"They are going to start this morning," the man said. "I crept in as soon as it became dark last night and made my way close up to them, and I gathered that they have decided to march this morning on to Wady El Bahr Nile. They could not stay where they were any longer as they had only brought with them sufficient food for the camels for the march to the wady, where they made sure they should find an abundant supply, and having given them a day's rest they were going to push forwards at once to the next wady, where they made certain of finding the fugitives."

"Will they be here to-night?" Edgar asked the sheik.

"I should think not, Muley. The regular halting-place is five miles away, and as that is about half-way they will probably stop there and start perhaps an hour before daybreak."

The scout was sent off to the wady with the news, and the little garrison spent the day in strengthening their fort, making another hedge of bushes three or four yards beyond the other, and gathering a large number of the heaviest stones they could find. These were laid on the grass rampart, which was thus raised in height nearly a foot, openings being left in the stones through which the defenders could thrust their guns and fire without exposing their heads to the shots of the assailants. This still further added to the confidence of the Arabs, and when all was completed they indulged in defiant gestures and wild yells signifying contempt, in the direction from which the enemy would probably advance.

At nightfall two of the men were posted as sentries, as it was possible the Mahdists might push straight forward. There was, however, no alarm during the night; but just as day broke the sentries reported that there were horsemen to be seen in the distance. As there was no object in concealment all leapt to their feet. Nine horsemen were seen on the brow of a sand-hill some two miles away. They were presently lost sight of as they descended into a dip, and a minute or two later the line of camels was seen following in their steps. The spear with the cloth was elevated as a flag; and when the horsemen appeared on the next sand-hill, it was evident by the suddenness with which they pulled up their horses that they saw it.

Half a minute later they started again, this time at a canter. When they came within half a mile the sheik asked, "Why do you not fire, Muley? Your gun will carry that distance easily."

"Double that distance if necessary, sheik. It is better not to let them know that we have such a gun here until they get close. It will be better for you to fire."

The sheik levelled his long gun and fired, and the horsemen at once drew up, and after a little consultation two or three of them rode off on each flank so as to make a circuit of this unlooked-for obstacle, while one of the others rode back at full speed to meet the camel train. As soon as it arrived, the riders, of whom there were two on each animal, dismounted. The camels were led back to a hollow where they would be safe from any stray bullet, and after a short pause one of the horsemen again advanced and at a rapid pace made a circle round the fort at a distance of two or three hundred yards only. A scattered fire was opened by the defenders, but the speed at which he was riding disconcerted their aim, and having completed the circuit he rode off with a yell of defiance to rejoin the party.

THE DASH FOR KHARTOUM

For half an hour no move was made. It was evident that the strength of the position had disconcerted the dervishes, who had expected to gain an almost bloodless victory. As, however, Hamish assured them that at the very utmost the sheik could put but twenty men in the field, including several boys and old men, it was finally decided to attack, and headed by the horsemen the dervishes started forward at a run, uttering shrill yells as they did so. Edgar had persuaded the chief that it would be useless to open fire until they were within two or three hundred yards, as but few shots would tell, and the men would be discouraged by finding that their fire did not check the advance. The sheik therefore commanded his followers on no account to fire until he gave the order. The dervishes, however, were not sparing of their ammunition, and fired as they ran, the balls going for the most part wide, although a few whistled over the heads of the defenders and two or three struck the rampart.

"Now I think they are near enough, sheik," Edgar, who had levelled his rifle at one of the horsemen, said. As he spoke he pulled the trigger, and simultaneously with the sharp crack of the piece the Arab threw up his arms and fell from his horse. The sheik and five of his men fired almost at the same moment. Kneeling as closely as they could, there was room for but seven along the face of the fort fronting the enemy, and at Edgar's suggestion the chief had divided the men into three parties, each of which after firing was to fall to the rear and reload, their places being taken by the others in succession. Thus there would always be a reserve and the fire could be kept up without interruption. Volley after volley was fired, Edgar loading quickly enough to repeat his fire with each squad.

So rapidly did the Arabs pass over the intervening ground that they reached the outside hedge of thorns just as the party who had first fired had again taken their places in front. Five of the dervishes had fallen and several were wounded, but this had not checked their speed for a moment, and under the orders of their leaders they at once fell to work with their swords and knives to destroy the hedge. The work was done far more rapidly than Edgar had thought possible, and they then fell upon the more formidable obstacle piled up against the rocks, attacking it on three sides simultaneously. The defenders now fired independently, each as fast as he could load, Edgar shouting continuously, "Steady! steady! take a good aim each time," and the sheik re-echoing his words. The Arabs, however, were too excited to obey, and the greater part of their shots were thrown away. Several of the dervishes had fallen, but the process of clearing away the hedge proceeded with alarming rapidity. The work was, however, speedily abandoned at the face where Edgar was stationed, for at each crack of his rifle a dervish fell. Leaving three of the men to defend that face the rest joined the defenders at the sides, the sheik taking the command on one side, Edgar on the other. The fire now became more steady, the sheik enforcing his orders by vigorous blows with the staff of his spear, while Edgar's rifle on his side more than made up for his want of influence with the men.

In their fury several of the dervishes sprang boldly into the midst of the thorns and strove to climb up, but they were met by the spears of the defenders, and not one gained an entrance. It was less than ten minutes after the first shot had been fired when the leader of the dervishes, seeing how fast his men were falling and that they would soon be no stronger than the defenders of the fort, called them off from the attack. As they turned and ran the defenders leapt to their feet with yells of triumph; but the dervishes, turning round, fired several shots. The sheik received a ball in his shoulder and two of his companions fell dead. The others at once took to their shelter again, and kept up their fire until long after the last of the dervishes was out of range. The moment the retreat began Edgar looked out for his man, of whom he had not hitherto caught a glimpse in the heat of the conflict. He soon caught sight of him, and taking a steady and careful aim with his rifle on a stone fired, and Hamish fell headlong forward, the ball having struck him fair between the shoulders.

A yell of triumph rose from the Arabs. The traitor who had brought the Mahdists down upon them was punished; the one man who could guide the foe to the wady was killed. As soon as the enemy got out of reach of shot they gathered in consultation. The defenders could see that the discussion was excited and violent; they waved their arms, stamped, and seemed on the point of coming to blows with each other. While they were so engaged the garrison looked out at the field of battle round the fort. No less than fifteen of the assailants had been killed, while of the defenders but two, the one an old man and the other a boy, had fallen. The sheik begged Edgar to bandage his shoulder; he seemed to feel the pain but little, so delighted was he with the issue of the contest. Edgar soaked a pad of the cotton cloth and laid it on the wound, and then with long strips of the same material bandaged the arm tightly to the side, and with other strips fastened as well as he could the pad in its place.

"They are scattering over the sand-hills," one of the Arabs said just as he had finished, and in a short time a dropping fire was opened at the fort. The Arabs would have replied, but the sheik said that it was a waste of powder, for their guns would not carry as far as the rifles in the hands of the dervishes, and it was better that they should lie quiet behind their shelter and allow the enemy to throw away their fire.

"What will they do next, do you think, sheik?"

"I do not think they will make another attack, Muley; at any rate not in the daytime. They must know they are not greatly superior to us in force, being now but twenty-five to our eighteen, and no doubt many of them are wounded. They may try to besiege us. They will know that we have a supply of water – we should never have shut ourselves up here without it – but that will fail in time."

"But their own supply will fail," Edgar said. "Probably they have only brought enough with them for what they supposed would be a two days' march to the wady."

THE ZAREBA

"I should think, Muley, they will send all their camels back to the wells, perhaps with one of their wounded men and another. The wounded man will remain there in charge of them, the other will bring two or three of them out with full water-skins; he can make the journey there and back every two days and can bring enough water for the men and horses. I don't think they will send the horses away. They will do with a small portion of water, and if greatly needed they could start from here at sunset, keeping among the sand-hills until out of sight, reach the wells, drink their fill, and be back in the morning. If they attack at night it will be between the setting of the moon and daybreak."

"I should hardly think they would do that," Edgar said. "We shall soon restore the thorn hedge, and they would scarcely be mad enough to attack us when they know that we have that protection and are almost as strong as they are. If it were not that we do not want them to know the way to the wady I should say that we could venture to sally out and march back, but that would cost us a good many lives, for the horsemen could ride on ahead, dismount, open fire on us from the sand-hills and be off again on their horses when we went up to attack them. No, I think we cannot do better than follow our original plan. Our water will hold out for a week, and by putting ourselves on short allowance at the end of a day or two if we find that they are determined to wait, we can make it last for nearly a fortnight, and long before that your tribesmen ought to be here, and in that case only the mounted men will escape us. Three of their horses lie dead outside, so there are but five left."

"Ah! if we could but cut them all off," the sheik said in a tone of fury, "then we might be safe for a long time. If any of them get back to tell the tale the Mahdi will send a force next time that there will be no resisting."

Edgar sat thinking for a minute or two.

"I have an idea, sheik," he said at last. "Send off one of your boys as soon as the moon sets, let him go to El Bahr Nile. When your friends arrive he will tell them of the repulse we have given the dervishes, and that there are now but

311

twenty-five of them, several of whom are doubtless wounded. Tell them that if but ten men come to aid us we can defeat them; let the other ten, that is if twenty arrive, start first, and turning off the track make a detour and come down at night upon the wady. There they will find but one man with the camels; but they must not show themselves, but must hide close at hand. Then when the horsemen arrive they must make an ambush, and either shoot them down as they pass or let them go through to the wells. They are sure to wait there for a few hours, and they can fall upon them there. Let the men be ordered to fire only at the horses; they can deal with the men after they have dismounted. The great thing is to prevent the horsemen getting away."

"Mashallah, Muley, your plan is a grand one. Had you been bred in the desert you could not have better understood our warfare. What a pity it is that you are a Kaffir! You would have been a great sheik had you been a true believer."

"Gordon Pasha was a Kaffir," Edgar replied, "but he was greater than any sheik."

"He was a great man indeed," the sheik said; "he was a very father to the people; there was no withstanding him. We fought against him, for our interest lay with the slave-dealing, but he scattered us like sheep. Yes, Gordon was a great man though, as you say, he was a Kaffir;" and the sheik sat in silence, meditating upon what seemed to him an inscrutable problem.

While the conversation had been going on, the bullets of the enemy continued to whistle round the zareba.

"I will try and put a stop to that," Edgar said; "we have a rifle here as much better than theirs, as theirs are superior to the guns of your tribesmen."

The nearest hill was some four or five hundred yards away, and on this several of the Arabs could be seen. Sure that they were nearly out of gun-shot, they took but little pains to conceal themselves. Edgar rested his rifle on a stone and took a steady aim at three of them who were sitting together. He fired. A yell of dismay came across the air; two of the figures leapt to their feet and ran back. A moment later four or five others who had been firing from among the bushes also dashed away, while a triumphant yell rose from the zareba.

"That is one enemy the less," Edgar said, "and I don't think the others will trouble us much in future. They must know that they can be doing us no harm, and now they discover they are not going to have it all their own way we shall not hear much more of them."

Shots were indeed fired occasionally from the bushes and eminences, but the discharges were far apart, and seemed to be intended rather to show the defenders of the zareba that they were surrounded than for any other purpose. The day passed without any further event. As soon as the sun had fairly set the defenders sallied out and repaired the hedge. The enemy probably guessed that they were so employed, and kept up a much heavier fire than they had done during the day. Edgar, lying in the zareba, replied, steadily firing at the flashes, and after a time the firing of the enemy slackened, and the defenders, when they had completed the hedge, re-entered the zareba through a very narrow gap that had been left for the purpose, carrying with them one of their number whose leg had been broken just above the ankle by one of the enemy's bullets.

Under the sheik's instructions some rough splints were made to keep the bone in its proper position, and bandages were then applied.

Four sentries were posted, one at each corner of the fort, and the rest of the garrison lay down to sleep. Twice during the night they sprang to their feet at the discharge of the gun of one of the sentries, but as no movement of the enemy followed they soon lay down again, supposing that either the alarm had been a false one, and that the sentry had fired at some low bush, or that, if he had really seen a man, the latter had made off as soon as he had discovered that the garrison were awake and vigilant. As soon as the moon set the sheik despatched one of the young men to the wady. His instructions were to crawl carefully, taking advantage of every bush until he deemed himself well beyond any of the enemy who might be watching, and then to start at full speed. If he were fired at, he was, if the enemy were still in front of him, to run back to the zareba; if they were behind him, to press forward at full speed.

For an hour after he had left the garrison listened anxiously. They were all under arms now, lest the enemy should try and attack during the darkness. No sounds, however, broke the stillness of the plain, and they were at last assured that their messenger had got safely through. For four days the blockade continued, an occasional exchange of shots being kept up. The dervishes, however, since they had learnt the range of Edgar's rifle, seldom showed themselves, but crept among the rocks and bushes, fired a shot, and then crawled off again to repeat the operation fifty or a hundred yards away. When the hedge had been repaired on the night after the fight the defenders buried their own dead in the sand a short distance off, and had dragged the bodies of their fallen enemies fifty yards away, as, had the siege lasted many days, the fort would have otherwise become uninhabitable.

In the morning one of the Arabs had yelled to the besiegers that the bodies were lying fifty yards away in front of the fort, and that four of them were free to come and carry them away or bury them as they chose. The invitation passed unregarded, but during the next night the bodies were all removed. The sentries were ordered not to fire if they heard any noise in that direction, for, as Edgar pointed out to the sheik, it was important that the bodies should be carried away. The next day several of the Arabs went out and raised heaps of sand over the horses that still lay just outside the hedge. The fourth night after his departure the messenger returned with the news that the tribesmen, eighteen in number, had arrived in the afternoon. They would carry out the sheik's orders. They were mounting fresh camels just as he started. Nine of them would hide among the sand-hills two or three miles away, and would there remain for twenty-four hours so as to give time for the others to get up to the wells. The sheik commanding the party had suggested that soon after daybreak the defenders of the fort should sally out and advance in the direction where the dervishes' camp was situated, as if intending to make an attack. This would bring in all the enemy who might be scattered among the sand-hills near the zareba. As soon as the engagement began he, with his men, would fall upon the rear of the dervishes.

"Do you think that that is a good plan, Muley?"

"I think so, sheik. You see, if we merely wanted to defeat them one would not wish them to rally into one body; but as our great object is to prevent any from returning, it is much better to do as the sheik suggests and let them get all together."

The day passed as usual, and the next morning shortly before sunrise the defenders of the fort issued out. The assailants were on the watch, and from four or five different points round the zareba shots were fired. Taking advantage of every bush the Arabs advanced slowly under the direction of their sheik. The dervishes, believing that the garrison must have been driven from their defences by thirst, and that they were now in their power, rapidly gathered their force and advanced to meet their opponents. At first they did so carelessly, but they were checked by the fall of one of their leaders by a ball from Edgar's rifle. They then advanced a little more cautiously. Edgar kept close to the sheik.

"They will make a rush soon," he said; "tell the men not to fire till they rise to their feet."

"Where are the others?" the sheik growled; "if they do not come we shall be outnumbered."

"Not by much, sheik; one or two of their men are certainly away with the camels, and we shall drop two or three more of them at least when they make their rush; the others are sure to be up directly. There, look! There they are on the top of the sand-hills the dervishes have been firing from."

The enemy had now approached to within a hundred yards, and were just preparing for a rush when a shout of welcome broke from the party in front of them and was at once echoed from the rear. The dervishes sprang to their feet in surprise and alarm, but one of their leaders exclaimed, "There are but a few of them! Slay these in front first, then we will destroy those in our rear!"

With a yell of defiance the dervishes dashed forward. The sheik's party poured in a volley as they did so, and then grasping their spears sprang to their feet, Edgar alone remaining prone, and firing four more shots as the dervishes traversed the intervening space. There was little disparity of numbers when the parties met. The sheik had, at Edgar's suggestion, ordered his men to form in a compact group with their spears pointing outward, as the great point was to withstand the rush until their friends came up. But the dervishes recklessly threw themselves upon the spears, and in a moment all were engaged in a hand-to-hand fight. Edgar, feeling that with a clubbed rifle he should have no chance against the spears and swords of the Arabs, kept between the sheik and two of his most trusted followers, and loading as quickly as he could throw out and drop in the cartridges, brought down four men who rushed one after another upon them.

It seemed an age to him, but it was scarce more than a minute after the combatants had closed that, with a shout, the ten new-comers arrived on the scene. Edgar dropped a fresh cartridge into his rifle and stood quiet; he had no wish to join in the slaughter. The dervishes fought desperately, and none asked for quarter, and in two or three minutes the combat was over and all had fallen, save three or four men who had extricated themselves from the fight and dashed off at the top of their speed, quickly pursued by the exultant victors. To Edgar's surprise they did not run in the direction of the sand-hill behind which he had thought their camp was made, but bore away to the south. Pursuers and pursued were soon out of sight, and Edgar turned to see how his companions had fared. Three of them had been killed and six of the others had received spear-thrusts or sword-cuts more or less severe.

"It would have gone hard with us, sheik, if our friends had not come up."

"We should have beaten them," the sheik said. "That gun of yours would have turned the scale. Had it not been for that they would have been too strong for us, for they were all fighting men in their prime, and five or six of my men were no match for them in a hand-to-hand fight. Mashallah! it has been a great day; it will be talked of long in our tribe, how, with but twenty men, and many of these not at their best, we withstood forty dervishes, and so beat them that when a reinforcement of eight men came to us we destroyed them altogether."

"Four may have got away," Edgar said; "they must have left their horses in the direction in which they fled. I suppose they feared that some of us might crawl out and hamstring them did they picket them near their camp. When I first saw our friends on the hill my first thought was that we had done wrong not to bid them secure the horses before they attacked. Now I see that they could not have found them; and it was well you sent no such orders, for had you done so they might have lost time looking for them and have arrived late."

For half an hour those unwounded of the party were occupied in bandaging up the wounds of the others. At the end of that time the men who had pursued the fugitives had arrived.

"Have you caught them?" the sheik asked as they approached.

"We overtook two and killed them, but the others reached the horses. A man was waiting there in charge of them, and the three rode off leading the fourth horse; but never fear, our men will catch them at the next wells."

The bodies of the fallen dervishes had been examined, and it was found that among the fallen were all the leaders, these being distinguishable by their gay garments from the others, who simply wore the long white shirt that formed, with a coloured straw skull-cap, the uniform of the Mahdi's men. The two men who had escaped belonged to the rank and file. The joy of the Arabs was extreme. They loaded and fired off their muskets, yelled, danced, and gesticulated. They did not believe in the Mahdi, but his followers had come to be considered among them as invincible. It was therefore a triumph indeed for the tribe that this invading party had been annihilated.

The new-comers were surprised at finding a white man among the defenders of the fort; and the sheik was so proud of his possession that he did not hesitate to say that their successful defence was chiefly due to the advice of this slave, whom he described as being, although so young, a great captain. Preparations were now made for a start. The camels of the new-comers were brought up from the spot where they had left them on advancing to take part in the fight. The six wounded men each mounted a camel behind its rider. The sheik and three of his principal followers mounted behind the riders of the other four camels. The rest proceeded on foot, two men being left behind at the fort with instructions that when the eight men who had gone on to the other wady returned with their own camels and the seventeen camels of the dervishes, all were to be loaded up to the extent of their power with the bundles of forage that had done such good service as the basis of the fort, for the supply at the wady had been very nearly all cut down, and food would be required for the camels until a fresh supply sprang up.

The wady was reached at sunset, and a messenger was at once sent off to the spot where, in accordance with the sheik's orders, the women and children with the camels were halted until news should arrive of the result of the fight. It was six miles away, and it was midnight when the party arrived.

Great fires had been lighted, and there was a scene of the liveliest rejoicing as the women and children arrived. There was no thought of sleep that night. The story of the battle was told over and over again, every incident being rehearsed with appropriate gesture, and even the friends of the six who had fallen restrained their grief for the time,

318

partly from pride that they had died so honourably, partly because any show of grief would have been out of place amid the rejoicings for so great an exploit.

With the exception of the children Edgar was the only occupant of the douar who closed an eye that night. He had waited up until the return of the camels and women, had assisted to unload the animals with the sheik's tent and baggage, and to put things into something like order, and had then withdrawn himself from the groups of excited talkers by the fire, and thrown himself down among the bushes some distance away.

He had had but little sleep from the time the party had marched to meet the dervishes. It was upon his advice that they had gone, and he felt himself to some extent responsible for the result. During the time the siege had lasted scarce half an hour had passed without his rising to see that the sentries were vigilant, and to assure himself that the silence of the desert was unbroken. The night before he had not thought of sleep. He had no doubt that the Arabs who were coming to their assistance would do their best to arrive at the right moment; still, something might occur to detain them a little, and although the Arabs had behaved with great bravery hitherto, he felt sure that in a fight in the open they would be no match against the fanatical dervishes, who always fought with a full assurance of victory, and were absolutely indifferent as to their own lives. He had seen them three times at work, and held their courage in the deepest respect.

The next day there was a grand feast, several kids being slaughtered for the purpose. The following morning a caravan was seen approaching, and the whole encampment turned out to meet it, the men discharging their guns and shouting cries of triumph and welcome, to which the new-comers replied with many shouts. In front of the caravan two horses were led; then followed the camels of the dervishes, behind which came those of their captors.

The sheik pressed forward to the leader of the party.

"There were four horses and three men," he said; "have you them all?"

"Two of the horses and the men were killed," he replied. "The others, as you see, we captured."

"Allah be praised!" the sheik said fervently; "then not one of the dervishes has escaped, and the secret of our place of refuge here is preserved."

Some more kids were killed and another grand feast was held. The captured camels were divided between the two parties. The sheik took one of the horses and the leader of the other party the second, and on the following morning the rescuing party started on their return journey to the wady they had left a week before, greatly satisfied with their journey. They had lost three men in the fight with the dervishes, but were the richer by eight camels, a horse, and the arms and ammunition of ten of the dervishes, that being the number they had accounted for, while thirty had been killed by the defenders of the zareba.

Edgar had been fully occupied during those days assisting the negro slave who had remained with the party left behind in looking after the camels, drawing water, and fetching wood for the fire. The sheik had spoken little to him since his return, being busied with the duties of entertaining his guests; but it was evident that he had highly commended him to his wife, who bestowed upon him night and morning a bowl of camel's milk in addition to his ordinary rations. After the caravan had started the sheik called him into his tent.

"Muley," he said, "you have done us great service. I acted upon your advice and it has turned out well; and you have shown that you are a brave fighter as well as one strong in counsel. I have no son, and if you are willing to accept the true faith I will adopt you as my son, and you will be no longer a slave but one of the tribe."

Edgar was silent for a minute or two, thinking over how he had best couch his refusal in terms that would not anger the sheik. Then he said, "I am indeed grateful for your offer, sheik, which does me great honour, but were I to accept it I know that even in your eyes I should be viewed with contempt. Had our people captured Metemmeh when you were there, and carried you off a prisoner, I know well that you would have treated with scorn any offer my people might have made you of a post of honour and wealth among us if you would have abjured Mohammed and become a Christian. You would have died first."

"That would I indeed!" the sheik exclaimed hotly.

"Honourable men do not change their religion for profit, sheik. You were born a follower of the Prophet, I was born a Christian. We both believe what we were taught as children; it is in our blood and cannot be changed. Were I to say the words that would make me a Mohammedan, you know well that I should say them with my lips and not with my heart, that I should be a false Mohammedan as well as a false Christian. I could as easily change the colour of my skin as my religion, and you in your heart would be the first to condemn and despise me did I do so."

The sheik sat for some time stroking his chin in silence. "You are right, Muley," he said at last; "a man cannot change his religion as he can his coat. I did not think of it when I made the offer; but as you say, I would rather die a thousand deaths than abjure Mohammed; and though I now think you worthy to be my son, and to become a sheik after me, I might not think you worthy did you become a renegade."

"Believe me, sheik," Edgar said, rising, "I feel deeply the kindness of your offer, and so long as I remain with you I shall take as much interest in the tribe as if I were a member of it, and I shall do my best to prove myself your faithful slave. You saved my life by refusing to hand me over to the Mahdi. I shall never forget it, and shall be ready at all times to risk it for you, for my kind mistress, and for the tribe."

"You have spoken well, Muley, and although I am sorry, I cannot feel angered at your decision."

Edgar saw that the interview was over, and left the tent, well content that he had been able to refuse the offer without exciting the anger of the sheik. For another two months the tribe remained in the wady. By that time forage was running short, and the sheik announced his intention of leaving it for a time and of going to El-Obeid, where he might obtain employment for his camels by some trader. Edgar was pleased at the news. His chances of escape from their present position in the desert were small indeed, but opportunities might present themselves during a trading journey.

He knew that some time must yet elapse before he could speak the language sufficiently well to hope to pass as a native, although he could make himself understood fairly and comprehend the purport of all that was said to him; still he would gain an acquaintance with the country and learn more of its peoples. He saw that he could not hope to pass as one of the Arab tribesmen, but that if his escape was to be made at all it must be in the disguise of a trader in one of the towns. Four days later the tents were levelled, the belongings of the tribes packed on the camels, and the caravan left the wady on its march across the desert.

CHAPTER XIX
A LONG SEARCH

IT was with mixed feelings that Rupert turned on his camel to take a last view of the camp at Korti. When should he see his countrymen again? Should he ever see them? His journey was sure to be a long one, and there would be the constant danger of discovery. He had to trust entirely in the fidelity of the three men riding ahead of him. It was true that their love of gain was also enlisted on his side, but it might well be that they would in time conclude it would be as well to be contented with the goods they had already received in part payment and with the two valuable camels, instead of continuing to run the risk of a prolonged journey in his company in order to earn the sum promised upon his arrival in Egypt or at a port on the Red Sea. However the die was cast, and he had no wish to withdraw from the task he had undertaken; and, with a wave of his hand towards the distant camp, he turned and set his face forwards to the desert.

The sheik was seated upon one of the heiries, two laden camels followed, each tied with his head-rope to the tail of the one in front. Then followed one of the tribesmen on the other heirie with two laden camels; three more were led by the other Arab. Rupert himself and Ibrahim brought up the rear of the procession, each with three loaded camels following that upon which he was riding. He wore a cotton cloth which passed over one shoulder and was wrapped round the waist, while a second formed a sort of petticoat. The sheik would have preferred that he should have dispensed with the cloth over his shoulder, but Rupert

323

pointed out that this was really essential to him, as he could while travelling wrap it round both shoulders and so protect his skin from the rays of the sun, which, were he naked from the waist, would in a very short time raise blisters over the whole of his body. His wig, with its wild tangle of long hair, acted as a capital protection to his head.

On the saddle was fastened a long Arab gun, a sword and knife were stuck into his girdle, and he carried a long spear in his hand. One of the baggage camels was laden with stores for his personal use on the journey, consisting of a number of jars of Liebig, cocoa, and milk, some tins of tea, a box or two of biscuits, some tins of preserved vegetables, a case or two of arrow-root, and a store of medicine, chiefly saline draughts, quinine, and ipecacuanha. The eatables he calculated would afford him a morning meal for many months – for the main articles of his diet, he depended of course upon such food as the Arabs would obtain – by the end of which time he hoped to have fallen completely into native habits, and to be able to content himself with such food as his guides might subsist upon.

At nightfall they halted at some wells. These were farther to the east than those which the desert column had used in its march to Metemmeh. Rupert had observed that a short time after they had got fairly into the desert the sheik had altered the line on which he was proceeding. He had had but little talk with him since the bargain had been concluded, as the Arab had considered it better that they should not be seen together, as some of the other natives in camp might notice it, and should they meet afterwards the circumstance might lead to his detection.

To Rupert the course taken was absolutely indifferent. He knew that the journey must be a very long one, and as he had only to trust to chance and the sagacity of his companions, there had been no discussion whatever as to the route to be taken. After a time Ibrahim, weary of the silence, urged his camel on until he came up level with that of Rupert.

"Well, Ibrahim, we are fairly on our way."

"Yes, my lord, we have cut our stick and no mistake."

Rupert smiled. Ibrahim had picked up his knowledge of English at Alexandria, and his conversation abounded with slang phrases which he used in perfect seriousness.

"There is no objection to your calling me my lord when we speak in English, Ibrahim, but when we are talking in Arabic be sure you always call me Hamza; that is what I am now. What do you think of this journey, Ibrahim?"

Ibrahim shrugged his shoulders. "It is all the same to me; better here than in boat. Soldier man good to fight, but very rough in tongue; call Ibrahim all sorts of names, sometimes Darkie, sometimes Mate, sometimes call him Nigger, that very bad, sah. One man call him Cockalorham. What is Cockalorham, sah?"

Rupert laughed. "Cockalorum means nothing in particular, Ibrahim; it is rather a friendly sort of address: it means good sort of fellow. That wasn't so bad."

"No. That not so bad. Then one soldier call him Jocko; that name for a monkey, sah; these things very unpleasant."

"But they don't mean anything, Ibrahim. They call each other all sorts of names too."

"That so," Ibrahim said, nodding his head, "very funny names; often call each other blooming something or other. Ibrahim always carry a dictionary; he look out blooming; blooming same as blossoming, means plants out in flower. Ibrahim could not make head or tail of them. Lots of other words, bad words, Ibrahim could not understand."

"They do not mean anything, Ibrahim; it is just an ugly way of talking. They all mean the same, 'very much' or 'very great,' nothing more or less. Now we had better go on talking Arabic."

"No words like those in Arabic," Ibrahim said. "Arab man say what he wants to say, proper words."

"I don't know, Ibrahim. When I have seen Arabs quarrelling they shout and scream at each other, and though I don't know what they say I should think they were using pretty strong expressions whatever they may be."

"Yes, when angry call bad names, one understand that, my lord; but white soldier and sailor use bad words when not angry at all."

"It is habit, Ibrahim, and a very bad habit; but, as I tell you, it doesn't really mean anything. You see we have turned east," he went on in Arabic.

Ibrahim nodded. "Not go straight to Metemmeh," he said. "I expect the sheik is going round by Berber."

Such proved to be the case, for when they halted for the night the sheik explained to Rupert, by means of Ibrahim, that he intended to follow the course of the river for the present. He should keep on the edge of the desert until they had passed the point at which the boat expedition had arrived. There would be no chance of the prisoner having been brought down anywhere in the neighbourhood of the British, but as most of the tribes had sent contingents to fight the whites as they advanced against Metemmeh, the captive might be anywhere beyond the point reached by the expedition, and it would be better to search regularly on their way up, as they might otherwise leave him behind them.

Another advantage was that the regular caravan track left the Nile a hundred miles below Dongola, and struck across the desert to the elbow of the river below Berber, and that when he got upon that route it would be supposed that he had travelled all along by it, and he would thereby avoid the suspicion of having been trading with the British camp. Rupert quite agreed with the justice of this reasoning. The sheik selected a route that led them through a desolate country, and they reached the elbow of the Nile without encountering any natives, save two or three small parties at wells, from the time they left camp. This course was dictated not only by the reason that he had given Rupert, but by a fear for the safety of the caravan.

The tribes along the main routes of travel respected the traders that passed along them; free passage was essential to all the towns and peoples lying further in the interior, and any interference with the caravan routes would have been resented and punished; but the tribes lying within the great loop formed by the bend of the river were true Ishmaelites, whose hand was against every one, and who regarded all passing through their territory as lawful prey. The sheik therefore conducted the march by routes but little traversed even by the natives, avoiding all localities where they were likely to be met with, and he was greatly pleased when, after ten days' travel, they encamped on the banks of the river just above the elbow. The main caravan track lay upon the opposite side, but at this season of the year, when the Nile was very low, it was fordable at several points, and caravans often selected the western bank of the river for their passage. They were now again in a comparatively populous country; villages surrounded by belts of cultivated land occurred at short intervals, and at these they were received with a hearty welcome, for since the war had begun trade had come almost to a stand-still.

Two or three of the camels were loaded with merchandise specially fitted for the wants of the natives: cheap cottons, tinware, trinkets, iron heads of tools, knives, cheap silk handkerchiefs and scarves for the women. These had been bought from some enterprising traders who had set up a store at Korti. A few of the bales were unpacked at the first village at which they arrived; small presents were given as usual to the chief man of the place, and a brisk trade at once commenced. As the camels were fully loaded, Rupert wondered what the sheik would do with the goods he obtained in exchange, which consisted chiefly of native cottons and other articles considerably more bulky than those which he gave for them; but he found that he had entered into an arrangement with the head of the village by which the latter agreed to take charge of all the merchandise until his return.

"It will be perfectly safe," the sheik said, "if I do not return for a couple of years. If I never return it will be no great loss, since I have purchased the goods with the monies I have received from you. If I return this way my camels will be unloaded, and I shall pick up the goods at the various villages through which I pass and bring them all down here, and then sell them to some trader who has boats in which he will take them down the river."

Rupert was now called upon to play his part in earnest. He and Ibrahim were treated by the sheik when in the villages as two slaves, and while he and his companions exhibited their goods and drove bargains with the villagers, Rupert and Ibrahim unloaded the camels, drove them out to pasture, and took them down to the river to drink, taking their meals as they could apart from the rest. On these occasions the stores were untouched, and Rupert and his companion made their meals on dry dates and cakes of coarse flour baked in the ashes of their fire. Ibrahim was fortunately a light-hearted fellow and made the best of matters, joking at the idea of the Arabs feasting upon their stew of kid or mutton while they had to content themselves with coarse fare.

Rupert cared nothing about the food one way or the other. He was now really engaged in the search for Edgar. There was, moreover, the excitement caused by the risk of discovery. When in the villages he seldom opened his lips except to reply briefly to his companion's talk, for a chance word might be overheard. When he spoke it was in a guttural voice, as if he suffered from some affection of the tongue or malformation of the mouth which prevented him speaking clearly; and thus, had any villager overheard the conversation between him and Ibrahim, his defective Arabic would pass unnoticed. Each day after getting away from their halting-place he learned from the sheik what he had gathered in the village. The natives were all heartily sick of the present state of affairs. They had no market for their goods, and were deprived of the trade upon which they had hitherto relied. A few restless spirits had joined the Mahdi's people and had gone to the war; but the cultivators in general sighed for a return of the old state of things, and of the peaceful days they enjoyed while under the rule of Egypt.

Even the tribesmen of the interior were highly dissatisfied. None had gained anything from the war except those who had taken an actual part in the capture of Berber,

Khartoum, or other cities. These had obtained a considerable amount of plunder. But beyond this all were worse off than before. There was no longer any profitable employment for their camels for trade purposes, and the promises of the Mahdi had been altogether falsified. Many of the tribes on the other side of the river had gone down to fight under Osman Digma at Suakim, but instead of the promises of victory being fulfilled they had suffered terribly, had lost vast numbers of men, and Suakim was as far off being taken as ever. Berber itself, the great market and centre of trade of that part of the country, was, all said, like a dead city. The shops were closed, the traders had been either killed or fled, the markets were empty; the Mahdi's soldiers treated the inhabitants as slaves. The sheik satisfied himself that there was no rumour current of there being any white prisoners in the hands of the tribesmen.

"There are white prisoners at Khartoum," the people said. "Gordon was killed, and great numbers with him; but others of the Egyptian officers and traders with their wives and families were made slaves and divided among the Mahdi's officers. But of the white soldiers who had come across the desert, they had heard of no prisoners being taken."

"Why should there be?" they asked. "They beat the Arabs in two battles, they carried off their wounded on their camels, and had any been left behind them they would have been killed at once. Why do you ask?"

The sheik had replied that the merchant far down the river from whom he had purchased his goods had told him that the whites were always ready to pay a good ransom to recover any of their colour who might have been taken captive, and had advised him if he should hear of any prisoners in the hands of the Arabs to ask what they would sell them for, so that on his next journey he might bring money or goods to redeem them.

The villagers had told him that this could not be, for that the Madhi required all captives to be sent to him, and that all who refused to acknowledge him as the Prophet were at once put to death. He had always appeared perfectly satisfied with this explanation, and had turned the conversation to other topics.

"This does not show," he said to Rupert, "that there are no captives in the hands of the tribesmen in the interior. If they had them they would keep it secret, at any rate as long as the white troops are on the river. They can only be holding them for the sake of obtaining a ransom, but I do not think that there would be much chance that your brother is in these parts, for had he been his captors would before now have sent in a messenger to one of your camps saying that he was in their hands and asking what ransom would be given for him. It is far to the south that we must look for him; but at the same time it is wise to make every inquiry as we go along, so that we shall be always looking before us and not wondering whether we have left him behind."

When they reached a village a few miles below Berber they stopped for three or four days. The sheik's two followers went alone into the city to make inquiries. They returned after being absent for three days, saying that it was certain that there was no white captive in the hands of the Mahdi's people there. They had talked to several tribesmen who had fought at Metemmeh. These knew that a white prisoner had been taken by a party of Arabs of the Jahrin tribe. Trouble had arisen owing to the sheik refusing to give him up, and he had fled in the night with his party, taking the prisoner with him; but beyond the fact that he had crossed the river none had heard anything of him.

As there was now no motive for going to Berber, and permission to trade could only be obtained by a large present to the Mahdi's governor, the party started early the next morning, struck out into the desert, and made a long detour before, two days later, they came down again upon the river bank above the city. Then they continued their journey, and some days later crossed the river at a ford some miles below Metemmeh. It was certain, wherever Edgar might be, it would not be in the neighbourhood of that town.

A LONG SEARCH

For some weeks the journey continued. At times they left the river bank and journeyed considerable distances to visit tribes or villages situated in the interior. Sometimes the caravan was divided in two, a portion remaining in charge of one of the sheik's followers with Ibrahim and Rupert with the bulk of the camels and baggage, while the sheik with his other follower and two or three camels made excursions to villages at a distance. In that case he took but few goods with him, so as not to tempt the cupidity of the tribesmen or of any parties of the Mahdi's men he might come across.

By this time Rupert had made considerable progress in Arabic, thanks to his continually conversing in that language, and his risk of detection had greatly decreased. Once or twice a week fresh dye was applied to him from head to foot. He was now accustomed to the scantiness of his clothing, and had completely caught the manners and gestures of the natives. The colour of his eyes was the sole point that even a close observer would detect as being peculiar in his appearance, and he had fallen into the habit of keeping them partly closed and the darkened eye-lashes greatly lessened the chance of their colour being noticed. He had, moreover, by the advice of one of the doctors before leaving, taken with him a bottle of belladonna, and a small dose of this prior to entering any populous village had the effect of enlarging the pupils and thus of darkening the general effect of the eyes. The sheik frequently crossed the river with one of his followers and made excursions among the tribes on the opposite bank, but with all their inquiries no news whatever was obtained of any white captive. It was not until three months after leaving Korti that the caravan approached Khartoum. It was more likely that news would be obtained here than elsewhere, but the sheik had been unwilling to enter the town until Rupert's Arabic would fairly pass muster; but even he now agreed that there was little chance of his detection in any sort of casual conversation. In Khartoum there would be people from all parts of the Soudan, and any slight peculiarity of accent would be little likely to be noticed; besides, in a city there would be less chance of anyone closely questioning the slave of a passing merchant than would be the case in a village. Before going into the town one of the sheik's followers was sent on ahead with a camel with presents for some of the Mahdi's officials, and upon his return with a document authorizing the sheik to enter the city and dispose of his merchandise the caravan set forward.

It was with mingled emotions that Rupert entered the town. Here perhaps Edgar was a captive, or had possibly been put to death for refusing to acknowledge the Mahdi. Here Gordon had fallen a victim to fanatical zeal, the hesitation of the English government, and the treachery of some of the troops he had led to victory. Here hundreds of Egyptian men, women, and children had been slain. Here were the head-quarters of the false Prophet who had brought such ruin and destruction over fertile provinces.

Upon showing the pass to the officials at the ferry leading across to the city a soldier had been told off to accompany them, and he conducted them to an empty caravansary in the city. One of the Arabs was despatched with two unladen camels to the market-place, where he bought a store of provender brought in by the country people. On his return Rupert and Ibrahim fed the animals, which were fastened by ropes from their head-stalls to rings in the wall of the court-yard, and then sallied out with one of the Arabs into the town.

It was still a busy place, although its aspect had greatly changed since its capture. There were no Egyptian soldiers in their gray cotton uniforms and fezes, no officials or traders in European costume in the streets, and the shops which had formerly held large assortments of goods brought up from Egypt were occupied by natives vending the absolute necessaries of life. The Mahdi's soldiers in their cotton shirts, decorated with rags of coloured cloth, and carrying guns, lounged about the streets, and the poorer part of the native population went about with a cowed and dejected air. Food was scarce and dear, for although the Mahdi by promising protection to all coming in to trade had endeavoured to induce the agricultural population to bring in their produce for sale, the invitation was very partially accepted. The country round, indeed, had been swept clean of its grain during the progress of the siege, and the fear of the Mahdi's followers was so great that the peasants contented themselves with tilling only sufficient for their needs. The Arab muttered curses beneath his breath as he walked along, while Rupert and Ibrahim followed in silence, seemingly paying no attention to what was going on around them. When they returned to the caravansary they found the sheik with several of the native shop-keepers engaged with him in conversation. At his orders Rupert and Ibrahim at once began to undo some of the bales and held up the goods for inspection. The sheik named the prices he required. These were at once declared by the natives to be impossible. The sheik simply ordered his assistants to fasten up the bales again. "I have brought them all the way from Egypt and I am not going to give them away. It is not every one in times like this who will risk his beasts and his goods on such an adventure. The traders have all gone down the river with the white men. It may be months or years before a caravan route is open again. Who is going to bring up goods to sell when there is nothing for his camels to carry down again and when the whole country is disturbed? There is neither law nor order in the land. I shall journey on to El-Obeid or Kassaia; I shall get what price I like to ask there."

The traders poured out a torrent of expostulation. They would see the goods again; doubtless they were of a better quality than they supposed; and so the bargain was recommenced, and after some hours a considerable portion of the goods that had been brought up were disposed off. In each case the traders arranged to come late in the evening with their servants to fetch away the goods they had bought.

"It would never do," one said, "to let it be known that we had money sufficient to make such purchases. It is only by assuming the greatest poverty that we can carry on our business unmolested, and only a few of the cheapest goods can be displayed to the eyes of the public, the rest being hidden away to be brought out privately for the benefit of some special customer."

The sheik was well pleased with the result of his traffic. The prices he had charged were five or six fold more than those that the goods had cost, and he sent out one of his followers to purchase a kid, which was presently converted into a stew. After this was eaten he went out with one of his followers, leaving the other to deliver the goods to their purchasers. When it became quite dark the traders arrived one by one, each with one or two porters to carry away the goods. These were paid for in cash drawn from buried hoards.

The sheik was late before he returned. He told Rupert that he had met a kinsman of his who was now an officer of the Mahdi, and had had a long conversation with him. "He believes in the Mahdi," he said, "and has faith that he is going to conquer the world. I told him that finding no traders would hire my camels I had this time brought up a load on my own account, and that it seemed to me there was money to be made if one could purchase some of the people who had been enslaved when the city was taken. He said that this could not be, that the greater part of the traders had been killed, and that all who remained were now zealous followers of the Mahdi. Lupton Bey was held as a slave by the Mahdi himself, and had to run before him when he rode. There would be no possibility of releasing him or the others in the Mahdi's hands.

"I inquired whether any of the Kaffirs who had come to Metemmeh had been taken prisoners. He said they had heard of but one, who was reported by a black slave to be in the hands of a petty sheik who was living at an oasis in the desert some nine days' journey from here. It had already been reported to the Mahdi that this man had taken a Kaffir prisoner at Metemmeh and had refused to give him up, and had escaped with the Kaffir in the night; and strict orders had been issued for his arrest, but nothing had been heard of him until the slave brought the news. The Mahdi sent off three officers and forty men on camels with orders to destroy everything, and to kill all they found with the exception of the sheik himself and his white captive, who were to be brought here to await his pleasure. They went, but though this is two months ago they have never returned.

"Another party was sent three weeks later to the place to order them to return instantly, but when they arrived there they found the oasis deserted. Two skeletons were found, but the sun and the vultures had done their work, and whether they had belonged to the troop that went or to the Arabs there none could say. It may be they found that this sheik and his party had travelled to El-Obeid or elsewhere and had pursued them, but so far no news has been heard of them and the whole matter is a mystery."

"What do you think has happened, sheik?"

"I know not what to think. My kinsman said that the black slave reported there were but twenty men in all with the sheik, and not more than half of these could be considered as fighting men, therefore they could not have resisted for a moment the force against them. It is possible they may have fled into the desert. The tribes know of wells whose existence is kept a secret from all, and it may be that such a well was known to the sheik and that he has made for it. It may be that the negro guide led the party in pursuit. Misfortune may have happened; they may have lost their way and all perished from thirst, though it would be strange indeed were none able to make their way back to the oasis."

"What think you we had better do, sheik? This gives us some indication at least of a direction in which my brother was taken."

The sheik sat for some minutes without answering. "It is difficult," he said at last; "this sheik El Bakhat is, as I have told you, a wanderer. I have heard of him though I have never met him. His father was a powerful sheik, but as a young man El Bakhat killed the son of another sheik of the same tribe and fled. Later on he gathered a few followers and was in the service of the slave-dealers who go down to the great lakes. Of late years, since Gordon broke up the slave-trade, he has returned at times and remained for weeks and sometimes for months in the part of the country occupied by his tribe, for it is so many years now since he killed his man that vengeance is no longer hot against him. He has the name of being a headstrong man, and indeed he must be so or he would never have embroiled himself with the Mahdi's people, for if he had been driven out of his oasis he would know that there is no safety for him anywhere near here; but where he has gone to no man could say. One might as well try to follow the flight of a vulture. He may have gone down near the coast; he may have made his way to the confines of Abyssinia; he may have journeyed away towards the lakes where Emin Pasha still rules in the name of Egypt. There is just one chance, he may be hiding in the desert, and before he starts on a long journey he may return to the oasis or may send a messenger to see if it is still occupied by the Mahdi's men. I think that our best chance is to proceed thither at once, and to wait there for a while to see if any come from him. If at the end of a fortnight or three weeks none come we can then decide in which direction to set out upon the search again."

This proposal seemed to Rupert to offer more prospect of success than any other, and on the following morning the caravan started, the camels now carrying scarce half the weight with which they had left Korti. As the sheik had learned from his kinsman the name of the oasis to which the troop had been sent, he had no difficulty in obtaining from some of the tribesmen in the city precise directions as to the route to be pursued, and ten days after leaving Khartoum they arrived there. The place was absolutely deserted, but they established themselves near the well, and the camels found abundant grazing, as the crops had shot up again with great vigour during the time that had elapsed since they had been cut.

The sheik at once pointed out to Rupert that although El Bakhat and some of his followers were down at Metemmeh, the probability was that his people had occupied the place for some time, as cultivation had been carried on to a considerable extent. "Here are where the tents stood," he said; "and see, he evidently brought back a good deal of plunder, for here are some empty tins and jars scattered about."

They remained for three weeks in camp. One of the party had been always on the watch, but no human being had been seen to approach. During that time the sheik and Rupert had many discussions as to the direction in which the fugitives had probably travelled, and finally decided that the probabilities were in favour of his having taken the southern route and made for the country ruled over by Emin. In the first place he was familiar with this line, and in the second he would be safe from the Mahdi when he reached Emin's country.

"It is rich and fertile," he said; "and probably Emin when he finds he is altogether cut off from the north will try to open a way down to Zanzibar, and El Bakhat may find good employment for his camels." As at any rate there were reasons why the fugitives should have chosen this route more than any other, it was decided to follow it.

CHAPTER XX
FOUND !

BEFORE starting upon their journey the sheik said to Edgar, "On our journey here we travelled by unfrequented tracks, and it was sufficient to cover you up so that none who passed us should notice you; but it will be different now, therefore we must dress you in our own fashion. Your hair can never be made to look like ours and must be bound in a turban. With that and a burnoose your face and hands only will be visible. These are now so darkened by the sun that their fairness will scarce be noticed, but the women will prepare a dye which will darken you to our shade. I wish you to dress like us for another reason. You have done us great service, and though you will not change your religion I regard you almost as one of the tribe, and do not wish you henceforth to consider yourself as a slave. You are improving fast in our language, and if you speak but little you will pass unnoticed. Some men are more silent than others, and you need speak but little when strangers are with us. As one of ourselves you will attract less notice than as a slave. None will say, 'Where did you get that fellow? To what part did he belong? Was he brought from the Great Lakes? Are you inclined to sell him? He is a likely youth. What will you take for him?' "

"I am ready to do what you think best, sheik," Edgar said, "and indeed there can be no doubt that I am far less likely to be noticed if wrapped up in your fashion than if I went half clothed as a slave."

FOUND !

Accordingly a low close-fitting turban was wound round Edgar's head, and he was wrapped up in loose cotton garments covered with a burnoose, the hood of which came over his head. His face, hands, and neck were slightly stained, and when this was done the Arabs admitted that they would not for a moment have suspected him of being other than he seemed. Most of the women, children, and old men were left behind at the wady; the goats and sheep would supply them with milk and cheese; there was a sufficient supply of grain for their use until the crops that had been sown as soon as they arrived should come into bearing; and when all preparations were complete the party started on its way.

It consisted of twelve men mounted on camels, while two other animals followed behind each of these. The sheik rode at the head of the party upon the horse that had been captured from the Mahdists. Amina also had a camel to herself, while the four other women who accompanied the party rode two on a camel. Yussuf and five or six lads of from fifteen to seventeen years old walked by the side of the camels. The led camels were but lightly loaded, carrying only the tents, cooking utensils, provender for the journey, and food and water for the party; and Edgar could see no reason why Yussuf and the boys should not have ridden, except that it was the custom for slaves and lads to walk.

It was a six days' journey to the point they aimed at, and the marches were long ones. The supply of water carried was ample for the wants of the party, and the camels were given a good drink before starting on the fourth day's journey. They were turned loose each evening on arriving at a halting-place, and left to pick up what subsistence they could from the bushes, a good feed being given to them each morning from the provender they carried. As they could have carried much more, Edgar inquired why enough had not been brought to give them a feed at night as well; but the Arab of whom he had asked the question said that it was better for them to browse at night, as the moisture in the herbage enabled them to do with much less water than if they had been fed entirely upon grain.

THE DASH FOR KHARTOUM

Edgar was very glad when the desert journey was over. The glare of the sun from the sand and rocks was almost blinding, and the wraps in which he was muffled up greatly added to his discomfort. On arriving at the cultivated land the same picture presented itself that he had seen near Khartoum. Everywhere the villages were almost entirely deserted and the fields lay waste; the blighting influence of the Mahdi seemed to weigh upon the whole country. The few natives that remained fled in fear at the sight of the strangers, and the old people they met with in the villages were crushed with grief and despondency. Of what use to cultivate the land when the Mahdists might at any moment sweep off the crops? Even should they gather the grain, where could they sell it? There were markets indeed still open, but the Mahdi's tax-gatherers would demand a proportion of the proceeds, which would sweep away all their profits. What was to become of them Allah alone knew.

Edgar was filled with pity for these poor creatures, and over and over again thought with astonishment of the policy which, after sending a force to within a short distance of Khartoum amply sufficient to have crushed the Mahdi and to have restored peace and comfort to the population of the Soudan, had withdrawn them when the goal was all but reached, and left the unhappy people to their fate.

After journeying for some days they passed a plain strewn with skeletons.

"You see these," the sheik said; "they are the remains of the army of Hicks Pasha. Here they were attacked by the Mahdi's army. They defended themselves bravely, but they could neither advance nor retreat, and at last they were vanquished by thirst and fatigue. They were slaughtered as they stood. Hicks Pasha and a band of officers rode right into the midst of the Mahdists, and died fighting there. There were, I heard, two or three Kaffirs with him, besides many Egyptian officers. The black troops fought splendidly, but the Egyptians made a poor stand; but it came to the same in the end. What could they do against the followers of Allah!"

FOUND !

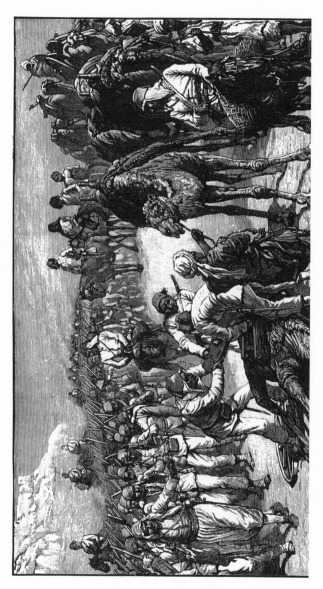

The army of Hicks Pasha on the march.

"But the Egyptians are followers of Allah too," Edgar said, "and yet, as you say, they are but poor fighters. No, no, sheik; I admit the extraordinary bravery of the tribesmen. I fought against them at Suakim and saw them charge down upon our square at Abu Klea. They had no fear of death, and no men ever fought more bravely. But it was a matter of race rather than religion. Your people have always been free, for the rule of Egypt was after all a nominal one. The Egyptians have been slaves for centuries and have lost their fighting power. In the old, old days, thousands of years ago, of which we have records in our sacred book, and which we have learned from other sources, the Egyptians were among the most warlike of people and carried their arms far and wide, but for many hundreds of years now they have been ruled by strangers. It was not very long ago that our people fought a great tribe in the south of Africa – a tribe who knew nothing of Allah, who had in fact no religion at all, and yet they fought as stoutly and as well as your people have done here. It is a matter of race. They were just as ready to die as were your tribesmen, and that not because they believed, as you do, that death in battle would open the gates of paradise to them, but simply because it was the will of their king."

"Mashallah!" the sheik said, stroking his beard, "they must have been brave indeed to throw away their lives if they knew nothing of paradise, merely at the will of one man. That was folly indeed. A man has but one life, it is his all; why should he part with it? Did they love this king of theirs?"

"I do not know that they loved him," Edgar said, "but they feared him. Their laws were very cruel ones, and it was death to turn back in battle."

"They had better have cut his throat and have gone about their own business," the sheik said. "Why should one man be master of the lives of all his people? Is this so among the whites?"

"It is so in some countries, but not in others," Edgar said. "Some countries are ruled over by men chosen by the people themselves, and the power of peace and war and of making laws of all kinds is in the hands of these men, and the king has very little power. In other countries the king is absolute; if he says it is war, it is war."

The sheik was silent.

"But why should people fight and die because one man tells them?" he said after a pause; "it is astonishing."

"But it is just the same thing with the people here and the Mahdi," Edgar said; "he tells them to fight, and they fight; if he told them to scatter to their homes they would do so."

The sheik made no further remark, but it was evident to Edgar that he was thinking out the problems that had presented themselves to him, for some hours afterwards he suddenly remarked, "We who live in tents and wander where we will are the only free men; it is more clear to me than ever."

When they were within a day's journey of El-Obeid they met one of the sheik's followers who had left the wady four days before the rest with instructions to go to the city and find out whether it would be safe to enter. He halted his camel when he reached that of the sheik.

"You must go no nearer the city, my father," he said. "I have learned that orders have been received by the Mahdi's governor to arrest you and all with you should you present yourselves there. There is much talk about a party of soldiers who went into the desert to arrest you having disappeared altogether; others have been sent to find them, but have discovered no traces of them, so there are orders that any of our tribe from the desert are to be closely questioned. Any who admit a knowledge of you are to be sent to Khartoum. I was questioned at the gates, but as I said that I had come straight from Khartoum and knew nought of what was passing in the desert I was passed in without further inquiry. I took up my abode with the people you told me of, and they have found out for me what I have told you. It is but three days since the orders concerning you were received."

THE DASH FOR KHARTOUM

"I thought there might be danger at El-Obeid," the sheik said calmly. "We will turn off so as to avoid the city, and will make south to join the white pasha. For a while it would not be safe anywhere here."

Without further words he turned his camel from the track they had been following, and bore away more to the south.

"Think you that the white pasha will be able to maintain his position?"

The sheik shook his head.

"For a time he may, but in the end he must either surrender or try to strike down to the sea. His troops will weary at last even if they are not beaten by the army the Mahdi will send against them. They will say, 'Why should we go on fighting? What good can come of our holding out when no aid can possibly reach us from Egypt?' The Mahdi will be glad to come to terms with them and allow them to live there in quiet with their wives and families and their possessions, if they will acknowledge him and hand over the white pasha with the two or three white officers he has with him. But that will make no difference to me. I know all the country by the Great Lakes. There are Arab traders there in plenty who buy slaves and ivory and take them down to the coast. I can find employment with them for my camels, and can stay with them until it is safe to return. This cannot go on for ever. Besides, in times of trouble events pass quickly out of men's minds, and in a year the Mahdists will have forgotten my name. As to the loss of their forty men, what is it? They have lost thousands since the war began."

"When we get to the white pasha, sheik, would you hand me over to him if he offered you a ransom for me?"

"No," the sheik said decidedly, "I should not take you near him. Why should I part with you? You have brought us good fortune. Thanks to you we defeated the Mahdists and captured their camels and all that they had. Besides, I like you. Why should I part with you? What good would it do you? With me you are no longer treated as a slave, but as one of my own people. What would you be with the white pasha? An officer of his troops, getting no pay, and running the risk of being one day seized and sent with the others a prisoner to Khartoum."

"I have no desire to stay with the white pasha," Edgar said; "I would rather be with you than in so hopeless a position as he is; but I might make my way down to the coast?"

"Never," the sheik said; "at least never alone. There are fierce tribes between the lakes and the sea. No white man could get through alone. He could only do it by going with a great band of fighting men and carriers, and by buying his way by presents through the great tribes and fighting his way through the small ones. You may travel down to the sea some day with me if I join the caravans of the Arabs, and then if there are countrymen of yours on the coast, as I have heard, and they would pay me a good ransom for you, we may see about it. You are ungrateful to wish to leave me."

"Not ungrateful, sheik, for you and your wife have treated me with great kindness; but it is natural that one should wish to go to one's own people. Had you been taken a prisoner and carried to England, however well you were treated you would sigh for your free life in the desert, for your people and friends, and would escape if you saw a chance. It is human nature to love the land where one was born, whatever that land may be."

"That is true," El Bakhat admitted; "but you cannot escape now; there is nowhere for you to go to."

"That is true, sheik; and I should be well content did I know that you were travelling straight either for Suakim or Zanzibar, for at either place I know that I could obtain from my countrymen money to pay any ransom you might set upon me, even a sum that would buy you fast camels and much goods, and make you a wealthy man in your tribe; but I am not content to wait for years."

"You are not thinking of making your escape now?" El Bakhat asked, looking scrutinizingly at Edgar under his heavy eyebrows.

"No, sheik," Edgar answered. "From the day that you captured me I made up my mind that I would escape sooner or later, whatever the risk; but I knew well that I could never traverse the country until I could speak the language like a native. I have made great progress, and can now understand all that is said and can talk freely and easily, but not so that I could travel alone as a native. It will be months yet before I can do that. Nor, after the kindness with which you have treated me, would I leave you suddenly without warning. When I feel that I can safely travel alone I shall give you fair warning. I shall say to you, Sheik, if you will now travel with me to Suakim or some other port where I can obtain money for paying you a fair ransom I will remain with you until such ransom is paid into your hands; if you will not do so I shall consider myself free to escape when I can. Of course it will be open to you to treat me again as a slave, and to use all vigilance to prevent my leaving you, but I shall consider that by giving you fair warning I shall be free to use my best endeavours to get away."

"You speak boldly," the sheik said, "but you speak fairly. Do you give me your promise not to attempt to escape until after warning me?"

"Yes, I give you that promise, sheik."

"It is well," El Bakhat said gravely. "I know that you would not lie to me. After you have given me warning I shall know what to do." So saying he got up and walked away to his tent.

Three days later, as the caravan was halting at a well, Yussuf, who had gone out with the camels, ran in.

"There is a large body of men, some on foot and some on horses, approaching from the south."

"How far are they off?" the sheik asked as he leapt to his feet.

"Scarce half a mile," the negro replied.

FOUND !

"Then it is too late for flight," the sheik said, reseating himself; "they would be here long before we could saddle our camels. It is doubtless a body of the Mahdi's troops, but if they come from the south they will have heard nothing against us."

When the Mahdists rode up the sheik rose and saluted their commander.

"Who are you?" the officer asked. "I am an humble person, one El Bakhat of the Jahrin tribe, travelling with my camels and some little merchandise."

"Have you the permit of one of the Mahdi's officers to trade?"

"No, my lord, I did not know that it was needful."

"Assuredly it is needful," the officer said. "Your camels and goods are forfeited, and you yourself and your people must travel with us to El-Obeid, where inquiries will be made about you."

"My lord," the sheik said, "I am a poor man and have done no harm. After fighting against the infidels I went back to my people with such spoil as we had taken and have dwelt there quietly, and was ignorant that it needed a permission for me to journey with my camels."

"Well, if you can prove that when you get to the city," the officer said, "the governor may take a lenient view of the case, and may content himself by taking a portion only of your camels as a fine; but if you are lying it will be worse for you. Remember now that you are prisoners, and will be shot down if one of you attempts to escape."

The sheik bowed submissively. The officer ordered some of his men to keep a rigid watch over the prisoners, and then paid no further attention to them.

The sheik re-entered his tent and sat down stern and silent without speaking. Amina, who had heard what had passed, was in the greatest state of alarm, but saw that her husband was not to be spoken to at present. She went to the door of her tent and beckoned to Edgar, in whom she felt the most implicit confidence, to enter.

"You heard what has passed, Muley?"

347

"I heard, lady; the position is full of danger."

"You are fertile in expedients. Can you not suggest something? You see if we are taken to El-Obeid, where they have had news of the expedition sent from Khartoum, and its disappearance in the desert, my husband would be sent in chains to the Mahdi, and you know what his fate would then be, while the least that will befall us all will be to be sold into slavery. What then do you advise?"

"With your permission I will think it over," Edgar replied. "The position is a difficult one; the danger is, as you say, great."

"Go, then, and think it over, Muley."

Edgar went out of the tent and squatted down (a position which had at first been very fatiguing, but to which he was now accustomed) by the embers of the fire before it, and thought over what had best be done. For himself, he felt sure that he could make his escape, for though a general watch might be kept, one man could doubtless crawl away in the darkness; but he felt that he could not abandon the sheik in a moment of danger. It was, in fact, owing to himself that the sheik was now in his present position. It was true that the Arab had refused to give him up to the Mahdi's people at Metemmeh, not from any love towards him, but of his own obstinate and headstrong disposition. However, that refusal, whatever its motives, had undoubtedly saved his life; and, moreover, the sheik had behaved with great kindness to him since, and he felt that it was clearly his duty to do all in his power to assist him now; but how?

It was upwards of an hour before he rose from the fire and again entered the sheik's tent. The sheik was sitting smoking gravely. Amina was baking some bread over the embers in the middle of the tent.

"What is your counsel, Muley?" she asked.

"I see no plan," he said, "by which my lord can get away with all his followers and camels. One or two might steal out from the camp, and I thought at first that if Yussuf and myself – who would not be so closely watched as he will be, for there are two sentries outside the tent – could manage to steal out with our guns and to open fire in the darkness upon the camp, the Mahdists, thinking they were attacked, would seize their arms and run out, and in the confusion my lord and you and some of the others might make their escape. But this plan is full of danger, and it might not succeed, for they might suspect that those who attacked them were of your party, and a portion would remain to keep guard over you. This, then, should be the last resource, for if the attempt was made and failed, escape would be more difficult than ever.

"It appears to me that the first thing to do is to try and bribe the chief. At present he only suspects you of trading without a license, and were my lord to see him and to offer him half the camels and the burdens, to let him go free with the remainder, he might accept it. If that failed, we can still try my plan. I would take my gun and crawl out with Yussuf. I would go two or three hundred yards away to the right, and would then fire as quickly as I could, moving while I did so; so that they might think that there were many attacking them. Then, my lord, in the confusion you and your wife with the child should try to make your escape. As soon as the camp is aroused and they are advancing against us we would move round to the left of the camp, and you would join us there and make straight across the country and be far away by daylight."

"But how could we travel without camels?" the sheik broke in impatiently; "they would surely overtake us before long."

"There are deserted villages in which we might hide until the pursuit is over," Edgar said. "As they would gain all the camels and goods it would matter little to them that three or four persons had escaped."

"Not until they reached El-Obeid," the sheik said. "Then they would learn who we were, and would scour the country for us. Camels we must have if we are to escape. Besides, I should be a ruined man, and might as well be killed at once."

"Not altogether ruined, sheik," Edgar said. "You remember that we buried many of your valuables and arms at the wady."

"We could never get there without camels," the sheik said gloomily.

"It might be done, sheik. Several men accompanied the camels on foot, and we could perform the journey so on our way back; but I should not counsel that. My idea was that we should get as far away from here as possible, and should then leave your wife and child in some village. We could take with us goods which would be quite sufficient to ensure a welcome for her until you return. Then I should propose that you and I with Yussuf, who is certainly faithful, should make our way down on foot as Arab fighting men to Berber, and then on to Osman Digma, who is, we know, close to Suakim. Thence we might readily find means of escaping him and entering the town, and then, as I told you, I can promise you a ransom that would enable you to buy more camels and goods than you have lost here, to return to your wife and child and take them with you to your wady. As to camels, I do not altogether despair of getting some. They are, as usual, grazing outside the camp, they know Yussuf's voice and mine, and when we first escape we might lead four of them away and take them to the left of the camp, where you are afterwards to meet us. Before morning we could be very many miles away."

"Ah! if you could do that!" the chief said, showing for the first time a lively interest in the matter, "it might be possible. However, I will try first of all if the officer will accept a bribe. If he will do so it will give us two days' start, and we can then arrange matters as you say."

Without another word he rose and went to the door of the tent. The two sentries placed there stepped forward and told him that their orders were that he was not to leave it.

"I wish not to leave it," he said; "I desire only to speak to your commander. I have something of importance to say to him. Will you pray him to come to me?"

FOUND !

One of the sentries at once went across to the commander's tent and shortly returned with him.

"Master," the sheik said, "I have done wrong in journeying without a license, but I came from the desert and did not know the law. I must pay for my fault, though I cannot think that the commander at El-Obeid would be hard upon one who has erred from ignorance. However, as it is urgent for me to press on my journey, I will relinquish to you one-third of my camels and their burdens if you will let us travel on with the others, and give us a permit from yourself so that none may molest us in future."

As the officer had no suspicion that the Arab's first story was untrue he hesitated; then he said, "Not so; all your camels are forfeited for breaking the laws of the Mahdi."

"But those who err in ignorance are surely not punished like those who err wilfully," the sheik urged. "But I am pressed for time. I am journeying south to the tents of my wife's father, who has sent to say that he is sick unto death and wishes to see her before he dies. Be content, my lord, and take half the camels." The officer thought that the offer was a good one. It was probable that the governor of El-Obeid would not fine the Arab more than half his camels, seeing that he had broken the law inadvertently, and in that case he himself would have but a small share in the spoil; whereas if he consented to the proposal, the camels would all fall to himself, saving one or two he might give to his officers to induce them to keep silence as to the affair.

"I will be more merciful than you deserve, Arab," he said; "I will take half your camels with their loads; but see that you cheat me not; if you do, it will be worse for you. Divide the animals and goods to-morrow morning in two equal parts. I will take that which pleases me most. I have spoken;" and turning upon his heel he went back to his tent.

Edgar, standing within, heard the conversation. "You have heard," the sheik said when he had entered; "half my property is gone, but I have freedom and the other half. I have had worse misfortunes than this. So far your counsel has turned out well, Muley. Now about the future. We shall

351

have but four days' start. He will reach El-Obeid by evening the day after to-morrow. There he will hear that he has let slip through his fingers the man for whom all the country is in search, and horsemen will be despatched instantly in pursuit; probably they will be here the next evening; it is but a reprieve. Journey as fast as we will they will soon overtake us."

"Yes, if we pursue our course in the same direction, sheik, but this we must not do. I should say that as soon as the division is made we should start south; it is as well that they should see the direction in which we are travelling. Then as soon as we are well out of sight of the camp I should say let us break up the party into six or eight parts and bid them travel in different directions east and west, and then make to the point where we arrived from the desert, and strike across to the wady. A party like ours would be noticed at once, but two or three persons each with a camel carrying their belongings would be scarce observed; and the Mahdi's horsemen, asking if a caravan of ten camels had passed, would be told that no such party had been seen. At any rate most of your men would be able to regain the wady and there to await your return. Then I should propose that you on one camel and your wife and child on another, with such goods as you require to pay your way, with myself on foot dressed as formerly as a slave, should strike in the direction of Khartoum, but keeping this side of the river until we reach Berber. Of course you could take Yussuf with you or not as you might choose; but I think that you would find him useful."

"You would like him to go?" the sheik asked in a tone of suspicion, for it flashed across him that if Edgar and Yussuf made common cause he would be at their mercy.

"I should like him to go, sheik. The negro has always been civil and obliging to me from the day when I thrashed his companion, and if when we arrive at a port on the Red Sea you are willing to part with him I will gladly arrange to buy him of you at any reasonable price that you might name."

"So be it," the sheik said; "the matter is settled."

FOUND !

Next morning the sheik and his followers were on foot early. They divided the camels with the greatest care into two portions, debating earnestly on the merits of each animal; then the goods, which were of but trifling value, were also divided. When all was done the Mahdi's officer came down and closely inspected both lots of animals.

"There is nothing to choose between them," he said; "you have made a just division. I will take the right-hand lot, and the horse is of course mine;" and to the disgust of the sheik he ordered one of the followers to take it to his tent. "Here is a permit for you to journey and trade as you will." The soldiers were already under arms, the Arabs hastily packed their tents and cooking-pots on the camels that remained to them, and the two parties set off almost at the same instant in two opposite directions. When they had travelled for an hour the sheik halted his caravan and explained the situation to his followers.

"As soon as the Mahdists reach the town they will hear of us, and hot pursuit will be instantly set on foot; therefore it is necessary for the present to abandon our plans and for you to return at once to the wady from which we started. But if our pursuers obtain news of a caravan of our size they will be sure to overtake us; therefore it is also necessary that we should separate at once. Let each man, therefore, take his camel, his wife, and his belongings, and journey singly. Let some go east and some west, and making a circuit to avoid El-Obeid reach the edge of the desert as best you may. Do not wait there for each other, but let each as he reaches it strike across to the wells. When you reach the wady wait there for me. I go with my wife and Muley and Yussuf. We shall take two camels and journey north. There I hope to obtain a sum for the surrender of Muley, which will more than repay us the loss we have suffered to-day."

The Arabs at once obeyed the orders of the sheik and in a few minutes were speeding across the country.

"We will go on for another three or four hours' march," the sheik said, "before we turn to the east. Our pursuers will be sure to inquire for us at every place they pass, and if they hear that solitary camel-men have been seen making their way across the country they will turn off at once in pursuit. It is therefore better that they should move off some distance before we turn off." The sheik had chosen two camels which, though not remarkable for their looks, were of better blood than the rest, and more capable of performing long journeys. He and his wife and child rode on one of the animals, Edgar with Yussuf behind him on the other. At noon they turned off from the southern course they had before been pursuing. They continued their journey until long after sunset, and then halted for a few hours to rest the camels.

The moon rose at eight o'clock, and as soon as it was up they started again, travelling now in a north-easterly direction in order to throw their pursuers off their track. At daybreak they halted again, this time in a grove. A fire was lit and Yussuf cooked some meal cakes, and a bountiful feed of grain was given to each animal. As speed was less an object than secrecy no move was made until nightfall, in order that they might pass through the villages unobserved. The journey was continued until the following morning, when they again halted. They were now following a track which would, the sheik said, lead them after a few miles into the main road between El-Obeid and Khartoum.

This time the halt was of but a few hours' duration, as they hoped that they had baffled their pursuers and could now travel without attracting any special attention. They had reached the road and were proceeding along it when Yussuf saw dust rising in the distance. He called the attention of the sheik to it, and the camels were pressed forward to their utmost speed. But camels will seldom go far beyond their accustomed walk; and it soon became apparent that they were being rapidly overtaken by the strangers who were pressing on behind. By this time it could be seen that the party following them were also mounted on camels. Two riders had detached themselves from the main body and were coming on at a rapid pace.

"They must be mounted on heiries," the sheik said; "see how they come along! There is no avoiding them."

"They are not the Mahdi's men," Yussuf said presently; "I can see by their dress that they are in Arab robes."

"They are riding for a purpose," the sheik said, "or they would not travel so fast, and yet if their purpose were hostile they would hardly leave their followers so far behind. If they know aught of El Bakhat they will know that he is not a man to surrender without resistance. Prepare your gun, Muley. Methinks there are but two men with the four camels behind, and if we slay these first we shall have no difficulty with them."

The strangers came rapidly up, and as they approached the sheik saw that they were an Arab trader and a wild-looking native. As they came up they reined in their camels and the trader gave the usual Arab salutation, which was responded to by the sheik. Two or three of the usual ceremonial sentences were repeated on both sides.

"My brother's name is El Bakhat?" the new-comer said. "My name is my own," the sheik replied, "and is no concern of strangers."

"I come as a friend," the Arab said. "I arrived at El-Obeid yesterday and heard that a body of horsemen had set out in pursuit of you. Yesterday evening some returned with a prisoner, who said that your party had separated and that you were travelling north. Two parties of horsemen were ordered to start at daybreak. Thinking that you might make for Khartoum, I set out at once to warn you."

By this time the wild-looking young native had slipped from his camel and walked up to Edgar, staring fixedly at him. Edgar, not knowing what to make of the movement, shifted his rifle forward, when the native gave a wild cry, "Edgar!"

Edgar gazed at him with stupefaction. It was Rupert's voice; but how could this wild figure be Rupert? how could he be here?

"Edgar, do you not know me? I am Rupert!" Edgar could doubt no longer. He flung himself from his camel and rushed into his brother's arms.

"It's Rupert's voice, but it cannot be Rupert!"

FOUND !

"Am I mad or dreaming?" he exclaimed, as he still failed altogether to recognize Rupert in his disguise. "It is Rupert's voice surely, but it cannot be Rupert."

"It is me, sure enough, Edgar; and you are neither mad nor dreaming."

"But this hair?" Edgar said, still bewildered, gazing at the wild, unkempt locks.

"It is a wig, neither more nor less, Edgar, made for me at Cairo; and a first-rate job too."

Edgar could doubt no longer, but with the certainty and joy a strange weakness seemed to come over him, and he would have fallen had not Rupert seized him.

"Stand up, old boy; it is all right, and natural enough. We heard at Metemmeh of your having been carried away, and as of course I wasn't going to let you remain a slave among these fellows, I got leave of absence from Wolseley, got a disguise and a first-rate guide, and, thank God, I have come to you at last."

The surprise of El Bakhat at seeing this meeting between Muley and this young native was much greater than that of the other Arab, who had heard at El-Obeid the evening before that the white slave was journeying in disguise with his captor.

"This is my brother, sheik," Edgar said to him. "He has come all this way in disguise to look for and rescue me."

"He has done well," the sheik said warmly, while Amina clapped her hands in pleasure.

"Is the story about the pursuit after us true?" Edgar asked.

"Yes, quite true. The horsemen will not be many hours before they overtake us."

A hurried consultation was held between the two sheiks, and it was decided to strike off to the south-east again, and as soon as the followers arrived with the camels the united parties left the road and made across the country, Edgar taking his place on the camel behind Rupert. He still felt like one in a dream, and even now could scarce believe that it was really Rupert who was riding before him. The latter, who had been looking forward to the meeting, was yet scarcely less surprised at what had taken place. It had seemed such a hopeless task looking for Edgar over so wide an expanse of country that he could scarcely credit that he had succeeded in finding him, and for a time the feelings were so deep on both sides that hardly a word was spoken. It was not, indeed, until the camels came to a halt late in the evening that they began to talk naturally.

CHAPTER XXI
HOME !

"YOU are a nice fellow, ain't you, Edgar, to give us all this trouble," Rupert said, as he held him at arm's-length and gazed at him in the light of the fire that Yussuf had lighted.

"I see now that I made an awful fool of myself," Edgar said; "but I think you would have done the same if you had been in my place, Rupert, and had heard what I heard."

"I have no doubt I should," Rupert agreed; "it must have been an awful thing to hear. Still you must have seen by the advertisements that father did not believe the woman's story."

"I did not see the advertisements," Edgar said. "I would not look at a paper, because I thought he would advertise for me to come back, and I felt I could not do so, and it would have been harder to keep away if I had seen them. You told me they were all well at home."

This was the first question he had asked after he had mounted Rupert's camel.

"Quite well when I last heard. I wrote and told them all about you."

"Then the sergeant was found, and did not die?"

"He died the first day after we found him," Rupert said gravely. "He was insensible when we discovered him; and I should have known nothing about him if they hadn't found two letters upon him, one to me and one to father, saying that his wife's story was a lie, and that he could swear that neither of them could in any way identify either of us from the other. He recovered consciousness before he died, and signed in the presence of witnesses a deposition to the same effect. So you saw me at Korti, Edgar, and would not make yourself known? I would not have believed it of you."

"Well, you see, Rupert, I did not know at the time that the sergeant was who he was, and still believed the woman's story to be true. Besides, I had gone my own way, and did not mean to see any of you again until I had got on and could do without assistance. It seemed to me to be like asking for help, and after all that I had had under false pretences I would have rather died than do that."

"But you see it wasn't under false pretences, Edgar, and you had as much right to consider yourself father's son as I had. You must have known that from the sergeant afterwards."

"Yes, I did learn that," Edgar allowed, "but I think that made me even more disinclined than before to show myself; it would have looked as if I had come back only to put in a claim."

"You are the most pig-headed fellow I ever saw, Edgar. However, I hope you have got out of all that feeling now."

"Quite, Rupert; I am quite ready to go back with you and beg their pardon at home for all the trouble I have given them. And to think that you have run all this awful risk to find me!"

"Stuff and nonsense, Edgar! When I found that you had been carried away as a slave, as a matter of course I determined to get you out as soon as possible, just as you would have done had I been caught by them; but I could have done nothing if it hadn't been for this Arab I am travelling with. Of course he will be well paid; but still men are often tempted to be unfaithful however well they are paid;" and then he went on to tell Edgar of the arrangement that had been made with the sheik. Edgar in return gave him a short sketch of his life since they had parted at Cheltenham, and told him of the promises he had made to El Bakhat if he would take him down to one of the Red Sea ports.

"I suppose they are discussing the matter together," he said, glancing at the two Arabs, who were deep in conversation on the other side of the fire.

"Well, sheik, what plan have you determined upon?"

"We both think that it will be impossible for us to travel north either to Egypt, or to Berber and thence to Suakim. They will be on the watch for us everywhere. Our best plan will be to make for Massowah."

"Well, sheik, you have heard that Ben Ibyn has agreed to deliver us at one of the ports for a handsome reward. He knows that Englishmen's words can be relied upon, and that there is no fear of his not getting the amount promised him. My brother and I agree to give you an equal sum to that which he will receive there."

"He has not told me the sum," El Bakhat said.

"Tell him the terms, Ben Ibyn," Rupert put in. "Not of course those you have already received for your expenses, but the sum that is to be paid you when you arrive at a port."

The sheik repeated the terms to El Bakhat, who at once expressed himself as perfectly satisfied with them.

"The English are rich and generous," he said. "El Bakhat will do his best to take them where they wish to go."

"Are you thinking of travelling with all this train?" Rupert asked Ben Ibyn.

"No, there is no occasion to do so. I have friends at a village on the Nile, and there my followers and their camels will remain, and El Bakhat's wife and child will remain with them also. We four will then travel on alone, taking with us Yussuf to cook for us and look after the camels. We shall separate from the others at once, as it will be much safer to travel in two small parties. There will be no fear as to their safety, as they will take my regular permit to trade, and no one will connect them in any way with El Bakhat. You and your brother will ride the heiries. I have a half-bred camel that will carry me well, although it will not compare in speed with yours. El Bakhat's camel is also a good one. If we are pursued, we have agreed that our best plan will be to turn off and find a hiding-place, and for you to push on alone.

On those camels you may defy pursuit. If pushed they will travel a hundred and fifty miles a day. When you get to Massowah you will wait until we join you there. We are content to trust to your word. Still we hope that we may keep together; for although your brother now speaks Arabic so well that he could pass as a native in casual conversation, it is better that we should be together, in which case it will be we who will do the talking."

"Have you two heiries?" Edgar asked Rupert.

"They are not quite full bred. It is very rare to meet with them, and the price is extremely high; but these are nearly full bred, and can swing along as fast as a horse can trot, and keep it up for twelve hours at a stretch."

The march was resumed at midnight. The two sheiks rode ahead, Edgar and Rupert followed on the heiries, while Yussuf was mounted on one of the spare camels, and rode with the other Arab in the rear. The two brothers talked by turns, and both were surprised when the first streak of daylight appeared. The party now separated, the sheik's wife and child taking their seats on one of the camels. She took a warm farewell of Edgar.

"Amina will never forget the young white man who has lived in her tents," she said. "He is brave in war, and is a wise counsellor; he will be a great man among his own people."

"And I shall never forget you," Edgar replied, "and your kindness to the white slave. When the sheik returns from Massowah he shall bring with him tokens of my remembrance."

As soon as the party had separated the sheiks put their camels to their best speed. Yussuf had been taken up by Edgar and rode behind him, the heiries carrying the double weight with ease. At sunset they halted.

"We are now," El Bakhat said to Edgar, "beyond the reach of pursuit. We may be stopped and arrested by others, but those from El-Obeid will never see the tails of our camels."

HOME !

"I wish," Edgar said as they were riding along the next morning, "that you could get rid of that wig and your dye for five minutes, Rupert, so that I could see what you really look like. You are such an awful object with that bush of hair that I do not seem to recognize you at all. It is different with me. I am only brown, while you are a sort of dirty black, and when this cloth round my head is off you really see me as I am."

"We should not have known each other by our figures. It is nearly three years since you left Cheltenham, and of course we have both widened out a lot since then. You have widened more than I have, but I have grown most."

"Yes, you are quite two inches taller than I am, Rupert. What are you – six feet?"

"About half an inch under."

"Ah! then you are just the two inches taller. I am forty, chest measurement."

"I am not more than thirty-seven, Edgar."

"Ah! I expect you will be forty before you have done, Rupert; you see neither of us is anything like his full width yet. I have had harder work than you have."

"Ah! Edgar, if we could both play in the house team now it would make a difference, wouldn't it? You remember how Skinner was always lamenting our want of weight."

"I don't think," Edgar said with a laugh, "that he has gained much in weight. He was about our size before, but he looked to me quite a little chap when I saw him on the march."

"He is tough," Rupert said; "he is like whip-cord all over; he is a capital fellow, not a bit changed. Easton has turned out first-rate; he was awfully good to me after you went away, and took no end of pains to cheer me up, had me down to his place in the holidays, and was a real friend. He is a big fellow now, and in another two or three years will make a splendid man. They will be delighted when we both turn up again. I don't think either of them thought, when they said good-bye to me, that I should ever get back. They

363

thought the language would floor me, I think. You have got on wonderfully that way. I thought I had picked it up pretty quickly, but you jaw away as if you had been years at it."

"I have been more with them, Rupert; besides, I had picked up a little in the year I was at Cairo. You see I had nearly four months start of you, and in the life I led among them of course I had a lot more occasion to talk than you have had, always on camel back and only talking in the encampment at night. El Bakhat says that in a casual conversation now no one would notice that I was not a native. So if we do get into any mess and have to ride for it by ourselves, we shall have no difficulty in making our way across the country; but I do not see much chance of that. If we should fall in with the Mahdists your sheik can give his name and appear to be the head of the party, and as there is nothing against him I don't see why we should have any trouble."

"I daresay we shall fall in with some Mahdists," Rupert said. "I got up the maps thoroughly before I started, and specially studied the routes leading to the coast. I fancy the line we shall travel will take us down by Kassala. The Mahdists were besieging it, but I don't know whether it has fallen or not. The safest route would certainly be to go through Abyssinia, but the Arabs wouldn't like to travel that way if they could help it. There have been troubles for years between Abyssinia and the Soudan, and it is by no means certain what sort of treatment we should meet if we got there. Massowah is certainly the best place to strike for. Suakim would have been the best place in some respects, because there are lots of English there and we should have no difficulty in getting money to pay the sheiks; but after all it is only a question of a week or two's delay at the most. I have letters from my father authorizing me to draw upon him for any amount, and if we cannot get it at Massowah we shall only have to send up to the officer in command at Suakim; he would cash a draft out of the pay-chest; or if he could not do it that way, would get some merchant there to do it."

HOME !

They no longer hurried, but made moderate marches, stopping only at small villages. There was no difficulty in obtaining food and shelter, as Rupert's conductor had brought on with him a sufficient store of merchandise to pay their way down to the coast. On these occasions Edgar and Rupert kept in the background looking after the camels, while Yussuf waited upon the sheiks, and afterwards cooked a meal for the two Englishmen. He did most of the talking with the poorer villagers, gossiped with them about the state of the country, the chance of peace being re-established, and retailed all sorts of wonderful stories of the doings of the Mahdists.

Both branches of the Nile were crossed in their journey, but no incident of any kind occurred until they had passed the eastern arm. They were now getting into a more dangerous country. Bodies of the Mahdi's troops going to and from Kassala, which had, they learned, at last surrendered, were encountered, and questions were asked as to where they were going and what was the object of their journey.

Upon these occasions Ben Ibyn acted as spokesman and represented that they had friends among the Hadendowah tribesmen, and wished to learn whether any trade could be opened with the coast. When within a day's march of Kassala they met a number of camels laden with spoil from that town on their way to Khartoum, accompanied by a number of foot soldiers and ten or twelve horsemen. Riding twenty or thirty yards behind the sheiks Edgar saw one of the horsemen look earnestly at El Bakhat, and then spur forward to speak to the others who were a short distance ahead.

"That fellow has recognized El Bakhat!" he exclaimed; "ride on, Rupert!"

They both shook the halters and the heiries broke into a trot.

"Ride, sheiks!" Edgar exclaimed as he came up to the others; "one of the horsemen has recognized El Bakhat."

A minute or two later they heard a shout behind them, but paid no attention.

THE DASH FOR KHARTOUM

"We have got four or five hundred yards start," Rupert said, looking back, "but the horsemen will overtake us; they can go faster than the camels for a burst. Ride, sheik," he said; "push on to the utmost. If we can get a mile away from the footmen before they come up to us we can thrash the horsemen."

The start they had obtained while the man who had recognized El Bakhat was explaining to the others who he was and how much his capture was desired at Khartoum, was invaluable to the fugitives, and the horsemen started in a body, shouting and yelling and firing their guns. The bullets whistled harmlessly round the fugitives.

"Make for that clump of trees on rising ground," Edgar said; "then spring off the camels and fight them on foot. What arms have you, Rupert?"

"I have two revolvers besides this rifle. You take one of them; we shall beat them off easily enough, they are only about two to one."

When they reached the trees they were but a hundred yards ahead and less than a mile from the caravan, which had halted when the horsemen commenced the pursuit. They leapt from their camels.

"Do you hold their bridles, Yussuf," Edgar said; "we will beat them off," and steadying his rifle against the trunk of a tree he fired at the nearest horseman, who fell instantly from the saddle.

Rupert's rifle cracked a moment later, and the two sheiks added their fire. Had the horsemen been coming up in a close body they would have gained the wood, for the leader was but fifty yards away when Edgar fired; but they were scattered, and the leaders being shot down the others wheeled their horses and galloped back towards the caravan at full speed.

"Now we will be off again," Rupert said, and in a minute they had mounted and continued their flight.

"There is no fear of the footmen overtaking us," Ben Ibyn remarked. "Our camels are not like yours, but they can trot at a good pace for forty miles. It is fortunate we had

366

them, for they would soon have been up to them had we only had common camels. Of course we must strike off straight for Massowah now. The danger is not over; some of the horsemen will bear the news to Kassala and a troop will be sent out in pursuit of us. It is well that we have journeyed quietly and that the beasts are in good condition."

Hour after hour passed. The camels kept on with unswerving gait until long after nightfall.

"My beast smells water," Ben Ibyn said as his camel, after waving his head backwards and forwards, suddenly quickened its pace.

Another quarter of an hour they stopped at a small pool in what during the rainy season was the bed of a river, and here they halted. The camels having drunk their fill were given an ample allowance of corn from the saddle-bags, and were then picketed close at hand, while Yussuf prepared a meal for their masters.

"What is the country like that we have to traverse?" Edgar asked.

"By to-morrow night," Ben Ibyn said, "we shall have reached the mountains. We are on very high land now, and have a great descent to make to reach the coast. We must inquire the way to the pass by which the road from Kassala descends to Massowah. If we strike it without failure we shall be safe; but if we miss our way, and the horsemen from Kassala get there first, we shall be in a bad position. They will have heard of our arms and strength, and are sure to have too strong a force for us to attack. If we fail to find the road at once, our best plan would be to turn and travel north until we reach a road going down to Suakim."

"Would that one of us had travelled here before!" El Bakhat said. "If we could but have continued our journey to-night we should be safe. Upon the desert one can travel by the stars, but the ground is getting far too broken to cross at night; we should only weary our camels in vain."

"How far is it to the gorge you speak of, El Bakhat?"

THE DASH FOR KHARTOUM

"I know not for certain. Those who travel the road have told me that it is three or four days' journey with laden camels from Kassala. Our camels can easily do three days' march in one, and if we have the good fortune to strike the road near the mouth of the pass we may pass through it before dark to-morrow; but by that time they may be there from Kassala."

"Well, I suppose we must take our chances," Rupert said.

He and Edgar soon lay down and were fast asleep, but the two Arabs talked together for a long time before they followed their example. At daybreak the party were on their feet.

"We talked it over last night," Ben Ibyn said; "and we both think that it were best not to proceed. The horsemen would have reached the town with the news three hours after noon, and had they sent off at once horsemen and fast camel-men down the road to Massowah, we think that they would be at the pass before we could possibly reach it. Had we known the country and could have travelled all night, we should have been there long before them. As it is, the risk would be too great. We are already some distance north of the Massowah road, and it will not be so many days longer a journey to Suakim than to Massowah. Osman Digma is lying at Handoub and Tamai, so we cannot come down by the Berber road; but there are passes by which we can descend to the low country near Tokar. Once down there we can cross from the foot of the hills to the sea by night, and then follow the coast until we arrive at Suakim."

"I think that is the best plan, sheik," Edgar said. "A few days will make no difference, and it would be as well to avoid all risks."

Accordingly, on mounting, the camels' heads were turned to the north-east. Yussuf rode behind Rupert and Edgar by turns, so as to divide the labour between the two heiries. A few villages were passed, but the inhabitants fled into their houses or into the fields on seeing the approach of the party, the arrival of strangers meaning extortion and demands for tribute. So they journeyed for several days, until one afternoon they came to a large village, which was evidently inhabited. They alighted and knocked at the door of the principal house. No answer was at first returned, but on El Bakhat shouting that he would break down the door if it was not opened, bolts were heard to unfasten. The door opened, and an old man presented himself.

"Why did you not reply to our knocking?" El Bakhat asked angrily. "Is this your hospitality to strangers?"

"My lord must pardon me," he said submissively; "but it was but last week that a party of the Mahdi's soldiers came along here and stripped the village of all it possessed, and drove off its bullocks and sheep. Save our grain, we have nought that we can call our own."

"We do not belong to the Mahdi," Ben Ibyn said, "but are peaceful travellers. We desire only to fill our bags with grain for the animals, for which we will pay you the full value. For ourselves we need nothing, although, if you have peradventure a kid or a sheep left among you we will gladly purchase it."

"Enter, my lord," the old man replied briskly, evidently much relieved at the announcement; "all that the village still possesses is at your service."

He gave an order, and a boy brought out a basket of grain, which he emptied before the camels, while the two Arabs, Edgar, and Rupert entered the house. Ten minutes later a villager brought in a freshly-killed kid, which Yussuf, after lighting a fire in the court-yard, proceeded to cut up and cook. In the meantime the Arabs had entered into a conversation with the peasant as to the routes down to the sea. They learned that so far they had been coming in the right direction, and that some thirty miles farther they would come upon a track leading down to Tokar.

"You must look well for it," he said; "it is never greatly traversed, and since the troubles all trade has ceased, and you may well cross the track without noticing it."

"Have you any in the village who know the track?" Edgar asked.

"There are several here who have been down to Tokar, my lord."

"We will give ten yards of good cloth to one who will go and set us on the road. We will take him behind one of our camels, and as we shall start at daybreak he can be back here before nightfall. I suppose when we once find the track it will not be difficult to follow it."

"I can doubtless find a guide," the peasant said; "he can give you instructions as to the path, or he could go with you, if you choose, still further, to show you the way. I will go and find you such a man."

An active-looking young native presently arrived, and said that he was willing to be their guide to the point where the track left the high lands and entered the gorges leading down towards the sea. It was, he said, four days camels' march beyond the point where they would strike the track, and he would accompany them this distance for forty yards of cotton cloth. The bargain was struck at once, and the following morning they started, the guide riding behind Edgar.

As there was no occasion for haste, and the camels might be required to exert their utmost speed when they reached the low country, the journey was performed by three easy stages, the distances being about forty miles each day. It was well that they had a guide with them, for the track was in most places entirely obliterated.

"You cannot miss your way now," the native said at their last halting-place by some shallow wells. "This depression leads straight down to the pass. It is two days' march hence to the lower plains. When the valley at last opens on them you will be about ten miles west of Tokar."

The next morning the guide started on his return journey. The cloth had been given to him before starting, and he now carried a few pounds of grain and a small bag full of dried dates for his five days' journey back to his village.

The journey down the gorges was an arduous one. The path had been swept away by the last season's rains, and in some places where the valley narrowed to a gorge but a few yards wide, with the rocks rising sheer up hundreds of feet on either side, the bottom was filled with large blocks of stone brought down by the floods, whose highest level could be seen forty or fifty feet above them on the rocks. Occasionally it was necessary to build a sloping platform with small boulders of stones to enable the camels to get over the vast blocks that filled the space between the walls. It took them three days of arduous labour; but the valley at last opened out, and they saw a broad expanse of country stretching before them. No one had either met or passed them on the way down; but here in the lower valley there were several flocks of sheep and goats watched over by Arab boys. These, at the sight of strangers, hastily collected their animals and drove them up the hillside, but at a shout from Ben Ibyn, saying that they were friends and would do them no harm, two of them presently came down.

On hearing that the travellers intended to camp for the night they led the way to the wells, and for three yards of cotton killed and brought in a sheep. Presently the rest of the lads came down and squatted near the fire that Yussuf had kindled, and after the party had dined were rejoiced by the present of some wheaten cakes and a portion of the cooked meat. They now became very communicative. They belonged to the Hadendowah tribe. There were three or four hundred of the dervishes at Tokar. Osman Digma had in all four or five thousand men at Handoub, and was soon going to drive the Kaffirs into the sea. Many of their tribe were with him, but others were disheartened at the long delay to carry his promise into effect. They had lost, too, a great many of their best fighting men in the battles with the Kaffirs, but no doubt when Osman Digma announced that the favourable time had arrived, all would again join him in order to have their share of the plunder of Suakim.

The next day they stopped at the wells, telling the boys that the camels were sorely wearied by their journey down the gorge, and that they needed a day's rest. In the evening as soon as the meal was over they mounted their camels, much to the surprise of the native boys, and started. Edgar could judge of the general position, for though he had not been as far as Tokar he could tell pretty well the line they should take to come down upon Trinkitat. As soon as they were fairly out of the valley the camels were put to their full speed, and in four hours the sea shining in the bright moonlight lay before them. Crossing a shallow lagoon they were upon the sandy beach.

The pace of the camels was now slackened, as it was useless to arrive at Suakim before daybreak, as they would have been liable to be shot by the sentries in the forts if they approached in the darkness. When day broke Edgar and Rupert gave a shout of joy, for three or four miles away could be seen the masts of shipping. Again the camels broke into a trot, and in half an hour they approached the forts raised to defend the town on the land side from the attacks by Osman Digma's followers. No questions were asked them, for natives belonging to friendly tribes frequently entered or left the town.

As they crossed the ground between the forts and the town they saw a party of marines marching out to relieve those who had occupied the fort at night. They reined in their camels, and Rupert addressed the officer marching at the head of the party.

"Can you tell me, sir, if Lieutenant Skinner is at Suakim at present?"

The officer was astounded at being thus addressed in pure English by a wild looking native, and the men following him were no less astonished.

"Is it possible," the officer exclaimed, "that you are Mr. Clinton?"

"That is my name," Rupert replied.

The officer advanced and grasped his hand warmly. "I am glad indeed to see you," he said; "Skinner is my subaltern, and has often spoken to me of what he considered your hopeless journey to try to find your brother, and said that if you did get through it alive you were as likely as not to turn up here. I congratulate you indeed. Have you been successful?" and he looked doubtfully at Rupert's companions.

"Yes, thank God, I have succeeded. This is my brother Edgar."

The officer shook hands warmly with Edgar, and even the men who had heard what was said raised a shout of welcome.

"I forgot; Skinner is in the rear," the officer said; and raising his voice shouted his name.

Skinner came running up. He had been wondering what the halt was for. Edgar and Rupert had dismounted by this time and ran forward to meet him. He stopped in surprise and then recognized Rupert, whom he had already seen in his present disguise.

"Clinton!" he exclaimed with a, joyous shout; "is it really you? Thank God, you have got back again, and – and –"

"And this is Edgar," Rupert put in.

For a minute or two the three stood shaking each other's hands, too excited and joyous to speak, while the soldiers cheered lustily. The captain in command came up.

"Look here, Skinner; it would be too bad to take you away from your friends now, so I will take it upon myself to give you leave off duty. I will get Thomson to stay out until to-morrow morning in your place. He won't mind when I tell him why, and you can take his turn on duty on shore next time."

Talking excitedly together they entered the town, the Arabs following on their camels and Yussuf leading the two heiries.

"The first thing to do," Skinner said, "is to get you rigged out decently. I suppose it will be some time before you can get rid of your dye, but at any rate you can get dressed like Christians; and you can get rid of that fearful wig, Rupert. I will send off a boat to my ship with a note, and they will soon send you on shore a couple of suits of clothes. Mine would be of no use; you could not get into them. This is the only hotel in the place."

THE DASH FOR KHARTOUM

"First of all we must see about these Arabs being made comfortable. Where can they put up their camels?"

"Oh! that will be all right," Skinner said; "one of the fellows here will take them under his charge."

Skinner entered and came out with a servant. "You can put your camels in the court-yard here, El Bakhat," Edgar said after speaking to the men. "Yussuf will look after them. You had better find a lodging for yourselves. You will be more at home there than you would here. Get everything you want; you will have no difficulty in finding everything in the Arab quarter. Skinner, lend me a sovereign, will you? We have been living on barter for a long time, but they will want money here."

"This is worth five dollars," he said as he handed the money to El Bakhat; "but, ah! I forgot, Ben Ibyn knows about the value of English money. If you will come here at noon I may be able to tell you something about the money."

They then entered the hotel with Skinner.

"Get breakfast, the best you can get," Skinner ordered; "and show me to a room where there is plenty of water and towels. These are Englishmen, though you would not think so from their appearance."

The young fellows enjoyed a thorough wash, and Rupert got rid of his wig, but they had to attire themselves in their former garments for breakfast. After existing for months upon native fare the breakfast was a luxury indeed. By the time they had finished, the messenger Skinner sent off returned with two suits of clothes sent ashore by the officers of his ship, and having attired themselves in these they went with Skinner to the political officer. When he understood who they were he received them with much warmth.

"I have had letters from Captain Clinton," he said, "respecting you; saying that it was possible that you might turn up here, and requesting me to assist you in getting any bills you might draw on him cashed. I will go with you to the principal merchant here. No doubt he will do it, but if not I can manage the affair with one of the ships' paymasters."

HOME !

The merchant, however, was perfectly willing to honour their draft upon their father for a thousand pounds upon the statement of the officer that he would himself guarantee its payment, and he told them that his servants should bring the money in silver to the hotel. Four hundred pounds was the amount that Ben Ibyn had been promised on delivering Rupert in safety at one of the ports, and an equal sum was to be given to El Bakhat. This left them two hundred pounds for getting to England, for Edgar had learned that his regiment had a month previously sailed for India, and he considered that under the circumstances he was perfectly justified in reporting himself at the depot at home.

The sheiks on their arrival at the hotel received with great satisfaction the bags of money containing the stipulated amount. To these were added a brace of revolvers each, being the two Rupert had carried and two they had purchased in Suakim, together with ten boxes of ammunition. Edgar also gave to El Bakhat a set of jewellery and several silk scarves for Amina.

"Now, sheik," he said, "I should like to purchase the freedom of Yussuf. What do you value him at?" "I will give him to you," the sheik said. "You have treated me well and honourably."

"No, I will not have that, sheik; he is your property, and is a very useful slave.

I will give you two hundred dollars for him."

"It is well," El Bakhat said; "he is yours."

"Now," Rupert said, "there are the two heiries; they are yours by right, Ben Ibyn, but I would fain give one to El Bakhat. I will give you three hundred dollars to forego your claim to it. I know the beast is worth more; but if you possess one of them it will suffice for your needs, and you will oblige me if you will part with the other."

"I can refuse my lord nothing," Ben Ibyn said, "and the possession of two such heiries might well draw envy and enmity upon me. I will accept his offer."

THE DASH FOR KHARTOUM

"Then the other heirie is yours, El Bakhat," Rupert said, "as a special present from me for the kindness you have shown my brother. What do you both mean to do now?"

"We have agreed to journey up the coast together and then to travel across the mountains to Assouan, and there buy camels and goods, or we may buy them here if we see bargains to suit us. Then we shall turn south. I shall go on alone to Khartoum; I know many of the Mahdi's officers, and shall by presents to them obtain a pardon for El Bakhat, and permission for him to return to his tribe. Money will do as much among the Mahdi's people as elsewhere."

"We shall see you again to-morrow, sheiks. A steamer sails in the afternoon for Suez, and we shall go in her. Come here to say good-bye to us in the morning."

When the sheiks had left Yussuf was called in, and Edgar told him that he had purchased his freedom from El Bakhat. The negro threw himself on his knees in an ecstasy of delight and poured out his thanks.

"Now, what would you like to do, Yussuf?" Edgar went on when the negro had quieted down. "I can recommend you here to some merchant as a faithful man whom he can trust, or if you would like to set up a shop here I will give you two hundred dollars with which to trade. Or I can take you up with us to Suez and give you strong letters of recommendation with which you can obtain employment there."

"No, my lord," Yussuf cried, "none of these things. I would go with you and be your servant; I will never leave you."

"But I don't want a servant, Yussuf," Edgar said. "As I have told you, I am a soldier, and soldiers do not have servants."

"Oh, that is nonsense!" Rupert put in. "You are not going on as a private soldier. You know you need not reckon upon that, Edgar. You like the fellow, and there is no doubt he would make you a faithful servant; and anyhow they could find something to do for him at home."

HOME !

Edgar pointed out to Yussuf that the life would be strange to him, the climate altogether different to that to which he was accustomed, and that he would find no one who could speak his language. But Yussuf was unmoved, and entreated so earnestly to be taken that Edgar gave in, saying that after all, if he repented afterwards, he could be sent back to Egypt. Just as this was settled a messenger entered with a telegram from Captain Clinton in answer to that they had despatched before they had sat down to breakfast announcing their safe arrival. It contained simply the words, "Thank God! Come home at once."

They went off to dinner with Skinner on board ship, and the story of their adventures excited immense interest among the officers. Skinner returned with them on shore, and remained with them until the steamer left in the afternoon, Yussuf, who had been rigged out in white trousers and jacket, a checked shirt, and straw hat, accompanying them. The two sheiks saw them off, and stood looking after them with grave regret until the steamer was far from land. At Suez Edgar and Rupert provided themselves with a stock of linen and clothing; two days later they took passage to Brindisi in a P. and O. steamer, and travelled rapidly across Europe. Their colour excited much surprise among the passengers on board the steamer, but as they had no wish to keep on telling their story they kept themselves apart, and made no acquaintances during the short voyage. Yussuf was astounded at everything he saw: the ship and her machinery, the trains, the fertile country through which they travelled, the frequent villages, and great towns. There was no stay in London. They drove across from Charing Cross to Paddington, and went down by the first train. A telegram had been despatched from Dover, and a carriage was at the station to meet them, and the servant handed Rupert a note. It contained a few words from his father, saying that he had not come to meet them, as he thought it better that they should all meet together at home. It was Edgar who received the first greeting from father, mother, and sister, while Rupert stood by, well content that his brother should on this occasion come first. It was little over a year since he had said good-bye to them, while it was more than three since Edgar had seen them, and his own greeting, though delayed for a moment, was no less warm than that of Edgar.

"Father and mother," Edgar began as soon as they turned again from Rupert, "I want to say that I feel how wrong I was –"

"Then don't say it," Captain Clinton broke in. "We won't talk about that time at all. You suffered, and we have all suffered; but good has come out of it. Thank God the matter is settled now for ever, and we know there is nothing more to be found out about it, and that there is no fear of our ever having to look at one or other of you in a different light to that with which we regard you, as our two sons, of both of whom we have every reason to be proud. There now, let us talk of other things. You have both gone through wonderful adventures, which we are burning to hear about."

"You have changed a great deal, Edgar," Mrs. Clinton said. "Of course we have seen Rupert comparatively lately; but I think that you have changed more than he has from what you both were three years ago. You look older than he does, and your figure is more set."

"He has gone through so much more," Rupert said; "he has been doing man's work for three years. I have only had a year and a half of it."

"You need not be in a hurry to look old, Rupert," Captain Clinton laughed; "that will come soon enough, and you have widened out a good deal in this last year. You had got very weedy, and I am glad to see that you are filling up.

"I have some news for you, Edgar. I saw Lord Wolseley on his return to England, and he spoke very kindly of you both, and when I got your telegram from Suakim I wrote to him again and received a very warm letter of congratulation from him in reply. He told me that he had received a most favourable report of you from your colonel, who said that your conduct had been most exemplary since you had entered the regiment, and that as you had been recommended for the Victoria Cross he had intended to recommend you for a commission as soon as you had served a qualifying time as a sergeant. But Lord Wolseley said that he thought it would be a great pity for you to lose four or five years' seniority by waiting to get your commission from the ranks, and that he had that morning spoken to the Duke of Cambridge about you, and that the latter had put your name down for a Queen's Cadetship, so that if you could pass the mere qualifying examination you could have a commission at once. There will be an examination in two months' time, and if you go up to a crammer and work hard you will be able to brush up your school work and get through; if not, of course you can go in again six months later. I am afraid you will hardly get ready in time for the first."

"I don't know, father," Rupert said; while Edgar expressed his lively satisfaction. "Edgar speaks Arabic like a native, and if he takes that up as a subject he is sure to get full marks for it, and that will help him tremendously. Of course he would have no chance of getting through if he had to go in for the competition; but something like half the number of marks are enough for the qualifying examination."

"Well, we mustn't be too sanguine," Captain Clinton said; "and eight months' quiet study won't hurt him after campaigning in Egypt for two years. By the way, Edgar, I paid in the money for you to buy out, and sent in an application in your name. These things take some little time before they are carried out, but no doubt we shall soon hear. But in the meantime you had better write at once to the officer commanding your depot, saying that you have returned home, and asking for a month's leave of absence. You are sure to get your discharge before that is over."

Edgar remained at home for a week, spending much of his time, however, over his old school-books. Then he went up to town and worked at a crammer's until the examination came off, when, thanks in no small degree to the number of marks he obtained for his Arabic, he just managed to get the number necessary to qualify him. To his great satisfaction he was at once gazetted to a regiment as if he had been promoted from the ranks, instead of having to go through the course at Sandhurst, and thus gained several months' seniority. Three months' leave was granted him, and at the end of that time he joined his regiment, which was stationed at Malta.

No question as to which of the Clintons is the legitimate son of the captain and his wife has ever again troubled them. Edgar and Rupert know that they are equally dear to those at home, and all are happy in the knowledge that nothing henceforth can break the closeness of their tie, and that it can never be known which is the lawful heir of the estates. What is much more important to them both, neither of them can say which has the first claim on the love and affection of Captain and Mrs. Clinton, and of their sister.

THE END.

Camp Life in Abyssinia.

by G. A. Henty

This article was written by Mr. Henty during his
career as a war correspondent

G. A. Henty age 48

Camp Life in Abyssinia.
Antalo, March 10. 1868

THE public are kept so thoroughly informed by the despatches of the authorities, and by the letters of the special correspondents, as to the general progress of this expedition, and the main features of the people and country through which we are passing, that any details upon these subjects would appear to be quite superfluous. But there is one phase of the expedition, and that a very important one to those engaged in it, which has been hitherto but little touched upon. I mean the actual routine of camp life, the food we eat, and the way we live. It is my intention, therefore, in this article, while speaking of the expedition generally, to endeavour to keep that ground more strongly than any other in view. Let me first depict the tent I am writing in, one of the ordinary English military tents of bell shape. Our party is three in number, known by the *sobriquets* of the "Drayman," so called from his general build and especial development of leg; "the Jockey," or "Lightweight," of about half the weight of the preceding occupant; and the "Professor," so called from a charming egotism, peculiar to himself, of expressing himself in an *ex cathedrâ* manner upon every imaginable point. Three in a bell-tent is very close work. Fortunately, two of us sleep upon the ground, the third enjoying the luxury of a portable bedstead. Boxes form our chairs and tables. One revolver, and a looking-glass, a thoroughly useless article in this tent, hang from the central pole, and, as the wind is blowing sharply, the whole fabric keeps up a confused flapping and roaring, which renders conversation almost an impossibility. The tent is in comparative darkness, as candles are very precious, and I have the only one alight stuck in a bottle upon the ground beside me; and all three men are smoking with great steadiness. The party present have messed together since we landed at Zoula, more than two months ago; but it is only lately that we have been three in a tent. But to begin at Zoula. It was early in December when we landed, and the dead and dying mules and camels were horrible to see—and

383

worse than that, dense clouds of sand enveloped everything; and a hundred or so of tents, and some piles of commissariat stores, were the solo precursors of what was to be in a short time a large canvas town. It certainly was a wrench to leave our comfortable and well appointed transport, and to land upon that shifting sand desert. However, there was no help for it, and, with our band playing, and the men cheering as we left the ship's side, we landed as gaily as it if we were entering a favourite garrison town. We had heard so much of Zoula, and what had been done there, that I think we were almost as surprised at seeing only a few tents, a couple of dozen at the most, scattered about with no native huts or sign of habitation, as was young Martin Chuzzlewit when he found what the thriving town of Eden was in reality. But for the next hour or so we were too busy seeing our own and the men's tents pitched to think about the country. When this was done, and our duties all over, we strolled out together to inspect our new land of promise. It would be difficult to say whether the sense of smell or sight was most offended. We arrived there at the worst time, and dying and dead mules and camels were met with everywhere. The scenes were frightful—worst of all by the waterside. Here half maddened mules would dash into the sea and drink, and then stagger back to die in the low scrub. By the edge of the sea were camels dead and dying, camels picked clean by vultures, camels half buried, camels which ought to have been buried days before. Farther out in the sea were objects which looked like huge birds, but which were camels lying down in the shallow water. Here they had been lowered from the native dacs in which they had come from Aden; and here very many died, either from pure weakness or drowned by the tide when it rose. In among the bushes other camels were lying—living skeletons. They had struggled to shore, and there they had sunk down, feebly cropping the scanty leaves within reach. It was so horrible that we could talk but little. Then—for it was just watering time—we went to the troughs—miserable-looking things—at which five or six animals at most could be watered. There was a guard to preserve order, but order could not have been kept by ten times as many men. There were hundreds of transport animals, with one driver to each four or five of them. But what could one driver do with five half-mad animals? They struggled, they kicked, they bit, they fought like wild beasts for a drink of the precious water for which they were dying. Besides these led animals were numerous other waifs, which, having broken their head-ropes, had gone out on the plain to seek a living on their own account. For these there was no water. They were beaten off. Most of them, after a repulse or two, submitted to their fate, and went off to die; others fought for their lives, cleared a way to the trough with heels and teeth, and drank regardless of the blows showered on them. It was the most painful sight I ever witnessed in my life. We went back to our tent to eat our dinner in silence, unmindful of the fact that the meat was hard as leather, and full of grit; and then lighting our pipes and cigars, our indignation found words.

"By Jove," the Drayman said, "if I knew who was responsible for all this, I should be inclined to horsewhip him to the last inch of his wretched life, even if I were dismissed the service five minutes afterwards."

"My dear fellow," the Jockey said mildly—he has a hateful way of being sarcastic at times— "you are threatening a non-existent personage. We are in the blame. No one will be blamed. Everyone has done his duty in an exemplary way. Some little conflict of departments has occurred, and a few animals suffer. Voilà tout."

"Nonsense!" the Drayman said, angrily. "This is not an ordinary case. Someone must be to blame, some one must be made to suffer for the torture his gross neglect has inflicted on these poor brutes."

"My dear fellow," Lightweight replied, "you take such a hasty view of things! The public does not suffer torture and takes no account of feelings. If you had said the public will demand a strict investigation into the pecuniary loss consequent on the death of so great a number of animals, you might perhaps be nearer the mark. But who is he?"

"The commanding officer, to begin with," the Drayman said.

"Who is the commanding officer?" the Jockey asked. "I mean who was he before—— and ——came into harbour?"

There was a pause.

"I have taken some little pains to find out," the professor rejoined, taking his cigar from his lips, and speaking in the oracular and deliberate way usual to him— "I have taken some little pains to find out, and I am told that there was no officer whatever in command."

"Nonsense, man! there must have been some one in command."

"I can assure you that there was no one in command. There was a head of the commissariat, a head of the quartermaster's department, a head of the transport train, each of whom did his best for himself; but there was no one in command, no one to direct operations."

"But," the Drayman cried, impatiently, "there are lots of colonels—there's A, B, C, and D, for instance—one of them must have been in command."

"The four officers you have named," the Professor answered placidly, "started a fortnight since for Senafé, leaving things here to take care of themselves."

"Do you mean to tell me that these men went off at a time when two or three ships a day, full of men and animals, were arriving; that they every one went away, and, as you put it, left things to take care of themselves, and did not even put any one in command to keep them straight?"

The Professor nodded.

"Then, by Jove," the Drayman furiously exclaimed, "the British public will insist on these men explaining their conduct."

"Well," said the Jockey, "I will bet you three to one that there is nothing whatever said about it."

But the Drayman thought that impossible—proving to his own satisfaction that the present was the very grossest case of mismanagement which ever happened in the annals of the British army.

Perhaps it was so; but for all that, four months have elapsed, and the Jockey has been justified. Every one has been praised and thanked, and some soldiers have been promoted. The dead animals have been buried, and so has the disposition for inquiry.

"What is this nastiness I am drinking?" one of our party asked, when the conversation had at last exhausted itself upon the horrible state of things around us.

After two or three tastings, it was unanimously agreed that we were drinking salt-water, mixed with brandy. Our servant was called. He, in his turn, summoned the water-carrier, who declared that it was obtained from the tanks. There was nothing more to be said so we threw away the contents of our glasses and ordered tea. Then a black mixture was brought, intensely bitter, and with no taste whatever of tea. We gave up in despair, and resolved to go to bed.

Lightweight had got on his pyjamas, and was about to get into his blankets, when the Professor said quietly,— "I should advise you to examine your bed before you lie down; there is something running across it now." The something was a scorpion. After a sharp hunt the creature was killed, and after a careful examination we wrapped ourselves in our rugs, the Jockey making anxious inquiries of the Professor as to the effects of a bite of a scorpion, and the remedies. "I fancy by what I have heard," he said finally, "that the best plan, if one is bitten, is to cut the place out. Look here, Professor, I have put my open knife, matches, and a candle, on this box. If you hear me holla, you jump out and strike a light, and lose no time in cutting away before it spreads."

Our duties at Zoula could hardly be termed light. The men were constantly on fatiguing duty—unloading stores from the lighters, carrying railway-sleepers, furnishing guards at the water-tanks, and so forth. The heat was great, but not overpowering; but the dust was almost appalling. Had it not been for the morning and evening bath in the sea, I do not know what we should have done. Barbers were in great request. Every one had his hair cut as short as scissors could cut it; and any one landing might have guessed, from our appearance, that he had just arrived at a convict settlement. For the first week we struggled for existence upon food cooked by our soldier servants, eked out with preserved meats, ham, and sticks of chocolate. The united invention of our three servants could only produce three dishes, which they called Irish stew, beefsteak, and roast-beef. The extreme toughness of the stew, the leathery nature of the steak, and the perfect dryness of the beef rendered them alike abominable. They worked our jaws to a standstill; and had it not been for the aid of the preserved meats, I believe we should have starved. "My dear fellows," the Lightweight said, after one of these banquets, "you may say what you like, but this cannot go on. We must get a native servant, cost us what it may." For once there was perfect accord among us; and three days afterwards we were fortunate enough to receive a Goa Portuguese, whose late master had brought more servants than he was able to take on with him. He proved to be a capital fellow, and a first-rate cook; and our little mess was the admiration of the regiment. Fortunately the Professor combined with his other admirable qualities that of a good shot, and many a guinea-fowl has he brought in as an addition to our larder. There is no better bird eaten than a Guinea-fowl when well cooked. It is larger than a pheasant, and more tender.

387

It has a much more decidedly game flavour and tastes indeed somewhat between a pheasant and a grouse.

Long before we left Zoula we had the satisfaction of seeing the terrible state of things I have described entirely altered. Sir Charles Staveley took matters in hand, and ere long everything was going on smoothly. Troughs were set up at which fifty animals could drink at once; and remembering the scenes we had witnessed when we first landed, it was now a pleasure to go down and see the long lines of mules come up and drink their fill. The bad days through which they had passed had, however, done their work. Disease was engendered, which sooner or later told upon the animals; and although a large number, no doubt, died of disease engendered in the country itself, it is certain that a much larger number died of lung-disease brought on by insufficient water and food. Accordingly, the transport train was crippled; and instead of the troops for the advanced division being at Senafé with a good supply of stores by the end of December, they were not ready for an advance until the first week in February. This, however, is not a subject to be entered into in a letter the object of which is to give a picture of camp life.

If the supply of water of these animals increased before we left Zoula, that issued to us decreased greatly. Very stringent regulations were made according to which three quarts of water became our daily allowance. This was for cooking, drinking, and washing. At most, a quart remained for the latter purpose; and this in a climate where the thermometer in our tent stood at 105, where one was in a permanent state of perspiration, and where the dust blew in such thick clouds that one could not see twenty yards! When we stopped in our tent it was well enough; but we came in from fatigue-work so covered with a crust of dirt as to be absolutely unrecognizable. The Drayman and the Professor, who took their swim twice a day, were able to bear this philosophically. Lightweight, however a man of delicate habits, and very particular as to his dress and get-up and who, moreover, did not swim, and had an objection to salt-water, because, he said, it made him sticky all over, became positively plaintive over this state of things. He would come in from a fatigue-party, sit down upon a box, take down the looking-glass, and groan out his usual complaint: "Good heavens! here am I, a gentleman by birth and education living to see myself with my hair cut off; and my face a mask, an absolute mask of dirt. I am positively gritty all over with sand, and am asked to wash in a teaspoonful of water!"

We were all delighted when we got the order to march forward. Anything more dusty than the march to Koomaylo can hardly be conceived; but we did not mind it, for we knew we could get as much water as we liked there. We stopped at Koomaylo for nearly a week, and the change from Zoula was delightful; the heat perhaps was nearly as great, but there was a perfect absence of dust. The Professor brought in several deer. The soldiers used to go off across the hill in chase of troops of enormous baboons, which it is unnecessary to say they never caught. The dogs came up with them several times; but the minute they seized one of their number, his companions attacked them and beat them off. The number of transport animals at Koomaylo was enormous; but, fortunately, the supply of water from the little American pumps was unfailing. The water, too, excellent, and actually quenched one's thirst; whereas the distilled water at Zoula had no such effect. The Professor found quartz in abundance scattered about, as indeed there was no difficulty doing, and affirmed that he was of opinion that gold would be found in the bed rock of the stream; but as he could give no acceptable reason for his belief, and never found a trace of gold— although he was always going out with his basin to wash—his assertion was received with incredulity, especially as we never saw any gold ornaments whatever upon the native women. I have not yet spoken of the natives. I should say that their principal characteristics were laziness and dirt. Still it must be said for the Shohos that in the first respect they are beaten hollow, and in the latter at least rivalled, by their Abyssinian brethren upon the plateau lands. The Shohos could be got to do some sorts of work. They would stand in a chain down to the water in the wells where there were no pumps, and would pass buckets from hand to hand. They would, too, assist to dig wells; whereas an Abyssinian considered it beneath his dignity to do any work whatever. As a general thing, however, the principal occupation of the lives of both people is loafing, pure and simple. They wander about listlessly with their clubs or spears over their shoulders, or squat for hours upon the ground, with their faces pressed hard against their chests and their dirty cotton robes tightly wrapped round both limbs and body. The effect of this is very curious; for the legs of these natives are fairly comparable to pipestems, their bodies are little thicker than their legs, and so they look like troops of strange birds, squatting together in groups of five or six.

At last we got the order to move forward in earnest. The bugles were to sound at half-past five in the morning. Why at half-past five in the morning was more than to this moment any one has been able to discover. Every one has to get up before it is light; every one is out of temper; the tents are wet with dew; no one has time to get breakfast before starting; the mules, too, are unfed and unwatered; the tents have to be struck and the packing done before it is fairly light. And why? No one can tell. It is all very well in India, where it is too hot to march in the middle of the day, but here there is no reason whatever for it. The hottest portion of the twenty-four hours by far is between eight and ten, before the breeze springs up. If our march was twenty or five-and-twenty miles in length there would be some reason in it; but as, since we reached the plateau land, they have not averaged more than eleven or twelve, one is at a loss to understand the motive of getting the troops up and off so early. We have often talked this over in our tent, and always without arriving at any satisfactory explanation. The Professor says that " the official mind is a wonderful and complicated machine." The Drayman remarks that "he wishes he had the command for a week or two." The Professor says, "Then, in that case, his mind, which is now a singularly simple one, would also become a complicated machine." The Drayman cries "Balderdash!"

I do not describe the gorge up to Sono—what with description and prints you must know all about it by this time. At Sono the Lightweight came in triumphant, but breathless, with a goat he had purchased for a rupee, and which he had had a great struggle with on his way to the tent. The Drayman expressed his admiration of the purchase in suitable terms. The Professor was silent: but at last inquired, "What do you mean to do with that goat?" "Eat him, of course." "Let me know what day you propose the feast shall take place," the Professor said calmly; "I will dine in some other man's tent. That is a he-goat, and fifty years old at least."

Lightweight did not say any more on the subject, nor do I know what he did with the goat; but it certainly never appeared at table. That night was not a peaceful one. We had two alarms—the one from without, the other from within the tent. We were awoke by the sentry posted not far behind us shouting something. That we heeded little. Then came a tremendous jerking at the ropes of the tent, which threatened to bring the whole affair to the ground. We all jumped up and rushed out. There stood a camel, who had strayed up and in his wanderings had nearly brought down our tent. We rushed out and drove him off with stones; the ground, however, being stony, and strewn over with small pieces of the thorny wood, we suffered severely in so doing. The camel appeared to have a peculiar affection for our tent, for he was continually returning throughout the night, and keeping us on the *qui vive* by getting close to the tent-ropes. At one time, however, we really thought he was gone, and were just getting off to sleep when the Lightweight woke us with a piercing cry, "Good gracious, something is biting me horribly! By Jove, I can't get him off! Strike a light, you fellows." We struck a light hastily, and found that the assailant was a large camel-tick, which had fastened upon our friend's leg, and had to be taken off piecemeal, for he would not let go his hold. Several others of his species were also discovered wandering about on the bed, and we found that we had encamped on a spot where camels had been at some time or other stationed, and that the place swarmed with their abominable vermin. They are about the size of sheep-ticks, and are of leaden colour; their bite is very severe, as the Jockey's leg, which was very much swollen up by the morning, sufficiently testified. We did not sleep any more that night, but kept the candle alight, rolled up our beds, and spreading our white waterproof sheets upon the ground, sat on the middle of them, so as to be able to perceive any insect advancing to attack us. I shall not speedily forget that night at Sono.

The next two marches to Rayraz Guddy were wearisome and monotonous in the extreme, round and round endless turnings and windings of the valley, every mile being just like the last. The men, too, felt their marches very much; there was no water to be had on the way, and they soon drank up that in their canteens. In addition, many of them not having had any marching for weeks, began to be footsore. And at Rayraz Guddy we felt a sensation which we had not experienced for some time: this was cold. The first to remark upon it was the Lightweight, who is a chilly subject, having no flesh to speak of on his bones. He came in from duty just as dinner was ready, rubbing his hands, "I say, you fellows, it's awfully cold." " Nonsense! Cold?" the Drayman said. "It's glorious, it's refreshing; I have not felt so jolly for months." But as the evening wore on even the Drayman was obliged to confess that it was very cold indeed. The native servants went about the camp with their teeth chattering, and kept up such a coughing and groaning all night as only a chilly Hindoo can. Even in the tent, rolled up in rugs, it was undeniably very cold; and at daybreak cold water was indulged in far more sparingly than usual. Lightweight was quite touching on the subject. He had, he said, exchanged into a regiment in India entirely because he could not bear an English winter, and to be sent to a place which he was certain was nearly as cold as the North Pole, and to have to sleep with only the protection of a thin canvas tent, was very hard upon him. That night, however, was certainly the coldest we experienced, for even at Senafé the thermometer never went below freezing-point, whereas at Rayraz Guddy a film of ice formed over water in the open air. On the bare plain of Senafé we stopped for some time. There we bargained with the natives, did a little shooting, finished our stock of preserved meats and liquors, and had to subsist entirely upon rations, varied occasionally by game and commissariat rum. This last was at first declared to be undrinkable; but as time wore on it was astonishing how we took to it, and how great a privation it would have been had the issue been stopped. At last, when we were all getting very sick of Senafé, Sir Robert Napier came up, and in less than a week afterwards we received the welcome order to advance. Our first day's march was an easy one, for the sappers had cleared the road; the second was long but not difficult; the third, into Attegrat, was short, but there was our tremendous descent. Here we had occasion to admire the exertions of the Professor, who happened to be our baggage-guard. The baggage had started first, but the number of breakdowns was so great that we came upon them at the top of this descent. All down the narrow road on the face of the hill animals were lying down or standing with their loads on their necks. Half-way down, in a most precipitous spot, a mule was on the point of falling, the load having got nearly on his ears. Two soldiers had by the Professor's direction got in front, and were almost carrying the load, which at that place it was impossible to remove. The weight, however, was too great upon such difficult ground, and mule, baggage, and men had a fair chance of a very ugly tumble— when the Professor, who was behind this mule, seized it by its tail, hung on with all his weight, and so acted as a skid till the animal reached a more level spot, where the load could be taken off. We had a laugh at him as we passed, but he replied imperturbably, "That animal carried my aneroid barometer and our last dozen of brandy." We were too grateful to the Professor to say another word. Attegrat was more infested by jackals and hyenas that any other place we came to. They made the night hideous with their yells and whinings, and we several times went outside the lines to terrify them with a stone. Of course fire-arms were not allowed. The fair here was very amusing, with its closely packed squatting figures, its animals, cloth, and vegetable markets. The two great events at Attegrat were the visit of Tigré's ambassador and a thunder-storm. The first, as a public event, was perhaps the more important, the second interested us personally very much the more. The ambassador's visit, however, was the prior event, and should therefore be first spoken of. Breakfast was just over, and we were discussing whether or not we should go out for a stroll, when the Professor entered. He had gone out towards Attegrat, he said, to collect antiquities, but that was of course humbug, for up to the present time he had only bought a prayer-book or two, or an old ham, for a dollar each. However, the Professor, as the Jockey says, "fancies himself" upon the subject of antiquarianism, as well as a dozen other-isms, and maintains that his prayer-books are quite different, and very much superior, to any others which either have been or could be purchased in Abyssinia. The Professor does not, even according to his own confession, understand more than three Abyssinian words, and he gives no reasons for the great superiority of his purchases over ours. He says we should not understand him; and I think this possible. The Professor, then, entered, and put an end to our discussion. "If you fellows want to see the King of Tigré, you had better come out at once." And we accordingly went, and found a strange procession approaching the camp, preceded by the warlike music of the stirring tom-tom, surrounded by a *cortège* of warriors, arrayed in dirty cotton, and armed with spears and with matchlocks, probably purchased from Chinese traders about the era

3000 B.C. Of the ambassador himself it can only be said that he was like unto his following, as dirty and as vagabond-looking as the rest of them. Presently our bugles sounded, and we had to buckle on our swords and form up in front of the camp. Thence we were marched in front of the Commander-in-Chief's tent, and were drawn up with our bands behind us at a distance of about fifty yards. The rest of the troops also formed in line, and then the mongrel procession marched up and the ambassador entered the tent, the two military bands playing as loudly as they could, and entirely different airs. However, I do not suppose he noticed anything extraordinary about it. The Professor, who was not on duty, was in the tent, and told us afterwards that the conversation which ensued was the very dullest thing he ever listened to. He suggested a number of topics of interest which might have been advantageously discussed; among others, some scientific point, which we understood to be the relation which the ancient Coptic language had, in the opinion of the ambassador, in the formation, modification, and origin of the primitive Abyssinian dialects. Some of his other suggestions were equally remarkable for abstruseness, and he was strongly advised to embody them in a memo, and to present them to Sir Robert Napier in case of another interview. The rain affected us much more intimately than the durbar had done. It had threatened rain for two previous days, and we therefore paid little attention to the heavy black cloud. When it began, however, it came down in a sheet, and in five minutes we had a stream three inches deep rushing through the tent. Before we had time to prepare, the beds upon the ground were under water, and everything was soaked through. The Professor— who alone had stuck to his bed— sat upon it, chuckling, at his superior sagacity; but the laugh went against him afterwards, when it was discovered, upon turning out everything after the shower was over, that some tobacco which he had that morning, taken from his trunk, and put upon the ground under his bed to be out of the way, was quite saturated. Up to Attegrat we had been very well off for tent accommodation, as we had been only three in one of the large tents known as "native routies;" but these were now to be left behind, and we were packed three in a bell-tent. It was at Ad Abaga, however, three days' march farther on—where we waited for five days for the King of Tigré—that our ideas of comfort received the rudest shock. The Drayman brought in the news. (The Drayman is perhaps too devoted to his personal comforts; he is a peaceful man, but is apt to get extremely irate if interfered with.) He came in red hot; he was in a passion; something serious had evidently happened. "Have you seen the general order?" We had not. What was it? The Drayman steadied himself to tell us: it was evidently most serious. At last he spoke. "It is proposed that the troops march forward without either rum, tea, or sugar." We were silent; the news was bad beyond our worst anticipation. No rum, tea, or sugar! it seemed impossible. The Professor spoke, "For myself," he said, with that calmness which distinguishes him, and which was only disturbed upon the great occasion of the destruction of his tobacco at Attegrat— "For myself, I care little; but the troops will all be in hospital in a fortnight. No constitution in the world can stand hard work and nothing but dirty water to drink." "I am very sorry for the troops," the Jockey said, "but I am quite as sorry for myself. The tea and sugar I should not mind." As indeed he would not; for his tastes having been vitiated by an early life among sporting associates, he eschews milder drinks, and even at breakfast drinks arrack and water, utterly disregarding any hints upon our part as to the fair allowance of spirits. "What a fool I was to come into the army! To think; that I should have to come to drink nothing but dirty water. I consider that Government took the price of my commission under false pretenses. I paid so much for the honor of fighting, of doing innumerable parades and other hateful work; and all this for the mere interest of my own money. But I did not bargain for drinking dirty water. I never read the Articles of War, but I am certain that dirty water is not as much as mentioned." Lightweight's lament was so earnest and pathetic that we had a laugh, and felt better tempered at once. This Draconian decree, which, if carried out, would certainly have been attended with the worst results as to the health of the troops, was never enforced; for such an abundance of stores and native carriage was obtained at Antalo, that rations, although upon a reduced scale, are still issued to the troops of both rum and tea and sugar. One of the greatest privations, as far as officers are concerned, is want of candles. None have been issued since we landed, and the consequence is, that there are now hardly any left in camp. Substitutes have, of course, been improvised: empty tins of chocolate have been converted into rough lamps; and in these, ghee, or native butter, is consumed with a more or less satisfactory result. A consequence is, that very early hours are perforce kept, and by nine o'clock the great majority of officers are in bed. Indeed there is little to promote conviviality. Many brought cards with them; but even a rubber is hardly a sociable game when played almost in the dark, and without any accompanying refreshment. I have only seen one game attempted since we landed. Until we reached this place, the prospects of the campaign looked dreary indeed. We could bring no supplies except meat at any price. The transport train was taxed to the utmost to keep our immediate wants supplied, and no one could see the end of the business at all. Thanks, however, to the enormous supplies of flour and other stores which we have purchased here, thanks to the unlimited amount of native transport which has been offered to us, we shall go forward in a few days with every hope of being at Magdala in three days from the date of starting hence. Every one has the greatest confidence in Sir Robert Napier; and we look forward to being out of this country by June. All are especially anticipating a fight at Magdala. The Jockey says that he shall not mind even short commons of rum if King Theodore does but fight. The Drayman pooh-poohs the idea of fighting with such followers as these. The Professor utters mysterious sayings about manuscripts and antiquities he expects, or says he expects, to find at Magdala. Why King Theodore should bother himself with manuscripts and antiquities is known only to the Professor himself.